List of personnel of the Defence Forces dismissed for desertion in time of National Emergency pursuant to the terms of Emergency Powers (No. 362) Order 1945 (S.R. & O. 1945, No. 198) or of Section 13 of the Defence Forces (Temporary Provisions) Act, 1946 (No. 7/1946).

The Naval & Military Press Ltd

Published by
The Naval & Military Press Ltd
Unit 10 Ridgewood Industrial Park,
Uckfield, East Sussex,
TN22 5QE England
Tel: +44 (0) 1825 749494
Fax: +44 (0) 1825 765701
www.naval-military-press.com
www.military-genealogy.com
www.militarymaproom.com

Army No.	Name.	Last Recorded Address.	Date of Birth.	Declared Occupation prior to enlistment in Defence Forces.	Date of Dismissal from Defence Forces.
A/46326	ABEL, Robert	7 Westland Row, Dublin.	13-5-1900	Labourer	8-8-1945
E/422014	ADAMS, Louis	Fermanagh St., Clones, Co. Monaghan	13-9-1906	Cattle Dealer	8-8-1945
A/80652	ADDERLEY, John	Main Street, Leixlip, Co. Kildare.	27-6-1921	Labourer	8-8-1945
A/80651	ADDERLEY, Peter	Main Street, Leixlip, Co. Kildare.	10-4-1922	French Polisher	8-8-1945
E/403960	AGNEW, Seamus	15 Cavendish St., Belfast.	11-1-1917	Student	8-8-1945
A/82359	AHERN, Cornelius	2 Merrypole Lane, Cork.	22-9-1922	Messenger Boy	8-8-1945
79814	AHERNE, John	6 Bengal Tce., Limerick.	3-7-1921	Shop-Boy	8-8-1945
V/205084	AHERNE, Patrick	20 Belvedere Pce. Dublin.	10-5-1918	Painter	8-8-1945
E/424297	AIKEN, Edward	40 Abbeyford Pce., South Side, Glasgow.	16-8-1918	Farm Labourer	17-9-1945
E/434127	ALDRIDGE, Joseph	Offaly Street, Athy.	8-9-1922	Farm Labourer	8-8-1945
74768	ALFRED, George	Graigue, Adare, Co. Limerick.	12-5-1920	Motor Driver and Mechanic	8-8-1945
E/423192	ALLEN, Arthur	12 Holywell Street, Derry.	22-6-1922	Labourer	8-8-1945
E/430096	ALLEN, George	1 Fairgate, New Ross, Co. Wexford.	1-11-1921	Waiter	8-8-1945
75869	ALLEN, John Michael	Convent Road, Newcastle West, Co. Limerick.	27-4-1918	Labourer	2-2-1946
83471	ALWARD, Patrick	10 Carrow Road, Crumlin, Dublin.	10-1-1922	Labourer	8-8-1945
E/423392	ANDERSON, John	Acre Hill, Killala, Co. Mayo.	16-10-1921	Farm Labourer	8-8-1945
A/83680	ANDERSON, Laurence	St. Brigid's Cottages, Blanchardstown, Co. Dublin.	11-4-1922	Labourer	8-8-1945
E/425473	ANDERSON, Patrick J.	33 Walkers Place, Derry.	5-1-1917	Labourer	8-8-1945
E/421715	ANDERSON, Thomas	21 Thomas Street, Derry.	4-2-1904	Mason	8-8-1945
E/406675	ANDREWS, John	10 Grove Road, Dublin.	13-6-1922	Lumbering	8-8-1945
E/410008	ANDREWS, Stephen	4 Dean St., West, Cork.	18-12-1910	Fish Filleter	8-8-1945
L/500286	ANDREWS, William	2 Magee's Court, Charlotte Street, Dublin.	20-6-1921	Labourer	8-8-1945
E/404608	ANSBRO, John Raymond	265 Griffith Ave., Dublin.	22-8-1914	Shop Assistant	8-8-1945
A/73558	ARBUTHNOT, John	Beauparc, Slane, Co. Meath.	10-7-1914	Tech. School Student	8-8-1945
206553	ARMSTRONG, Francis	11 Waterford St., Dublin.	28-5-1922	Labourer	8-8-1945
E/406348	ARMSTRONG, George	41 Up. Mount St., Dublin.	4-11-1921	Bricklayer	8-8-1945
E/437631	ARMSTRONG, Gerard	20 Hamill Street, Belfast.	9-8-1925	Motor Mechanic Apprentice	8-8-1945
75281	ARMSTRONG, Michael	Lisadell, Ballinfull, Co. Sligo.	30-1-1915	Hotel Porter	8-8-1945
E/406363	ARROW, William Brendan	27 Parkgate St., Dublin.	2-10-1909	Caterer	8-8-1945
79664	ARTHURS, Anthony	Kilgarve, Dungannon.	2-6-1920	Labourer	8-8-1945
78728	ASHE, Bernard	125 Thistle St., Glasgow.	17-2-1921	Messenger	8-8-1945
E/403074	ASHE, John	40D Corporation Place, Dublin.	28-5-1922	Poulterer	8-8-1945
A/76602	ASHE, Michael	16 Vicar Street, Dublin.	23-10-1919	Hotel Kitchen Boy	8-8-1945
83472	ASHE, Patrick	32 J Pearse House, Dublin.	20-9-1920	Labourer	8-8-1945
E/413803	ASHMAN, Michael	5 Mahoney's Square, Blackpool,, Cork.	23-9-1914	Labourer	8-8-1945
E/403180	ASHMORE, Francis	18 Upr. Oriel St., Dublin.	13-7-1922	Labourer	8-8-1945
209145	ASKINS, Michael	The Shannon, Enniscorthy.	18-1-1900	Cook	8-8-1945
E/207851	AUSTER, Roger	91 St. Peter's Rd., Howth, Co. Dublin.	22-2-1918	Seaman	8-8-1945
77346	AYLMER, Patrick	8 Bank Place, Limerick.	24-10-1919	Farm Labourer	8-8-1945
A/73917	AYLWARD, John	Tinteskin, Kilmuckridge, Gorey, Co. Wexford.	18-10-1911	General Farm Work	8-8-1945
A/73997	BAGENAL, Patrick	Downings, Prosperous, Co. Kildare.	1-1-1916	Farm Labourer	8-8-1945
E/401347	BAILEY, Joseph	88 Oliver St., Portadown.	1-11-1915	Butcher	8-8-1945
E/407679	BAKER, Frank	255 Larkfield Rd., Dublin	3-7-1923	Motor Mechanic	8-8-1945
A/79182	BAKER, Martin	Sentry Hill, Letterkenny, Co. Donegal.	3-12-1913	Farm Labourer	8-8-1945

Army No.	Name.	Last Recorded Address.	Date of Birth.	Declared Occupation prior to enlistment in Defence Forces.	Date of Dismissal from Defence Forces.
E/406311	BALFE, Brendan	24 Bredin St., Drogheda.	22-6-1922	Gen. Labourer	8-8-1945
V/207073	BALL, John	59 Mountjoy Sq., Dublin.	10-1-1920	Storeman	8-8-1945
83473	BALL, Peadar	59 Mountjoy Sq., Dublin.	2-7-1922	Groundsman	8-8-1945
E/402083	BALL, Thomas	3 Nt. Portland St., Dublin.	1-6-1922	Messenger	8-8-1945
E/423037	BANAGHAN, William	St. Eithne's Road, Cabra, Dublin.	28-2-1922	Messenger	8-8-1945
E/424000	BANNON, Francis	Kilmore, Lisnaskea, Co. Fermanagh.	1-3-1921	Farm Labourer	8-8-1945
V/208831	BANNON, James	Harbour Street, Mount-mellick, Leix.	9-6-1921	Labourer	8-8-1945
V/203220	BANNON, Michael	13 Adelaide Road, Dublin.	12-1-1916	Student	8-8-1945
E/433144	BANON, Edward A.	Broughall, Castle, Kilcor-mac, Co. Offaly.	22-12-1913	Farmer	8-8-1945
E/434810	BARBER, Kevin	Ballysax, Curragh Camp.	22-9-1922	Baker	8-8-1945
208994	BARBOUR, Alex.	Drumscar, Bailieboro', Co. Cavan.	12-8-1914	Gardener	8-8-1945
A/72240	BARCOE, John	11 William St., Kilkenny.	1-4-1912	Labourer	8-8-1945
E/437726	BARKEY, Henry	Tunnis Coffey, Dunrny-mond, Monaghan.	23-9-1923	Farmer	27-8-1945
73795	BARNS, Patrick	Ballinamona, Blackwater, Wexford.	10-11-1915	Labourer	8-8-1945
E/422316	BARR, Patrick L.	Rooskey, Fahan, Co. Donegal.	10-11-1919	Labourer	8-8-1945
E/413226	BARRETT, Frederick	8 D Road, Janesboro, Limerick.	10-5-1922	Embosser	8-8-1945
E/415353	BARRETT, John A.	Rosenheim, Magazine Rd., Cork.	3-4-1912	Bank Clerk	8-8-1945
209711	BARRETT, John	Rahelnagh, Ballaugh, Co. Limerick.	15-11-1916	Motor Driver	8-8-1945
E/414414	BARRETT, Kevin	66 Watercourse Rd., Cork.	15-2-1921	Motor Driver	8-8-1945
A/84090	BARRETT, Martin	Church, Street, Gort. Co. Galway.	12-1-1919	Gen. Labourer	8-8-1945
E/413867	BARRETT, Patrick	Drumcommer, Banteer, Co. Cork.	1-3-1916	Farm Labourer	8-8-1945
V/213041	BARRETT, William	Dirha, Listowel.	3-9-1921	Labourer	8-8-1945
V/205599	BARRON, John	The Square, Ballindrait, Co. Donegal.	26-6-1921	Labourer	8-8-1945
V/206762	BARRY, Christopher	Summerhill, Co. Meath.	12-1-1915	Farm Labourer	8-8-1945
70403	BARRY, Christopher	72 St. Ita's Road, Island Field, Limerick.	2-12-1911	Labourer	8-8-1945
A/77674	BARRY, David	19 Corporation Buildings, Clonmel.	24-11-1919	Labourer	8-8-1945
A/76648	BARRY, James	Kilfrush, Knocklong, Co. Limerick	21-11-1919	Gardener	8-8-1945
L/502835	BARRY, John	142 Annamoe Drive, Cabra, Dublin.	16-1-1927	Carrier	8-8-1945
E/416752	BARRY, Joseph	Curoleigh, Ballyporeen, Co. Tipperary.	18-5-1916	Labourer	8-8-1945
E/434854	BARRY, Maurice	Owbeg, Lismore, Co. Waterford.	17-7-1917	Rivetter	8-8-1945
E/401949	BARRY, Michael	1 James's Terrace, Dublin.	3-11-1918	Builders' Labourer	8-8-194
83175	BARRY, Michael	2 Newtown Ctgs., Raheny, Dublin.	20-1-1920	Gardener	8-8-194
77319	BARRY, Patrick	63 Connolly St., Fermoy, Co. Cork.	20-6-1920	Farm Labourer	8-8-194
81450	BARRY, Patrick	64 Bridgefoot St., Dublin.	9-10-1926	Messenger	3-5-194
A/71730	BARRY, Richard	Thomond Gate, Limerick.	7-1-1906	Co. Council Labourer	8-8-194
E/415248	BARRY, William	2 Harrison's Place, Charle-ville, Co. Cork.	8-8-1923	Garage Hand	8-8-194
E/414481	BARY, Michael	Kells, Co. Kilkenny.	15-6-1908	Labourer	8-8-19
E/424717	BASQUILL, James	Station Road, Swinford, Co. Mayo.	11-1-1920	Aircraft Factory Hand	8-8-19

Army No.	Name.	Last Recorded Address.	Date of Birth.	Declared Occupation prior to enlistment in Defence Forces.	Date of Dismissal from Defence Forces.
79105	BASS, John	22 Woodlawn House, Rutland Ave., Dublin.	28-6-1920	Messenger	8-8-1945
E/431736	BATCHELOR, Robert	3 Woodstock Street, Athy, Co. Kildare.	15-4-1922	Farm Labourer	8-8-1945
E/431287	BATEMAN, Joseph	18 Patrick St., Kilkenny.	27-5-1922	Mechanic	8-8-1945
E/420342	BAXTER, Thomas	Drumcarry, Creesclough, Co. Donegal.	4-3-1910	Dock Labourer	18-11-1945
E/400650	BEATTIE, William	Scots House, Clones, Co. Monaghan.	8-7-1917	Butcher	8-8-1945
83839	BEATTIE, William	27 Hill Street, Newry.	25-5-1917	Shoemaker	8-8-1945
72463	BEATTY, Andrew	Tough, Adare, Co. Limerick	11-10-1914	Labourer	8-8-1945
75595	BEATTY, Richard	23 Ard Righ Rd., Dublin.	18-2-1918	Solicitor's Clerk	8-8-1945
76828	BEECH, Edward	7 May Lane, Waterford.	24-5-1918	Shop Assistant	8-8-1945
L/502049	BEGLEY, Anthony	50 The Coombe, Dublin.	26-6-1925	Labourer	8-8-1945
E/400767	BEGLEY, Timothy	33 Pimlico, Dublin.	29-11-1921	Labourer	8-8-1945
E/402113	BEHAN, Christopher	21 Golden Lane, Dublin.	8-8-1922	Porter	8-8-1945
78795	BEHAN, Frederick	1 Up. Stephen St. Dublin.	22-3-1917	Labourer	8-8-1945
E/400955	BEHAN, Matthew	3 Emerald Place, Dublin.	29-8-1910	Labourer	8-8-1945
E/407423	BEHAN, Patrick B.	68 Downpatrick Rd. Dublin	3-1-1924	Messenger	8-8-1945
E/400378	BEHAN, Patrick	Carnew, Co. Wicklow.	27-1-1921	Labourer	8-8-1945
E/429628	BEIRNE, Joseph	St. Patrick's Park, Carrick-on-Shannon.	13-12-1916	Labourer	8-8-1945
V/202265	BELL, Matthew	10 St. Brigid's Tce., Kells.	17-2-1917	Labourer	8-8-1945
E/405502	BELL, Michael	12 St. Brigid's Road, Killester, Co. Dublin.	26-9-1916	Labourer	8-8-1945
V/207621	BELLAMY, Seán	27 Pearse Street, Dublin.	14-12-1917	Translator	8-8-1945
A/77297	BENNETT, James	34 St. Brigid's Terrace, Mullingar.	8-7-1918	Labourer	8-8-1945
77265	BENNETT, Patrick	77 Eden Villas, Glasthule, Dun Laoghaire.	13-7-1917	Carter and Blacksmith	8-8-1945
E/414403	BENSON, Thomas	13 Cash's Range, Thomondgate, Limerick.	22-8-1922	Factory Worker	8-8-1945
77391	BERGIN, Francis	Shinrone, Offaly.	20-2-1919	Motor Driver	8-8-1945
E/434861	BERGIN, Joseph	2 Michael St., Kilkenny.	21-3-1914	Carpenter	8-8-1945
E/434952	BERGIN, Timothy	Skough, Callan, Co. Kilkenny.	2-8-1922	Farm Labourer	8-8-1945
E/434383	BERGIN, William	138 Lr. George's Street, Dun Laoghaire.	12-8-1918	Labourer	8-8-1945
34454	BERMINGHAM, John	31 Chancery House, Charles Street, Dublin.	3-8-1899	Motor Driver	8-8-1945
E/434292	BERMINGHAM, Michael	Sragh, Tullamore.	10-6-1916	Labourer	8-8-1945
E/438023	BERNE, Vincent	31 Harrowgate St., Belfast.	4-11-1925	Storeman	8-8-1945
E/405188	BERRILL, George	Old Hill, Drogheda.	14-5-1922	Labourer	8-8-1945
E/430136	BERRY, John	Model Lane, Off John St., Waterford.	2-6-1914	Labourer	8-8-1945
L/500223	BERRY, John	1 Peterson's Lane, City Quay, Dublin.	11-7-1920	Labourer	8-8-1945
E/407642	BIBBY, Thomas	119 Cooley Road, Dublin.	26-1-1908	Mechanic Driver	8-8-1945
E/406803	BIRD, Michael	Curkish, Bailieboro, Co. Cavan.	7-9-1922	Fruit Dealer	8-8-1945
L/502778	BIRD, Thomas	62 North King St., Dublin.	21-4-1927	Moulder	8-8-1945
V/209954	BIRNEY, William	25 Ballymacool Terrace, Letterkenny.	7-6-1921	Labourer	8-8-1945
E/421655	BIRRANE, Joseph	The Lane, Crossmolina, Co. Mayo.	16-10-1918	Labourer	8-8-1945
E/435359	BISSETT, James	2 Waterford Rd., Kilkenny	10-2-1922	Labourer	8-8-1945
L/501460	BLACK, James	4 Lr. Dominick St., Dublin	11-1-1925	Packer	8-8-1945
L/503242	BLACK, Michael	34 Queen Street, Dublin.	6-4-1928	Bootmaker	30-3-1946
E/406893	BLACK, William	41 Monasterboice Road, Dublin.	8-1-1923	Tailor	8-8-1945
L/508748	BLACKBOURNE, William	Monarte, Enniscorthy.	22-6-1920	Labourer	8-8-1945
E/420804	BLAIR, John	Castlehamilton, Killeshandra, Co. Cavan.	23-2-1916	Motor Driver	8-8-1945
E/406690	BLAIR, William	12 John Martin Gardens, Newry.	18-5-1923	Factory Hand	8-8-1945

Army No.	Name.	Last Recorded Address.	Date of Birth.	Declared Occupation prior to enlistment in Defence Forces.	Date of Dismissal from Defence Forces.
L/507573	BLAKE, George	61 St. Munchin's, Island Field, Limerick.	20-2-1927	Labourer	8-8-1945
E/423354	BLAKE, Jerry	94 Jinks Avenue, Sligo.	22-5-1922	None	8-8-1945
E/403999	BLAKE, John	126 Capel Street, Dublin.	27-12-1910	Labourer	8-8-1945
E/403078	BLAKE, Joseph	29 Dominick Street, Dun Laoghaire.	29-9-1921	Labourer	8-8-1945
78349	BLAKE, Patrick	St. Senan's Street, Island Field, Limerick.	8-7-1920	Garage Assistant	8-8-1945
E/431893	BLANCHE, John	25 Stephen St., Kilkenny.	12-5-1896	Labourer	8-8-1945
83790	BLANEY, William	21 Ormond Rd., Dublin.	18-9-1921	Student	8-8-1945
E/425424	BLEE, Joseph	27 Ann Street, Derry.	25-1-1925	Labourer	8-8-1945
78709	BLEE, Joseph	17 Limewood St., Derry.	23-11-1916	Motor Driver	8-8-1945
E/424596	BLESSION, Francis	Drummandly, Rooskey, Co. Roscommon.	9-12-1922	Farm Labourer	8-8-1945
E/406089	BOGGAN, John Thomas	5 Emmet Rd., Inchicore, Dublin.	26-12-1894	Motor Driver	8-8-1945
E/422452	BOGGS, Leo	c/o H. Doherty, Foyle View House, Lifford.	2-8-1920	Barman	8-8-1945
E/424575	BOGGS, William	Lifford.	16-1-1918	Shop Assistant	8-8-1945
V/205993	BOLAND, John	Ballindrait, Lifford.	10-5-1915	Farm Labourer	8-8-1945
E/408047	BOLAND, Joseph	277 Cashel Road, Crumlin, Dublin.	13-4-1924	Messenger	8-8-1945
A/74653	BOLAND, Maurice	Faghan, Dingle, Co. Kerry.	10-5-1916	Farm Labourer	8-8-1945
E/404201	BOLAND, Robert	11 Ennis Road, Cabra, Dublin.	18-4-1918	Motor Driver	8-8-1945
E/402754	BOLGER, James	91 Francis Street, Dublin.	13-9-1907	Commercial Traveller	8-8-1945
E/402243	BOLGER, Thomas	124 Stanaway Road, Crumlin, Dublin.	22-4-1921	Slater	8-8-1945
A/76969	BOND, Daniel	Martry, Maurice's Mills, Co. Clare.	27-2-1919	Farm Labourer	8-8-1945
E/414100	BOND, Patrick	4 James St., Gerald Griffin St., Limerick.	11-2-1920	Labourer	8-8-1945
205655	BONNER, Frank	c/o Ml. Lynch, Leenamore, Muff, Co. Donegal.	2-6-1916	Musician	8-8-1945
E/424812	BONNER, James	Castlefin, Co. Donegal.	11-5-1921	Motor Driver	8-8-1945
77912	BONNER, John	Sessaghlong, Castlefin, Co. Donegal.	27-8-1916	Labourer	8-8-1945
E/423252	BONNER, John	104 St. Columb's Wells, Derry.	5-2-1919	Labourer	8-8-1945
E/408325	BONNER, Kenneth Hector	12 Up. Bridge St., Dublin.	3-5-1924	Carpenter	8-8-1945
E/422852	BONNER, Michael	Fahan Fort, Co. Donegal.	26-11-1922	Fisherman	8-8-1945
502598	BONNER, Terence	28 Golden Lane, Dublin.	1-5-1926	Barber	7-1-1946
A/73667	BOSHELL, William	8 Ellenborough Road, London, N.19.	22-12-1914	Labourer	8-8-1945
E/405293	BOTHWELL, Davis	Glasslough, Co. Monaghan.	6-8-1917	Motor Driver	8-8-1945
L/507291	BOURKE, Christopher	5 Keynon's Ave., Kileely, Limerick.	10-6-1925	Shoe-Maker	8-8-1945
75666	BOURKE, Daniel	31 Stephen's Place, Dublin.	1-8-1918	Butcher	8-8-1945
E/406278	BOURKE, Daniel	9 Waterford St., Dublin.	28-2-1922	Messenger	8-8-1945
A/76651	BOURKE, George	Thomastown, Kilmallock, Co. Limerick.	13-5-1919	Labourer	8-8-1945
E/414143	BOURKE, James	Kells, Drumcollogher, Co. Limerick.	16-7-1920	Labourer	8-8-1945
V/204876	BOURKE, Jerome	9 Rockfield Terrace, Killenaule, Thurles.	20-7-1920	Labourer	8-8-1945
A/83268	BOWDEN, Thomas	7 Stephen's Place, Dublin.	22-3-1922	Messenger	8-8-1945
A/79457	BOWE, Joseph	Moore St., Rathdowney, Leix.	3-7-1916	Labourer	8-8-1945
V/203948	BOWE, Patrick	16 Moore St., Rathdowney, Leix.	22-7-1919	Gen. Labourer	8-8-1945
A/57504	BOWE, Patrick	34 Pearse St., Kilkenny.	17-6-1902	Groom	8-8-1945
A/82228	BOWEN, Edward	6 School Av., Gurrane-braher, Cork.	15-2-1922	None	8-8-1945

Army No.	Name.	Last Recorded Address.	Date of Birth.	Declared Occupation prior to enlistment in Defence Forces.	Date of Dismissal from Defence Forces.
E/407655	BOWER, William	18 Upper Eden Road, Dun Laoghaire.	27-12-1923	Student	8-8-1945
A/77484	BOWES, Michael	Ashgrove, Bansha, Co. Tipperary.	2-10-1920	Farm Labourer	8-8-1945
E/408463	BOWLER, Patrick	Cuass, Dingle, Co. Kerry.	23-11-1920	Carpenter	8-8-1945
E/421211	BOYCE, John	Tullogh, Carrigart, Co. Donegal.	15-6-1904	Labourer	8-8-1945
E/400530	BOYD, James	Meath Street, Dublin.	4-2-1922	Labourer	8-8-1945
V/209440	BOYD, James	Boyle, Co. Roscommon.	6-1-1921	Labourer	8-8-1945
V/209383	BOYD, John	62 Foley Street, Dublin.	30-4-1918	Labourer	8-8-1945
E/404566	BOYLAN, Francis	Drumullen, Co. Cavan.	22-8-1922	Motor Driver	8-8-1945
V/206885	BOYLAN, James	31 Bangor Road, Dublin.	6-9-1920	Labourer	8-8-1945
208472	BOYLAN, John	11 Mitchell's St., Dublin.	22-8-1921	Labourer	8-8-1945
E/420167	BOYLAN, Patrick	Feenagh, Manorhamilton, Co. Leitrim.	18-3-1922	Labourer	8-8-1945
E/403435	BOYLAND, John	52 Paul Street, Dublin.	3-10-1921	Labourer	8-8-1945
207196	BOYLE, Bertie	Ballymacogh Terrace, Letterkenny.	15-6-1914	Labourer	8-8-1945
E/425126.	BOYLE, Charles	Port Rd., Letterkenny.	10-4-1924	Labourer	8-8-1945
E/424376	BOYLE, Francis	Meenaleck, Annagry, Co. Donegal.	26-1-1920	Shoemaker	8-8-1945
84172	BOYLE, James	c/o J. Molloy, Ballybofey, Co. Donegal.	28-4-1922	Apprentice Butcher	8-8-1945
E/421428	BOYLE, James Jos.	Innishfree, Burtonport, Co. Donegal.	23-1-1917	Farmer	8-8-1945
E/404394	BOYLE, John	23 Upton Ctgs., Belfast.	20-4-1920	Sheet Metal Worker	8-8-1945
E/424516	BOYLE, Joseph	Kilclooney, Portnoo, Glenties Co. Donegal.	12-10-1918	Labourer	8-8-1945
E/423041	BOYLE, Joseph	205 Keogh Sq., Inchicore, Dublin.	22-9-1920	Labourer	8-8-1945
E/437930	BOYLE, Joseph	3 Beechfield St., Belfast.	7-6-1925	Bricklayer	8-8-1945
E/433428	BOYLE, Neil	Kinnalough, Ballyla, Lifford	23-7-1922	Farm Labourer	8-8-1945
E/422948	BOYLE, Patrick	Carrigobyle, Derrybeg, Co. Donegal.	11-3-1921	Labourer	8-8-1945
E/423253	BOYLE, Patrick	26 Edenmore St., Derry.	20-3-1920	Clerk	8-8-1945
84198	BOYLE, Patrick	c/o Mrs. Hegarty, Bridge-end, Co. Donegal.	20-10-1921	Mason	8-8-1945
E/409182	BOYLE, Sean	2 Francis Street, Dublin.	20-9-1920	Labourer	8-8-1945
E/420462	BOYLE, William	Bridgend, Co. Donegal.	14-3-1920	Apprentice Motor Mechanic	8-8-1945
A/79967	BOYLE, William	14 Cross Street, Waterside, Derry.	11-8-1921	Messenger	8-8-1945
E/433114	BRABAZON, James	Tubber, Lucan, Co. Dublin	23-11-1916	French Polisher	8-8-1945
E/430307	BRABAZON, Martin	Westmanstown, Lucan, Co. Dublin.	27-11-1925	Messenger	27-8-1945
E/408258	BRACKEN, Patk. Joseph	Kilcock, Co. Kildare.	17-2-1920	Motor Driver	8-8-1945
V/206054	BRADLEY, Alexander	71 Belgium Pk., Monaghan	22-7-1922	Tailor	8-8-1945
E/420165	BRADLEY, Dominic	Newmills, Letterkenny.	23-12-1914	Farm Labourer	8-8-1945
V/205359	BRADLEY, Kevin	278 St. Attracta Road, Dublin.	23-1-1920	Messenger	8-8-1945
V/208802	BRADLEY, Michael	278 St. Attracta Road, Dublin.	31-12-1920	Messenger Boy	8-8-1945
E/408041	BRADLEY, Thomas	278 St. Attracta Road, Dublin.	29-9-1923	Cow Milker	8-8-1945
E/422015	BRADY, Bernard	Ballinacargie, Drung, Co. Cavan.	4-1-1919	Farm Labourer	8-8-1945
V/208028	BRADY, Bernard	32 Douglas St., Cork.	17-4-1916	Gen. Labourer	8-8-1945
A/83245	BRADY, Francis	74 Lr. Clanbrassil Street, Dublin.	26-6-1921	Labourer	8-8-1945
V/209332	BRADY, James	Ballinagh, Co. Cavan.	1-5-1917	Farm Labourer	8-8-1945
A/75749	BRADY, James	Aughalion, Ballyjamesduff, Co. Cavan.	13-6-1919	Farm Labourer	8-8-1945
E/422016	BRADY, John	Three Mile House, Monaghan.	12-6-1922	Labourer	8-8-1945

Army No.	Name.	Last Recorded Address.	Date of Birth.	Declared Occupation prior to enlistment in Defence Forces.	Date of Dismissal from Defence Forces.
V/203851	BRADY, John	Lr. Monkstown, Co. Cork.	22-6-1920	Gen. Labourer	8-8-1945
E/407043	BRADY, Joseph J.	65 Annamoe Tce., Dublin.	11-11-1921	Newsvendor	8-8-1945
A/83435	BRADY, Kevin Gerard	79 Larkhill Rd., Dublin.	9-8-1921	Pantry Boy	8-8-1945
E/403590	BRADY, Michael	11 Wilson's Lane, Newry.	5-9-1905	Painter	8-8-1945
L/503196	BRADY, Michael	62 Lr. Dominick Street, Dublin.	28-8-1927	Messenger	6-1-1946
E/422486	BRADY, Oliver	Cookstown, Kells.	23-7-1920	Labourer	8-8-1945
E/423697	BRADY, Patrick	Cranaghan, Ballyconnell, Co. Cavan.	19-8-1922	Farmer	8-8-1945
E/424703	BRADY, Patrick	Loisiorty, Lossitt P.O., Co. Cavan.	29-3-1918	Motor Driver	8-8-1945
E/422111	BRADY, Patrick	Clondergole, Monaghan.	22-8-1905	Labourer	8-8-1945
E/434426	BRADY, Thomas	233 Collins Ave., Dublin.	4-10-1913	Plasterer	8-8-1945
E/421808	BRADY, William	Lahernahone, Ballyconnell, Co. Cavan.	21-5-1922	Farm Labourer	8-8-1945
E/404863	BRANNIGAN, Charles C.	17 York Rd., Rathmines, Dublin.	17-8-1912	Fitter	8-8-1945
E/409615	BRANNIGAN, Gerard	224 Larkhill Rd., Dublin.	7-7-1923	Clerk	8-8-1945
E/403032	BRANNIGAN John	15 Inchicore Rd., Dublin.	5-9-1919	Student	8-8-1945
E/424676	BRAY, Thomas	Robinstown, Navan.	11-4-1922	Bar Assistant	8-8-1945
E/423039	BRAZIL, Joseph	30 Seafort Gardens, Sandymount, Dublin.	28-2-1919	Messenger	9-7-1946
E/431540	BRAZIL, Peter	Coolagarry, Walsh Island, Geashill, Offaly.	7-11-1921	Labourer	8-8-1945
E/433058	BRAZIL, William	15 Upr. Buckingham St., Dublin.	20-4-1921	Labourer	8-8-1945
77729	BREEN, Brendan Francis	41 Belvedere Pce., Dublin.	3-12-1918	Student	8-8-1945
V/201879	BREEN, Denis	New Road, Tipperary.	5-11-1916	Labourer	8-8-1945
76856	BREEN, Joseph	Pella Road, Kilrush, Co. Clare.	14-1-1920	Labourer	8-8-1945
E/404903	BREEN, Myles	44 Grenville Tce., Dublin.	19-11-1919	{Fitter's Mate, {Motor Mechanic	8-8-1945
E/430272	BREEN, Thomas	Ballycolla, Co. Leix.	7-10-1919	Labourer	8-8-1945
E/403253	BRENNAN, Anthony	30 Pearse Sq., Dublin.	17-8-1915	None	8-8-1945
E/432414	BRENNAN, Anthony	32 Bolton Street, Dublin.	5-9-1921	Gen. Labourer	8-8-1945
E/405218	BRENNAN, Cyril J.	13 Fortfield Rd., Terenure, Dublin.	25-7-1902	Clerk	8-8-1945
E/433533	BRENNAN, George	10 Kirwan St. Cottages, Dublin.	26-6-1912	Assembler	8-8-1945
E/422017	BRENNAN, Harry	Celbridge, Co. Kildare.	26-2-1916	Farm Labourer	8-8-1945
75403	BRENNAN, John	27 Stephen's St., Kilkenny.	1-4-1918	Labourer	8-8-1945
E/408458	BRENNAN, Michael	Sallins, Co. Kildare.	27-7-1924	Farmer	8-8-1945
E/431331	BRENNAN, Michael	35 Stephen's St., Kilkenny.	22-4-1922	Labourer	8-8-1945
L/507042	BRENNAN, Michael	3 Market Alley, Limerick.	3-4-1923	Labourer	8-8-1945
78441	BRENNAN, Michael	Main Street, Athlone.	25-2-1920	Weaver	8-8-1945
L/507686	BRENNAN, Michael	21 Doyle's Cottages, Garryowen, Limerick.	4-4-1926	Labourer	30-6-1946
E/434380	BRENNAN, Patrick	4 Hanover St. W., Dublin.	20-11-1915	Iron Moulder	8-8-1945
L/502566	BRENNAN, Sean	17 Annamoe Tce., Dublin.	16-7-1926	Bootmaker	16-9-1945
E/407791	BRENNAN, Thomas	30 Seán McDermott St., Dublin.	31-12-1922	Labourer	8-8-1945
E/431814	BRENNAN, Thomas	29 Pearse St., Kilkenny.	25-11-1916	Labourer	8-8-1945
L/501725	BRENNAN, Thomas	26 Cross Avenue, Dun Laoghaire.	5-7-1922	Messenger	8-8-1945
A/84086	BRESLIN, Charles	O'Connell's Tce., Longford.	30-8-1912	Labourer	8-8-1945
E/425188	BRESLIN, Gerald	45 Nelson Street, Derry.	23-9-1924	Motor Driver	8-8-1945
E/420673	BRESLIN, Robert	6 O'Connell's Terrace, Longford.	4-7-1922	Messenger	8-8-1945
L/503258	BRIDE, James	326 Kildare Rd., Crumlin, Dublin.	19-4-1928	Messenger	12-4-1946
L/502161	BRIDGEMAN, Ml. A.	31 Collins Av., Donnycarney, Dublin.	30-6-1923	Painter	8-8-1945
205916	BRIEN, Myles	Ballywalter, Kilmuckridge, Gorey.	18-6-1918	Labourer	8-8-1945

Army No.	Name.	Last Recorded Address.	Date of Birth.	Declared Occupation prior to enlistment in Defence Forces.	Date of Dismissal from Defence Forces.
A/80511	BRIEN, Thomas	Kilrock, Ballon, Tullow, Co. Carlow.	6-1-1922	Farm Labourer	8-8-1945
A/73715	BRODERICK, John	Newtownmountkennedy, Co. Wicklow.	30-6-1914	Apprentice to Motor Trade	8-8-1945
82285	BRODERICK, John	91 Oliver Plunkett Street, Cork.	28-2-1917	Motor Driver	8-8-1945
E/401586	BROGAN, Joseph	44 Foley Street, Dublin.	15-5-1912	Dairy Worker	8-8-1945
E/401626	BROHAN, Patrick	12 Emmet St., Blackrock, Co. Dublin.	28-3-1907	Gardener	8-8-1945
E/430811	BROODER, Joseph	Green Rd., Ballybrophy, Leix.	8-1-1912	Postman	8-8-1945
V/206525	BROPHY, James	41 Waterford St., Dublin.	22-2-1921	Factory Hand	8-8-1945
E/431566	BROPHY, Peter	Balland Ctgs., Tullamore.	17-3-1919	Gen. Labourer	8-8-1945
206793	BROSNAN, Patrick	5 Sandford Ave., Donore Ave., S.C.Rd., Dublin.	21-1-1920	Telegraphist	8-8-1945
75992	BROWN, Christopher	Patrick St., Mountrath, Leix.	25-7-1919	Labourer	8-8-1945
79667	BROWN, Eamon V.	2 Allen Street, Limerick.	14-7-1921	Clerk	8-8-1945
E/424528	BROWN, Emmet	8 Brackenagh, Ballinasloe, Co. Galway.	14-10-1922	Farm Labourer	9-8-1945
E/434801	BROWN, George	Ballysax, Curragh, Co. Kildare.	26-6-1920	Motor Driver	8-8-1945
V/207439	BROWN, James	8 St. Kevin's Tce., Arklow.	29-6-1913	Motor Driver	8-8-1945
E/415421	BROWN, John	2 Albert Street, Clonmel.	17-2-1923	Engineer's Tool Maker	8-8-1945
V/202426	BROWN, Martin	11 St. Bridget's Terrace, Bohermore, Co. Galway.	9-5-1920	Road Labourer	8-8-1945
83729	BROWN, Patrick	28 Elm Rd., Donnycarney, Dublin.	31-5-1922	Tailor's Assistant	8-8-1945
A/75828	BROWN, Patrick	39 St. Brendan's Terrace, Ballinasloe.	6-3-1918	Labourer	8-8-1945
79735	BROWN, Patrick	Fox and Geese, Clondalkin, Co. Dublin.	31-3-1921	Labourer	8-8-1945
V/203885	BROWN, Peter	7 Mount Eden Rd., Cork.	18-7-1919	Labourer	8-8-1945
E/424726	BROWN, William	Dernable, Strabane.	16-8-1922	Labourer	8-8-1945
L/507742	BROWN, William	34 Lacy's Villas, Tipperary.	2-7-1926	Labourer	9-6-1946
205069	BROWN, William	68 Galtymore Road, Crumlin, Dublin.	1-2-1918	Labourer	8-8-1945
A/106447	BROWNE, Denis	Lr. Main St., Letterkenny.	12-7-1912	Factory Worker	8-8-1945
E/433531	BROWNE, Denis	390 "S" Block, Oliver Bond House, Usher's Street, Dublin.	16-10-1918	Gen. Labourer	8-8-1945
E/423524	BROWNE, Edward	c/o Mrs. Gaughan, Mail Coach Road, Sligo.	19-5-1918	Labourer	8-8-1945
E/421599	BROWNE, George	Hill Street, Ballina.	14-1-1914	Shop Assistant	8-8-1945
V/207439	BROWNE, James	Turnpike, Moate, Co. Westmeath.	13-1-1920	Labourer	8-8-1945
A/110301	BROWNE, James	Mitchell Street, Cavan.	25-5-1916	Labourer	8-8-1945
E/413598	BROWNE, Patrick	1 Cathedral Pce., Limerick.	20-3-1920	Labourer	8-8-1945
72122	BROWNE, Thomas	24 High Road, Thomond Gate, Limerick.	4-7-1909	Farm Labourer	8-8-1945
E/404735	BROWNLOW, Patrick G.	St. Vincent's House, Glasnevin, Dublin.	2-3-1921	Clerk	8-8-1945
66961	BRUDER, Thomas	78 Gaskard Road, Balham Hill, London, S.W.	17-6-1907	Labourer	8-8-1945
83742	BRUNTZ, Frederick B. J.	38 Eastmoreland Lane, Haddington Rd., Dublin.	6-3-1918	Motor Mechanic Welder	8-8-1945
V/208769	BRUTON, James	84 Devenish Rd., Crumlin, Dublin.	16-9-1921	None	8-8-1945
E/434795	BRYAN, Patrick John	43 Connolly St., Kilkenny.	5-11-1913	Lorry Driver	8-8-1945
V/209535	BRYANT, George	5 Killiney Hill Cottages, Killiney, Co. Dublin.	15-4-1917	Seaman	8-8-1945
V/208466	BRYANT, Seamus	5 Killiney Hill Cottages, Killiney, Co. Dublin.	26-8-1921	Mess Room Steward	8-8-1945

Army No.	Name.	Last Recorded Address.	Date of Birth.	Declared Occupation prior to enlistment in Defence Forces.	Date of Dismissal from Defence Forces.
V/205997	BUCHANAN, Daniel	Argrey, Ballinadrait, Co. Donegal.	22-10-1916	Labourer	8-8-1945
E/407462	BUCKLEY, Bernard	15 Russell Avenue, Drumcondra, Dublin.	4-6-1923	Clerk	8-8-1945
78415	BUCKLEY, Michael	54 Ossory Park, Kilkenny.	30-8-1915	Gen. Labourer	8-8-1945
V/207215	BUCKLEY, Patrick	Smithfield, Lombardstown, Co. Cork.	6-5-1921	Labourer	8-8-1945
E/409365	BUCKLEY, Peter	Ballysax, Kilcullen, Co. Kildare.	10-6-1923	Farm Labourer	8-8-1945
E/424126	BUCKLEY, Peter.	Clooneagh, Dromod, Co. Leitrim.	27-11-1921	Blacksmith's Helper.	8-8-1945
V/206606	BUCKLEY, Richard	11 Blarney Street, Cork.	21-3-1921	Gen. Labourer	8-8-1945
A/75627	BUCKLEY, Thomas	3 Killarney Parade, Dublin.	1-6-1919	Farm Labourer	8-8-1945
L/500267	BULLMAN, Thomas	5 Dummy's Lawn, Shandon Street, Cork.	4-7-1922	Shoemaker	8-8-1945
E/415734	BULLMAN, Timothy	26 Cathedral Road, Cork.	19-5-1923	None	8-8-1945
L/500763	BURBIDGE, James	14 Camac Park, Bluebell, Inchicore, Dublin.	4-6-1923	Carter	8-8-1945
L/501789	BURDIS, Martin	185 Carnlough Rd., Cabra, Dublin.	1-7-1924	Messenger	8-8-1945
V/208812	BURKE, Andrew	3 St. James's St., Gorey.	17-2-1908	Motor Driver	8-8-1945
E/421716	BURKE, Bernard	Moness, Burt, Co. Donegal.	1-1-1922	Labourer	8-8-1945
E/410243	BURKE, Donald	Mallow Road, Doneraile, Co. Cork.	25-3-1921	Labourer	8-8-1945
L/502797	BURKE, Eugene	43 Lr. Seán McDermott Street, Dublin.	6-6-1927	Messenger	29-12-1945
78235	BURKE, George	Temple, Gurteen, Co. Galway.	18-3-1921	Labourer	8-8-1945
E/414442	BURKE, James	The Cross, Ballintemple, Cork.	1-8-1904	Machinist	8-8-1945
E/404431	BURKE, John	Newtown, Charleville, Co. Cork.	12-7-1906	Draper's Assistant	8-8-1945
V/205437	BURKE, John	27 Coombe Street, Dublin.	21-6-1921	Gen. Labourer	8-8-1945
V/207766	BURKE, John	3 Claddagh Quay, Galway.	6-2-1920	Gen. Labourer	8-8-1945
E/410773	BURKE, John	21 Lacey's Villas, Tipperary.	24-5-1921	Labourer	8-8-1945
L/507945	BURKE, John	5 Keynon's Ave., Kileely, Limerick.	12-3-1926	Labourer	28-4-1946
A/101207	BURKE, Joseph	Curratabain, Killene, Gorey, Co. Wexford.	30-5-1915	Labourer	8-8-1945
63256	BURKE, Joseph	17 Roche Mill Lane Brinwood Estate, Rochdale, England.	24-11-1906	Labourer	8-8-1945
74106	BURKE, Joseph	2 Havelock Tce., Sandymount, Dublin.	6-8-1915	Gen. Labourer	8-8-1945
A/78832	BURKE, Kevin	Curraghtubber, Killeena, Wexford.	6-3-1921	Farm Labourer	8-8-1945
E/421505	BURKE, Leslie	Ballygallon, Breenagh, Co. Donegal.	23-7-1919	Labourer and Road Worker	8-8-1945
64563	BURKE, Maurice	8 Sarsfield Sq., Athlone.	17-11-1902	Labourer	8-8-1945
A/73990	BURKE, Michael	2 Williams Cottages, Bracknell, Berks.	12-8-1914	Longshoreman	8-8-1945
E/423781	BURKE, Patrick	Drumcool P.O., Riverstown, Co. Sligo.	7-12-1921	Labourer	8-8-1945
E/416450	BURKE, Patrick	18 Strand Street, Tralee.	6-1-1923	Labourer	8-8-1945
V/210028	BURKE, Thomas	15 St. Patrick's Park, Carrick-on-Shannon.	18-4-1921	Labourer	8-8-1945
78710	BURNS, Bernard	29 Chapel Rd., Waterside, Derry.	25-7-1919	Storeman	8-8-1945
E/422453	BURNS, Hugh	c/o H. McInley, Glebe, Lenan Fort P.O., Buncrana, Co. Donegal.	16-10-1921	Shop Assistant	8-8-1945
L/507307	BURNS, Martin	Bayview, Gleninagh, Ballyvaughan, Co. Clare.	19-4-1925	Labourer	8-8-1945
78711	BURNS, Michael	29 Chapel St., Derry.	1-8-1920	Storeman	8-8-1945

Army No.	Name.	Last Recorded Address.	Date of Birth.	Declared Occupation prior to enlistment in Defence Forces.	Date of Dismissal from Defence Forces.
L/501935	BURNS, Thomas	Macks Road, Drogheda, Co. Louth	11-2-1922	Labourer	8-8-1945
E/420065	BURNSIDE, Robert	25 St. John's Tce., Sligo.	29-3-1915	Labourer	8-8-1945
A/73435	BURNSIDE, William	Holborn St., Sligo.	22-2-1911	Motor Driver	8-8-1945
E/421029	BUSHELL, Francis	4 Congress Tce., Longford	20-9-1917	Motor Driver	8-8-1945
77582	BUSTON, Christopher	Clonagh, Ardagh, Co. Limerick.	20-7-1920	Labourer	8-8-1945
76068	BUTLER, Augustine	Ballynock, Dungarvan, Co. Waterford.	28-8-1918	None	8-8-1945
V/208786	BUTLER, Edward	50 Mary St., Drogheda.	7-6-1914	Bus Conductor	8-8-1945
E/402653	BUTLER, Francis J.	Dublin Street, Monaghan.	8-4-1921	Labourer	8-8-1945
A/74831	BUTLER, James	17 Deane St., Kilkenny.	7-6-1914	Gen. Labourer	8-8-1945
A/72979	BUTLER, James	118 St. Ita's Street, Lr. Mary's Park, Limerick.	14-10-1910	Bar Assistant	8-8-1945
E/424128	BUTLER, James	Drumshambo, Co. Leitrim.	26-7-1922	Gen. Labourer	8-8-1945
V/213170	BUTLER, John	32 St. Declan's Road, Gurranebraher, Cork.	15-12-1920	Waiter	8-8-1945
74115	BUTLER, Nicholas	Kilmanagh, Callan, Co. Kilkenny.	27-11-1915	Labourer	8-8-1945
E/405697	BUTLER, Pierce	66 Oliver Plunkett Avenue, Dun Laoghaire	14-8-1910	Motor Driver	8-8-1945
V/207892	BUTLER, Thomas	Boheraclough, Cashel.	15-3-1918	Mason	8-8-1945
E/432592	BUTLER, Thomas	1 St. Patrick's Villas, Ringsend, Dublin.	20-6-1919	Labourer	8-8-1945
E/410774	BUTLER, Tobias	27 O'Connell Road, Tipperary.	13-6-1921	Glove Cutter	8-8-1945
E/411078	BUTLER, William	Burton St., Kilrush, Co. Clare.	25-9-1914	Motor Driver	8-8-1945
E/438053	BYRNE, Andrew	56 Hollyfield Buildings, Rathmines, Dublin.	27-4-1926	Messenger	* 8-8-1945
L/502962	BYRNE, Charles	176 Quarry Road, Cabra, Dublin.	12-11-1927	Gen. Labourer	8-8-1945
A/78453	BYRNE, Christopher	2 Hammond Lane, Dublin.	1-1-1918	Labourer	8-8-1945
E/432932	BYRNE, Christopher	47 Dolphin's Barn Street, Dublin.	15-12-1918	Labourer	8-8-1945
L/500351	BYRNE, Colman	24 Philipsburgh Terrace, Fairview, Dublin.	7-6-1919	Heating Engineer	8-8-1945
E/402392	BYRNE, Denis	162 Clonmacnoise Road, Kimmage, Dublin.	25-3-1922	None	8-8-1945
83370	BYRNE, Edward	14 St. John's Street, Pimlico, Dublin.	27-12-1919	Labourer	8-8-1945
L/502839	BYRNE, Edward	315 Ballybough House, Poplar Row, Dublin.	20-10-1926	Turf Worker	17-3-1946
V/203222	BYRNE, Edward	Knocklishen, Co. Carlow.	23-12-1916	Labourer	8-8-1945
E/408967	BYRNE, Edward	Newcastle, Co. Dublin.	13-10-1924	Builders' Labourer	8-8-1945
L/501958	BYRNE, Edward	27 Coleraine St., Dublin.	20-5-1925	Newsboy	8-8-1945
73182	BYRNE, Felix	7 Ryder's Row, Parnell Street, Dublin.	15-6-1914	Packer	8-8-1945
83127	BYRNE, Francis	3 Park Terrace, Francis Street, Dublin.	8-2-1922	Labourer	8-8-1945
E/405206	BYRNE, James	8 Bloomfield Cottages, Dublin.	9-5-1922	Window Dresser	8-8-1945
E/404489	BYRNE, James	6 Pleasants Street, Dublin.	5-11-1903	Office Cleaner	8-8-1945
81955	BYRNE, James	25 Sarsfield St., Thurles, Co. Tipperary.	29-4-1924	Labourer	8-8-1945
210024	BYRNE, James	3 Rathfadden, Waterford.	16-1-1923	None	8-8-1945
A/75539	BYRNE, John	37 Chancery Lane, Dublin.	10-5-1918	Messenger Boy	8-8-1945
E/401857	BYRNE, John	9 Linenhall St., Dublin.	15-5-1922	Packer	8-8-1945
V/206443	BYRNE, John	3 Eden Villas, Glasthule, Co. Dublin.	25-6-1923	Labourer	8-8-1945
V/209706	BYRNE, John	5 Middle Third, Kellester, Dublin.	17-8-1922	Messenger Boy	8-8-1945
202820	BYRNE, John	43 Coombe, Dublin.	8-1-1918	Butcher	8-8-1945

Army No.	Name.	Last Recorded Address.	Date of Birth.	Declared Occupation prior to enlistment in Defence Forces.	Date of Dismissal from Defence Forces.
E/430580	BYRNE, John P.	2 Plewman's Tce., Athy, Co. Kildare.	2-4-1914	Butcher	8-8-1945
400096	BYRNE, Joseph	13 Annaville, Ranelagh, Dublin.	1-6-1912	Barber	8-8-1945
79366	BYRNE, Joseph	26 Quarry Road, Cabra, Dublin.	2-6-1920	None	8-8-1945
77034	BYRNE, Martin	68 Irishtown Road, Ringsend, Dublin.	20-5-1919	Assistant on Lorry	8-8-1945
L/502337	BYRNE, Martin	26 York St., Dublin.	1-1-1922	Gen. Labourer	8-8-1945
V/205942	BYRNE, Michael	Mullice, Hollywood, Co. Wicklow.	27-4-1913	Farmer	8-8-1945
A/73137	BYRNE, Michael	52 Fenian St., Dublin.	2-9-1913	Labourer	8-8-1945
A/74383	BYRNE, Michael	2 New House B., Inacourty, Co. Waterford.	29-8-1916	Gen. Labourer	8-8-1945
L/502936	BYRNE, Nicholas	38 Desmond Ave., Dun Laoghaire.	10-9-1927	Hotel Waiter	18-4-1946
83265	BYRNE, Patrick	16 Upr. Buckingham St., Dublin.	16-11-1920	Shoemaker	8-8-1945
E/404737	BYRNE, Patrick S.	14 Georges Place, Dublin.	26-12-1900	Fitter's Helper	8-8-1945
V/206486	BYRNE, Patrick	52 Gulistan Cottages, Rathmines, Dublin.	23-1-1922	Labourer	8-8-1945
E/408556	BYRNE, Patrick	27 Sean McDermott St., Dublin.	6-6-1922	Lorry Driver	8-8-1945
205087	BYRNE, Patrick	133 Parnell St., Dublin.	25-6-1921	Labourer	8-8-1945
78417	BYRNE, Patrick	77 Patrick St., Kilkenny.	9-8-1915	Gen. Labourer	8-8-1945
75864	BYRNE, Peter	27 Belvedere Place, N.C.Road, Dublin.	4-4-1918	Gen. Labourer	8-8-1945
E/406167	BYRNE, Peter	10 Pearse Square, Bray.	8-3-1923	Messenger	8-8-1945
E/435522	BYRNE, Peter	27 Clonard Rd., Dublin.	16-12-1914	Labourer	8-8-1945
V/206450	BYRNE, Richard	3 Molesworth Pce., Dublin.	28-1-1922	Messenger	8-8-1945
78495	BYRNE, Robert	11 Railway Cottages, Lansdowne Rd., Dublin.	3-5-1918	Shop Assistant	8-8-1945
80325	BYRNE, Stephen	44A Beaumont Road, Drumcondra, Dublin.	2-3-1922	Labourer	8-8-1945
E/406650	BYRNE, Thomas	Ballindaragh, Markethill, Co. Armagh.	15-1-1923	Farm Labourer	8-8-1945
83187	BYRNE, Thomas	Newtown, Raheny, Dublin	18-12-1917	Mechanic	8-8-1945
400384	BYRNE, Thomas	Milltown, Ashford, Co. Wicklow.	25-3-1918	Butcher	8-8-1945
E/402986	BYRNE, Thomas	26 Northbrook Tce., North Strand, Dublin.	23-7-1913	Electrician	8-8-1945
E/405569	BYRNE, Thomas	6 St. Patrick's Tce., Navan	12-8-1922	Labourer	8-8-1945
L/502183	BYRNE, Thomas	45 St. Mary's Rd., East Wall, Dublin.	16-7-1923	Labourer	8-8-1945
75668	BYRNE, Vincent	93 Kilfenora Road, Kimmage, Dublin.	16-4-1919	Messenger	8-8-1945
E/406435	BYRNE, William	3 St. Mary's Tce., Dorset Street, Dublin.	23-1-1923	Grocer's Porter	8-8-1945
E/402159	BYRNE, William	3 Seatown, Dundalk, Co. Louth.	11-10-1920	Motor Mechanic	8-8-1945
V/206455	BYRNE, William	21 Hendrick St., Dublin.	5-1-1922	Labourer	8-8-1945
E/407323	BYRNE, William	44 Stanaway Road, Kimmage, Dublin.	29-6-1926	Farm Labourer	8-8-1945
E/433976	BYRNE, William	Ballaghmoon, Carlow.	18-2-1916	Farm Labourer	8-8-1945
83706	BYRNE, William	143 F Block, Iveagh Bldgs., New Bride St., Dublin.	2-7-1922	Engineering Apprentice	8-8-1945
E/412878	BYRNES, Joseph	78 St. Munchin's Street, Limerick.	15-2-1903	Labourer	8-8-1945
A/63260	BYRON, William	10 St. Columbcille Street, Island Field, Limerick.	28-11-1904	Labourer	8-8-1945
E/422119	CADDEN, William	Drumlownagh, Loughdough, Co. Cavan.	21-6-1915	Steel Erector	8-8-1945
A/83164	CAFFREY, Nicholas	Ballymun, Santry, Co. Dublin.	7-3-1922	Labourer	8-8-1945

Army No.	Name.	Last Recorded Address.	Date of Birth.	Declared Occupation prior to enlistment in Defence Forces.	Date of Dismissal from Defence Forces.
57739	CAFFREY, Philip	Stork Stables, Lambourn, Berks.	10-5-1903	Labourer, Groom	8-8-1945
E/424007	CAGNEY, John	5 St. Patrick's Tce., Sligo.	20-4-1920	Clerk	8-8-1945
L/506799	CAHERLANE, Michael	Ballylangley, Butlerstown, Timoleague, Co. Cork.	6-6-1925	Labourer	8-8-1945
74004	CAHILL, Arthur	20 Lr. Kevin St., Dublin.	6-1-1916	Messenger Boy	8-8-1945
E/407891	CAHILL, Eoin	Emmet St., Kilmallock, Co. Limerick.	28-12-1923	Farm Labourer	8-8-1945
V/206347	CAHILL, James	Tobinstown, Ramsgrange, Co. Wexford.	10-5-1920	Farm Labourer	8-8-1945
E/435283	CAHILL, John	Coolman, Ballyhale, Co. Kilkenny.	25-8-1915	Farm Labourer	8-8-1945
E/403730	CAHILL, John Francis	1 James's Street, Dublin.	13-12-1922	Labourer	8-8-1945
E/431623	CAHILL, Matthew	Main Street, Abbeyleix.	6-7-1916	Plasterer	8-8-1945
E/437768	CAHILL, Patrick	21 C Block, St. Joseph's Mansions, Killarney St., Dublin.	29-9-1925	Painter	8-8-1945
A/77485	CAHILL, Patrick	Bansha Rd., Tipperary.	20-9-1915	Gen. Labourer	8-8-1945
E/435281	CAHILL, Richard	Coolmeen, Ballyhale, Co. Kilkenny.	7-9-1917	Farm Labourer	8-8-1945
E/402892	CAHILL, Thomas	36 Lr. Rathmines Road, Dublin.	25-5-1900	Crane Driver	8-8-1945
E/416425	CAHILL, William	Dromsally, Cappamore, Co. Limerick.	22-11-1921	Labourer	8-8-1945
E/405302	CAHILLANE, Patrick	13 Fontenoy St., Dublin.	17-6-1919	Labourer	8-8-1945
E/423597	CALLAGHAN, Charles	6 Mitchell's Tce., Sligo.	18-8-1922	Messenger	8-8-1945
E/421168	CALLAGHAN, John	Sandyrow, Castlefin, Co. Donegal.	2-11-1915	Mill Worker	8-8-1945
E/424801	CALLAGHAN, Michael	Tournagh, Riverstown, Co. Sligo.	10-2-1923	Labourer	8-8-1945
E/423449	CALLAGHAN, Thomas	Shealmore, Mohill, Co. Leitrim.	16-1-1910	Motor Driver	8-8-1945
A/78433	CALLAN, Thomas	742 Iveagh Flats, Bride Street, Dublin.	1-1-1920	Sawyer's Apprentice	8-8-1945
A/77056	CALLANAN, Cornelius	Cabra, Holycross, Thurles.	15-7-1915	Labourer	8-8-1945
A/76577	CALLANAN, Thomas	Cabra, Holycross, Thurles.	19-6-1919	Labourer	8-8-1945
E/407620	CALLERY, John	13 Heytesbury St., Dublin.	4-8-1923	Page	8-8-1945
V/209334	CALPIN, Patrick	Caltra, Easkey, Co. Sligo.	5-4-1920	Labourer	8-8-1945
A/84363	CALVIN, Martin	Slieverue, Athenry.	8-10-1924	Gen. Labourer	22-1-1946
E/421718	CAMERON, Alan	Palace Street, Drogheda.	17-8-1921	Motor Engineering Apprentice	8-8-1945
E/433013	CAMP, James	75 Eccles Street, Dublin.	3-11-1918	Sheet Metal Worker	8-8-1945
E/422451	CAMPBELL, Charles	11 New Cottages, Cockhill, Buncrana, Co. Donegal.	24-8-1922	Moulder	8-8-1945
E/437847	CAMPBELL, Cyril	18A Albert Bridge Rd., Belfast.	26-12-1926	Hair Dresser's Assistant	8-10-1945
83624	CAMPBELL, Felix	221 North Circular Road, Dublin.	27-12-1921	Butcher	8-8-1945
E/424576	CAMPBELL, James	East End, Bundoran, Co. Donegal.	12-3-1923	Labourer	8-8-1945
E/408919	CAMPBELL, James	67 Dartmouth Sq., Dublin.	12-1-1919	Veterinary Student	8-8-1945
83730	CAMPBELL, John	1 Greenmount Court, Harold's Cross, Dublin.	2-6-1922	Messenger	8-8-1945
E/423193	CAMPBELL, John	5 Herbert Street, Derry.	6-4-1920	Shop Assistant	8-8-1945
E/406655	CAMPBELL, John	Annaghbeg, Dungannon, Co. Tyrone.	7-5-1922	Clerk	8-8-1945
E/425146	CAMPBELL, John	Cornlaughta, Leitrim P.O.	22-8-1922	Farmer	8-8-1945
78993	CAMPBELL, Joseph	Dungannon Road, Coalisland, Co. Tyrone.	24-10-1920	Shop Assistant	8-8-1945
75650	CAMPBELL, Joseph	Queen's Hotel, Harlech, North Wales.	6-3-1918	Labourer	8-8-1945
E/406562	CAMPBELL, Malachy	Railway St., Coalisland, Co. Tyrone.	24-6-1919	Electrical Improver	8-8-1945

Army No.	Name.	Last Recorded Address.	Date of Birth.	Declared Occupation prior to enlistment in Defence Forces.	Date of Dismissal from Defence Forces.
81820	CAMPBELL, Michael P.	34 Bannow Road, Cabra West, Dublin.	20-3-1927	Tailors' Presser	23-3-1946
E/400246	CAMPBELL, Peter	12A Corporation Buildings, Dublin.	11-1-1896	Cook	8-8-1945
A/83798	CAMPBELL, Thomas	Dungannon Road, Coalisland, Co. Tyrone.	27-9-1920	Butchers' Assistant	8-8-1945
E/401398	CAMPBELL, William P.	174 Cashel Rd., Kimmage, Dublin.	5-12-1901	Painter	8-8-1945
E/404379	CAMPBELL, William	47 Wellington St., Lurgan, & 41 Eccles St., Dublin.	2-5-1917	Aero-Fitter	8-8-1945
A/73086	CAMPION, Andrew	11 P Pearse House, Pearse Street, Dublin.	16-2-1914	Motor Driver	8-8-1945
L/507397	CAMPION, Eric	17 Arthur's Qy., Limerick.	24-3-1927	Labourer	8-8-1945
52134	CANAVAN, James	20 Townsend St., Dublin.	27-9-1905	Labourer	8-8-1945
E/404778	CANAVAN, Patrick	6 Mountjoy Pce., Dublin.	9-4-1919	Lorry Driver	8-8-1945
E/425596	CANNING, Edward	22 Cross Street, Derry.	6-3-1926	Horse-Van Driver	20-8-1945
E/423450	CANNING, Patrick	Treanmore, Mohill, Co. Leitrim.	24-4-1914	Farmer	8-8-1945
79043	CANNING, Patrick	4 Meehan's Row, Waterside, Derry.	12-2-1918	Labourer	8-8-1945
E/425077	CANNING, Thomas	Ardmeenan, Ballinamore, Co. Leitrim.	23-1-1924	Farm Labourer	8-8-1945
E/405125	CANNON, Desmond	Mill St., Balbriggan, Co. Dublin.	18-6-1922	Factory Worker	8-8-1945
E/400509	CANNON, Lawrence	60 Fenian St., Dublin.	2-7-1921	Baker	8-8-1945
E/421030	CANNON, Maurice	Ardbane, Downings, Co. Donegal.	16-6-1920	Labourer	8-8-1945
E/433857	CANNON, Patrick	Cloghanbeg, Lusmagh, Banagher, Co. Offaly.	21-4-1919	Farmer and Carpenter	8-8-1945
E/434731	CANTWELL, James	24 Gardiner's Pce., Dublin.	12-4-1922	Butcher's Apprentice	8-8-1945
E/411495	CANTY, Timothy	Mahona, Dunmanway, Co. Cork.	10-3-1916	Farm Labourer	20-5-1946
E/404109	CARBERRY, Chas. T.	46 Brown Street, Lurgan, Co. Armagh.	20-1-1920	Labourer	8-8-1945
V/211008	CAREY, Bernard	89 Bride Street, Dublin.	16-4-1918	Labourer	8-8-1945
E/434733	CAREY, Brendan	43 Dunmore St., Belfast.	17-5-1918	Mill Worker	8-8-1945
L/503155	CAREY, Francis J.	37 Kells Road, Crumlin.	7-3-1926	Motor Driver	8-10-1945
E/414632	CAREY, James	c/o Mrs. Raleigh, Ball's Lane, Charleville, Cork.	11-6-1906	Painter	8-8-1945
A/71224	CAREY, Jeremiah	6 Hardwicke St., Dublin.	23-9-1910	Labourer	8-8-1945
E/405435	CAREY, Patrick	43 Up. Mount St., Dublin.	17-11-1914	Lorry Driver	8-8-1945
E/436475	CAREY, Richard	7 Stapleton St., Carlow.	2-6-1925	Shoemaker	8-8-1945
E/406469	CARLEY, Eugene	Carneyhough, Newry.	26-1-1923	Law Clerk	8-8-1945
78749	CARLIN, Jas.	5 Lecky Road, Derry.	8-11-1918	Labourer	8-8-1945
E/422456	CARLIN, John	c/o P. McGlinchy, Cronlaghey, Ballybofey, Co. Donegal.	1-4-1920	Labourer	8-8-1945
E/421509	CARLIN, John	c/o Mrs. Kelly, Glenties, Co. Donegal.	29-11-1919	Apprentice Painter	8-8-1945
E/422854	CARLIN, John	Main Street, Buncrana, Co. Donegal.	5-11-1921	Labourer	8-8-1945
E/422909	CARLIN, Joseph	c/o Mary Gordon, Lettershambo, Co. Donegal.	16-5-1922	Labourer	8-8-1945
E/421507	CARLIN, Patrick	Kilmacrennan, Lifford.	3-6-1912	Ink Worker	8-8-1945
V/204711	CARNEY, Joseph	Castle Street, Castlebar, Co. Mayo.	20-1-1917	Student	8-8-1945
E/402646	CAROLAN, Anthony	Ballacornick, Ballina, Co. Mayo.	30-1-1922	Shop Assistant	8-8-1945
E/424129	CAROLAN, Bernard	Coragh, Belturbet, Co. Cavan.	27-2-1916	Farm Labourer	8-8-1945
80056	CAROLAN, James	56 Chapel St. Rd., Derry.	25-4-1918	Motor Driver, Mechanic	8-8-1945
83941	CAROLAN, Peter	10 Thomas St., Dundalk.	16-8-1922	Fitter	8-8-1945

Army No.	Name.	Last Recorded Address.	Date of Birth.	Declared Occupation prior to enlistment in Defence Forces.	Date of Dismissal from Defence Forces.
V/209085	CARPENTER, Bernard	43 Railway Av., Inchicore, Dublin.	11-2-1921	Labourer	8-8-1945
E/406041	CARPENTER, Felix	17 Nicholas Place, Dublin.	24-2-1922	Ticket Picker	8-8-1945
V/202419	CARPENTER, Patrick	Carlanstown, Kells.	17-3-1918	Labourer	8-8-1945
84773	CARR, Anthony	52 St. Patrick's Park, Carrick-on-Shannon.	5-8-1924	Shoemaker	8-8-1945
V/211332	CARR, James Leo	46 Grosvenor Sq., Dublin.	16-1-1916	Medical Student	8-8-1945
E/421852	CARR, John	Milltown, Barnesmore, Co. Donegal.	17-9-1910	Motor Driver	8-8-1945
V/209015	CARR, Kevin	16 Little Strand Street, Skerries, Co. Dublin.	27-9-1923	Shop Boy	8-8-1945
E/433093	CARR, Patrick	19 Sir John Rogerson's Quay, Dublin.	2-6-1922	Sailor	8-8-1945
E/83445	CARR, Peter	34A Pearse House, Dublin.	23-4-1922	Porter	8-8-1945
E/400885	CARR, Peter	78 Townsend St., Dublin.	26-12-1909	Labourer	8-8-1945
72438	CARR, William	19 Sir John Rogerson's Quay, Dublin.	5-11-1912	Labourer	8-8-1945
L/500939	CARRIE, Joseph	Town Park, Ardee, Co. Louth.	31-5-1916	Cook	8-8-1945
E/421764	CARRIGY, Edward	Killeenbore, Colehill, Co. Longford.	13-7-1922	Farmer	8-8-1945
V/202261	CARROLL, Conor	Lisduff, Kells.	2-3-1910	Labourer	8-8-1945
E/408112	CARROLL, David	15A Benburb Street Buildings, Dublin.	22-1-1908	Gen. Labourer	8-8-1945
80655	CARROLL, Denis	6 Pound Street, Maynooth.	2-6-1920	Labourer	8-8-1945
A/75741	CARROLL, James	1 Merchant's Road, East Wall, Dublin.	27-4-1919	Blacksmith's Helper	8-8-1945
E/423569	CARROLL, John	Fetard, Crossmolina, Co. Mayo.	15-7-1917	Labourer	8-8-1945
E/433060	CARROLL, John	19 Adelaide Terrace, Kilmainham, Dublin.	30-6-1922	Motor Driver	8-8-1945
E/434463	CARROLL, Joseph	52 J.K.L. Place, New Ross, Co. Wexford.	18-10-1917	Labourer	8-8-1945
A/79671	CARROLL, Patrick	Ballyhennessy, Lixnaw, Co. Kerry.	3-10-1919	Farm Labourer	8-8-1945
L/508541	CARROLL, Patrick	Brewel, Collinstown, Co. Wicklow.	25-5-1924	Labourer	8-8-1945
E/401671	CARROLL, Thomas	Newcastle, Co. Wicklow.	18-4-1915	Labourer	8-8-1945
E/424119	CARROLL, Thomas	Carnarea, Curry, Co. Sligo.	13-5-1917	Labourer	8-8-1945
76410	CARROLL, Thomas	Weaver's Point, Crosshaven, Co. Cork.	6-12-1919	Farm Labourer	8-8-1945
205744	CARROLL, Thomas	184 Stanaway Road, Kimmage, Dublin.	17-7-1919	Van Helper	8-8-1945
E/408647	CARROLL, William	143 Galtymore Road, Crumlin, Dublin.	6-6-1920	Bootmaker's Improver	8-8-1945
E/416134	CARROLL, William	Ballyheigue, Co. Kerry.	10-9-1923	Student	8-8-1945
E/422489	CARRY, Terence	Rosmeen, Kells.	1-9-1912	Labourer	8-8-1945
217070	CARSON, Eugene	28 Belquinn Park, Monaghan.	6-3-1922	Weaver	8-8-1945
E/432444	CARSON, Frank	Main St., Castleblaney.	5-3-1921	Motor Driver	8-8-1945
A/76611	CARSON, Henry	2 Nicholas Street, Dublin.	1-4-1919	Milk Server	8-8-1945
A/83449	CARTER, John Patrick	32 F Block, Oliver Bond House, Dublin.	5-11-1919	Labourer	8-8-1945
A/74229	CARTHY, Aidan	Ballygow, Bannow, Co. Waterford.	11-4-1916	General Farm Labourer	8-8-1945
A/73938	CARTON, Thomas	The Bungalows, St. Laurence Rd., Ballymoran, Co. Wicklow.	25-9-1912	Farm Labourer	8-8-1945
E/422738	CARTY, Francis	Corduff, Carriga P.O., Co. Leitrim.	11-5-1922	Farm Labourer	8-8-1945
E/434399	CARTY, Peter	2 Mountjoy Sq., Dublin.	11-7-1907	Fitter (Motor)	8-8-1945
79984	CARVILLE, Terence	278 Cupar Street, Belfast.	13-4-1915	Barman	8-8-1945
E/435838	CASEY, James	58 Ross Road, Enniscorthy, Co. Wexford.	26-10-1919	Lorry Driver	8-8-1945
V/210027	CASEY, John	36 Nicholas Av., Dundalk.	4-3-1921	Labourer	8-8-1945

Army No.	Name.	Last Recorded Address.	Date of Birth.	Declared Occupation prior to enlistment in Defence Forces.	Date of Dismissal from Defence Forces.
E/423254	CASEY, John	120 Bogside, Derry.	22-12-1922	Labourer	8-8-1945
E/434398	CASEY, Joseph	10a Camden St., Dublin.	24-7-1922	Factory Worker	8-8-1945
A/84019	CASEY, Michael	24 Bunree Road, Ballina.	8-7-1921	Labourer	8-8-1945
L/507824	CASEY, Patrick	19 Mountain View, Tipperary.	20-3-1928	Labourer	30-6-1946
E/406547	CASEY, Richard	Curran Rd., Dungannon.	23-5-1923	Tinter	8-8-1945
L/506176	CASEY, Thomas	2 Merrypole Lane, Blarney Street, Cork.	23-3-1924	Messenger	8-8-1945
V/208131	CASEY, William	Derryfad, Tourmakeedy, Co. Mayo.	3-2-1921	Labourer	8-8-1945
E/405750	CASHIN, Bernard	45 Hardwicke St., Dublin.	7-12-1916	Motor Driver	8-8-1945
200428	CASHIN, James	Kilbricken, Rossmuck, Co. Galway.	20-12-1914	Labourer	8-8-1945
E/423255	CASSIDY, Daniel	Bridge Street, Irvinstown, Co. Fermanagh.	4-5-1901	Labourer	8-8-1945
A/75041	CASSIDY, James	10 Aungier St., Dublin.	13-5-1917	Farm Labourer	8-8-1945
106123	CASSIDY, James	Emmet St., Cavan.	30-8-1914	Bricklayer	8-8-1945
84528	CASSIDY, John	7 Robinhood Road, Clondalkin, Co. Dublin.	24-12-1917	Clerk	8-8-1945
E/420348	CASSIDY, John	Derrylahan, Grangerlin, Co. Cavan.	19-7-1900	Farm Labourer	8-8-1945
V/200836	CASSIDY, John J.	15 Union Quay, Cork.	14-2-1921	Labourer	8-8-1945
E/415655	CASSIDY, Joseph	Courthouse, Killaloe, Co. Clare.	24-7-1922	Labourer	8-8-1945
79969	CASSIDY, Kevin	53 Rossvill Street, Derry.	6-2-1921	Labourer	8-8-1945
75829	CASSIDY, Patrick J.	Curoar, Dooger, Co. Cavan.	28-2-1912	Labourer	8-8-1945
E/421960	CASSIDY, William	c/o Mrs. M. Carbury, Newtownforbes, Co. Longford.	29-9-1913	Motor Driver	8-8-1945
V/204230	CASSIN, Peter	13C Oliver Bond Terrace, Dublin.	4-2-1919	Tinsmith	8-8-1945
E/407579	CATNEY, Michael	5 Brighton Street, Belfast.	14-1-1924	Upholsterer	8-8-1945
E/403890	CAULFIELD, John	14 Thomas Street, Warrenpoint, Co. Down.	20-6-1916	Labourer	8-8-1945
V/206280	CAULFIELD, Patrick	Castlefin, Co. Donegal.	31-3-1921	Labourer	8-8-1945
83722	CAULFIELD, Samuel	65 Ardilla Street, Belfast.	26-6-1922	Labourer	8-8-1945
E/422321	CAULFIELD, Thomas	Toran End St., Buncrana, Co. Donegal.	17-6-1921	Labourer	8-8-1945
E/403230	CAVANAGH, Bernard	37 Ardilla Street, Belfast.	11-11-1916	Labourer	8-8-1945
E/423947	CAVANAGH, John	Corrowhugh, Moville, Co. Donegal.	29-7-1912	Motor Driver	8-8-1945
E/408437	CAVANAGH, Peter	45 Ferguson Road, Drumcondra, Dublin.	7-7-1924	Clerk	8-8-1945
E/408743	CAWLEY, Francis	4 Windle Road, Drumcondra, Dublin.	5-8-1923	Milk Server	8-8-1945
E/421213	CAWLEY, Francis	Waste Gardens, Sligo.	15-2-1920	Messenger	8-8-1945
E/420068	CAWLEY, Kevin	Waste Gardens, Sligo.	3-6-1921	Labourer	8-8-1945
E/420931	CAWLEY, Michael	21 Fenian Tce., Ballina.	14-2-1922	Gen. Labourer	8-8-1945
V/202722	CHAMBERLAIN, John	135 Rathgar Rd., Dublin.	22-2-1918	Printer	8-8-1945
E/404059	CHAMBERS, Patrick	38 Aungier St., Dublin.	19-3-1918	Tailor	8-8-1945
A/78497	CHAMBERS, William	58 Cashel, Rd., Crumlin, Dublin.	20-3-1920	Messenger	8-8-1945
E/401168	CHAMPMAN, Edward	21 Island Street, Dublin.	22-10-1910	Motor Driver	8-8-1945
E/434430	CHAYTON, Joseph Michael	35 Benmadigan Rd., Nth. Crumlin, Dublin.	10-11-1922	Blacksmith's Apprentice	8-8-1945
E/406326	CHERRY, Joseph	Townrath, Drogheda.	18-6-1922	Weaver	8-8-1945
E/400407	CHRISTIE, Thomas	20 Park Pce., Islandbridge, Dublin.	26-12-1921	Labourer	8-8-1945
E/431990	CHRISTOPHER, James	104 Brandon Road, Drimnagh, Dublin.	14-3-1916	Labourer	19-1-1946
V/207749	CLANCY, Denis Lce.	Castlemoylan, Manorhamilton, Co. Leitrim.	2-3-1915	Labourer	8-8-1945
V/207750	CLANCY, John	Moneenashinnagh, Manorhamilton.	18-9-1920	Labourer	8-8-1945

Army No.	Name.	Last Recorded Address.	Date of Birth.	Declared Occupation prior to enlistment in Defence Forces.	Date of Dismissal from Defence Forces.
76860	CLANCY, Martin	4 Nagle's Tce., Kilrush, Co. Clare.	5-12-1919	Butcher's Helper	8-8-1945
75628	CLANCY, Matthew	Mullinahone, Co. Tipperary.	21-4-1919	Farm Labourer	8-8-1945
E/423194	CLANCY, Patrick	c/o Cyril McGriskin, Kiltyclougher, Co. Leitrim.	26-8-1922	Labourer	8-8-1945
E/421899	CLANCY, Stephen	Newtown Bond, Killoe, Co. Longford.	10-5-1922	Gen. Labourer	8-8-1945
V/206694	CLARE, Patrick	55 Ballybeg, Rathnew. Co. Wicklow.	30-5-1918	Clerk	8-8-1945
V/204036	CLARE, Thomas	1 Wood Lane, Benburb Street, Dublin.	26-3-1920	Labourer	8-8-1945
E/422986	CLARKE, Charles	31 Upper Seán McDermott Street, Dublin.	7-10-1919	Labourer	8-8-1945
E/421508	CLARKE, Charles	c/o Ml. Duffy, Carndonagh, Co. Donegal.	22-2-1916	Labourer	8-8-1945
A/79619	CLARKE, James	1 Jetty Street, Belfast.	28-12-1910	Labourer	8-8-1945
E/420932	CLARKE, James	5 Grawley Park, Ballina.	8-4-1905	Labourer	8-8-1945
L/507668	CLARKE, John	7 Tower View Terrace, Limerick.	14-6-1927	Labourer	28-2-1946
E/420011	CLARKE, John	43 McHale Rd., Castlebar.	13-7-1900	Labourer	8-8-1945
73566	CLARKE, John Joseph	c/o Mrs. B. Flynn, Kilmacthomas, Co. Waterford	28-2-1914	Farm Labourer	8-8-1945
E/422322	CLARKE, Joseph	c/o Martin Moyne, Drumhaggard, Muff, Co. Donegal.	14-1-1921	Labourer	8-8-1945
E/405303	CLARKE, Matthew	35 Cumberland Street, Dun Laoghaire.	21-5-1913	Fabric Finisher	8-8-1945
E/409635	CLARKE, Matthew	Kilcreevin House, Ballymote, Sligo.	2-4-1918	Motor Driver	8-8-1945
E/424851	CLARKE, Michael	Ballymote, Co. Sligo.	13-10-1923	Baker	8-8-1945
E/408713	CLARKE, Norman	35 Blessington St., Dublin.	13-9-1914	Quantity Surveyor	8-8-1945
E/405858	CLARKE, Patrick	Roebuck Road, Clonskea, Dublin.	30-10-1920	Motor Driver	8-8-1945
V/215015	CLARKE, Patrick	Corimbla, Ballina.	27-2-1920	Farmer	8-8-1945
A/72025	CLARKE, Patrick	12 Richmond, Nenagh, Co. Tipperary.	28-4-1913	Labourer	8-8-1945
E/420814	CLARKE, William	49, McHale Rd., Castlebar.	9-6-1909	Lorry Driver	8-8-1945
V/209189	CLARKE, William	c/o Mrs. Gorman, 112 St. Joseph's Tce., Sligo.	5-12-1918	Dock Labourer	8-8-1945
E/408016	CLASBY, William	Kefemore, Lenane, Co. Galway.	7-5-1921	Farm Labourer	8-8-1945
E/401404	CLAVIN, Thomas	116 Upr. Dorset Street, Dublin.	9-11-1912	Labourer	8-8-1945
77473	CLEARE, John	c/o Ellen Sweeney, Shinmore, Offaly.	20-8-1919	Labourer	8-8-1945
E/420741	CLEARY, Edward	Ballymagroorty, Ballintra, Co. Donegal.	7-6-1920	Labourer	8-8-1945
79031	CLEARY, John S.	Claremount Park, Blackrock, Dundalk.	26-12-1917	Farm Labourer	8-8-1945
E/430715	CLEARY, Nicholas	Webb's Lane, Gorey, Co. Wexford.	20-8-1914	Labourer	8-8-1945
V/210009	CLEARY, Patrick	Whitehall Cottages, Drumcondra, Dublin.	28-1-1923	Messenger Boy	8-8-1945
E/405705	CLEARY, Stanislaus	3 Sunbury Gardens, Rathgar, Dublin.	8-2-1917	Motor Driver	8-8-1945
E/416347	CLEARY, Thomas	Glassdrum, Cappawhite, Co. Tipperary.	12-3-1917	Farming	8-8-1945
84790	CLEERE, John J.	Hospital, Knocklong, Co. Limerick.	25-1-1924	Secondary School Student	8-8-1945
L/501464	CLEMENGER, Michael	53 Lismore Road, Kimmage, Dublin.	19-7-1922	Silver Polisher	8-8-1945
A/84175	CLERKIN, Patrick	66 St. Edward's Terrace, Sligo.	16-12-1921	Labourer	8-8-1945

Army No.	Name.	Last Recorded Address.	Date of Birth.	Declared Occupation prior to enlistment in Defence Forces.	Date of Dismissal from Defence Forces.
80720	CLERKIN, Thomas	Crosshill, Braddoe, Co. Monaghan.	11-8-1916	Plasterer	8-8-1945
E/421721	CLIFFORD, James	Moness, Burt, Co. Donegal.	28-7-1921	Labourer	8-8-1945
210030	CLIFFORD, James	Newtowncunningham, Co. Donegal.	2-4-1921	Student	8-8-1945
E/422984	CLIFFORD, John	Knocktemple, Virginia, Co. Cavan.	8-5-1908	Labourer	8-8-1945
V/201291	CLIFFORD, Timothy	27 Pearse St., Kilkenny.	26-9-1920	Gen. Labourer	8-8-1945
E/404004	CLINCH, Francis	68 Grace Park Road, Drumcondra, Dublin.	21-8-1919	Grocer's Assistant	8-8-1945
204297	CLINCH, Patrick	109 Lr. Gardiner Street, Dublin.	7-2-1922	Gen. Labourer	8-8-1945
V/203250	CLOHESSY, William	School House Lane, Limerick.	23-4-1921	Messenger Boy	8-8-1945
E/408671	CLOSE, Charles	31 Strathroy Pk., Belfast.	22-11-1923	Labourer	8-8-1945
E/408532	CLOSE, John	31 Strathroy Pk., Belfast.	22-2-1924	Cook	8-8-1945
V/208965	CLUNE, John	74 Fair Green, Limerick.	25-9-1922	Labourer	8-8-1945
E/425194	CLYNE, Peter	Braney, Carrickboy, Co. Longford.	1-5-1923	Gen. Labourer	8-8-1945
E/416216	COADE, Lawrence	138 St. Brendan's Road, Spangle Hill, Cork.	16-1-1923	Plumber's Assistant	2-12-1945
V/209229	COATES, Patrick	2 Fleet Street, Belfast.	20-12-1921	Labourer	8-8-1945
E/424761	COCHRANE, Cecil	Killucan, Co. Westmeath.	31-6-1923	Labourer	8-8-1945
E/421882	COCHRANE, Leslie	School House, Killucan, Co. Westmeath.	3-3-1921	Waiter	8-8-1945
A/76486	CODD, Patrick	Barrack St., Tullow, Co. Carlow.	18-9-1919	Labourer	8-8-1945
76232	CODD, Thomas	Belgrove, Drumcormack, Wexford.	9-4-1914	Labourer	8-8-1945
E/406324	CODDINGTON, John	50 Hand St., Drogheda.	6-9-1923	Gen. Labourer	8-8-1945
E/402440	COFFEY, Christopher	3 Park St., The Ranch, Dublin.	26-10-1921	Motor Driver	8-8-1945
V/213031	COFFEY, James	Chiplee Lodge, Ballintemple, Co. Cork.	13-5-1916	Labourer	8-8-1945
79919	COFFEY, James	25 Hanover Lane, Patrick Street, Dublin.	4-4-1921	Messenger	8-8-1945
E/423689	COFFEY, Joseph	Adamstown, Castletown-Geoghegan, Co. Westmeath.	17-5-1909	Labourer	8-8-1945
A/83662	COFFEY, Patrick	Fermont, Clane, Co. Kildare.	20-9-1921	None	8-8-1945
L/506212	COFFEY, Thomas	82 Boherbee, Tralee.	8-5-1924	Labourer	8-8-1945
E/423322	COFFEY, William	Danesfort, Ballymacormack, Co. Longford.	9-11-1909	Farm Labourer	8-8-1945
E/401934	COGAN, John	14 Woodroof Cottages, Islandbridge, Dublin.	18-7-1912	Labourer	8-8-1945
E/403702	COLE, James Joseph	Newry Street, Kilkeel, Co. Down.	11-7-1911	Butcher	8-8-1945
A/74927	COLE, Michael	6 Pender's Court, Dawson Street, Dublin.	8-3-1907	Labourer	8-8-1945
82466	COLEMAN, Christopher	Bohernarana, Pallasgreen, Co. Limerick.	15-12-1919	Labourer	8-8-1945
E/436038	COLEMAN, David	95 Cathedral Rd., Cork.	28-5-1921	Postman	8-8-1945
E/405434	COLEMAN, James	39 Lr. Baggot St., Dublin.	2-1-1923	Messenger	8-8-1945
A/79573	COLEMAN, James	Tower, St. Anne's Hill, Co. Cork.	10-8-1921	Labourer	8-8-1945
E/405892	COLEMAN, John J.	39 Lr. Baggot St., Dublin.	16-11-1922	Labourer	8-8-1945
79952	COLEMAN, Joseph	173 Annamoe Drive, Cabra, Dublin.	6-11-1921	Dairy-boy	8-8-1945
L/506127	COLEMAN, Michael	14 St. Bridget's Tce. Dungarvan, Co. Waterford.	21-3-1921	Labourer	8-8-1945
78430	COLFER, Joseph	Kilbrew, Ashbourne, Co. Meath.	12-10-1919	Gardener	8-8-1945
E/404981	COLGAN, Edward	133 St. Mary's Rd., East Wall, Dublin.	8-7-1922	Labourer	8-8-1945

Army No.	Name.	Last Recorded Address.	Date of Birth.	Declared Occupation prior to enlistment in Defence Forces.	Date of Dismissal from Defence Forces.
78750	COLL, Thomas	42 Cottage Road, Derry.	27-5-1916	Motor Driver	8-8-1945
83395	COLLIER, Matthew	Woodpark, Dunboyne, Co. Meath.	21-11-1916	Labourer	8-8-1945
E/422275	COLLINS, Arthur	Mill St., Kilbeggan, Co. Westmeath.	1-10-1915	Tinsmith	8-8-1945
E/415750	COLLINS, Daniel	Roughgrove, Bandon, Co. Cork.	28-11-1914	Shoemaker	8-8-1945
L/506738	COLLINS, Denis	Gragues, Charleville, Co. Cork.	20-1-1925	Labourer	8-8-1945
E/404717	COLLINS, Eamonn	236 Sundrive Rd., Crumlin, Dublin.	18-9-1921	Labourer	8-8-1945
E/424130	COLLINS, Edward	79 Cavendish Street, Falls Road, Belfast.	7-4-1922	Not stated	8-8-1945
A/83887	COLLINS, James	21 Priory Road, Harold's Cross, Dublin.	14-5-1920	Sheet Metal Worker	8-8-1945
E/420347	COLLINS, James	Pound St., Ramelton, Co. Donegal.	4-10-1921	Labourer	8-8-1945
80707	COLLINS, John	2 Park Villas, Castleknock, Co. Dublin.	24-4-1922	None	8-8-1945
E/404716	COLLINS, John	236 Sundrive Rd., Crumlin, Dublin.	29-9-1914	Mechanic	8-8-1945
62508	COLLINS, John	35 Summerhill Parade, Dublin.	28-5-1905	Labourer	8-8-1945
71073	COLLINS, John	Craigs, Charleville, Co. Cork.	24-12-1911	Labourer	8-8-1945
E/422019	COLLINS, Joseph	O'Neill's Park, Clones, Co. Monaghan.	18-11-1919	Lorry Helper	8-8-1945
V/211094	COLLINS, Kevin	Park Villas, Castleknock, Co. Dublin.	4-12-1921	Labourer	8-8-1945
E/438223	COLLINS, Louis	Gortaway, Ramelton, Co. Donegal.	26-6-1916	Farm Labourer	29-4-1946
A/84236	COLLINS, Martin	Churchill, Letterkenny.	11-11-1921	Farmer	8-8-1945
E/421122	COLLINS, Martin	6 St. Patrick's Avenue, Galway.	27-11-1921	General Labourer	8-8-1945
V/200905	COLLINS, Patrick	River Street, Ballinasloe,	2-1-1913	Motor Driver	8-8-1945
E/423622	COLLINS, Patrick	Tyrawley Terrace, Ballina.	10-10-1921	Hawker	8-8-1945
E/414775	COLLINS, Patrick	14 St. Philomena's Road, Gurranebraher, Cork.	1-3-1920	Assistant Chef	8-8-1945
E/413825	COLLINS, Timothy	34 Cecil Street, Limerick.	24-6-1919	Clerk	8-8-1945
E/430929	COLLINS, William	74 Doyle's St., Waterford.	13-8-1913	Labourer	8-8-1945
75173	COLMAN, Alfred	32 Darmount Rd., Longbridge Lane, Northfield, Birmingham.	16-6-1918	General Labourer	8-8-1945
A/78239	COLMAN, Peter	Abbey, Ballyshannon, Co. Donegal.	2-5-1921	Labourer	15-10-1945
E/402294	COLQUHOUN, James	51 Summerhill, Dublin.	3-11-1904	Labourer	8-8-1945
E/435203	COMERFORD, Patrick	Railyard, Castlecomer, Co. Kilkenny.	25-10-1916	Labourer	8-8-1945
V/209148	CONACHY, Owen	26 Birchfield Road, Bosworth, Birmingham.	14-10-1921	Labourer	8-8-1945
V/205648	CONAGHAN, Hugo	Ballintra, Arran More, Co. Donegal.	8-1-1920	Labourer	8-8-1945
83725	CONBOY, Seamus	101 Annamoe Drive, Cabra, Dublin.	27-10-1921	None	8-8-1945
E/422324	CONCANNON, Joseph	Ture, Redcastle, Co. Donegal.	10-7-1922	Labourer	8-8-1945
E/404156	CONDON, John	217 Clonard Road, Kimmage, Dublin.	24-3-1922	Carpenter	8-8-1945
L/502544	CONLON, Henry James	44 O'Hanlon Park, Dundalk.	19-4-1926	Labourer	8-8-1945
E/402190	CONLON, James	Lisdrumclare, Latton P.O., Castleblayney.	29-7-1920	Farming	8-8-1945
V/202393	CONLON, John	10 St. Michael's Terrace, Sligo.	27-5-1920	Labourer	8-8-1945

Army No.	Name.	Last Recorded Address.	Date of Birth.	Declared Occupation prior to enlistment in Defence Forces.	Date of Dismissal from Defence Forces.
L/503069	CONLON, Michael	10 St. Michael's Terrace, Sligo.	10-5-1928	Plasterer	13-2-1946
E/402651	CONLON, Patrick	18 Dobbin Street, Armagh.	22-4-1922	Motor Driver	8-8-1945
E/423893	CONNEELEY, John	Alnacolly, Ballinafad, Roundstone, Co. Galway.	25-5 1922	Farm Labourer	8-8-1945
V/203769	CONNEELEY, Patrick	Carraroe, Co. Galway.	10-2-1920	Labourer	8-8-1945
E/423786	CONNELL, Anthony	Tallagh, Belmullet, Co. Mayo.	10-6-1910	Blacksmith	8-8-1945
E/403595	CONNELL, John	92 Clonliffe Ave., Dublin.	8-3-1920	None	8-8-1945
73165	CONNERY, Michael	36 Pope's Quay, Cork.	5-4-1914	Clerk	8-8-1945
E/402648	CONNERY, Patrick Neil	96 St. Stephen's Green, Dublin.	10-5-1915	Electrician	8-8-1945
A/103025	CONNERY, William	The Green, Cashel.	13-1-1913	Labourer	8-8-1945
V/201790	CONNIFFE, Edward	Rahelty, Thurles.	17-5-1920	Labourer	8-8-1945
V/210211	CONNOLLY, Bernard	183 Golden Ball Cottages, Kilternan, Co. Dublin.	20-7-1921	Labourer	8-8-1945
E/408042	CONNOLLY, Charles	50 St. Michael's Park, Portarlington, Leix.	1-7-1920	General Labourer	8-8-1945
V/200434	CONNOLLY, Colum	Caslo, Co. Galway.	5-12-1911	Labourer	8-8-1945
A/104010	CONNOLLY, Denis	Ballinaveen, Emly, Knocklong, Co. Limerick.	8-12-1912	Farmer	8-8-1945
L/508930	CONNOLLY, Francis	50 St. Michael's Park, Portarlington.	22-7-1926	Messenger	8-8-1945
E/422131	CONNOLLY, Gerald	Kilcriary, Lislea P.O., Co. Armagh.	6-3-1920	Farm Labourer	8-8-1945
V/209882	CONNOLLY, James	Tullymongan, Cavan.	17-8-1921	Labourer	8-8-1945
E/411020	CONNOLLY, Jeremiah	8 Paul Street, Cork.	25-6-1905	Labourer	8-8-1945
E/407422	CONNOLLY, James	Moy Road, Armagh.	21-10-1920	Labourer	8-8-1945
E/437511	CONNOLLY, John	3 Varna Street, Belfast.	20-8-1919	Factory Machinist	8-8-1945
E/409153	CONNOLLY, John	29 Lr. Dominick Street, Dublin.	19-10-1924	Tailor	8-8-1945
E/422132	CONNOLLY, John	c/o B. Hughes, Market St., Monaghan.	3-6-1922	Labourer	8-8-1945
A/78211	CONNOLLY, John	Killsala, Kilkerrin, Carna, Co. Galway.	15-4-1917	Farm Worker	8-8-1945
V/208273	CONNOLLY, John C.	Ballyconry, Lisselton, Co. Kerry.	24-8-1921	Carpenter's Helper	8-8-1945
V/207214	CONNOLLY, John	Main Street, Hacketstown, Carlow.	25-5-1920	Farmer	8-8-1945
E/431588	CONNOLLY, John	O'Connell St., Tullamore.	3-11-1917	Labourer	8-8-1945
E/438110	CONNOLLY, Joseph	6 Caledonian Place, Limerick.	13-11-1924	Labourer	30-10-1945
E/432650	CONNOLLY, Kevin	10 Lake View Tce., Cavan.	1-4-1921	Labourer	8-8-1945
V/202308	CONNOLLY, Michael	18 St. Finbar's Terrace, Bohermore, Galway.	13-11-1913	Farm Labourer	8-8-1945
L/502500	CONNOLLY, Michael	9 Middle Gardiner Street, Dublin.	4-7-1926	Messenger	8-8-1945
V/206399	CONNOLLY, Patrick	The Diamond, Castlefin, Co. Donegal.	21-2-1921	Student	8-8-1945
A/69914	CONNOLLY, Patrick	Inverrin, Co. Galway.	6-3-1906	Farm Labourer	8-8-1945
E/425273	CONNOLLY, Patrick	Ladyswell, Glasson, Athlone.	7-11-1919	Bricklayer	8-8-1945
E/403109	CONNOLLY, Patrick	3 Blessington St., Dublin.	13-4-1922	Cinema Operator	8-8-1945
A/79813	CONNOLLY, Patrick	Termon Cottages, Boyle, Co. Roscommon.	10-6-1921	Labourer	8-8-1945
E/407334	CONNOLLY, Patrick J. G.	1A Hill Street, Newry.	2-10-1921	Student	8-8-1945
L/500404	CONNOLLY, Patrick	21 Corporation Buildings, Dublin.	1-5-1921	Labourer	8-8-1945
V/209972	CONNOLLY, Paul	c/o W. Morrison, Main St., Lifford, Co. Donegal.	26-6-1921	Motor Driver	8-8-1945
L/500529	CONNOLLY, Peter	29 Lr. Dominick Street, Dublin.	6-2-1922	Labourer	8-8-1945
E/422134	CONNOLLY, Thomas	Tullymongan, Cavan.	17-6-1917	Labourer	8-8-1945

Army No.	Name.	Last Recorded Address.	Date of Birth.	Declared Occupation prior to enlistment in Defence Forces.	Date of Dismissal from Defence Forces.
A/84808	CONNOLLY, Thomas	Ballynahown, Co. Galway.	11-8-1915	Farm Labourer	8-8-1945
74417	CONNOLLY, Thomas	Newroad East, Birr.	14-5-1916	General Labourer	8-8-1945
E/405145	CONNOLLY, Timothy	Morning Star Hostel, Nth. Brunswick St., Dublin.	3-1-1906	Plumber	8-8-1945
A/112779	CONNOLLY, William	New Cottage, Deerpark, Carrick-on-Suir.	18-9-1917	Farm Labourer	8-8-1945
E/422578	CONNOR, Arthur	137 Pierce Park, Drogheda.	6-10-1917	Factory Worker	8-8-1945
E/407471	CONNOR, Bernard	31B High Street, Newry.	2-11-1923	Auxiliary Postman	8-8-1945
E/402100	CONNOR, Eamonn	35 Sth. Gloucester Street, Dublin.	12-8-1922	Messenger	8-8-1945
E/422674	CONNOR, Edward	Rathcor, Carlingford, Co. Louth.	7-10-1907	Motor Mechanic	8-8-1945
75912	CONNOR, Edward	Castletown, Castleconnor, Co. Sligo.	7-7-1915	Motor Driver	8-8-1945
E/404832	CONNOR, Frank	137 Pearse Pk., Drogheda.	11-11-1920	Messenger	22-10-1945
E/408754	CONNOR, John	94 Benbrook Hill, Armagh.	4-4-1920	Postman	8-8-1945
84181	CONNORS, Desmond	c/o J. McMahon, Newtown Road, Clones.	27-5-1922	Lorry Helper	8-8-1945
A/72494	CONNORS, John	Bottomstown, Elton, Knocklong, Limerick.	21-4-1910	Labourer	8-8-1945
E/416283	CONNORS, Michael	8 Patrick's Tce., Nenagh.	29-6-1912	Motor Driver and Mechanic	8-8-1945
V/201162	CONNORS, Thomas	35 Millmount Terrace, Kilmallock, Co. Limerick.	14-12-1918	Farm Labourer	8-8-1945
E/403692	CONNORTON, George	5 Marrowbone Ln., Dublin.	23-11-1921	Farm Labourer	8-8-1945
E/416242	CONNORTON, James	Ballycorney, Killaloe, Co. Clare.	18-10-1907	Labourer	8-8-1945
E/405915	CONROY, Denis	37 Glasthule Road, Dun Laoghaire.	24-4-1916	Mechanic	8-8-1945
E/436432	CONROY, Edward	Donaguile, Castlecomer, Co. Kilkenny.	2-11-1924	Farm Labourer	15-2-1946
V/213076	CONROY, Francis	68 Stack's Villas, Tralee.	14-10-1920	Labourer	8-8-1945
83352	CONROY, John	23E Liberty House, Railway Street, Dublin.	19-6-1921	Labourer	8-8-1945
E/438218	CONROY, Joseph	24 Tangier Terrace, Boyle.	25-1-1920	Merchant Seaman	8-8-1945
80567	CONROY, Patk. Joseph	Borrislittle, Portlaoighise.	16-2-1922	Fitter's Assistant	8-8-1945
72810	CONROY, William	63 Goodinge Road, Islington, London.	1-7-1909	Labourer	8-8-1945
A/76710	CONSIDINE, Michael	9 Garvey Long Lane, Brook St., Limerick.	20-6-1919	General Labourer	8-8-1945
E/432446	CONVEY, Francis	c/o Miss M. Rooney, N.T., Tydovant, Co. Monaghan.	5-7-1914	Farm Labourer	8-8-1945
E/421917	CONVEY, Henry	Dowra P.O., Co. Cavan.	15-1-1915	Motor Driver	8-8-1945
E/421801	CONVEY, John Matthew	c/o John Gethins, Cleveragh Road, Sligo.	27-2-1921	Farm Labourer	8-8-1945
E/401871	CONWAY, Alfred	4 Church Avenue, Church Road, Dublin.	2-1-1921	Labourer	8-8-1945
E/400657	CONWAY, Andrew	Main Street, Castleblayney.	31-10-1897	Labourer	8-8-1945
E/405440	CONWAY, Arthur	1 St. Joseph Terrace, Dun Laoghaire.	19-1-1922	Student	8-8-1945
A/75407	CONWAY, James	29 Sutton's Blds., Cork.	29-12-1918	Messenger	8-8-1945
L/503045	CONWAY, James C.	43 Ferns Road, Kimmage, Dublin.	13-10-1928	General Labourer	28-1-1946
E/402683	CONWAY, John	38 St. Augustine Street, Dublin.	23-5-1918	Slater and Tiler	8-8-1945
E/429639	CONWAY, John	Ballard, Clonbur, Co. Galway.	15-6-1912	Farm Labourer	8-8-1945
E/432583	CONWAY, John	21 Church Avenue, Church Street, Dublin.	8-5-1920	Messenger	8-8-1945
A/82712	CONWAY, Martin	43 St. Munchin's Street, Island Field, Limerick.	20-1-1922	Messenger Boy	8-8-1945

Army No.	Name.	Last Recorded Address.	Date of Birth.	Declared Occupation prior to enlistment in Defence Forces.	Date of Dismissal from Defence Forces.
A/83732	CONWAY, Michael	Scart, Mullinavat, Co. Kilkenny.	5-11-1920	Labourer	8-8-1945
V/201471	CONWAY, Patrick	17 Ardee Street, Sligo.	18-12-1917	Labourer	8-8-1945
75333	CONWAY, Patrick	Newcastlewest, Co. Limerick.	4-3-1917	Labourer	8-8-1945
E/420345	CONWELL, Joseph	Corporation Cottages, Killybegs, Co. Donegal.	24-8-1920	Fish Packer	8-8-1945
E/422418	COOKE, Horace	Brackenagh, Ballinasloe, Co. Galway.	4-4-1922	Farmer	8-8-1945
A/75849	COONEY, James	Rahins, Castlebar, Co. Mayo.	12-6-1918	Nil	8-8-1945
E/433540	COONEY, Michael	15 Dodder View Cottages, Ballsbridge, Dublin.	30-2-1918	Groomer	8-8-1945
V/209233	COONEY, Patrick	57 Mellows Ave., Arklow, Co. Wicklow.	8-9-1917	Clerk	8-8-1945
V/210273	COONEY, Patrick	78 Charlemount St., Dublin	5-9-1921	Labourer	8-8-1945
E/409007	COOPER, Edward	252 Prosperous Rd., Clane, Co. Kildare.	29-7-1919	General Labourer	8-8-1945
E/404594	COOPER, George	48 Nansen St., Falls Rd., Belfast.	20-11-1918	Clerk	8-8-1945
L/508818	COOPER, John	Kilgarvan, Taghmon, Co. Wexford.	2-1-1925	Farm Labourer	8-8-1945
77584	COOTE, John	22 Connolly Villas, Ennis.	16-6-1920	Labourer	8-8-1945
81598	CORBETT, Daniel	Ballinderry, Borrisokane, Co. Tipperary.	20-11-1920	Labourer	8-8-1945
E/413774	CORBETT, Edmond	30 Glenville Sq., Tipperary	18-7-1906	Motor Mechanic	8-8-1945
A/81904	CORCORAN, John	Railstown, Fethard, Co. Tipperary.	29-10-1925	Student	26-7-1946
E/403103	CORCORAN, Michael	31 Lambay Rd., Glasnevin, Dublin.	11-6-1922	Sawyer's Helper	8-8-1945
E/409185	CORCORAN, Patrick	14 Bolton Street, Dublin.	27-3-1913	Labourer	8-8-1945
E/404786	CORCORAN, Peter	Bridge Street, Balbriggan, Co. Dublin.	18-5-1915	Butcher	8-8-1945
E/431525	CORCORAN, Richard	Greene Lane, Callan, Co. Kilkenny.	11-11-1922	Farm Labourer	8-8-1945
E/435074	CORCORAN, Richard	Millers March, St. John's, Waterford.	20-3-1923	Labourer	8-8-1945
E/414186	CORKERY, Patrick	Tooreen, Croom, Co. Limerick.	5-7-1919	Labourer	26-2-1946
A/75639	CORR, Francis	The Flats, Watling Street, Dublin	3-7-1917	Messenger	8-8-1945
E/406323	CORR, William	91 Pearse Park, Drogheda.	23-6-1922	Labourer	8-8-1945
204257	CORRIGAN, James	72 Mid. Abbey St., Dublin.	21-1-1919	Grocer's Porter	8-8-1945
84184	CORRIGAN, Joseph	c/o P. McKernan, Main St., Ballyconnell, Co. Cavan.	11-6-1920	Farm Labourer	8-8-1945
A/72825	CORRIGAN, Patrick	14 Kelleher's Bldgs., Cork.	25-9-1913	Labourer	8-8-1945
A/83870	CORRIGAN, Peter	Tullymore, Benburb, Co. Armagh.	23-6-1922	Motor Driver	8-8-1945
A/84165	CORRIGAN, William	c/o F. McGovern, Ballyconnell, Co. Cavan.	25-9-1917	Labourer	8-8-1945
11792	CORRY, Henry	29 Hospital St., Kildare.	18-10-1904	Clerk	8-8-1945
205950	CORRY, John	3 Owen Roe Tce., Cavan.	4-2-1913	Labourer	8-8-1945
E/403976	CORRY, Joseph	46 Rockmore Rd., Belfast.	1-1-1909	Motor Mechanic	8-8-1945
A/76974	CORRY, Patrick	Lisdeen, Co. Clare.	3-3-1919	Labourer	8-8-1945
E/424707	COSGROVE, Gerald	Cloncarrick, Carrigallen, Co. Leitrim.	11-5-1923	Shop Assistant	8-8-1945
E/400771	COSGRAVE, James	57 Summerhill, Dublin.	11-2-1922	Labourer	8-8-1945
V/205578	COSGRAVE, Philip	29 Greenmount Crescent, Cork.	14-9-1912	Labourer	8-8-1945
E/423052	COSGRAVE, Thomas	20 Terenure Pk., Terenure, Dublin.	17-10-1920	Labourer	8-8-1945
E/431806	COSS, Denis	10 Bridge Street, Portlaoighise, Co. Leix.	3-12-1919	Motor Driver	8-8-1945

Army No.	Name.	Last Recorded Address.	Date of Birth.	Declared Occupation prior to enlistment in Defence Forces.	Date of Dismissal from Defence Forces.
A/83310	COSTELLO, John	9 Middle Third, Killester, Dublin.	10-12-1921	Appren. Fitter and Turner	8-8-1945
E/408150	COSTELLO, Joseph	53 Lr. Wellington Street, Dublin.	21-3-1924	Labourer	8-8-1945
E/401531	COSTELLO, Michael	Baltoney, Gortahork, Co. Donegal.	5-2-1908	Hotel Porter	8-8-1945
209698	COSTELLO, Richard	Greenvill, Kilmacow, Co. Kilkenny.	9-10-1921	Labourer	8-8-1945
V/200515	COSTELLOE, James	48 Oliver Plunkett Street, Island Field, Limerick.	9-2-1923	Messenger Boy	8-8-1945
A/76621	COSTELLOE, Joseph	Harrison's Place, Charleville, Co. Cork.	7-6-1919	Farm Labourer	8-8-1945
E/412957	COSTELLOE, Michael	63 St. Munchin's Street, Island Field, Limerick.	26-9-1916	Labourer	8-8-1945
L/508730	COSTIGAN, Edward	Castlewarren, Co. Kilkenny	2-6-1925	Farm Labourer	8-8-1945
A/80558	COSTIGAN, John	Castlewarren, Co. Kilkenny	23-8-1918	Farm Labourer	8-8-1945
E/407696	COSTIGAN, Nigil	Mullinary, Carrickmacross, Co. Monaghan.	29-1-1924	Labourer	8-8-1945
E/423825	COTTER, Eamon	Glebe Street, Ballinrobe, Co. Mayo.	5-9-1920	Barman Labourer	8-8-1945
V/207205	COUCH, Timothy	9 Greenfield Lane, Cove Street, Cork.	25-7-1921	General Labourer	8-8-1945
E/405249	COUGHLAN, Daniel	44 Patrick Street, Dublin.	15-11-1922	Bootmaker	8-8-1945
E/422761	COUGHLAN, Martin	Lower New St., Ballinrobe, Co. Mayo.	23-10-1902	Tailor	8-8-1945
E/412716	COUGHLAN, Patrick	Mill Road, Corbally, Limerick.	3-12-1915	Motor Driver	8-8-1945
200081	COUGHLAN, Robert	3 Church Street, Dublin.	1-10-1918	Heel-tip Maker	8-8-1945
E/402598	COUNIHAN, Michael	5 Summerhill, Dublin.	9-7-1912	Labourer	8-8-1945
200285	COURTNEY, James	c/o Mrs. McCourille, 19 Beattystown, Faorhill, Co. Galway.	16-7-1917	Labourer	8-8-1945
E/407895	COURTNEY, John	Doon, Tierworker, Co. Meath.	9-10-1918	Labourer	8-8-1945
83721	COUSINS, James P.	Moneydarragh, Ballymartin, Co. Down.	3-12-1921	Pile Driver	8-8-1945
E/407656	COWAN, Frederick	15 Patrick's Sq., Bray.	8-6-1923	Farm Labourer	8-8-1945
E/432451	COWAN, James	c/o Mrs. E. McGovern, Glasslough, Co. Monaghan.	23-4-1914	Mechanic and Driver	8-8-1945
E/408520	COWAN, Patrick	30 Gillis Terrace, Armagh.	16-8-1924	Agricultural Worker	8-8-1945
A/58208	COWHIG, Denis	24 Bowman St., Limerick.	12-2-1905	Labourer	8-8-1945
L/500727	COWLEY, Joseph	4F Ross Road, Patrick St., Dublin.	5-7-1922	Agricultural Worker	8-8-1945
E/422022	COX, James	The Diamond, Belturbet, Co. Cavan.	6-7-1922	Labourer	8-8-1945
E/422740	COX, Patrick	Treanmore, Mohill, Co. Leitrim.	7-3-1905	Labourer	8-8-1945
E/422739	COX, Patrick	20 High Street, Birr	2-7-1922	Messenger Boy	8-8-1945
E/420015	COX, Thomas	8 O'Connell Terrace, Longford.	15-8-1922	Messenger	8-8-1945
A/75913	COYLE, Anthony	1 Erne Street, Ballyshannon, Co. Donegal.	15-8-1919	Bill Poster	8-8-1945
E/420465	COYLE, Charles	Dunneagh, Derrybeg, Co. Donegal.	26-6-1913	Motor Driver	8-8-1945
E/422856	COYLE, Denis	c/o Mark McLoughlin, Carrowliere, Fahan, Co. Donegal.	23-1-1922	Bread Server and Waiter	8-8-1945
A/75629	COYLE, Edward	Carrickadawson, Raphoe, Co. Donegal.	26-2-1919	Labourer	8-8-1945
E/422139	COYLE, Gerard	19 St. Columbs Avenue, Buncrana, Co. Donegal.	11-2-1921	Student	8-8-1945

Army No.	Name.	Last Recorded Address.	Date of Birth.	Declared Occupation prior to enlistment in Defence Forces.	Date of Dismissal from Defence Forces.
E/423257	COYLE, Henry	17 Artisan St., Rosemount, Derry,	16-7-1922	Labourer	8-8-1945
E/423419	COYLE, John	Oranmore, Co. Galway.	20-5-1922	Apprentice Mechanic	8-8-1945
E/420503	COYLE, Joseph	Lower Main Street, Letterkenny.	16-12-1917	Labourer	8-8-1945
E/401493	COYLE, Michael	22 Tolka Road, Drumcondra, Dublin.	17-1-1922	Messenger	8-8-1945
E/433063	COYLE, Patrick	22 Tolka Road, Drumcondra, Dublin.	27-3-1922	Metal Worker	8-8-1945
E/400537	COYLE, Thomas	22 Tolka Road, Drumcondra, Dublin.	9-6-1920	Labourer	8-8-1945
V/207581	COYNE, John	Claddagh, Galway.	15-8-1922	Gen. Labourer	8-8-1945
E/423838	CRAIG, Kevin	2 Newtown Cottages, Mullingar,	23-10-1921	Farm Labourer	8-8-1945
V/208850	CRAMPSEY, Patrick	Ballygorman, Malin Head, Co. Donegal.	19-3-1916	Labourer	8-8-1945
203053	CRAMPSIE, Roderick	Ballindrait, Lifford.	27-4-1914	Cycle Mechanic	8-8-1945
E/430178	CRAMPTON, Thomas	41 Irishtown, New Ross, Co. Wexford.	13-11-1919	Labourer	8-8-1945
V/209575	CRANEY, Patrick	Dublin Street, Monaghan.	15-2-1909	Motor Driver	8-8-1945
75174	CRANLEY, John	Bohercrow, Tipperary.	11-12-1912	Farm Labourer	8-8-1945
E/406285	CRANNY, Hugh B.	Drumsallagh, Loughbrickland, Co. Down.	15-10-1914	Clerk	8-8-1945
E/403774	CRAVEN, Michael	25 James's Street, Dublin.	21-5-1922	Slating Apprentice	8-8-1945
L/500042	CRAWLEY, Daniel	142 Upper Dorset Street, Dublin.	28-2-1922	Labourer	8-8-1945
E/401786	CRAWLEY, Peter	19 St. Clement's Park, Dundalk.	12-4-1908	Dock Labourer	8-8-1945
E/435131	CREAN, George	Gurraon, Blackwater, Co. Wexford.	15-5-1923	Farm Labourer	8-8-1945
E/423325	CREAN, John	Graffy, Attymass, Ballina.	15-4-1920	Farm Labourer	8-8-1945
E/422935	CREAN, Stephen	Behymore, Ballina.	6-9-1897	Carpenter	8-8-1945
E/405195	CREANEY, Kevin	90 Shankill St., Lurgan.	20-6-1921	Butcher	8-8-1945
E/437975	CREANEY, Patrick	54 Oranmore St., Belfast.	23-12-1923	Dairyman	8-8-1945
L/506558	CREEDON, Timothy	5 Townsend Place, Greenmount, Cork.	12-7-1924	Messenger Boy	8-8-1945
E/425490	CREGAN, Patrick	3 Fountain Hill, Derry.	1-10-1925	Messenger	8-8-1945
81875	CREHAN, William	Cush, Kilfinane, Co. Limerick.	13-12-1926	Farm Labourer	29-11-1945
V/200357	CREIGHAN, Thomas	Beligan Square, Monaghan.	1-8-1916	Labourer	8-8-1945
E/412718	CREMINS, Joseph	5D Kileely, Thomondgate, Limerick.	22-4-1917	Dry-Cleaner	8-8-1945
V/209947	CRILLY, Laurence	33 St. Nicholas Avenue, Dundalk.	30-11-1921	Labourer	28-3-1946
E/406332	CRIMMINS, Thomas	Linenhall Street, Dundalk.	26-7-1920	Merchant Seaman	8-8-1945
E/434290	CRINNION, Francis	8 Adelaide Road, Dublin.	21-2-1913	Carpenter	8-8-1945
E/415221	CROFTON, Patrick	13 Wallis Street, Newport, Monmouthshire.	12-3-1914	Motor Driver	8-8-1945
E/430968	CROKE, Michael	15 Georges St., Waterford.	17-6-1918	Labourer	8-8-1945
V/213033	CRONIN, Daniel	75 Hibernian Bldgs., Cork.	1-5-1921	Labourer	8-8-1945
E/414011	CRONIN, Denis	Killuragh, Cappamore, Co. Limerick.	1-6-1921	Labourer	8-8-1945
E/417716	CRONIN, Edward	1 Upper Cattle St., Cork.	12-1-1925	Labourer	8-8-1945
E/425121	CRONIN, John	Garda Bks., Roscommon.	17-2-1924	Student	8-8-1945
77999	CRONIN, John	12 Kyrl Street, Cork.	29-6-1919	Shoemaker	8-8-1945
V/206842	CRONIN, John	2 Strand St., Dungarvan, Co. Waterford.	21-2-1922	None	8-8-1945
E/434396	CRONIN, Joseph	20 Kells Road, Crumlin, Dublin.	26-1-1922	Messenger Boy	8-8-1945
E/414426	CRONIN, Mark	Custom Gap House, Bantry, Co. Cork.	6-9-1917	Carpenter	8-8-1945

Army No.	Name.	Last Recorded Address.	Date of Birth.	Declared Occupation prior to enlistment in Defence Forces.	Date of Dismissal from Defence Forces.
V/200439	CRONIN, Michael	Barrack Hill, Clonakilty, Co. Cork.	10-1-1917	Labourer	8-8-1945
V/209638	CRONIN, Michael	Knockanuire, Newtown-sands, Co. Kerry.	12-7-1921	Labourer	8-8-1945
A/76623	CRONIN, Mortimer	9 Married Quarters, Fort Camden, Cork.	29-11-1919	Baker	8-8-1945
A/69164	CRONIN, Patrick	10 McKeown Tce., Patrick Street, Mullingar.	3-10-1907	Labourer	8-8-1945
E/424680	CROSSAN, Henry	c/o Edward Ban, Bun-crana, Co. Donegal.	1-8-1922	Motor Driver	8-8-1945
E/412876	CROTTY, John	Rathdrum, Fethard, Co. Tipperary.	15-1-1922	Farm Labourer	8-8-1945
E/431836	CROTTY, Maurice	50 Ballybricken, Waterford	12-10-1916	Cook	8-8-1945
78634	CROTTY, Patrick	Mitchell St., Dungarvan, Co. Waterford.	3-3-1921	Messenger	8-8-1945
E/410874	CROWE, Cornelius	6 Rowland's Lane, Dominick Street, Cork.	26-12-1919	Labourer	8-8-1945
E/405220	CROWE, James	Ardleny, Kilnaleck, Co. Cavan.	11-2-1920	Farm Labourer	8-8-1945
A/76864	CROWE, Martin	Turnpike Road, Ennis.	2-2-1920	Labourer	8-8-1945
204365	CROWE, Thomas F.	Ballinacarrig, Carlow.	28-2-1919	Student	8-8-1945
E/422383	CROWLEY, Kevin	11 St. Lawrence's Terrace, Mullingar.	29-1-1922	Factory Worker	8-8-1945
E/403639	CROWLEY, John	Newtownmountkennedy, Co. Wicklow.	27-1-1893	Driver	8-8-1945
79929	CROWLEY, Michael	5 O'Brien Place, Blarney Street, Cork.	18-3-1922	Shop Assistant	8-8-1945
E/414375	CROWLEY, Michael	34 Evergreen Bldgs, Cork.	23-7-1922	Clerk	8-8-1945
E/410750	CROWLEY, Michael	Slievedooley, Labasheeda, Co. Clare.	1-9-1919	Farmer	8-8-1945
L/508654	CROWLEY, Patrick	25 Douglas Street, Cork.	24-2-1924	Labourer	8-8-1945
E/413792	CROWLEY, Thomas	3 Greenmount Crescent, Cork.	2-1-1922	Student	8-8-1945
L/507576	CROWLEY, William	15 Vicar Street, Cork.	2-9-1927	Labourer	8-8-1945
E/437885	CRUDDEN, Brian	Tyrone, Magheraveely, Newtownbutler, Co. Fermanagh.	28-10-1923	Electrical Apprentice	8-8-1945
E/425063	CRYAN, Michael	Cloonfaughtin, Ballymote, Co. Sligo.	3-6-1916	Farm Labourer	26-10-1945
E/403594	CULLEN, Christopher	60 East Arran St., Dublin.	8-12-1921	Labourer	8-8-1945
E/405066	CULLEN, Edward	Donard, Dunlavin, Co. Wicklow.	22-12-1916	Labourer	8-8-1945
E/425253	CULLEN, James	11 Rosemount Lane, Letterkenny, Co. Donegal	3-7-1911	Labourer	8-8-1945
E/432587	CULLEN, John	121 Upper Dorset Street, Dublin.	23-1-1920	Labourer	8-8-1945
E/423600	CULLEN, Lawrence	Cornaclone, Kiltyclogher, Co. Leitrim.	12-1-1922	Farm Labourer	8-8-1945
E/434873	CULLEN, Martin	Kiltre, Enniscorthy, Co. Wexford.	17-5-1921	Farm Labourer	8-8-1945
E, 409459	CULLEN, Michael	Bray Road, Stillorgan, Co. Dublin.	24-1-1925	Clerk	8-8-1945
A/79248	CULLEN, Michael	17 St. Augustine Street, Dublin.	22-6-1919	Motor Driver	8-8-1945
E/431101	CULLETON, Patrick	Chapel Lane, New Ross, Co. Wexford.	28-5-1921	Moulder	8-8-1945
A/79650	CULLIGAN, Benedict	Lake Field, Fethard, Co. Tipperary.	10-9-1914	General Labourer	8-8-1945
V/204527	CULLINANE, Michael	Carhue, White's Cross, Cork.	9-9-1910	None	8-8-1945
E/425080	CULLINANE, Patrick	8 Beatty's Town, Galway.	16-5-1923	Laboratory Attendant	8-8-1945
A/74718	CULLINANE, Patrick	Cockhill, Kilcummin, Killarney.	2-5-1919	Farm Labourer	8-8-1945

Army No.	Name.	Last Recorded Address.	Date of Birth.	Declared Occupation prior to enlistment in Defence Forces.	Date of Dismissal from Defence Forces.
78000	CULLINANE, Timothy	Main Street, Ballinacurra, Cork.	20-9-1920	Engine Mender	8-8-1945
E/421815	CULLIS, Clifford	Swanlinbar, Co. Cavan.	24-1-1914	Bricklayer	8-8-1945
E/407898	CULLY, John	Tunnyinn Hill, Cootehill, Co. Cavan.	15-12-1923	Farm Labourer	8-8-1945
79324	CUMMINGS, Frank	The Square, Bantry, Co. Cork.	28-5-1921	Motor Driver	8-8-1945
E/403254	CUMMINS, James	38 South Earl St., Dublin.	18-1-1922	Labourer	8-8-1945
E/408086	CUMMINS, James	27 Temple Cottages, Broadstone, Dublin.	24-10-1923	Clerk	8-8-1945
78304	CUMMINS, Kevin	38 Patrick Street, Dun Laoghaire.	20-5-1920	Messenger Boy	8-8-1945
A/80519	CUMMINS, Laurence	Kildrummry, Windgap, Co. Kilkenny.	1-2-1913	Farm Labourer	8-8-1945
84241	CUMMINS, Michael	Gleneely, Moville, Co. Donegal.	14-10-1922	Carpenter	8-8-1945
V/209710	CUMMINS, Patrick	Ticknock, Sandyford, Co. Dublin.	18-7-1915	Gardener	8-8-1945
V/201763	CUMMINS, Patrick	9 Thomas Ave., Waterford.	19-9-1919	Labourer	8-8-1945
V/204506	CUMMINS, Robert	103 North Main St., Cork.	24-9-1918	Metal Worker	8-8-1945
E/421676	CUNNANE, Patrick	Kildeema N.S., Loughrea, Co. Galway.	7-7-1920	Grocer's Assistant	8-8-1945
E/429700	CUNNANE, Philip	Minna, Indreaban, Co. Galway.	3-2-1920	Farm Worker	8-8-1945
A/83481	CUNNINGHAM, Andrew	18 Shelmalier Rd., Dublin.	8-6-1922	Storekeeper	8-8-1945
V/205156	CUNNINGHAM, Denis	153 Parnell St., Dublin.	15-5-1920	Tyre Fitter (Motor)	8-8-1945
83190	CUNNINGHAM, Edward	72 Mountpleasant Bldgs., Dublin.	1-5-1922	Messenger	8-8-1945
A/80947	CUNNINGHAM, James	Fahir, Kilmacthomas, Co. Waterford.	18-12-1923	Labourer	8-8-1945
83672	CUNNINGHAM, John	21 High Street, Newry.	29-6-1920	Butcher	8-8-1945
E/406345	CUNNINGHAM, John P.	24 Oxford Road, Ranelagh, Dublin.	6-7-1922	Dairy Assistant	8-8-1945
E/404875	CUNNINGHAM, Joseph	Omara, Kilnaleck, Co. Cavan.	5-3-1922	Farm Labourer	8-8-1945
E/403977	CUNNINGHAM, Malachy	27 O'Neill Ave., Newry.	21-3-1915	Electrician	8-8-1945
E/420398	CUNNINGHAM, Michael	1 Mons Terrace, Castlebar.	4-4-1922	Mechanic	8-8-1945
E/404940	CUNNINGHAM, Patk. J.	Corless, Crossmaglen, Co. Armagh.	17-3-1903	Stone Mason	8-8-1945
E/404715	CUNNINGHAM, Séamus	Lake View Ctge., Toomebridge, Co. Antrim.	14-8-1922	Motor Driver	8-8-1945
E/414012	CUNNINGHAM, Thomas	29 Tracey Park, Carrick-on-Suir.	2-2-1917	Labourer	8-8-1945
E/421581	CUNLISK, Patrick	Victoria Road, Sligo.	7-11-1915	House Painter	8-8-1945
E/409191	CURLEY, Charles	24 Lady Street, Belfast.	15-12-1924	Mill Labourer	8-8-1945
E/406279	CURLEY, James	Newtown, Rathcoole, Co. Dublin.	7-4-1920	General Storeman	8-8-1945
E/408376	CURLEY, John	40 Saul Road, Crumlin, Dublin.	25-3-1924	Plumber	8-8-1945
E/409943	CURLEY, Joseph	24 Lady Street, Belfast.	16-7-1922	Labourer	8-8-1945
E/423928	CURRAN, Charles Joseph	Meenderry, Falcarragh, Co. Donegal.	31-7-1921	Labourer	8-8-1945
E/421564	CURRAN, Denis	Barron, Co. Cavan.	1-6-1921	Labourer	8-8-1945
E/425288	CURRAN, Francis	Gurteenaville, Kiltormer, Ballinasloe, Co. Galway.	31-5-1924	Labourer	8-8-1945
E/402219	CURRAN, George	65 Kenilworth Road, Dublin.	17-4-1910	Electrician	8-8-1945
E/421324	CURRAN, Gerald	White Rose Cottage, Rathmullen, Co. Donegal.	6-3-1907	Electrician	8-8-1945
E/421814	CURRAN, Henry	1 Owen Roe Tce., Cavan.	12-9-1920	Motor Driver	8-8-1945
E/423195	CURRAN, John	25 Dunfield Tce., Derry.	30-12-1920	Apprentice Aircraft Fitter	8-8-1945
203046	CURRAN, John	Kildrum, Newtowncunningham, Co. Donegal.	1-6-1910	Labourer	8-8-1945

Army No.	Name.	Last Recorded Address.	Date of Birth.	Declared Occupation prior to enlistment in Defence Forces.	Date of Dismissal from Defence Forces.
E/434993	CURRAN, Joseph	Kildrenagh, Muinebeag, Co. Carlow.	18-3-1922	Farm Labourer	8-8-1945
A/75483	CURRAN, Patrick J.	Tievebrack, Castlefin, Co. Donegal.	19-7-1919	Dairy Worker	8-8-1945
E/423477	CURRAN, Peter	Woodside, Carndonagh, Co. Donegal.	19-2-1922	Labourer	8-8-1945
83767	CURRAN, Phelim	28 Cuffe Street, Dublin.	18-6-1915	None	8-8-1945
76779	CURTIS, John	5 Dolphin's Terrace, Crosshaven, Co. Cork.	8-2-1920	None	8-8-1945
E/404969	CURTIN, Jeremiah	3 Crumlin Village, Crumlin, Dublin.	9-10-1922	Apprentice to Bootmaking	8-8-1945
E/421664	CUSACK, Michael	Cashel, Foxford, Co. Mayo.	6-7-1918	Motor Mechanic	8-8-1945
V/205669	DALTON, Bernard	79 Fassaugh Ave., Cabra, Dublin.	12-8-1920	Publican's Porter	8-8-1945
V/213088	DALTON, Dominick	2 Railway Cottages, Anglesea Street, Cork.	6-1-1913	Barman	8-8-1945
E/422857	DALTON, Eugene	Ardlough, Co. Derry.	24-1-1904	Labourer	8-8-1945
E/404352	DALTON, Richard	52 Thatch Rd., Whitehall, Dublin.	3-6-1922	Motor Mechanic	8-8-1945
209681	DALTON, Thomas	32 Stanaway Road, Kimmage, Dublin.	6-1-1920	Labourer	8-8-1945
E/425246	DALY, Anthony	Clara Road, Moate, Co. Westmeath.	8-8-1924	Farm Labourer	8-8-1945
E/421725	DALY, Austin	14 Tangier, Boyle.	6-9-1922	Labourer	8-8-1945
V/207938	DALY, Christopher	78 Up. Church St., Dublin.	6-2-1921	Messenger Boy	8-8-1945
E/413525	DALY, Christopher	1 Wesley Pce., Wellington Road, Cork.	25-12-1918	Male-Nurse	8-8-1945
E/434146	DALY, Edward	5 The Terrace, Barrack St., Waterford.	15-8-1922	General Labourer	8-8-1945
72135	DALY, Edward	49 Parnell Sq., Athlone.	13-10-1912	Carter	8-8-1945
E/422831	DALY, Gavin	2 St. Bridget's Terrace, Mullingar.	31-1-1919	Bricklayer	8-8-1945
L/507925	DALY, Gerald	Coolnaleen, Listowel, Co. Kerry.	2-7-1926	Labourer	19-7-1946
L/502234	DALY, James	11 Lower Dominick Street, Dublin.	25-3-1925	None	8-8-1945
V/206476	DALY, John	27 Botharbuidhe, White-hall, Dublin.	17-12-1907	Grocer's Porter	8-8-1945
A/83474	DALY, John	8a St. Joseph Mansions, Dublin.	31-5-1922	None	8-8-1945
82033	DALY, John	c/o Ml. Buckley, Mullard Park, Youghal.	23-6-1916	Farm Labourer	8-8-1945
L/506282	DALY, John	98 Gurranebraher Avenue, Cork.	26-7-1924	Messenger Boy	8-8-1945
A/78373	DALY, Joseph	View House, Kilkee, Co. Clare.	8-12-1920	General Labourer	8-8-1945
E/420259	DALY, Joseph	69 Falcarragh Pk., Bally-shannon, Co. Donegal.	4-5-1922	Labourer	8-8-1945
E/430879	DALY, Martin	Broughal, Kilcormack, Offaly.	10-7-1906	Farm Labourer	8-8-1945
E/432185	DALY, Matthew	Ballytore, Co. Kildare.	9-6-1919	Labourer	8-8-1945
V/205610	DALY, Michael	117 The Cottages, Lifford.	9-12-1920	Cycle-Mechanic Apprentice	8-8-1945
A/73867	DALY, Michael	Connaught St., Kilcock, Co. Kildare.	28-2-1915	Farm Labourer	8-8-1945
E/400200	DALY, Patrick	6 Susan Place, Coombe Street, Dublin.	8-10-1906	Barber	8-8-1945
E/405048	DALY, Patrick	31 Carmel Hall, Francis Street, Dublin.	30-11-1912	Labourer	8-8-1945
E/451684	DALY, Patrick	Ballytore, Co. Kildare.	5-1-1916	Labourer	8-8-1945
E/424555	DALY, Patrick	Mount Everest, Newcastle Road, Galway.	17-3-1921	Shop Assistant	8-8-1945
E/432960	DALY, Peter	4 Villa Bank, Royal Canal, Phibsborough, Dublin.	8-10-1917	Labourer	8-8-1945

Army No.	Name.	Last Recorded Address.	Date of Birth.	Declared Occupation prior to enlistment in Defence Forces.	Date of Dismissal from Defence Forces.
E/412727	DALY, Stephen	6 Ryan's Place, off Watergate Street, Limerick.	19-7-1918	Labourer	8-8-1945
E/401497	DALY, Thomas	8 Longford Lane, Dublin.	22-11-1921	Coal Vendor	8-8-1945
V/208456	DALY, Thomas	14 Brian Boru Street, Clontarf, Dublin.	1-8-1920	Telegraph Messenger	8-8-1945
L/502853	DALY, Thomas	65 Bargy Road, East Wall, Dublin.	11-3-1927	Messenger	21-4-1946
E/421077	DALY, Thomas	Palace, Elphin, Co. Roscommon.	17-3-1905	Labourer	8-8-1945
E/415759	DALY, Timothy	Bealduvroga, Ballingarry, Co. Limerick.	20-4-1912	Motor Driver	8-8-1945
E/402903	DANSKY, Joseph	24 Lombard Street, West, Dublin.	3-7-1921	Cabinetmaker	8-8-1945
E/401877	DARBINSON, William	10 Kells Road, Kimmage, Dublin.	11-6-1922	Labourer	8-8-1945
L/501978	DARCY, Albert	Mill House, Douglas West, Cork.	3-5-1920	Saddler	8-8-1945
E/424697	DARCY, James	Redlivea, Castlegad P.O., Co. Sligo.	18-10-1922	Farm Labourer	8-8-1945
E/401139	DARCY, Liam A.	92 Gwynne Rd., Battersea, London	29-3-1922	Draper's Assistant	8-8-1945
204057	DARCY, Michael	Befolam, Ballycusack, Co. Cavan.	28-7-1912	Labourer	8-8-1945
E/405969	DARCY, Robert	144 Mountpleasant Bldgs., Dublin.	22-9-1918	Shop Assistant	8-8-1945
E/402444	DARCY, William	36 North Great George's Street, Dublin.	5-5-1922	None	8-8-1945
E/435068	DARCY, William	3 Jinkens Lane, Waterford.	24-2-1923	Messenger Boy	8-8-1945
V/207896	DARE, Joseph	Ballyhenny, Kilmallock, Co. Limerick.	15-8-1921	Farm Labourer	8-8-1945
A/75306	DARGAN, Edward	IA Block, Aldborough House, Dublin.	12-7-1918	Labourer	8-8-1945
E/407865	DARLING, Terence	53 Casimir Road, Harold's Cross, Dublin.	29-11-1919	Clerk	8-8-1945
E/433463	DAVIDSON, Samuel	94 Ardilea Street, Belfast.	30-6-1922	Labourer	8-8-1945
E/424042	DAVIS, Festus	Aughrisbeg, Cleggan, Co. Galway.	5-1-1909	Farm Labourer	8-8-1945
79249	DAVIS, Henry	49 St. Killian's Crescent, Carlow.	16-6-1920	Labourer	8-8-1945
78640	DAVIS, James	Killusty, Fethard, Co. Tipperary.	20-9-1920	Labourer	8-8-1945
E/402430	DAVIS, John	16 Ravensdale Rd., East Wall, Dublin.	28-7-1918	Trimmer	8-8-1945
E/409150	DAVIS, John	22 Athole St., Manchester.	8-5-1922	Builder's Labourer	8-8-1945
V/206504	DAVIS, Kevin	12 Mary Aikenhead, James Street, Dublin.	5-1-1922	Tailor	8-8-1945
E/403017	DAVIS, Louis	38 Bloomfield Av., Dublin.	3-2-1920	Salesman	8-8-1945
A/83256	DAVIS, Thomas	16 Upper Dominick Street, Dublin.	13-3-1921	Butcher's Helper	8-8-1945
E/435715	DAWSON, Michael	Freshford, Co. Kilkenny.	22-11-1923	Farm Labourer	8-8-1945
A/83174	DEASE, Peter	34 Dominick Street, Dun Laoghaire.	28-9-1921	Labourer	8-8-1945
A/12614	DE BOTTE, Augustine	312 Cooley Road, Crumlin, Dublin.	20-5-1899	Labourer	8-8-1945
V/210052	DEE, Michael	Knocklong, Co. Limerick.	4-10-1922	Labourer	8-8-1945
L/502146	DEEGAN, Christopher	23 St. Joseph's Place, Lr. Dorset Street, Dublin.	18-5-1925	Van Boy	8-8-1945
E/433065	DEEGAN, James	7 Hogan's Place, Dublin.	6-3-1918	Farm Labourer	8-8-1945
E/401632	DEEGAN, Patrick	4 Lr. Mercer St., Dublin.	27-4-1901	Ship's Fireman	8-8-1945
E/421961	DEEHAN, Patrick	c/o John Smith, Main St., Buncrana, Co. Donegal.	5-10-1921	Labourer	8-8-1945
E/421728	DEENEY, Alfred	Burnfoot P.O., Co. Donegal.	30-5-1922	Apprentice Electrician	8-8-1945
79044	DEENEY, Hugh	10 Beechwood St., Derry.	21-11-1919	Labourer	8-8-1945

Army No.	Name.	Last Recorded Address.	Date of Birth.	Declared Occupation prior to enlistment in Defence Forces.	Date of Dismissal from Defence Forces.
V/209238	DEENY, Cathal G.	Lifford.	20-5-1921	Student	8-8-1945
E/400926	DEERING, Christopher	12 Digges Street, Dublin.	27-12-1907	Labourer	8-8-1945
E/434405	DEERING, John	2 " B " Block, Countess Markievicz House, Townsend St., Dublin.	21-12-1905	Driller	8-8-1945
A/79186	DELAHUNT, Peter	Kinneagh, Curragh, Co. Kildare.	18-1-1921	Grocer's Porter	8-8-1945
V/201764	DELAHUNTY, James	Brandondale, Graiguenamanagh, Co. Kilkenny.	19-6-1910	Labourer	8-8-1945
E/433552	DELAHUNTY, Kevin	1 Mary's Lane, Dublin.	9-11-1920	None	8-8-1945
E/409786	DELANEY, Arthur	45 Ward Street, Belfast.	27-7-1922	Labourer	8-8-1945
E/434788	DELANEY, Brian	Ardhill, Carbury, Co. Kildare.	1-10-1910	Motor Driver	8-8-1945
E/402441	DELANEY, Edward	125 Clonliffe Ave., Dublin.	29-7-1920	Labourer	8-8-1945
E/421919	DELANEY, Ivor	c/o Rectory, Dromahair, Co. Leitrim.	14-10-1921	Shop Assistant	8-8-1945
E/401978	DELANEY, James	125 Clonliffe Ave., Dublin.	7-10-1918	Grocer's Apprentice	8-8-1945
E/409785	DELANEY, James	45 Ward Street, Belfast.	19-9-1924	Joiner	8-8-1945
77266	DELANEY, Liam	67 Saumby St., Garston, Liverpool.	20-11-1918	Student	8-8-1945
V/211526	DELANEY, Michael	127 Sperrin Road, Crumlin, Dublin.	12-1-1922	Labourer	8-8-1945
80559	DELANEY, Michael	50 Walkin St., Kilkenny.	1-7-1921	Baker's Apprentice	8-8-1945
E/403413	DELANEY, Patrick	415 Mourne Rd., Crumlin, Dublin.	22-2-1910	Labourer	8-8-1945
E/406472	DELANEY, Patrick	22 Ardee Street, Dublin.	10-9-1922	Labourer	8-8-1945
E/416160	DELANEY, Patrick	Windgap, Co. Kilkenny.	4-4-1921	Labourer	8-8-1945
V/204220	DELANEY, Patrick	10 Mary Street, Cork.	16-1-1921	Labourer	8-8-1945
E/422911	DELANEY, Patrick	Main Street, Kilkenny.	1-9-1917	Labourer	8-8-1945
E/404668	DELANEY, Richard	16 Engine Alley, Francis Street, Dublin.	18-7-1911	Motor Driver	8-8-1945
E/409787	DELANEY, Samuel	43 Gibson Street, Belfast.	12-2-1923	Mill Worker	8-8-1945
78715	DELANEY, Thomas	10 Clonfert Rd., Crumlin, Dublin.	21-2-1921	Farm Labourer	8-8-1945
L/502927	DELANEY, William	16 Summer Place, off Upr. Rutland Street, Dublin.	6-10-1927	Messenger	13-7-1946
L/500321	DELANEY, William	196 Phibsboro Road, Dublin.	11-4-1922	Motor Trimmer	8-8-1945
206848	DEMPSEY, John	1 Upper Pollerton Road, Carlow.	11-1-1919	Labourer	8-8-1945
80388	DEMPSEY, Jos.	Mirah, Turloughmore, Co. Galway.	26-10-1917	Farm Labourer	8-8-1945
E/435130	DEMPSEY, Patrick	Blackwater, Co. Wexford.	23-6-1922	Labourer	8-8-1945
78726	DEMPSEY, Sean	7 Greenville Street, Dublin.	13-6-1920	Labourer	8-8-1945
V/209909	DENNEHY, Denis	108 St. Colman's Road, Spangle Hill, Cork.	12-10-1919	Labourer	8-8-1945
E/403510	DENNIS, James	16 Charlemont Row, Dublin.	13-8-1907	Plumber	8-8-1945
E/406710	DENNISON, Thomas	96 Gregg Street, Lisburn.	27-10-1911	Mill Worker	8-8-1945
V/214097	DERWIN, John F.	4 Fontenoy Tce., Thurles.	5-1-1916	Painter and Mechanic	8-8-1945
E/420881	DEVANEY, Michael	122 Sarsfield Sq., Athlone.	9-6-1921	Gen. Labourer	8-8-1945
203011	DEVINE, James	19 Eire Street, Gorey, Co. Wexford.	16-2-1922	Leather Worker	8-8-1945
85420	DEVINE, John A.	Cornabracken, Lanny, Omagh, Co. Tyrone.	21-9-1927	Solicitors Clerk	18-7-1946
E/432023	DEVINE, John	Whitehall, Graiguenamanagh, Co. Kilkenny.	14-1-1915	Gardener	8-8-1945
E/421710	DEVINE, John	Moorstown, Castlepollard, Co. Westmeath.	5-2-1922	Labourer	8-8-1945
208611	DEVINE, Patrick	19 Eire Street, Gorey.	5-7-1922	Labourer	8-8-1945
E/437876	DEVITT, John B.	Blackrock College, Blackrock, Co. Dublin.	1-10-1921	Baker	8-8-1945

Army No.	Name.	Last Recorded Address.	Date of Birth.	Declared Occupation prior to enlistment in Defence Forces.	Date of Dismissal from Defence Forces.
E/404799	DEVLIN, Felix	6 Turvey Ave, Donabate, Co. Dublin.	18-6-1911	Motor Driver	8-8-1945
E/424246	DEVLIN, James	Leenan, Clonmany, Co. Donegal.	14-5-1910	Crane Driver	8-8-1945
E/404068	DEVLIN, Malachy	16 Castle Lane, Lurgan.	14-1-1910	Nurseryman	8-8-1945
E/404595	DEVLIN, Patrick	5 Andersonstown Park, Belfast.	12-7-1916	Clerk	8-8-1945
E/404485	DEVLIN, Patrick	4 Upper Gardiner Street, Dublin.	20-4-1920	Machine Tool Setter	8-8-1945
E/434934	DEVLIN, Raymond	Donaguile, Castlecomer, Co. Kilkenny.	22-11-1922	Farm Labourer	8-8-1945
E/438022	DIAMOND, Edward	80 Albert Street, Belfast.	26-3-1926	Upholsterer	8-8-1945
E/412320	DICKENSON, James	33 Island Street, Limerick.	9-10-1920	Factory Worker	8-8-1945
L/503219	DICKENSON, Michael	33 Avondale House, North Cumberland St., Dublin.	17-3-1928	Gen. Labourer	5-12-1945
E/435266	DIGNAN, William	River Street, Clara, Offaly.	1-2-1919	Machinist	8-8-1945
E/406612	DIGNEY, John G.	Ballinahatton, Kilkeel, Co. Down.	24-6-1921	Electrical Improver	8-8-1945
E/407182	DILLON, James J.	14 Linfield Street, Dungannon, Co. Tyrone.	22-6-1921	Poultry-Butcher	8-8-1945
E/400927	DILLON, Michael	7 Middle Mountjoy Street, Dublin.	21-3-1903	Labourer	8-8-1945
E/412059	DILLON, Michael	Ballyooneen, Kildimo, Co. Limerick.	30-6-1916	Labourer	8-8-1945
L/503122	DILLON, Michael	43 Wellington St., Dublin.	29-12-1927	Gen. Labourer	1-7-1946
E/416687	DILLON, Oliver	2 Fish Lane, Mary Street, Limerick.	28-7-1920	Labourer	8-8-1945
L/507967	DILLON, Thomas	2 Fish Lane, Mary Street, Limerick.	14-8-1922	Labourer	12-5-1946
V/203254	DILLON, Thomas	2 Fish Lane, Mary Street, Limerick.	5-3-1921	Labourer	8-8-1945
V/209806	DINAN, James	Ballyea, Darragh, Co. Clare.	9-5-1919	Farm Labourer	8-8-1945
E/412252	DINEEN, John	Richmond House, The Crescent, Limerick.	23-5-1920	Labourer	8-8-1945
79641	DINEEN, Michael	4 Ladyswell Hill, Cork.	28-10-1920	Gen. Labourer	8-8-1945
E/422391	DIRRIG, Walter John	Gurteen, Shrule, Claremorris, Co. Mayo.	28-7-1922	Farm Labourer	8-8-1945
E/421865	DIVER, Andrew	Carrickatasken, Gweedore, Co. Donegal.	1-11-1903	Labourer	8-8-1945
E/421866	DIVER, James	Coshclaudy, Dunbeg, Co. Donegal.	1-6-1913	Motor Driver	8-8-1945
E/432576	DIXON, Patrick	Edenmore Dairy, Raheny, Dublin.	10-5-1922	Dairy Labourer	8-8-1945
76931	DOBSON, Edward	Kilcool, Co. Wicklow.	4-10-1919	Labourer	8-8-1945
E/425356	DOCKERY, Martin	Kilboy, Mantua, Castlerea, Co. Roscommon.	1-3-1924	Farm Labourer	8-8-1945
E/425355	DOCKERY, Peter	Kilboy, Mantua, Castlerea, Co. Roscommon.	16-7-1919	Farm Labourer	8-8-1945
210231	DOHERTY, Alfred	13 "A" Block, Pearse Barracks, Curragh Camp.	22-5-1922	Labourer	8-8-1945
A/84136	DOHERTY, Bernard	Urrisnanagh, Clonmany, Co. Donegal.	21-9-1918	Labourer	8-8-1945
E/420470	DOHERTY, Brian	Ballyliffan, Clonmany, Co. Donegal.	8-3-1910	Labourer	8-8-1945
E/422145	DOHERTY, Cahal	c/o Neil W. Cranaghan, Main Street, Buncrana, Co. Donegal.	30-9-1921	Labourer	8-8-1945
84333	DOHERTY, Charles	Castlefin, Co. Donegal.	20-2-1923	Farm Labourer	8-8-1945
E/423259	DOHERTY, Charles	69 Lecky Road, Derry.	1-2-1898	Clerk	8-8-1945
208890	DOHERTY, Cornelius	Drummany, Letterkenny.	12-10-1919	Labourer	8-8-1945
79494	DOHERTY, Daniel	Mullins Cottages, Thurles.	18-1-1921	Shoemaker	8-8-1945
V/203783	DOHERTY, Daniel	14 Barrack St., Strabane, Co. Tyrone.	26-12-1920	Warehouse Porter	8-8-1945

Army No.	Name.	Last Recorded Address.	Date of Birth.	Declared Occupation prior to enlistment in Defence Forces.	Date of Dismissal from Defence Forces.
E/422860	DOHERTY, Daniel	c/o Wm. Henderson, Calhone, Fahan, Co. Donegal.	16-1-1919	Aero Machinist	8-8-1945
V/215175	DOHERTY, Daniel	Glenfad, Clonleigh, Lifford.	24-2-1922	Labourer	8-8-1945
V/215142	DOHERTY, George	Porthall, Lifford.	1-7-1922	Farm Labourer	8-8-1945
81825	DOHERTY, Gerald	Waterside, Derry.	21-3-1927	Grocer's Assistant	8-3-1946
E/407658	DOHERTY, James	Drumlee, Benburb, Co. Tyrone.	7-10-1923	Labourer	8-8-1945
E/422461	DOHERTY, James	c/o J. Bonner, Donegal St., Ballybofey, Co. Donegal.	26-7-1919	Labourer	8-8-1945
E/423196	DOHERTY, James	86 Lecky Road, Derry.	18-2-1922	Joiner	8-8-1945
209831	DOHERTY, James	Claggan, Clonmany, Co. Donegal.	10-7-1918	Farmer	8-8-1945
E/421731	DOHERTY, John	Drumhaggard, Muff, Co. Donegal.	24-2-1921	Apprentice Painter	8-8-1945
77372	DOHERTY, Joseph	Kerrykeel, Lifford.	28-3-1919	Motor Driver	8-8-1945
84938	DOHERTY, Joseph	Altclough, Carrick, Co. Donegal.	5-9-1923	Farm Labourer	28-2-1946
V/207200	DOHERTY, Joseph	30 Daly's Terrace, Letterkenny.	14-2-1922	Labourer	8-8-1945
E/420751	DOHERTY, Joseph	Barnes Road, Ballybofey, Co. Donegal.	18-6-1919	Farm Labourer	8-8-1945
E/423260	DOHERTY, Joseph	12 Creggan Terrace, Derry.	5-8-1920	Labourer	8-8-1945
E/417799	DOHERTY, Laurence	Gurrane, Charleville, Co. Cork.	28-10-1912	Farmer	8-8-1945
E/421818	DOHERTY, Maurice	Erne Tce., Ballyshannon, Co. Donegal.	8-4-1920	Student	8-8-1945
208848	DOHERTY, Michael	Umgal, Malin Head, Co. Donegal.	28-3-1921	Farm Labourer	8-8-1945
E/422851	DOHERTY, Neal	c/o E. McCallion, Glockmore, Ture P.O., Co. Donegal.	5-7-1919	Butcher	8-8-1945
E/425190	DOHERTY, Neil	61 Nelson Street, Derry.	29-12-1923	Motor Driver	8-8-1945
E/424248	DOHERTY, Patrick Jos.	Glebe, Clonmany,, Co. Donegal.	3-11-1920	Lorry Driver	8-8-1945
V/208846	DOHERTY, Patrick	Ballygorman, Malin Head, Co. Donegal.	15-4-1921	Farm Labourer	8-8-1945
84360	DOHERTY, Patrick	Lisnakelly, Buncrana, Co. Donegal.	28-3-1917	Labourer	8-8-1945
E/421816	DOHERTY, Patrick	Tiernasligo, Clonmany, Co. Donegal.	25-3-1908	Labourer	8-8-1945
75878	DOHERTY, Robert	c/o Miss L. Melia, 3 Hallicks Rd., Curragh.	11-7-1920	Labourer	8-8-1945
80341	DOHERTY, Roddy	Clonleagh, Parkhall, Co. Donegal.	31-3-1921	Carpenter	8-8-1945
E/420399	DOHERTY, Samuel	Church Lane, Letterkenny.	9-2-1897	Labourer	8-8-1945
A/78752	DOHERTY, Seamus	18 Tyrconnell St., Derry.	21-10-1919	Labourer	8-8-1945
83939	DOHERTY, Terence	56 McSweeney Street, Dundalk.	20-8-1922	Motor Engineer	8-8-1945
E/406569	DOHERTY, Thomas	8 Church Street, Sligo.	22-5-1909	Clerk	8-8-1945
E/425213	DOHERTY, Thomas	Carrigullen, Strabane, Co. Tyrone.	17-5-1924	Factory Hand	8-8-1945
E/434024	DOHERTY, William	31 York Street, Dublin.	15-1-1912	None	8-8-1945
V/215128	DOLAN, Joseph	Killyacreagh, Ballinamuck, Co. Longford.	13-1-1923	Motor Mechanic	8-8-1945
A/71392	DOLAN, Leo	54 Ard Righ Road, Arbour Hill, Dublin.	2-3-1911	Bus Conductor	8-8-1945
E/413788	DOLAN, Patrick	36 Harrisons Place, Charleville, Co. Cork.	13-12-1921	None	8-8-1945
E/404395	DOMEGAN, Christopher	Iveagh Hostel, Bride St., Dublin.	23-12-1903	Steel Worker	8-8-1945
E/432903	DONAGHUE, James	1 Old Court Road, Tallaght, Co. Dublin.	27-12-1922	Gardener	8-8-1945

Army No.	Name.	Last Recorded Address.	Date of Birth.	Declared Occupation prior to enlistment in Defence Forces.	Date of Dismissal from Defence Forces.
E/407187	DONAGHY, Francis P.	Cornaney, Pomeroy, Co. Tyrone.	5-3-1922	Driver	8-8-1945
E/424021	DONAGHY, Hugh	Station Road, Mohill, Co. Leitrim.	31-7-1920	Farm Labourer	8-8-1945
83086	DONAGHY, John	4 Ryder's Row, Capel St., Dublin.	14-3-1918	Butcher (Shop-assistant)	8-8-1945
E/421575	DONAGHY, John	Magherhart, Dromore, Omagh.	13-3-1918	Motor Driver & Dock Labourer	8-8-1945
E/424692	DONAGHY, John	Banone, Donemanagh, Co. Tyrone.	24-10-1920	Farm Labourer	8-8-1945
E/404486	DONAGHY, Joseph	Cavanmore, Emyvale, Co. Monaghan.	24-12-1919	Motor Driver	8-8-1945
E/406487	DONAGHY, Patrick J.	18 King Street, Newry.	17-4-1921	Motor Mechanic	8-8-1945
83848	DONAGHY, Philip	27 James Street, Bessbrook, Co. Armagh.	13-1-1920	Lorry Driver	8-8-1945
E/422023	DONAGHY, Thomas	Westport, Ballyshannon, Co. Donegal.	25-10-1914	Gen. Labourer	8-8-1945
E/432466	DONALDSON, Daniel	Market Street, Monaghan.	9-12-1907	Labourer	8-8-1945
E/424977	DONEGAN, John	Old Town, Letterkenny.	8-1-1911	Labourer	8-8-1945
E/432365	DONEGAN, Michael	17 Sth. Earl St., Dublin.	18-3-1918	Labourer	8-8-1945
E/420072	DONLON, Luke	Moher, Lanesboro. Co. Louth.	27-9-1917	Farm Labourer	8-8-1945
83674	DONNELLAN, Henry J.	Stackallen, Navan.	19-5-1922	None	8-8-1945
E/407130	DONNELLAN, Martin	Feggaron, Cookstown, Co. Tyrone.	23-6-1922	Farmer	8-8-1945
E/406883	DONNELLAN, Peter	44 Annesley Place, North Strand, Dublin.	14-7-1923	Apprentice Electrician	8-8-1945
E/434487	DONNELLY, Daniel J.	Derrybuoy, Corr, Coalisland, Co. Tyrone.	8-11-1918	Farm Labourer	8-8-1945
E/407640	DONNELLY, James	19 Railway Tce., Armagh.	8-2-1919	Driver	8-8-1945
E/422861	DONNELLY, James	Carrown, Burt, Co. Donegal.	22-6-1922	Labourer	8-8-1945
E/409824	DONNELLY, John	Annagher, Coalisland, Co. Tyrone.	3-5-1924	Lorry Driver	8-8-1945
E/403172	DONNELLY, John	Market St., Ballycastle, Co. Antrim.	9-6-1894	Farrier and Blacksmith	8-8-1945
E/423467	DONNELLY, John	Aughinney, Drumshambo, Co. Leitrim.	20-10-1919	Farm Labourer	8-8-1945
E/401067	DONNELLY, Michael	89 Upr. Dorset St., Dublin	5-5-1917	Painter	8-8-1945
E/409638	DONNELLY, Patrick	29 Hand Street, Drogheda.	2-2-1925	Messenger Boy	8-8-1945
E/405104	DONNELLY, Sean	Fire Station, Lower Buckingham St., Dublin.	15-3-1922	Labourer	8-8-1945
E/421170	DONNELLY, Thomas	Ballykerrigan, Cloghan, Co. Donegal.	18-4-1919	Motor Driver	8-8-1945
E/405833	DONNELLY, Thomas	Dublin Street, Swords, Co. Dublin.	16-3-1917	Labourer	8-8-1945
E/406480	DONNELLY, Vincent M.	17 St. James Pde., Donegal Road, Belfast.	22-7-1915	Brass Moulder	8-8-1945
79943	DONNOLLY, John	30 Vulcan Street, Mount Pottinger, Belfast.	20-10-1921	Tailor's Helper	8-8-1945
E/413515	DONOGHUE, James	Ballingarry, Shinrone, Offaly.	4-9-1915	Hackney Driver	8-8-1945
76660	DONOGHUE, Thomas	20 Carmen's Hall, Francis Street, Dublin.	2-2-1918	Labourer	8-8-1945
E/407888	DONOHOE, Thomas	5 Churchtown Little, Rathgar, Dublin.	16-3-1924	Messenger	8-8-1945
75449	DONOHUE, William	c/o Mrs. McMahon, Ardnacrusha, Co. Clare.	8-12-1918	Labourer	8-8-1945
E/411356	DONOVAN, Patrick	Main Street, Ballincollig, Co. Cork.	16-3-1901	Labourer	8-8-1945
V/201188	DONOVAN, Richard	73 Wolfe Tone St., Cork.	22-5-1917	Labourer	8-8-1945
L/502374	DONOVAN, Thomas	Ballymackean, Oldhead, Kinsale, Co. Cork.	27-12-1921	Seaman	8-8-1945
E/414447	DONOVAN, Thomas	23 Seminary Road, Cork.	13-3-1922	Messenger Boy	8-8-1945
V/205967	DONOVAN, William	9 Ladyswell Hill, Cork.	16-6-1921	Messenger	8-8-1945

Army No.	Name.	Last Recorded Address.	Date of Birth.	Declared Occupation prior to enlistment in Defence Forces.	Date of Dismissal from Defence Forces.
V/204860	DONOVAN, William	Raffeen, Monkstown, Co. Cork.	3-8-1919	Labourer	8-8-1945
E/408230	DOODY, Joseph	2 Morgan's Place, Dublin.	31-1-1923	Schoolboy	8-8-1945
A/83847	DOOEY, Patrick	Cloughmills, Co. Antrim.	11-11-1921	Butcher	8-8-1945
79325	DOOLAN, Joseph	Lisclooney, Belmont, Offaly.	12-5-1919	Farm Labourer	8-8-1945
E/412538	DOOLAN, Patrick	50 Hennessy's Avenue, Clancy's Pk., Limerick.	17-3-1922	None	8-8-1945
81489	DOOLEY, Patrick	Johnstown, Bennykerry, Co. Carlow.	6-8-1926	Farm Labourer	7-1-1946
A/78685	DOOLEY, Terence	Dromahane, Mallow, Co. Cork.	24-4-1916	Labourer	8-8-1945
V/201815	DOONA, Daniel	Upper Dunloe, Beaufort, Co. Kerry.	28-12-1920	Farmer	8-8-1945
E/403746	DOONAN, John	Newry Street, Kilkeel, Co. Down.	3-2-1914	Dock Labourer	8-8-1945
V/209551	DOONAN, John	10 Lake View Tce., Cavan.	13-9-1913	Labourer	8-8-1945
E/422149	DOONAN, Patrick	Lake View Terrace, Cavan.	10-4-1917	Labourer	8-8-1945
E/422065	DOONAN, Terence	Lettercran, Pettigo, Co. Donegal.	10-8-1914	Labourer	8-8-1945
V/209286	DOONAN, Wm.	10 Lake View Tce., Cavan.	16-4-1920	Labourer	8-8-1945
A/67586	DOONE, John	Cloughendough, Coon, Bagenalstown, Co. Carlow.	28-9-1905	Labourer	8-8-1945
E/401259	DORAN, Bernard	117 Lr. George's Street, Dun Laoghaire.	29-2-1920	Railway Clerk	8-8-1945
E/403747	DORAN, Henry	Newry Street, Kilkeel, Co. Down.	28-8-1919	Labourer	8-8-1945
83647	DORAN, James	Hynstown, Newcastle, Co. Dublin.	7-5-1921	Dyer	8-8-1945
V/217017	DORAN, John	32 Pearse St., Kilkenny.	2-3-1919	Labourer	8-8-1945
83849	DORAN, Joseph	Mullartown, Annalong, Co. Down.	21-8-1914	Stone Mason	8-8-1945
E/423896	DORAN, Joseph	Keagh, Manorcunningham, Co. Donegal.	9-12-1921	Labourer	8-8-1945
L/507637	DORAN, Joseph	St. Joseph's Industrial School, Clonmel.	29-12-1926	Labourer	20-1-1946
E/432950	DORAN, Joseph	61 Lr. Dominick Street, Dublin.	30-6-1922	Silversmith	8-8-1945
202723	DORAN, Joseph	6 Sth. Summer St., Dublin.	11-6-1918	Labourer	8-8-1945
65569	DORAN, Samuel	Riverstown, Cork.	24-2-1901	Barber	8-8-1945
E/400659	DORAN, Thomas	Coolderry, Carrickmacross, Co. Monaghan.	24-5-1915	Labourer	8-8-1945
E/423984	DORAN, William	Killyussey, Newtown-cunningham, Co. Donegal.	27-1-1904	Labourer	8-8-1945
A/110117	DORMAN, John	Morgaws, Borrigone, Co. Limerick.	17-7-1916	Labourer	8-8-1945
E/421034	DORRIAN, Joseph	Ross, Rossnakill, Co. Donegal.	11-4-1913	Farmer	8-8-1945
E/402705	DOUGAN, Michael	18 Portmore Road, Port-stewart, Co. Derry.	31-1-1922	Bar Attendant	8-8-1945
204293	DOWLING, Cecil	61 Larkfield Grove, Kimmage, Dublin.	27-6-1919	Clerk	8-8-1945
A/83539	DOWLING, Joseph	545 North Circular Road, Dublin.	2-1-1922	Labourer	8-8-1945
L/508564	DOWLING, Joseph	Borris Rd., Portlaoighise.	2-2-1927	Labourer	8-8-1945
E/434406	DOWLING, Michael	6 Poole's Tce., Dolphin's Barn, Dublin.	20-12-1919	Motor Mechanic	8-8-1945
A/79143	DOWLING, Michael	26 Stephen's Road, New Kilmainham, Dublin.	19-7-1919	Clock Assembler	8-8-1945
E/434103	DOWLING, Patrick	Kilcoursey, Clara, Offaly.	23-12-1913	Waiter	8-8-1945
E/403175	DOWLING, Richard	2 Hughes Cotts., off Pearse Street, Dublin.	7-2-1921	Messenger	22-12-1945

Army No.	Name.	Last Recorded Address.	Date of Birth.	Declared Occupation prior to enlistment in Defence Forces.	Date of Dismissal from Defence Forces.
79755	DOWLING, Richard	Ballintubrid House, Newcastle West, Co. Limerick.	29-3-1912	Farmer	8-8-1945
A/76162	DOWLING, Valentine	1 Excise Street, Athlone.	8-1-1920	Messenger Boy	8-8-1945
E/405139	DOWNES, Donald	13 Upper Mountpleasant Buildings, Dublin.	4-6-1922	None	8-8-1945
E/405730	DOWNES, Michael P.	Old Bawn, Tallaght, Co. Dublin.	7-3-1918	Motor Driver	8-8-1945
77933	DOWNES, Nicholas	Crinkle, Birr, Offaly.	20-11-1920	Labourer	8-8-1945
E/404705	DOWNEY, Edward	28 Frederick Street, Bessbrook, Co. Armagh.	18-7-1920	Weaver	8-8-1945
E/422283	DOWNEY, Ed. A.	Castlecurry, Moville, Co. Donegal.	19-5-1913	Wood Joiner	8-8-1945
E/423261	DOWNEY, George	1 Townsend Street, Derry.	11-11-1912	Joiner	8-8-1945
E/422284	DOWNEY, James	Castlecurry, Moville, Co. Donegal.	10-2-1922	Labourer	8-8-1945
V/205123	DOWNEY, John	67 Railway Street, Dublin.	29-9-1920	Bootmaker	8-8-1945
A/67447	DOWNEY, John	251 Cathedral Road, Gurranebraher, Cork.	16-7-1906	Labourer	8-8-1945
E/422282	DOWNEY, William	Ture, Muff, Co. Donegal.	11-2-1914	Builder's Labourer	8-8-1945
79888	DOWNS, Ml. J.	Tubbers Lane, Carrigans, Co. Donegal.	22-10-1920	Labourer	8-8-1945
L/508749	DOYLE, Andrew	Finchogue, Enniscorthy, Co. Wexford.	8-9-1925	Farm Labourer	8-8-1945
85241	DOYLE, Daniel	The Commons, Lusk, Co. Dublin.	7-8-1923	Gen. Labourer	8-8-1945
75557	DOYLE, Daniel	Waterstown, Sallins, Co. Kildare.	6-1-1918	Labourer	8-8-1945
E/407604	DOYLE, Desmond	20 St. James Av., Clonliffe Road, Dublin.	12-1-1924	Painter and Decorator	8-8-1945
L/502796	DOYLE, Edward	15 St. Joseph's Place, Dorset Street, Dublin.	17-2-1927	Fitter	9-8-1945
V/217216	DOYLE, Francis J.	8 Stanaway Road, Kimmage, Dublin.	10-4-1916	Tailor's Cutter	22-9-1945
81463	DOYLE, Francis	28 Hollydene Gardens, Belfast.	21-8-1926	Butcher	28-5-1946
E/403748	DOYLE, George	154 Tolka Road, Dublin.	8-7-1911	Tailor's Presser	8-8-1945
E/423878	DOYLE, George	Newport, Rathowen, Co. Westmeath	23-6-1917	Farm Labourer	27-1-1946
E/434988	DOYLE, Geo. Kevin	12 Killarmount Street, Glasgow	29-8-1921	Student	8-8-1945
E/409710	DOYLE, Henry	6 Westmoreland Park, Ranelagh, Dublin.	1-5-1924	Messenger Boy	8-8-1945
E/408630	DOYLE, James A.	37 New Street, Dublin.	10-8-1924	Clerk	8-8-1945
E/424769	DOYLE, James	c/o Mrs. Toal, Bridge St., Dundalk.	4-9-1914	Street Singer	8-8-1945
E/416971	DOYLE, James	35 St. Ita's Street, Island Field, Limerick.	3-1-1923	Labourer	8-8-1945
79426	DOYLE, Jas.	Ballaghaderreen, Bagenalstown, Co. Carlow.	31-10-1919	Labourer	8-8-1945
E/431163	DOYLE, James	Finchogue, Enniscorthy, Co. Wexford.	14-5-1922	Gen. Labourer	12-9-1945
V/201435	DOYLE, John	10 Glencorp Road, Whitehall, Dublin.	10-7-1919	Typewriter Mechanic	8-8-1945
E/408611	DOYLE, John G.	28 Holmdene Gds., Belfast.	24-8-1924	Joiner	8-8-1945
E/432910	DOYLE, John	Killananny, Blue Ball, Tullamore.	16-5-1921	Sailor	8-8-1945
E/408284	DOYLE, Joseph	27 Clowney St., Falls Rd., Belfast.	15-10-1923	Aircraft Fitter	8-8-1945
E/407103	DOYLE, Joseph	Taney Villas, Dundrum, Co. Dublin.	8-11-1920	Motor Driver	8-8-1945
A/69942	DOYLE, Laurence	Castletown, Inch, Co. Waterford.	24-12-1911	Sailor	8-8-1945

Army No.	Name.	Last Recorded Address.	Date of Birth.	Declared Occupation prior to enlistment in Defence Forces.	Date of Dismissal from Defence Forces.
E/84711	DOYLE, Leo M.	335 St. Attracta Road, Dublin.	16-7-1923	Bricklayer	8-8-1945
E/434675	DOYLE, Leo	37 York Street, Dublin.	5-1-1922	Printer	8-8-1945
78617	DOYLE, Matthew	Wood Park, Castleconnell, Co. Limerick	7-5-1918	Labourer	8-8-1945
E/405281	DOYLE, Michael D.	11 Devitt Villas, Sandycove, Dublin.	21-2-1920	Press Photographer	8-8-1945
E/423064	DOYLE, Michael	27 Larkfield Pk., Dublin.	18-1-1915	Fitter	8-8-1945
E/434677	DOYLE, Michael	2 Kennedy's Cottages, Spa Rd., Inchicore, Dublin.	24-4-1922	Labourer	8-8-1945
E/433899	DOYLE, Owen	6 Centenary Place, Gorey, Co. Wexford.	17-9-1915	Motor Driver	8-8-1945
E/431972	DOYLE, Patrick J.	Whitelog, Athy, Co. Kildare.	28-7-1918	Labourer	8-8-1945
77801	DOYLE, Patrick W.	75 Whitemill, Wolfe Tone Villas, Wexford.	6-5-1919	Labourer (Docks)	8-8-1945
E/401793	DOYLE, Peter	High Street, Wicklow.	24-1-1921	Labourer	8-8-1945
A/80366	DOYLE, Philip	64 Leighlin Rd., Crumlin, Dublin.	23-8-1918	Labourer	8-8-1945
72418	DOYLE, Philip	261 Upr. Erne St., Dublin.	17-1-1913	Labourer	8-8-1945
L/503077	DOYLE, Terence	Ballsbridge Guest House, 47 Wellington Road, Dublin.	10-3-1928	Grocer's Assistant	2-2-1946
E/405585	DOYLE, Thomas	1 Upper Erne St., Dublin.	18-4-1915	Painter	8-8-1945
L/501649	DOYLE, Thomas	128 Oliver Plunkett Road, Monkstown, Dublin.	11-2-1923	Painter	8-8-1945
74894	DOYLE, William	2 Ranelagh Ave., Dublin.	19-3-1917	Labourer	8-8-1945
E/404121	DOYLE, William	66 Derry Road, Crumlin, Dublin.	28-8-1907	Lorry Driver	8-8-1945
E/431451	DOYLE, William	Tobinstown, Rathcrilly, Co. Carlow.	7-4-1920	Labourer	8-8-1945
208235	DOYLE, William	Rosetown, Rosslare, Co. Wexford.	22-11-1916	Farm Labourer	8-8-1945
A/79959	DREW, Robert	5 O'Donnell Gardens, Glasthule, Co. Dublin.	14-10-1919	Garage-hand	8-8-1945
E/434950	DREW, Timothy	Skough, Callan, Co. Kilkenny.	10-11-1922	Farm Labourer	29-11-1945
E/414916	DRONEY, Robert	Friarstown, Ballysheedy, Co. Limerick.	16-10-1922	Labourer	8-8-1945
A/79465	DRUMM, John	1 Kilbride St., Tullamore.	20-5-1921	Labourer	8-8-1945
E/415694	DRUMMOND, Virgie	9 Anglesea Road, London, S.E.18.	13-9-1921	Motor Driver	8-8-1945
E/425001	DUANE, Patrick	c/o Mrs. Fahy, Kilrickle, Loughrea, Co. Galway.	7-1-1924	Shoe Maker	8-8-1945
77466	DUDDY, John	3 Harbour Row, Cobh.	4-9-1920	General Labourer	8-8-1945
E/422150	DUDDY, Patrick	Gortusskea, Burnfoot, Co. Donegal.	7-3-1921	Labourer	8-8-1945
L/503332	DUDLEY, John	91 Lower Gardiner Street, Dublin.	28-8-1928	Messenger	29-5-1946
E/408622	DUFF, Francis	119 Annamoe Dr., Dublin.	2-6-1924	Student	8-8-1945
E/413205	DUFF, John J.	Carrigaline, Co. Cork.	30-4-1909	Meat Factory Employee	8-8-1945
83386	DUFF, Philip	Cloran, Athboy, Co. Meath	27-5-1922	Labourer	8-8-1945
E/404155	DUFFY, Alfred K.	5 Effra Road, Rathmines, Dublin.	7-4-1911	Motor Engineer	8-8-1945
E/422588	DUFFY, Arthur	15 William St., Drogheda.	12-5-1906	General Labourer	8-8-1945
V/208302	DUFFY, Donal	132 Cooley Road, Crumlin, Dublin.	11-9-1920	Seaman	8-8-1945
E/432438	DUFFY, Eamon	c/o Owen Swift, Glasslough, Co. Monaghan.	10-3-1922	Plumber's Assistant	8-8-1945
E/408614	DUFFY, Eugene	213 Cashel Rd., Kimmage, Dublin.	15-4-1924	Labourer	8-8-1945

Army No.	Name.	Last Recorded Address.	Date of Birth.	Declared Occupation prior to enlistment in Defence Forces.	Date of Dismissal from Defence Forces.
V/209793	DUFFY, Francis	c/o Mr. H. McGrane, Lifford.	4-1-1922	Labourer	8-8-1945
82415	DUFFY, Frederick Gavin	4 Castle View, Youghal.	30-11-1921	Garage Worker	8-8-1945
83466	DUFFY, Gerald	Dublin Street, Monaghan.	7-7-1921	Labourer	8-8-1945
78309	DUFFY, James	Cooleen, Moate, Co. Westmeath.	1-1-1921	Labourer	8-8-1945
83402	DUFFY, James	Newcastle, Oldcastle, Co. Meath.	16-5-1922	Labourer	8-8-1945
E/423344	DUFFY, James	33 Springfield, Mullingar.	29-6-1922	Labourer	8-8-1945
V/211015	DUFFY, John	14 New Cottages, Clondalkin, Dublin.	16-9-1920	Labourer	8-8-1945
84313	DUFFY, John	c/o J. McGuire, Lisbally, Ballyshannon, Co. Donegal.	22-9-1922	Farm Labourer	8-8-1945
A/77441	DUFFY, John	Cooldowngha, Ballinahown, Athlone.	5-7-1919	Farm Labourer	8-8-1945
E/434918	DUFFY, Joseph	11 Soldiers' Cottages, Ballysax, Co. Kildare.	8-5-1925	Messenger Boy	8-8-1945
E/400475	DUFFY, Kevin	29 St. Patrick's Villas, Ringsend, Dublin.	11-5-1921	Butcher	8-8-1945
84404	DUFFY, Michael	Dunaff, Clonmany, Co. Donegal.	10-3-1920	Farmer	8-8-1945
E/408411	DUFFY, Patrick	29 Churchtown Great, Rathgar, Dublin.	23-7-1924	Clerk	8-8-1945
74951	DUFFY, Patrick	34 Kiernan Street, Dublin.	17-4-1916	Pharmaceutical Assistant	8-8-1945
E/423884	DUFFY, Patrick	c/o J. McGloin, Loughty-bar, Kiltyclogher, Co. Leitrim.	21-2-1921	Farm Labourer	8-8-1945
E/433457	DUFFY, Patrick	Kilmeague Rd., Kilmeague, Co. Kildare.	25-10-1921	Packing Case Maker	8-8-1945
L/503331	DUFFY, Patrick	23 Dunmanus Road, Cabra West, Dublin.	11-8-1927	Plasterer	22-4-1946
L/502561	DUFFY, Thomas	10 Rampart St., Dundalk.	19-5-1926	Shop Assistant	14-10-1945
A/79879	DUFFY, Thomas	4 Sheriff Place, North Wall, Dublin.	19-5-1917	Carter	8-8-1945
E/420469	DUFFY, William	Elaghbeg, Burnfoot, Co. Donegal.	12-8-1921	Labourer	8-8-1945
205646	DUFFY, William	16 Fountain St., Strabane, Co. Tyrone.	15-9-1919	General Labourer	8-8-1945
E/431998	DUGDALE, John	26 John's Street, Ennis-corthy, Co. Wexford.	20-2-1919	Labourer	8-8-1945
B/1647	DUGGAN, James	194 Old Youghal Road, Cork.	29-5-1911	Labourer	8-8-1945
81818	DUGGAN, Michael A.	The Rear 36 St. Augustine Street, Dublin.	6-11-1926	Bootmaker	24-1-1946
V/208824	DUGGAN, Peter	Rosslare.	10-5-1921	Fisherman	11-11-1945
A/74743	DUGGAN, Sean	Falcarragh, Co. Donegal.	15-7-1918	Student	8-8-1945
E/433785	DUGGAN, William	Merton, Ballyhogue, Ennis-corthy, Co. Wexford.	29-3-1913	Farmer	8-8-1945
E/401794	DUIGNAN, Michael	150 Botanic Road, Dublin.	3-7-1902	Groom	8-8-1945
V/203884	DULEA, Daniel	3 Gould's Terrace, Cork.	5-3-1914	General Labourer	8-8-1945
209544	DUNDAS, James	c/o F. McGrisein, Kilty-clogher, Co. Leitrim.	7-4-1912	Farm Labourer	8-8-1945
E/424354	DUNDAS, William	Kiltyclogher, Co. Leitrim.	1-5-1916	Lorry Driver	8-8-1945
A/83871	DUNK, George	14 St. Thomas's Road, S.C.Rd., Dublin.	15-4-1922	Messenger	8-8-1945
V/203255	DUNLEA, Michael	Ballyvoreen, Murroe, Co. Limerick.	19-6-1919	Labourer	8-8-1945
V/209219	DUNLEA, William	Ballyvoreen, Murroe, Co. Limerick.	9-2-1922	Farm Labourer	8-8-1945
V/213003	DUNLEA, William	24 Roche's Buildings, Blarney Street, Cork.	13-5-1914	Labourer	8-8-1945

Army No.	Name.	Last Recorded Address.	Date of Birth.	Declared Occupation prior to enlistment in Defence Forces.	Date of Dismissal from Defence Forces.
E/420228	DUNLEAVY, Anthony	Corlough West, Belmullet, Co. Mayo.	16-6-1922	Labourer	8-8-1945
E/422147	DUNLEAVY, William	c/o B. Hughes, Market St., Monaghan.	3-11-1922	Labourer	8-8-1945
A/74993	DUNNE, Andrew	Coolecla, Kanturk, Co. Cork.	21-12-1914	Labourer	8-8-1945
85105	DUNNE, Anthony	6 Margaret Sq., Newry.	29-12-1925	Mechanic	8-8-1945
L/508526	DUNNE, Christopher	333 Boyne Street, Dublin.	17-3-1922	Dock Worker	8-8-1945
A/73716	DUNNE, Edward	Newtownmountkennedy, Co. Wicklow.	22-1-1915	Motor Van Driver	8-8-1945
E/431578	DUNNE, Edward	c/o Mrs. Czyzyk, 10 Wilton Road, Charlton, Cum-Hardy, Manchester, England.	6-1-1922	Student	8-8-1945
E/403706	DUNNE, Ernest	Dublin Union, James's St., Dublin.	15-3-1914	Labourer	8-8-1945
75972	DUNNE, Frederick	Farnacardy, Sligo.	2-6-1918	Farm Labourer	8-8-1945
A/83271	DUNNE, James	10 Middle Third, Killester, Dublin.	9-6-1922	Labourer	8-8-1945
E/455822	DUNNE, James	Russellstown, Innistigue, Co. Kilkenny.	8-8-1916	Farm Labourer	8-8-1945
E/417339	DUNNE, John	Brewery Ave., Dungarvan.	20-6-1924	Farm Labourer	8-8-1945
E/415246	DUNNE, John	17 Limerick St., Roscrea.	25-6-1920	Shoemaker Apprentice	8-8-1945
E/424368	DUNNE, John	Larah, Ballymoe, Co. Roscommon.	17-4-1922	Labourer	8-8-1945
E/400461	DUNNE, Joseph	20 Parks Place, Islandbridge, Dublin.	9-10-1910	Waiter	8-8-1945
E/407264	DUNNE, Martin	Camp, Tralee.	6-2-1917	Clerk	8-8-1945
E/404249	DUNNE, Michael	135 Parnell Street, Dublin.	25-3-1921	Labourer	8-8-1945
E/404110	DUNNE, Michael J.	10 Lower Dominick Street, Dublin.	13-10-1919	Fitter's Helper	8-8-1945
V/208672	DUNNE, Michael	Dromina, Charleville, Co. Cork.	13-5-1917	Labourer	8-8-1945
79601	DUNNE, Michael	61 Railway St., Dublin.	1-9-1921	Vanboy	8-8-1945
B/5853	DUNNE, Patrick	20 Warde's Tce., Longford.	12-3-1911	Farm Labourer	8-8-1945
E/435274	DUNNE, Patrick	c/o Mrs. Reddin, Garryowen, Mount-mellick, Co. Leix.	15-6-1922	Labourer	8-8-1945
E/431315	DUNNE, Richard	2 The Ring, Kilkenny.	6-11-1921	Messenger Boy	8-8-1945
E/404426	DUNNE, William	19 Upper Sean McDermott Street, Dublin.	3-12-1903	Labourer	8-8-1945
E/402368	DUNSTER, Reuben	62 Smith Villas, York Rd., Dublin.	7-6-1910	Process chemical worker	8-8-1945
A/82572	DUNWORTH, Denis	Kingsland, Bruree, Co. Limerick.	16-5-1922	Farm Labourer	8-8-1945
E/421786	DURCAN, Thos. Jos.	Cloonrane, Curry, Co. Sligo.	4-2-1920	Labourer	8-8-1945
V/215163	DWODICAN, Daniel	Mullaghmore, Co. Sligo.	22-2-1915	Fisherman	8-8-1945
E/404570	DWYER, David	33 Oaklands Park, Balls-bridge, Dublin.	18-12-1909	Motor Driver	8-8-1945
A/80474	DWYER, Denis	6 Lower Shannon, Ennis-corthy, Co. Wexford.	18-1-1922	Labourer	8-8-1945
E/432308	DWYER, Desmond	100 Farm Road, Dun Laoghaire.	1-3-1922	Carpenter	8-8-1945
E/412882	DWYER, Martin	3 Roseboro Rd., Tipperary.	21-10-1911	Labourer	8-8-1945
L/507252	DWYER, Michael	28 River Street, Clonmel.	13-10-1926	Labourer	29-12-1945
E/438328	DWYER, Patrick	5 Seán Terrace, Thurles.	24-5-1925	Labourer	8-8-1945
A/76662	EAKINS, John	New Road, Tipperary.	16-9-1919	Messenger Boy	8-8-1945
A/74468	EAMES, James	Lenamore, Carndonagh, Co. Donegal.	1-8-1915	Assistant Baker	8-8-1945
E/405200	EARLEY, James	College Street, Cavan.	6-1-1907	Shoemaker	8-8-1945
79245	EARLEY, James	91 Lower Gardiner Street, Dublin.	7-2-1920	Messenger	8-8-1945

Army No.	Name.	Last Recorded Address.	Date of Birth.	Declared Occupation prior to enlistment in Defence Forces.	Date of Dismissal from Defence Forces.
506873	EARLS, Michael	11 " B " Road, Killeely, Limerick.	10-6-1926	Labourer	8-5-1946
E/409940	EARLY, George	19 Baker Street, Belfast.	30-3-1925	Labourer	8-8-1945
E/407295	EARLY, John	2 Oxmantown Lane, Blackhall Place, Dublin.	23-2-1914	Driver	8-8-1945
E/434374	EARLY, Joseph	91 Lower Gardiner Street, Dublin.	29-9-1921	Delivery Van Helper	8-8-1945
V/211322	EARNSHAW, Desmond	28 Adelaide Road, Dublin.	5-1-1922	Engineer Student	8-8-1945
E/408324	EASTWOOD, Samuel	22 H Nicholas St., Dublin.	12-9-1922	Labourer	8-8-1945
V/211222	EBBS, Brendan	132 South Circular Road, Dublin.	20-3-1914	Upholsterer	8-8-1945
V/211376	EBBS, Kevin	132 South Circular Road, Dublin.	22-8-1917	Tailor	8-8-1945
A/74926	EDGEWORTH, Michael	Lyrecrompane, Listowel.	26-12-1915	Farm Labourer	8-8-1945
E/405356	EDMONDS, Charles	19 Churchtown Great, Rathgar, Dublin.	2-1-1923	Packer	8-8-1945
E/414907	EDWARDS, Daniel	67 Gurranebraher, Cork.	4-8-1922	None	8-8-1945
E/404452	EDWARDS, Patrick G.	75 Slievemore Road, Drimnagh, Dublin.	29-3-1920	Helper on Lorry	8-8-1945
E/430669	EGAN, Edward	6 Green Street, Birr.	2-6-1920	Clerk	8-8-1945
E/434740	EGAN, Joseph	3 Up. Fownes St., Dublin.	6-3-1916	House Painter	8-8-1945
E/430743	EGAN, Patrick	Dunnycross, Tullamore.	5-2-1922	Labourer	8-8-1945
E/438209	EGAN, Philip	Brannockstown, Trim.	16-7-1922	Farmer	8-8-1945
E/409271	EGAN, Thos.	20 O'Donovan Rd., S.C.R., Dublin.	26-5-1921	Blacksmith	8-8-1945
206931	EGAN, Thomas	Mullinahone, Co. Tipperary.	20-9-1916	Nurse Attendant	8-8-1945
A/73235	EGAN, Timothy	Cuskinny, Ballymore, Co. Cork.	30-9-1915	Labourer	8-8-1945
E/425261	EGAN, William	19 Pound Street, Birr.	20-8-1923	Farm Labourer	8-8-1945
E/408244	ELLIOTT, Alfred	1 High Street, Dublin.	9-4-1924	Tailor	8-8-1945
E/420177	ELLIOTT, Charles	Cloughfin, Castlefin, Co. Donegal.	18-1-1912	Labourer	8-8-1945
85323	ELLIOTT, John F.	33 Francis Street, Lurgan, Armagh.	6-8-1926	Painter	9-5-1946
E/409176	ELLIOTT, Joseph	33 Silverwood Terrace, Lurgan, Co. Armagh.	6-8-1924	Shop Assistant	8-8-1945
E/402381	ELLIS, John	19 Georges Place, Dublin.	10-4-1922	Kitchen Man	8-8-1945
E/402661	ELLIS, John	7 Galtymore Drive, Crumlin, Dublin.	3-6-1922	Labourer	8-8-1945
A/83020	ELMES, Thomas	23 St. Jarlath Rd., Cabra, Dublin.	21-7-1918	Labourer	8-8-1945
L/502795	EMERSON, Francis	3 Fitzgibbon Lane, Dublin.	10-2-1926	News Vendor	8-8-1945
E/410525	ENGLAND, Patrick	16 Francis Street, Cork.	2-6-1916	Labourer	8-8-1945
82486	ENGLISH, Francis	Lodge, Hospital, Co. Limerick.	23-3-1923	Farmer	8-8-1945
210195	ENGLISH, William	31 Peter Street, Waterford.	10-10-1921	Messenger Boy	8-8-1945
E/430436	ENNIS, Frederick	Eyre Street, Newbridge, Co. Kildare.	20-6-1922	Labourer	8-8-1945
E/402080	ENNIS, Hubert	11 Langrishe Place, Summerhill, Dublin.	23-7-1922	Carter	8-8-1945
E/435458	ENNIS, Patrick	Ballycashlane, Broadway, Wexford.	27-8-1919	Labourer	8-8-1945
E/406368	ENNIS, Patrick	173 Bangor Rd., Crumlin, Dublin.	15-3-1922	Motor Driver	25-11-1945
E/414180	ENRIGHT, Thomas	Tullerboy, Athlacca, Co. Limerick.	22-4-1916	Valet	8-8-1945
78382	ENRIGHT, Thomas	Clogher, Bruree, Limerick.	28-10-1919	Farm Labourer	8-8-1945
L/502688	EUSTACE, Wm.	176 Lismore Road, Kimmage, Dublin.	17-11-1926	Messenger	20-10-1945
E/402001	EVANS, John	100 Summerhill, Dublin.	1-1-1922	Messenger	8-8-1945
A/80706	EVANS, William	95 Abbeyfield, Killester, Dublin.	12-7-1921	None	8-8-1945

Army No.	Name.	Last Recorded Address.	Date of Birth.	Declared Occupation prior to enlistment in Defence Forces.	Date of Dismissal from Defence Forces.
V/208452	EVERETT, Chris.	85 Keogh Sq., Inchicore, Dublin.	1-12-1921	Labourer	8-8-1945
E/407609	FAGAN, James A.	12 St. Alban's Park, Ballsbridge, Dublin.	19-4-1916	Publican	8-8-1945
V/204188	FAGAN, Michael	26 North Cumberland St., Dublin.	15-4-1918	News Vendor	8-8-1945
E/423760	FAGAN, Patrick	Bridgend, East Port, Ballyshannon, Co. Donegal.	15-5-1906	Motor Driver	8-8-1945
E/402005	FAGAN, Sydney	27 York Street, Dublin.	30-1-1907	Framer	8-8-1945
V/207777	FAHERTY, Thomas	Flood Street, Galway.	5-9-1922	General Labourer	8-8-1945
E/433566	FAHY, Aiden Pk.	1 St. Michael's, Sarsfield Rd., Inchicore, Dublin.	6-2-1922	Labourer	8-8-1945
E/424482	FAIR, Alfred	Ballina Street, Crossmolina, Co. Mayo.	24-4-1922	Farm Labourer	8-8-1945
E/405189	FALLON, Leo	44 Trinity Gds., Drogheda.	23-10-1922	Butcher's Apprentice	8-8-1945
75684	FALLON, Peter G.	11 Summerhill Place, Dublin.	2-2-1918	Iron Moulder	8-8-1945
V/204062	FALLON, Timothy	43 Jinks Avenue, Sligo.	14-4-1920	General Labourer	8-8-1945
E/434778	FALOONA, James	Main St., Portarlington.	15-6-1907	Shop Assistant and Clerk	8-8-1945
L/508924	FARNAN, Patrick	Kilkea, Castledermot, Co. Kildare.	18-5-1922	Farm Labourer	8-8-1945
E/422864	FARRAN, Seán	Muff, Lifford.	17-8-1922	General Labourer	8-8-1945
E/415061	FARRELL, Edward	Silver Street, Nenagh.	21-1-1923	Labourer	8-8-1945
E/402003	FARRELL, James	6 Willet Place, Rutland Street, Dublin.	18-11-1903	Labourer	8-8-1945
E/402002	FARRELL, James	543 North Circular Road, Dublin.	7-6-1922	None	8-8-1945
E/408429	FARRELL, John J.	17 King's Av., Ballybough Road, Dublin.	13-1-1924	Show Card Painter	8-8-1945
E/420753	FARRELL, John	Crossmolina, Ballina.	4-6-1913	Labourer	8-8-1945
A/80352	FARRELL, John	12 Mount Drummond Sq., Dublin.	14-12-1921	General Labourer	8-8-1945
V/205192	FARRELL, John	90 Cork Street, Dublin.	—-2-1921	Metal, Tin and Sheet Worker	8-8-1945
203601	FARRELL, John	147 Upper Abbey Street, Dublin.	19-1-1918	Labourer (Dock)	8-8-1945
E/405339	FARRELL, Joseph	5 Ardmore Avenue, North Circular Road, Dublin.	12-3-1919	Motor Driver	8-8-1945
V/206176	FARRELL, Kevin	26 Hughes Pk., Dundalk.	11-9-1921	Labourer	8-8-1945
L/501234	FARRELL, Laurence	3 St. Michan's Flats, Greek Street, Dublin.	6-7-1924	Sheet Metal Worker	8-8-1945
E/408624	FARRELL, Michael	41 Leix Road, Cabra, Dublin.	9-6-1924	Van Boy	8-8-1945
A/77505	FARRELL, Michael	Cloonsheeran, Kilashee, Co. Longford.	10-12-1917	Labourer	8-8-1945
E/423482	FARRELL, Michael	7 Ballymahon Street, Longford.	15-3-1920	Labourer	8-8-1945
A/75540	FARRELL, Michael	45 St. Jarlath Rd., Cabra, Dublin.	8-3-1919	Shop Assistant	8-8-1945
E/438341	FARRELL, Patrick	Woodbrook, Mountrath, Leix.	10-9-1925	Labourer	8-8-1945
E/401540	FARRELL, Patrick	2 Tram Tce., Sandymount, Dublin.	24-10-1909	Labourer	8-8-1945
E/424607	FARRELL, Peter	21 Parnell Sq., Athlone.	8-10-1921	General Labourer	8-10-1945
L/502764	FARRELL, Philip	5B Liberty House, Railway Street, Dublin.	21-5-1927	Messenger	30-1-1946
V/202776	FARRELL, Thomas	70 Cook Street, Dublin.	15-8-1914	Sheet Metal Worker	8-8-1945

Army No.	Name.	Last Recorded Address.	Date of Birth.	Declared Occupation prior to enlistment in Defence Forces.	Date of Dismissal from Defence Forces.
L/500691	FARRELL, Thomas	619 North Circular Road, Dublin.	31-8-1918	Carpenter	8-8-1945
A/77783	FARRELL, Thomas	Kilbrush, Knocklong, Co. Limerick.	23-5-1917	General Labourer	8-8-1945
207429	FARRELL, Thomas	3 Clogher Rd., Kimmage, Dublin.	27-4-1921	Messenger Boy	8-8-1945
83226	FARRELL, William	185 Keogh Sq., Inchicore, Dublin.	10-4-1920	Labourer	8-8-1945
77953	FARRELL, William	Canaveen, Laurencetown, Ballinasloe.	7-10-1920	Farm Labourer	8-8-1945
V/211110	FARRELLY, James	142 Clonmacnoise Road, Crumlin, Dublin.	10-2-1922	Messenger	8-8-1945
A/67263	FARRELLY, John	Doolan, Ennistymon, Co. Clare.	13-6-1899	Farm Labourer	8-8-1945
A/75759	FARRELLY, John J.	6 Up. Stephen St., Dublin.	1-7-1919	Motor Driver	8-8-1945
L/501393	FARRELLY, Joseph	8 Lower Dominick Street, Dublin.	15-3-1921	Labourer	8-8-1945
E/402925	FARRELLY, Patrick	4 Charleville Mall, Dublin.	25-11-1915	Carpenter	8-8-1945
E/421965	FARREN, John	Carrigans, Co. Donegal.	10-8-1898	Sailor	8-8-1945
203918	FARREN, Patrick	Altaghaderry, Carrigans, Co. Donegal.	16-9-1920	Labourer	8-8-1945
E/422542	FARRIAN, Patrick	Boyne Cottages, Trim.	29-2-1920	Labourer	8-8-1945
V/202385	FAULKNER, Michael	56 Clanbrassil Street, Dundalk.	5-5-1909	Cycle Mechanic	8-8-1945
A/79818	FAWCETT, Vincent	2 North King St., Dublin.	23-4-1921	Labourer	8-8-1945
83954	FAY, Patrick	142 Mourne Road, Drimnagh, Dublin.	19-6-1922	Machine Minder (Printer)	8-8-1945
E/438269	FAY, Patrick	Lisbodiff, Cootehill, Co. Cavan.	20-9-1924	Labourer	8-8-1945
E/432636	FAY, Patrick	19 Owen Roe Tce., Cavan.	6-11-1897	Foreman Labourer	8-8-1945
E/400973	FAY, Peter	30 Hardwicke St., Dublin.	3-5-1922	Labourer	8-8-1945
A/76491	FAY, Thomas J.	23 Middle Gardiner Street, Dublin.	7-4-1919	Labourer	8-8-1945
82041	FEARON, Anthony	143 Lower Road, Cork.	4-10-1919	Hair-dresser	8-8-1945
E/408781	FEARON, Bernard C.	78 Coast Guard Station, Ringsend, Dublin.	20-8-1916	Hair-dresser	8-8-1945
83886	FEARON, James	23 Lower Gardiner Street, Dublin.	24-10-1921	Labourer	8-8-1945
E/404678	FEARON, Peter	20 Park Street, Dundalk.	24-1-1921	Farmer	8-8-1945
211387	FEARON, Stephen	24 Berkeley Road, Dublin.	1-12-1914	Unemployed	8-8-1945
77403	FEATHERSTONE, Thos.	Crinkle, Birr, Offaly.	16-9-1920	Farm Labourer	8-8-1945
E/420906	FEE, James	c/o O. Fee, Swanlinbar, Co. Cavan.	24-3-1920	Student	8-8-1945
E/408869	FEE, Peter	Drumbroches, Lisnaskea, Co. Fermanagh.	21-7-1924	Farm Labourer	8-8-1945
A/77109	FEEHAN, Patrick M.	Mayne, Clonee, Co. Meath.	1-6-1919	Dairy Worker	8-8-1945
A/75879	FEELY, John	Westport, Ballyshannon, Co. Donegal.	23-2-1919	Labourer	8-8-1945
A/80370	FEELY, Thomas	1 Connolly Pce., Kilkenny.	3-2-1922	Weaver	8-8-1945
E/437841	FEELY, William	1 Henrietta St., Dublin.	22-11-1925	Butcher's Assistant	8-8-1945
E/421305	FEENAY, Thomas	Blockpark, Manorhamilton, Co. Leitrim.	20-7-1920	Motor Mechanic	8-8-1945
E/420978	FEENEY, Andrew	Gurtermore, Killorgue, Co. Leitrim.	31-8-1913	Bus Driver	8-8-1945
L/508610	FEENEY, George	Forrest, Athy.	9-7-1923	Labourer	8-8-1945
V/200426	FEENEY, Martin	Clynagh, Costello, Co. Galway.	15-1-1913	Farm Labourer	8-8-1945
82442	FEENEY, John	Hillside, Ballyduff Upper, Co. Waterford.	18-1-1923	Shoemaker	8-8-1945
E/406166	FEHILY, Brian	14 Vevay Road, Bray, Co. Wicklow.	17-4-1922	Labourer	8-8-1945
V/217089	FEHILY, Fridolin	14 Vevay Road, Bray, Co. Wicklow.	10-12-1921	None	8-8-1945

Army No.	Name.	Last Recorded Address.	Date of Birth.	Declared Occupation prior to enlistment in Defence Forces.	Date of Dismissal from Defence Forces.
E/437606	FENLON, Dermot	Fort View Cottages, Ballyboro, Tagoat, Wexford.	30-5-1919	Carpenter	8-8-1945
L/500316	FENLON, Peter	16 Coombe Street, Dublin.	5-4-1921	Labourer	8-8-1945
E/435545	FENNELL, James	41 Dealy's Terrace, Athy.	15-11-1923	Labourer	8-8-1945
E/433145	FENNELL, James	Grange Cottage, Tullow, Co. Carlow.	9-10-1913	Motor Transport Driver	8-8-1945
A/83097	FENNELL, William	29 Our Lady's Road, Maryland, Dublin.	19-10-1921	Labourer	8-8-1945
85606	FENNESSY, Matthew	50 St. Patrick's Terrace, Navan.	27-12-1927	Gen. Labourer	17-8-1946
E/424439	FERGUS, James	20 McHale Rd., Castlebar.	2-3-1923	Student	8-8-1945
V/215158	FERGUSON, Thomas	Holborn Street, Sligo.	23-4-1921	Motor Mechanic	8-8-1945
A/83850	FERRAN, Anthony	12 Clare St., Dungannon.	28-1-1922	Iron Moulder	8-8-1945
E/421435	FERRY, Patrick	Murroe, Dunfanaghy, Co. Donegal.	14-3-1920	Farm Labourer	8-8-1945
40263	FIDDIS, Richard	27 Arysdale St., Hoxton, London.	24-4-1905	Labourer	8-8-1945
E/418197	FIELD, Michael	4 Gillahugh Cottages, Barrack Street, Cork.	27-1-1926	Dock Labourer	3-8-1946
L/502818	FIELDS, George	26 Glenaan Rd., Whitehall, Dublin.	15-4-1927	Porter	8-8-1945
A/83467	...FIELDS, Joseph	46 Hill Street, Millford, Co. Armagh.	28-3-1920	Labourer	8-8-1945
V/207086	FIELDS, Stephen	19 Georges Place, Blackrock, Co. Dublin.	Dec., 1921	Messenger	8-8-1945
A/79592	FINAN, William	Carowmore, Castlerea, Co. Roscommon.	24-3-1921	Fitter	8-8-1945
V/209901	FINEGAN, Thomas	62 Stanaway Road, Kimmage, Dublin.	17-12-1921	Messenger Boy	8-8-1945
77219	FINGLETON, Thomas	Belview Lodge, Athy.	8-6-1916	Farm Labourer	8-8-1945
E/421966	FINLAY, James	Cloughfin, Castlefin, Co. Donegal.	19-11-1913	Motor Driver	8-8-1945
83583	FINLAY, Michael J.	7 Mountjoy Sq., Dublin.	17-6-1922	Seaman	8-8-1945
V/206056	FINLAY, Richmond	Grange, Emyvale, Monaghan.	6-7-1919	Farm Labourer	8-8-1945
E/402345	FINLAY, William	2 Watling Street, Dublin.	4-2-1922	Labourer	8-8-1945
206632	FINN, Cornelius	34 Lower Gardiner Street, Dublin	27-2-1913	Labourer	8-8-1945
E/400371	FINN, Gerard	15 Lr. Mount St., Dublin.	15-1-1914	Engineering Dept., G.P.O.	8-8-1945
E/425010	FINN, James	Castle Avenue, Buncrana, Co. Donegal.	17-11-1921	Labourer	8-8-1945
E/421036	FINN, John	Marlow, Ballymote, Co. Sligo.	14-11-1909	Labourer and Baker	8-8-1945
E/433567	FINN, John	c/o Mrs. Maher, 17 Grenville St., Dublin.	19-5-1911	Engineer's Handyman	8-8-1945
72209	FINN, Patrick	2 Marrowbone Lane, Dublin.	8-2-1910	Labourer	8-8-1945
E/407299	FINNEGAN, Bernard J.	7 Forrest Street, Belfast.	8-5-1923	Window Cleaner	8-8-1945
200951	FINEGAN, Denis	Knocknadite, Tournafulla, Co. Limerick.	2-4-1919	Farmer	8-8-1945
V/204994	FINNEGAN, Felix	Emmet Street, Carrickmacross, Co. Monaghan.	26-7-1917	Labourer	8-8-1945
208879	FINNEGAN, James	Carrigavanty Cottage, Tramore, Co. Waterford.	2-5-1921	Telephone Operator	8-8-1945
V/209732	FINNEGAN, Michael	Rathcline, Lanesboro, Co. Longford.	12-4-1916	Labourer	27-1-1946
V/208085	FINNEGAN, Patrick	20 Emmet Street, Carrickmacross, Co. Monaghan.	11-9-1919	Farm Labourer	8-8-1945
E/406991	FINNEGAN, Sean	Main Street, Castleblaney, Co. Monaghan.	18-6-1923	Draper's Assistant	8-8-1945
A/84003	FINNEN, Bernard	19 Scrabby Road, Granard, Co. Longford.	27-10-1918	Farm Labourer	8-8-1945
E/402897	FINNERTY, John	84 Bulfin Road, Dublin.	20-6-1922	Labourer	8-8-1945

Army No.	Name.	Last Recorded Address.	Date of Birth.	Declared Occupation prior to enlistment in Defence Forces.	Date of Dismissal from Defence Forces.
E/411717	FINNIN, William	4 Flay Lane, Off Sand Mall, Limerick.	2-8-1900	Fireman	8-8-1945
E/405192	FINNISON, Patrick J.	Knocknagoran, Omeath, Co. Louth.	22-4-1920	Insurance Agent	8-8-1945
E/407235	FISHER, John J.	Tennoghmore, Loughlin Island, Co. Down.	18-5-1921	Metal-Spinner	8-8-1945
78338	FISHER, Patrick J.	62 St. Nicholas Avenue, Dundalk.	15-3-1920	Messenger	8-8-1945
V/209762	FITZGERALD, Frank	Ballinteggart, Screen, Co. Wexford.	22-5-1917	Farm Labourer	8-8-1945
E/402501	FITZGERALD, George	30 Annamoe Drive, Cabra, Dublin.	4-5-1922	Mechanical Engineer	8-8-1945
77351	FITZGERALD, James	Orr Street, Kilmallock, Co. Limerick.	22-4-1920	Labourer	8-8-1945
V/201861	FITZGERALD, James	Ballylusky, Ballydavid, Dingle, Co. Kerry.	—-7-1915	Labourer	8-8-1945
V/201382	FITZGERALD, James	Coad, Castlecove, Co. Kerry.	10-5-1920	Farmer	8-8-1945
V/208690	FITZGERALD, James	Suncroft, Lr. Salthill, Galway.	13-1-1918	Student	8-8-1945
E/406468	FITZGERALD, John	9 Grenville St., Mountjoy Street, Dublin.	21-5-1923	Slater (Apprentice)	8-8-1945
E/414663	FITZGERALD, John	Kilmore, Ballyduff, Co. Kerry.	11-8-1922	Labourer	8-8-1945
E/412545	FITZGERALD, John	Feenagh, Co. Limerick.	14-5-1910	Farmer	8-8-1945
82058	FITZGERALD, John	41 Friar's Road, Turner's Cross, Cork.	27-5-1920	Baker	8-8-1945
V/217032	FITZGERALD, John	14 Rathfadden Villas, Waterford.	26-10-1921	Dairyman	8-8-1945
L/501525	FITZGERALD, John	6 Cloghey Rd., Kimmage, Dublin.	8-10-1924	Messenger	8-8-1945
200950	FITZGERALD, Joseph	129 Keogh, Sq., Inchicore, Dublin.	21-1-1921	Messenger Boy	8-8-1945
E/415665	FITZGERALD, Michael	Collorus, Lauragh, Killarney.	2-12-1920	Wireless Operator	8-8-1945
A/69280	FITZGERALD, Michael	5 Red Abbey Place, Cork.	20-8-1909	Labourer	8-8-1945
A/111838	FITZGERALD, Michael	Mary Street, Templemore.	19-4-1916	Labourer	8-8-1945
L/502738	FITZGERALD, Stephen	6 Clogher Rd., Crumlin, Dublin.	20-11-1926	Labourer	8-8-1945
E/412253	FITZGERALD, Thomas	Abbey Street, Cahir, Co. Tipperary.	12-1-1922	Messenger	8-8-1945
E/412736	FITZGERALD, Timothy	1 Korwick's Rd., Off Lr. Gerald Griffin Street, Limerick.	2-9-1922	Labourer	8-8-1945
V/207875	FITZGERALD, William	Ballinode, Co. Monaghan.	7-6-1910	Farmer	8-8-1945
A/64762	FITZGERALD, William	Ballyconrad, Cashel, Co. Tipperary.	1-5-1902	Gen. Labourer	8-8-1945
V/204952	FITZGERALD, William	3 Bushy Lane, Gerald Griffin St., Limerick.	26-1-1921	Messenger Boy	8-8-1945
207997	FITZGERALD, William	Ballydavid, Dingle, Co. Kerry.	6-6-1917	Farmer	8-8-1945
V/201088	FITZGIBBON, George	Milford, Charleville, Co. Cork.	1-10-1916	Shoemaker	8-8-1945
207151	FITZHUGH, Michael	18 Upr. Drumcondra Rd., Dublin.	28-4-1919	Cycle Mechanic	8-8-1945
E/434036	FITZPATRICK, Chris.	33 Upr. Sean McDermott Street, Dublin.	22-8-1917	Labourer	8-8-1945
E/403037	FITZPATRICK, Desmond	5B Patrick Street, Dublin.	30-3-1922	Tailor	8-8-1945
V/214159	FITZPATRICK, Edward	Glengoole, Newbermingham, Thurles.	3-1-1923	Labourer	8-8-1945
69817	FITZPATRICK, Edward	20 Southend Row, London, W.8.	7-5-1912	Grocer's Assistant	8-8-1945
79579	FITZPATRICK, Francis	39 Tolka Rd., Ballybough, Dublin.	6-6-1921	Labourer	8-8-1945
E/404196	FITZPATRICK, George	73 Ranelagh Road, Dublin.	1-8-1915	Lorry Driver	8-8-1945

Army No.	Name.	Last Recorded Address.	Date of Birth.	Declared Occupation prior to enlistment in Defence Forces.	Date of Dismissal from Defence Forces.
E/406465	FITZPATRICK, John	74 Queen Street, Dublin.	30-12-1922	Messenger	8-8-1945
E/415270	FITZPATRICK, John	15 Lower Road, Cork.	3-5-1922	Labourer	8-8-1945
78420	FITZPATRICK, John	45 St. Nicholas Avenue, Dundalk.	22-6-1920	Boot Maker	8-8-1945
E/406853	FITZPATRICK, John	7 Offaly Road, Cabra, Dublin.	13-6-1922	Metal Worker	8-8-1945
E/408423	FITZPATRICK, Joseph	34 Hogan's Place, Grand Canal Street, Dublin.	31-10-1923	Apprentice Pumber	8-8-1945
A/83540	FITZPATRICK, Kevin	13 Ranelagh Road, Dublin.	6-5-1922	Labourer	8-8-1945
E/402535	FITZPATRICK, Patrick	187 Botanic Rd., Dublin.	23-4-1921	Window Dresser	8-8-1945
E/406111	FITZPATRICK, Patrick	Aughadreena, Crosskeys, Co. Cavan.	22-1-1916	Farm Labourer	8-8-1945
E/434141	FITZPATRICK, Patrick	Tyles, Abbeyleix	1-10-1922	Farm Labourer	8-8-1945
E/403848	FITZPATRICK, Patrick	Donishall, Carnew, Co. Wicklow.	19-4-1920	Motor Driver	8-8-1945
A/83640	FITZPATRICK, Pearse	6 O'Neill Avenue, Newry.	18-1-1922	Shop Assistant	8-8-1945
76801	FITZPATRICK, Terence P.	Ardona, Milltown, Co. Cavan.	10-11-1916	Farm Labourer	8-8-1945
L/502956	FITZPATRICK, William	35K Pearse House, Hanover Street, Dublin.	23-10-1927	General Labourer	8-8-1945
E/407763	FITZSIMONS, Chris.	46 Russell Avenue, East Wall, Dublin.	15-1-1924	Messenger	8-8-1945
V/207100	FITZSIMONS, Patrick	15 Upr. Buckingham St., Dublin.	26-3-1921	None	8-8-1945
72271	FITZSIMONS, Patrick	54A Netherwood Street, Kilburn, London, N.W.	19-7-1910	Grocer's Assistant	8-8-1945
E/429574	FLAHERTY, Laurence	75 St. Dominick's Terrace, Galway.	6-6-1906	Tailor	8-8-1945
82319	FLAHERTY, Thomas	Oyster Hill, Spa, Tralee.	15-2-1917	Farm Labourer	8-8-1945
E/407582	FLANAGAN, Francis	Boyne Road, Navan.	15-10-1915	Upholsterer	8-8-1945
75219	FLANAGAN, Hugh	12 Fitzgibbon St., Dublin.	26-2-1918	Labourer	8-8-1945
E/425501	FLANAGAN, James	Creevy, Ballyshannon, Co. Donegal.	6-4-1922	Farm Labourer	8-8-1945
E/403962	FLANAGAN, James	Ballinahattan, Kilkeel, Co. Down.	1-4-1910	Motor Driver	8-8-1945
E/420641	FLANAGAN, John	Finnalaughta, Dromod, Co. Leitrim.	23-6-1900	Labourer	8-8-1945
V/214127	FLANAGAN, Martin	Lisatunna, Ennistymon, Co. Clare.	2-4-1916	Labourer	8-8-1945
E/414857	FLANAGAN, Patrick	Carhunagry, Mullagh, Miltown Malbay, Co. Clare.	13-3-1921	Labourer	8-8-1945
A/77080	FLANAGAN, Philip	Stamullen Road, Gormanston, Co. Meath.	11-11-1917	Farm Labourer	8-8-1945
E/402895	FLANAGAN, William	11 Temple Pce., Ranelagh, Dublin.	21-9-1921	None	8-8-1945
L/507937	FLANNERY, Martin	Ashmount Terrace, Dingle, Co. Kerry.	26-7-1928	Fisherman	22-7-1946
E/406290	FLATMAN, Brendan	17 Temple Street, Dublin.	12-2-1918	Tailor's Presser	8-8-1945
75852	FLEMING, Arthur	Healy Terrace, Ardnaree, Ballina.	10-7-1919	Labourer	8-8-1945
E/409008	FLEMING, Bernard	Church St., Castleblaney, Co. Monaghan.	7-3-1923	Boot Factory Worker	8-8-1945
V/208695	FLEMING, Gerard	University Rd., Galway.	30-3-1916	Student	8-8-1945
L/502944	FLEMING, Gerard	3 Clonmacnoise Road, Kimmage, Dublin.	12-5-1927	Schoolboy	8-8-1945
E/404080	FLEMING, John	279 Farranboley Cottages, Dundrum, Co. Dublin.	15-6-1917	Tent Maker	8-8-1945
A/72932	FLEMING, Michael	3 Kellagher Bks., Battery Road, Longford.	2-10-1913	Labourer	8-8-1945
E/432116	FLEMING, Michael J.	143 St. Brigid's Parade, Clara, Offaly.	20-10-1919	Carpenter	8-8-1945
E/421384	FLEMING, Patrick	Brackloonagh, Charlestown, Co. Mayo.	8-3-1918	Farm Labourer	8-8-1945
E/412885	FLEMING, Robert	1 Lelia Place, Limerick.	3-2-1919	Assistant Cook	8-8-1945

Army No.	Name.	Last Recorded Address.	Date of Birth.	Declared Occupation prior to enlistment in Defence Forces.	Date of Dismissal from Defence Forces.
V/204604	FLETCHER, Patrick	3 Grove Street, Roscrea.	10-1-1921	Labourer	8-8-1945
E/401638	FLOOD, John	24 Peter Street, Drogheda.	9-11-1916	Labourer	8-8-1945
E/401018	FLOOD, Patrick	155 Nth. King St., Dublin.	5-6-1911	Fitter's Helper	8-8-1945
84764	FLOOD, Patrick	2 Gardiner Lane, Middle Gardiner Street, Dublin.	20-6-1924	Gen. Labourer	8-8-1945
E/409149	FLOOD, Richard	1 Smithfield Tce., Dublin.	1-7-1908	Grocer's Porter	8-8-1945
204175	FLOOD, William	125 Pembroke Lane, Lr. Baggot Street, Dublin.	22-9-1920	None	8-8-1945
A/76493	FLOODY, Patrick	17 Bredin St., Drogheda.	15-1-1920	Messenger	8-8-1945
V/211576	FLOWERS, Patrick	4 Dunbar Tce., Wicklow.	6-4-1923	Grocer's Assistant	8-8-1945
V/207753	FLYNN, Andrew	9 St. John's Terrace, Sligo.	6-5-1920	Labourer	8-8-1945
E/415391	FLYNN, Doney	Churchill, Ennistymon, Co. Clare.	10-1-1923	Boot Repairer	8-8-1945
L/506440	FLYNN, James	Jail Lane, Charleville, Co. Cork.	3-1-1922	Labourer	8-8-1945
A/77547	FLYNN, John	4 Parnell Street, Dublin.	1-10-1920	Labourer	8-8-1945
E/425172	FLYNN, John	Collinstown, Clara.	2-8-1924	Factory Worker	8-8-1945
203008	FLYNN, John	Palace East, New Ross, Co. Wexford.	28-4-1918	Labourer	8-8-1945
E/407568	FLYNN, Kevin	89 Knockbreda Road, Belfast.	16-6-1920	Labourer	8-8-1945
E/420298	FLYNN, Mark	9 Castlemaine St., Athlone.	22-3-1894	Motor Mechanic and Driver	8-8-1945
E/434789	FLYNN, Matthew	70 Fair Green, Clara.	1-1-1921	Factory Worker	8-8-1945
E/431180	FLYNN, Michael	Glenbrine, Enniscorthy, Co. Wexford.	5-3-1916	Labourer	8-8-1945
V/206772	FLYNN, Nicholas	Leixlip, Co. Kildare.	19-10-1914	Labourer	8-8-1945
84679	FLYNN, Patrick	16 Lourdes Road, Maryland, Dublin.	10-2-1924	Watchmaker	8-8-1945
200954	FLYNN, Patrick	Ballinvana, Kilmallock, Co. Limerick.	7-3-1916	Labourer	8-8-1945
A/80392	FLYNN, Patrick	Collinstown, Clara.	12-11-1921	Labourer	8-8-1945
A/80420	FLYNN, Peter	Mole House, Oldcastle, Co. Meath.	17-11-1912	None	8-8-1945
V/201464	FLYNN, Thomas	9 St. John's Tce., Sligo.	10-10-1918	Labourer	8-8-1945
L/508380	FLYNN, William	8 Dillon St., Tullamore, Offaly.	2-7-1924	Labourer	8-8-1945
84601	FOGARTY, Desmond	40 St. Declan's Road, Marino, Dublin.	18-2-1921	Clerk	8-8-1945
205057	FOGARTY, John	25 Beaufield Park, Stillorgan, Co. Dublin.	2-1-1922	None	8-8-1945
V/210210	FOGARTY, Lawrence	30 Ranelagh Road, Dublin.	16-9-1921	Painter	8-8-1945
78141	FOLAN, Colm	Teac Mór, Inverrin, Co. Galway.	17-12-1917	Farm Labourer	8-8-1945
E/429641	FOLAN, Michael	Teach Mór, Indreabhán, Co. Galway.	—-7-1922	Farm Labourer	8-8-1945
E/406559	FOLEY, Chris.	9 Meath Place, Meath St., Dublin.	10-12-1911	Storeman	8-8-1945
A/83238	FOLEY, Gerald	134 Caledon Road, East Wall, Dublin.	10-4-1922	Labourer	8-8-1945
E/433096	FOLEY, James	44 Yellow Rd., Beaumont, Drumcondra, Dublin.	1-11-1921	Umbrella Maker	8-8-1945
77087	FOLEY, John	Dooks, Glenbeigh, Co. Kerry.	6-1-1920	Farm Labourer	8-8-1945
E/430167	FOLEY, John	Green Villa Lane, Enniscorthy, Co. Wexford.	11-7-1912	Labourer	8-8-1945
V/213107	FOLEY, John	Shanna Upper, Kilgobnet, Killorglin, Co. Kerry.	21-5-1915	Labourer	8-8-1945
V/203471	FOODY, Sean	Salthill, Galway.	24-1-1916	Student	8-8-1945

Army No.	Name.	Last Recorded Address.	Date of Birth.	Declared Occupation prior to enlistment in Defence Forces.	Date of Dismissal from Defence Forces.
L/502698	FORAN, Michael	74 Marlboro' St., Dublin.	12-10-1925	Labourer	8-8-1945
200956	FORD, William	Knocklong, Co. Limerick.	4-5-1918	Carpenter	8-8-1945
L/506809	FORDE, Michael F.	4 Cottage, Limerick Road, Charleville, Co. Cork.	7-11-1926	Labourer	8-8-1945
L/506784	FORDE, Patrick J.	4 Cottage, Limerick Road, Charleville, Co. Cork.	25-2-1921	Cattledriver	8-8-1945
E/417233	FORDE, Richard	27 Harrison's Place, Charleville, Co. Cork.	13-11-1924	Labourer	8-8-1945
E/432153	FORDE, Thomas	Bridge Street, Callan, Co. Kilkenny.	28-2-1922	Baker	8-8-1945
L/507305	FORESTER, James	4 McCann's Street, Cashel, Co. Tipperary.	27-3-1927	Labourer	4-12-1945
E/431776	FORRESTAL, John	11 Convent View, Tullamore.	23-11-1920	Carpenter	8-8-1945
E/415614	FORRESTAL, Thos.	25 McDonagh Avenue, Janesboro', Limerick.	21-6-1922	Film Operator	8-8-1945
L/502750	FORRESTER, John	35 Nth. Cumberland St., Dublin.	5-4-1927	Messenger	8-8-1945
83878	FORSYTHE, Gerald	4B Beggars Bush Bks., Shelbourne Rd., Dublin.	4-9-1922	Clerk	8-8-1945
L/502298	FORTUNE, John	8 St. Laurence Terrace, Chapelizod, Dublin.	20-7-1925	Labourer	8-8-1945
E/404480	FORWOOD, James	47 I Block, Marshalsea Bks., Thomas St., Dublin.	20-10-1922	Waiter	8-8-1945
E/405036	FOSTER, Alfred	3 Ridgemount Gardens, Torrington Pce., London.	1-8-1922	Clerk	8-8-1945
E/408613	FOSTER, Francis	51 Brookfield St., Belfast.	17-9-1924	Carter	8-8-1945
E/405031	FOSTER, Horace	3 Ridgemount Gardens, Torrington Pce., London.	2-4-1920	Clerk	8-8-1945
A/83094	FOSTER, Joseph	Lea House, Portarlington.	4-8-1920	Motor Driver	8-8-1945
72713	FOSTER, Richard	2 Dailly Road Crescent, Maybole, Ayrshire.	4-10-1912	Labourer	8-8-1945
A/70613	FOSTER, Thomas	Clough Rd., Baltinglass, Co. Wicklow.	19-9-1911	Farm Labourer	8-8-1945
E/422865	FOSTER, Wm.	c/o Mgt. Duffy, Elaghabeg, Burnfoot, Co. Donegal.	5-2-1921	Labourer	8-8-1945
E/402446	FOWLER, Patrick	36 Clarendon St., Dublin.	4-3-1918	Labourer	8-8-1945
E/423263	FOX, Charles	114 Bishop St., Derry.	18-10-1909	Labourer	8-8-1945
202777	FOX, John	100 Walsh Road, Dublin.	10-2-1921	Unemployed	8-8-1945
V/200718	FOX, Martin	Derrynaseeha, Cranny, Co. Clare.	9-5-1913	Farm Labourer	8-8-1945
A/83800	FOX, Patrick	6 Corny's Sq., Newry.	15-6-1921	Butcher	8-8-1945
V/206919	FOY, Peter	New Lane, Church Street, Cootehill, Co. Cavan.	11-5-1920	Egg-Packer	8-8-1945
E/416757	FOX, Michael	Loughloher, Cahir, Co. Tipperary.	18-6-1923	Messenger	8-8-1945
E/437819	FOYNES, Donal J.	19 Rathgar Road, Dublin.	2-2-1922	Clerk	8-8-1945
A/79956	FRAHER, Michael	Mayharling, Kelvdon. Colchester, Essex.	13-10-1921	Student	8-8-1945
215019	FRAIN, Christopher	Knocknacurry, Ballaghaderreen, Co. Roscommon.	18-12-1920	Farm Labourer	8-8-1945
V/200519	FRAWLEY, John	5 Bank Place, Limerick.	11-1-1921	Messenger Boy	8-8-1945
E/410580	FRAY, Patrick	18 Steps Lane, Shandon Street, Cork.	12-8-1912	Labourer	8-8-1945
L/502127	FREER, Chris.	43 Monasterboice Road, Crumlin, Dublin.	4-12-1924	Foundry Helper	8-8-1945
L/501076	FRENCH, Patrick	169 North Circular Road, Dublin.	3-2-1922	Motor Engineer	8-8-1945
V/200129	FRENCH, Samuel	Braid, Rorthall, Lifford.	10-8-1910	Labourer	8-8-1945
V/202418	FRIARY, Thomas	Nobber, Co. Meath.	5-5-1911	Labourer	8-8-1945
A/113299	FRIEL, Hugh	Mill Brae, Buncrana, Co. Donegal.	12-11-1914	Labourer	8-8-1945
79636	FRIEL, James	Kilton, Killygordon, Co. Donegal.	24-8-1916	Motor Driver	8-8-1945
E/422866	FRIEL, Manasses,	10 High Street, Derry.	4-6-1905	Motor Driver	8-8-1945

Army No.	Name.	Last Recorded Address.	Date of Birth.	Declared Occupation prior to enlistment in Defence Forces.	Date of Dismissal from Defence Forces.
77105	FRIEND, Harry	Hospital Strteet, Kildare.	9-1-1918	Labourer	8-8-1945
E/421261	FUERY, Edward	15 St. Finbar's Terrace, Bohermore, Co. Galway.	3-3-1921	General Labourer	8-8-1945
75452	FUERY, Henry	Crowenstown, Delvin, Co. Westmeath.	19-11-1918	Labourer	8-8-1945
A/72059	FULHAM, Joseph	4 Marshalsea Ln., Dublin.	24-4-1905	Labourer	8-8-1945
E/421732	FULTON, Joseph	Lynch Road, Fawn, Co. Donegal.	11-11-1904	Labourer	8-8-1945
79134	FULTON, Patrick	Main Street, Pomeroy, Co. Tyrone.	2-5-1921	Farm Labourer	8-8-1945
E/401542	FURLONG, Edward J.	14 The Rear, Herbert St., Dublin.	16-9-1916	Messenger	8-8-1945
E/408165	FURLONG, James	106 Church Road, East Wall, Dublin.	14-5-1924	Schoolboy	8-8-1945
80793	FURLONG, James	Castaheaney, Clonsilla, Co. Dublin.	17-6-1922	Labourer	8-8-1945
E/405168	FURLONG, Thomas	5 Emmet Place, Wexford.	16-1-1920	Clerk	8-8-1945
V/208651	GAFFALY, Charles	Eldergole, Cloone, Co. Leitrim.	25-7-1911	Farm Labourer	8-8-1945
E/423748	GAFFEY, Martin	35 St. Patrick's Terrace, Athlone.	8-9-1922	Messenger	8-8-1945
E/403458	GAFFNEY, Andrew	12 Lambay Road, Drumcondra, Dublin.	3-10-1920	Labourer	8-8-1945
E/425618	GAFFNEY, Joseph	Callintra, Castletara, Co. Cavan.	17-11-1923	Shop Assistant	8-8-1945
E/406342	GAFFNEY, Michael	Campbell's Park, Ardee, Co. Louth.	10-4-1923	Labourer	8-8-1945
E/404020	GAFFNEY, Patrick	15 North Georges Street, Dublin.	1-9-1908	Seaman	8-8-1945
69754	GAFFNEY, Peter	59 Crumlin Road, Dublin.	15-10-1915	Schoolboy	8-8-1945
E/424899	GAHAN, John	Ballybromhill, Fenagh, Bagenalstown, Co. Carlow.	18-2-1922	Lorry Driver	8-8-1945
L/501510	GAHAN, William	Ludford Park Lodge, Ballinteer Road, Co. Dublin.	11-9-1924	Messenger	8-8-1945
V/206561	GALBRAITH, Thomas	33 Kevin Street, Dublin.	5-8-1914	Labourer	8-8-1945
203921	GALLAGHER, Andrew	Lusticle, Carrigans, Donegal.	25-1-1920	Farm Labourer	8-8-1945
E/421733	GALLAGHER, Bernard	15 Sloan's Terrace, Derry.	31-10-1903	Labourer	8-8-1945
E/420566	GALLAGHER, Bernard	Glebe, Carndonagh, Co. Donegal.	12-6-1900	Road Worker	8-8-1945
E/406399	GALLAGHER, Charles	133 Ligoniel Road, Belfast.	25-7-1907	Motor Driver	8-8-1945
A/78754	GALLAGHER, Charles	31 Orchard Row, Derry.	25-11-1917	Electrician	8-8-1945
205605	GALLAGHER, Charles	Butcher Street, Lifford.	28-12-1918	Labourer	8-8-1945
79937	GALLAGHER, Charles	Aughoo, Tullyrosmearn, Co. Fermanagh.	15-10-1921	Farm Labourer	8-8-1945
E/400227	GALLAGHER, Chris.	5 Summerhill, Dublin.	15-10-1919	Labourer	8-8-1945
E/421968	GALLAGHER, Denis	c/o R. McLoughlin, Ballycliffen, Co. Donegal.	25-9-1921	Barman	8-8-1945
79955	GALLAGHER, Francis	Aughoo, Tullyrosmearn, Co. Fermanagh.	16-8-1917	Labourer	8-8-1945
E/420477	GALLAGHER, Frank	Sheskinarone, Dungloe, Co. Donegal.	30-4-1910	Car Driver	8-8-1945
209122	GALLAGHER, George	c/o J. Bonar, Augheygant, Drumkeen, Co. Donegal.	23-12-1920	Labourer	8-8-1945
E/438403	GALLAGHER, George G.	Castletown, Castleconnor, Co. Sligo.	10-4-1920	Gen. Labourer	26-10-1945
E/424917	GALLAGHER, Gerald	Tully, Ballyshannon, Co. Donegal.	22-12-1922	Labourer	8-8-1945
77892	GALLAGHER, Henry	6 Brittons Parade, Belfast.	31-1-1917	Shop Assistant	8-8-1945
E/425164	GALLAGHER, James	Glebe, Cullian, Co. Derry.	11-7-1923	Builder's Labourer	8-8-1945
E/425235	GALLAGHER, James	Clogher, Barnesmore, Co. Donegal.	9-4-1910	Labourer	8-8-1945

Army No.	Name.	Last Recorded Address.	Date of Birth.	Declared Occupation prior to enlistment in Defence Forces.	Date of Dismissal from Defence Forces.
V/206289	GALLAGHER, James	Dunmore, Carrigans, Co. Donegal.	22-1-1922	Clerk	8-8-1945
V/204418	GALLAGHER, James	Chapel Street, Stranorlar, Co. Donegal.	14-7-1920	Labourer	8-8-1945
E/425566	GALLAGHER, Jeremiah	Urney, Clady, Co. Derry.	23-11-1925	Farm Labourer	8-8-1945
E/416330	GALLAGHER, John	44 Cross Road, Thomondgate, Limerick.	5-1-1923	Labourer	8-8-1945
V/203919	GALLAGHER, John J.	Listmintigal, Raphoe, Co. Co. Donegal.	9-10-1921	Labourer	8-8-1945
L/507763	GALLAGHER, John	34 Abbey Street, Cork.	18-12-1927	Messenger	3-2-1946
79936	GALLAGHER, John P.	Aughoo, Tullyrosmearn, Co. Fermanagh.	21-3-1915	Farm Labourer	8-8-1945
E/405627	GALLAGHER, Joseph	16 Lr. Rathmines Road, Dublin.	28-3-1909	Shirt and Collar Cutter	8-8-1945
79971	GALLAGHER, Joseph	2 Stewarts Close, Lower Road, Derry.	20-12-1919	Labourer	8-8-1945
V/214117	GALLAGHER, Joseph	Clunefinglas, Bansha, Co. Tipperary.	2-5-1922	Labourer	8-8-1945
E/422867	GALLAGHER, Joseph	Tooban, Burnfort, Co. Donegal.	15-3-1922	Labourer	8-8-1945
E/423265	GALLAGHER, Michael	132 Bogside, Derry.	25-8-1915	Labourer	8-8-1945
36143	GALLAGHER, Michael	7 King's Ave., Ballybough, Dublin.	16-6-1907	Shop Assistant	8-8-1945
V/210109	GALLAGHER, Nial	Upper Inchiney, Lifford.	4-4-1920	Flax Boiler	8-8-1945
E/406725	GALLAGHER, Patrick J.	Carr Point, Lettermacward, Donegal.	10-12-1921	Shop Assistant	8-8-1945
84047	GALLAGHER, Patrick	Meenanmiller, Gweedore, Co. Donegal.	12-2-1922	Labourer	8-8-1945
E/424355	GALLAGHER, Peter	Kiltyclogher, Co. Leitrim.	26-9-1919	Farm Labourer	8-8-1945
79045	GALLAGHER, Philip	75 Wellington St., Derry.	21-1-1921	Butcher	8-8-1945
E/421971	GALLAGHER, Robert	c/o Mr. Gallagher, 2 North Strand, Dublin.	26-9-1912	Ship's Fireman	8-8-1945
E/425150	GALLAGHER, Stephen	64 Townsend Street, Strabane, Co. Tyrone.	22-12-1920	Machine Operator	8-8-1945
V/209130	GALLAGHER, Stephen	St. Patrick's Tce., Athlone.	8-7-1922	Labourer	8-8-1945
206290	GALLAGHER, Terence	Dunmone, Carrigans, Co. Donegal.	31-10-1920	Labourer	8-8-1945
78755	GALLAGHER, Vincent	Ballyholey, Co. Donegal.	4-10-1920	Labourer	8-8-1945
E/406201	GALLAGHER, William	43 Charles Street, Warrenpoint, Co. Down.	6-10-1913	Labourer	8-8-1945
A/78995	GALLAGHER, William	32 Church Street, Warrenpoint, Co. Down.	5-4-1921	Messenger Boy	8-8-1945
E/400120	GALLAGHER, William	133 Lr. Rathmines Road, Dublin.	28-5-1909	Labourer	8-8-1945
V/203790	GALLAGHER, William	Gort House, Ballindrait, Co. Donegal.	22-4-1921	Fowl Dealer	8-8-1945
E/433118	GALLAGHER, William	Glasslock St., Monaghan.	26-2-1915	Labourer	8-8-1945
E/422335	GALLAGHER, William	c/o Bridgend P.O., Burnfoot, Co. Donegal.	2-4-1912	Labourer	8-8-1945
E/421734	GALLAGHER, William	Drumtaggart, Muff, Co. Donegal.	9-1-1919	Labourer	8-8-1945
V/211075	GALLIGAN, James	56 Errigal Rd., Drimnagh, Dublin.	7-2-1914	Barman	8-8-1945
V/206420	GALLOWAY, Samuel	4 St. Kevin's Sq., Bray.	16-6-1922	Motor Mechanic	8-8-1945
E/423865	GALVIN, Michael	31 St. Patrick's Terrace, Athlone.	16-1-1902	Labourer	8-8-1945
E/403979	GALWAY, Patrick J.	142 Falls Road, Belfast.	9-12-1908	Fitter	8-8-1945
A/75248	GALWEY, Francis	39 Park Parade, London, W.10.	20-1-1918	Farm Labourer	8-8-1945
E/406700	GAMBON, Leo	Richmond Hospital, North Brunswick St., Dublin.	24-6-1920	Tailor	8-8-1945
E/423454	GANNON, Charles	Kilbarry, Ruskey, Co. Leitrim.	21-1-1922	Waiter	8-8-1945

Army No.	Name.	Last Recorded Address.	Date of Birth.	Declared Occupation prior to enlistment in Defence Forces.	Date of Dismissal from Defence Forces.
84315	GANNON, Ernest	c/o M. Kelleher, Drumburness, Corriga, Co. Leitrim.	4-12-1918	Farm Labourer	8-8-1945
79046	GANNON, John	Mountain View, Myrtleville Road, Crosshaven, Co. Cork.	18-9-1916	Farm Labourer	8-8-1945
E/425383	GANNON, Lawrence	Clooneybeirne, Strokestown, Co. Roscommon.	26-2-1923	Farm Labourer	8-8-1945
A/76437	GANNON, Patrick	Shumbert, St., Tubercurry, Co. Sligo.	1-1-1919	Labourer	8-8-1945
E/405568	GANNON, William	37 Chancery Lane, Dublin.	31-8-1922	Messenger	8-8-1945
V/202224	GARLAND, James	35 O'Hanlon's Park, Dundalk.	25-3-1910	Labourer	8-8-1945
E/435739	GARLAND, Norman	St. Corban's Place, Naas.	6-9-1917	Motor Driver	8-8-1945
83913	GARRAHAN, John P.	51 Abbeyfield, Killester, Dublin.	15-4-1922	Carpenter	8-8-1945
E/406533	GARRIGAN, Peter	5 Upper Gardiner Street, Dublin.	1-7-1906	Labourer	8-8-1945
E/406020	GARTLAND, John	c/o Mr. J. Soraghan, Prospect, Dundalk.	11-7-1922	Farm Labourer	8-8-1945
E/404374	GARVEY, James	12 St. Margaret's Street, Newry.	3-1-1902	Labourer	8-8-1945
E/424472	GARVEY, Michael	55 Garravogue Villas, Sligo.	16-7-1923	Messenger Boy	8-8-1945
E/422438	GARVEY, Thomas	Holborn Street, Sligo.	23-11-1916	Baker and Confectioner	8-8-1945
E/421922	GARVIN, John	Muingnabo, Rosport, Ballina.	9-4-1906	Labourer	8-8-1945
E/409942	GATES, James	Drumkee, Coalisland, Co. Tyrone.	28-1-1925	Labourer	8-8-1945
E/421601	GAVAGHAN, Peter	30 Dublin Road, Swinford, Co. Mayo.	14-6-1910	Labourer	8-8-1945
85423	GAVAN, Robert	Killur, Clonmellon, Co. Westmeath.	17-5-1927	Turf Cutter	25-7-1946
L/508045	GAVIN, John	Tusker, Philipstown, Offaly.	1-7-1920	Labourer	8-8-1945
E/423247	GAVIN, Martin	Dublin Bridge, Mullingar.	5-9-1922	Tinsmith	8-8-1945
E/423248	GAVIN, Patrick	41 St. Finbarr's Terrace, Galway.	14-6-1908	Tinsmith	8-8-1945
205018	GAVIN, William	Tara Street, Tullamore.	16-5-1921	Labourer	8-8-1945
E/406377	GAVIN, Thomas	Garron, Newbliss, Co. Monaghan.	26-5-1922	Labourer	8-8-1945
E/422547	GAVIN, Thomas	Loughcrene, Oldcastle, Co. Meath.	20-10-1921	Gardener	8-8-1945
E/420407	GAYLAND, James	11 St. Kiernan's Terrace, Athlone.	28-4-1922	Labourer and Messenger Boy	8-8-1945
V/205146	GAYNOR, Patrick	25 Summerhill, Dublin.	29-11-1918	Labourer	8-8-1945
A/78994	GAYNOR, Thomas	Castletown, Dundalk.	17-3-1921	Farm Labourer	8-8-1945
E/412407	GEARNS, Thomas	2 Rutland Street, Cork.	16-6-1920	Apprentice Machinist	8-8-1945
E/420032	GEARY, John	41 St. Dominick's Terrace, Fair Hill, Galway.	14-6-1915	Dock Labourer	8-8-1945
204627	GEARY, Patrick	12 Stafford Street, Dublin.	25-9-1917	Moulder	8-8-1945
E/409381	GEOGHEGAN, Edward	21 Monck Pce., Phibsboro', Dublin.	9-4-1924	Labourer	8-8-1945
E/406474	GEOGHEGAN, Laurence	17 Old Camden St., Dublin.	17-5-1923	Labourer	8-8-1945
A/78456	GEOGHEGAN, Stephen	55½ Pimlico Street, Dublin.	17-9-1920	Messenger	8-8-1945
E/408151	GERAGHTY, Edward	229 Cashel Road, Crumlin, Dublin.	9-8-1923	Gen. Labourer	8-8-1945
A/75660	GERAGHTY, James	5 Eccles Street, Dublin.	14-1-1919	Shoe Repairer	8-8-1945
E/434416	GERAGHTY, John	3 Peterson's Lane, City Quay, Dublin.	19-11-1922	None	8-8-1945
V/209236	GERAGHTY, Stanley	86 St. Joseph's Terrace, Banbrook Hill, Armagh.	17-3-1920	Barber	8-8-1945

Army No.	Name.	Last Recorded Address.	Date of Birth.	Declared Occupation prior to enlistment in Defence Forces.	Date of Dismissal from Defence Forces.
E/408462	GERARD, Harold V.	Church Street, Duleek, Co. Meath.	4-6-1924	Student	8-8-1945
V/203204	GERRARD, Charles J.	297 Lower Kimmage Road, Dublin.	1-4-1914	Engineering Student	8-8-1945
E/422005	GETHINS, Thomas	Mail Coach Road, Sligo.	22-7-1922	Gen. Labourer	8-8-1945
E/404877	GIBBINS, Daniel	Cavoney, Scots House, Clones, Co. Monaghan.	16-6-1922	Farm Labourer	8-8-1945
E/434488	GIBBONS, Eugene	c/o Garda J. J. Gibben, Royal Hospital, Kilmainham, Dublin.	16-5-1916	Farmer	8-8-1945
L/502747	GIBBONS, Francis	113 Bangor Road, Crumlin, Dublin.	8-10-1926	Messenger	25-1-1946
V/211021	GIBBONS, James P.	129 Annamoe Dr., Dublin.	15-6-1920	Variety Artist	8-8-1945
V/209920	GIBBONS, John	Church St., Tubbercurry, Co. Sligo.	3-5-1921	Labourer	8-8-1945
79990	GIBBONS, Jos.	22 Turvey Ave., Inchicore, Dublin.	16-3-1922	Labourer	8-8-1945
E/420305	GIBBONS, Michael	Crowe Street, Gort, Co. Galway.	7-8-1921	Tailor	8-8-1945
V/204357	GIBBONS, Sean	Middle House, Cleggan, Westport, Co. Mayo.	15-7-1918	Student	8-8-1945
84242	GIBBONS, Thomas	Gurteen, Shrule, Co. Galway.	9-11-1913	Labourer	8-8-1945
E/404575	GIBSON, David	58 O'Hanlon Park, Dundalk.	7-10-1902	Driver	8-8-1945
81362	GIBSON, Hugh	Cloughrea, Bessbrook, Co. Armagh.	8-11-1926	Gen. Labourer	1-9-1945
E/42292	GIBSON, Martin	203 Emmet Bldgs, Watling Street, Dublin.	17-7-1911	Labourer	8-8-1945
E/437584	GIBSON, William	Cloughrea, Bessbrook, Co. Armagh.	20-7-1923	Labourer	8-8-1945
E/424135	GILBANE, James	Aughrimen, Drumsna, Co. Leitrim.	18-8-1919	Farm Labourer	8-8-1945
A/83586	GILBERT, Joseph	19 St. Patrick's Terrace, The Barracks, Newbridge, Co. Kildare.	16-3-1920	Plumber's Improver	8-8-1945
L/501604	GILBERT, Pierce	Glencullen, Kilternan, Co. Dublin.	1-2-1923	Farm Labourer	8-8-1945
E/423362	GILHEANY, John	Swanlinbar, Co. Cavan.	23-11-1914	Farm Labourer	8-8-1945
84782	GILL, Charles	4 Lacey Ave., Templemore.	24-2-1924	Butcher	8-8-1945
E/424890	GILL, Eugene	Rossam, Corriga, Carrigallon, Co. Leitrim.	12-7-1922	Shop Assistant	8-8-1945
E/405478	GILLAN, Cornelius	23 Grosvenor Place, Rathmines, Dublin.	3-12-1921	Farm Labourer	8-8-1945
E/420911	GILLEECE, John	Drumcondra, Swanlinbar, Co Cavan.	23-6-1922	Farmer	8-8-1945
A/80343	GILLEN, Brendan	Drum East, Co. Sligo.	18-1-1922	Labourer	8-8-1945
E/405623	GILLEN, Francis	23 Grosvenor Pce., Dublin.	28-1-1920	Carpenter	8-8-1945
70042	GILLESPIE, Thomas	Ballykeeran Lodge, Athlone.	12-5-1912	Labourer	8-8-1945
A/113243	GILLICK, James	Clonarney Road, Delvin, Co. Westmeath.	6-4-1916	Farm Labourer	8-8-1945
E/403184	GILLIGAN, Chris.	7 St. Anthony's Place, Dublin.	5-12-1921	Carter	8-8-1945
78883	GILLIGAN, Joseph	45 St. Flannan's Terrace, Ennis, Co. Clare.	8-2-1920	Farm Labourer	8-8-1945
79296	GILLIGAN, Stephen	21 Anner Road, Inchicore, Dublin.	17-11-1917	Labourer	8-8-1945
V/202314	GILMARTIN, Patrick	41 Temple Street, Sligo.	5-7-1920	Labourer	8-8-1945
E/422869	GILMOUR, Patrick	c/o Mrs. Ramsey, Rose Cottage, Fahan, Co. Donegal.	3-6-1921	Labourer	8-8-1945
E/421566	GILMURRAY, Thomas	Main St., Manorhamilton, Co. Leitrim.	10-4-1898	Painter	8-8-1945

Army No.	Name.	Last Recorded Address.	Date of Birth.	Declared Occupation prior to enlistment in Defence Forces.	Date of Dismissal from Defence Forces.
E/424605	GILROY, Albert	c/o M. Healy, Knockgravia, Ballymote, Co. Leitrim.	19-2-1922	None	8-8-1945
E/424802	GILROY, Edwin	Knockgrama, Rathmullen P.O., Ballymote, Co. Sligo.	30-3-1918	Car Driver	8-8-1945
84153	GILROY, William	Swanlinbar, Co. Cavan.	9-10-1914	Farmer	8-8-1945
L/507630	GILTRAP, James	24 Drumgoold Villas, Enniscorthy, Co. Wexford.	28-5-1927	Student	13-5-1946
E/437787	GINNELLY, Michael	Rostuck, Westport.	7-10-1913	Plasterer	8-8-1945
L/508304	GLEESON, Philip	8 Accommodation Road, Carlow.	10-1-1923	Labourer	8-8-1945
A/83719	GLENNON, Christopher	30 Upr. Dorset St., Dublin.	10-7-1922	Labourer	8-8-1945
L/507764	GLENNON, Peter	36 Abbey Street, Cork.	14-9-1927	Student	8-8-1945
A/83820	GLOVER, Raymond	18 Talbot Street, Dublin.	9-8-1921	Shipping Clerk	8-8-1945
77407	GLYNN, Martin	Doolingate, Ennistymon, Co. Clare.	8-2-1919	Labourer	8-8-1945
E/420703	GLYNN, Thomas	Glebe Street, Ballinrobe, Co. Mayo.	8-3-1920	Plasterer	8-8-1945
A/113055	GOAN, John	Drumboyle, Lifford.	20-11-1917	Labourer	8-8-1945
79250	GOFF, Robert	4 Honey Pk., Sallynoggin, Co. Dublin.	23-1-1921	Messenger	8-8-1945
202386	GOFF, Roy	Blackrock, Dundalk.	23-5-1918	Insurance Agent	8-8-1945
E/407742	GOGARTY, Patrick	Carranross, Kells.	12-5-1920	Labourer	8-8-1945
E/413728	GOGGIN, Patrick	71 Mount Eaden Road, Gurranebraher, Cork.	7-7-1900	Labourer	8-8-1945
E/403004	GOGGINS, Gerald	4 Upr. Buckingham Street, Dublin.	8-5-1913	Hosiery-Machinist	8-8-1945
V/207831	GOLDNEY, William	1M Maitland Ctge., Bray.	8-7-1917	Labourer	8-8-1945
202652	GOODISON, Thomas	Blackwater, Enniscorthy.	31-3-1917	Labourer	8-8-1945
A/78833	GORDON, Edward	Killincooley, Kilmuckridge, Wexford.	11-6-1920	Farm Labourer	8-8-1945
79708	GORDON, Patrick	Tinnack, Campile, Co. Co. Wexford.	23-9-1918	Labourer	8-8-1945
A/78809	GORDON, Patrick	Treamore, Mohill, Co. Leitrim.	26-2-1921	Labourer	8-8-1945
A/82671	GOREY, Michael	Granagh, Bruree, Co. Limerick.	20-7-1920	Domestic Worker	8-8-1945
E/421217	GORMAN, Eamonn	Hazelwood, Sligo.	4-10-1921	Labourer	8-8-1945
E/403182	GORMAN, John	c/o Mrs. J. Coyle, 17 Leinster Street, Dublin.	9-6-1917	Lorry Driver	8-8-1945
205612	GORMAN, John	Leenamore, Muff, Co. Donegal.	9-8-1920	Labourer	8-8-1945
E/423169	GORMAN, Michael	65 St. Patrick's Park, Carrick-on-Shannon.	16-1-1922	Motor Driver	8-8-1945
E/423624	GORMAN, Patrick	61 Lord Edward Street, Ballina.	22-2-1922	Labourer (Messenger Boy)	8-8-1945
A/70624	GORMAN, William	O'Molloy St., Tullamore.	20-4-1907	Labourer	8-8-1945
74732	GORMLEY, Cecil	Drumullagh, Omeath, Co. Louth.	3-8-1915	Student	8-8-1945
V/217076	GORMLEY, Denis J.	2 Church St., Cootehill, Co. Cavan.	6-7-1922	Shop Assistant	8-8-1945
74294	GORMLEY, Francis	9 Lr. Camden St., Dublin.	21-8-1914	House Painter	8-8-1945
E/422167	GORMLEY, John	Corvalley, Co. Monaghan.	5-9-1917	Mason and Driver	8-8-1945
E/423493	GORMLEY, Martin	7 Manor Park, Ballymote, Co. Sligo.	16-9-1904	Labourer	8-8-1945
E/422267	GORMLEY, William	Main Street, Lifford.	15-1-1916	Builder	8-8-1945
A/76805	GOSLING, James	34 Hughes Park, Hill St., Dundalk.	20-3-1919	Shoemaker	8-8-1945
E/432570	GOUCHER, Michael	27 Rosary Road, Dolphin's Barn, Dublin.	5-4-1922	Labourer	8-8-1945
A/80546	GOUGH, Thomas	Confey, Leixlip, Co. Kildare.	23-4-1922	Labourer	8-8-1945

Army No.	Name.	Last Recorded Address.	Date of Birth.	Declared Occupation prior to enlistment in Defence Forces.	Date of Dismissal from Defence Forces.
L/503150	GOUGH, Thomas	4 Honey Park Cottages, Dun Laoghaire.	17-2-1927	Messenger	30-3-1946
E/414854	GOULD, James	26 Rochford's Lane, Cork.	18-12-1916	Labourer	8-8-1945
77673	GOULDING, John	10 Grattan Tce., Galway.	11-2-1920	Labourer	8-8-1945
61908	GOURLEY, Patrick	c/o Miss M. Moloney, 18 Lavitt's Lane, Cork.	19-9-1906	Labourer	8-8-1945
E/407942	GRACE, John	Glenamaddy, Castlerea, Co. Roscommon.	30-10-1919	Wireless Operator	8-8-1945
E/430332	GRACE, Thomas	Bohercessia, Freshford, Co. Kilkenny.	10-7-1922	Labourer	8-8-1945
83026	GRAGHAN, James S.	59 Saul Road, Crumlin, Dublin.	31-1-1922	Labourer	8-8-1945
205644	GRAHAM, Anthony	c/o Patrick Conroy, Lifford, Co. Donegal.	25-3-1921	Shop Assistant	8-8-1945
V/205270	GRAHAM, Andrew	32 D Block, Liberty Hall, Marlboro' Street, Dublin.	23-4-1922	Gen. Labourer	8-8-1945
E/407144	GRAHAM, Patrick	91 C Block, Mercer House, Mercer Street, Dublin.	3-4-1922	Baker	8-8-1945
E/403260	GRAHAM, Peter	14 Brim's Rd., Liverpool.	22-1-1922	Chain Tester	8-8-1945
83247	GRAHAM, Vincent	c/o Jos. Kane, Grand Central Hotel, Omeath, Co. Louth.	25-4-1917	Motor Driver	8-8-1945
V/204467	GRAHAM, William	18 Ave Maria Road, Maryland, Dublin.	18-6-1920	Student Electrician	8-8-1945
205611	GRAHAM, William	c/o Miss M. Kelvey, The Bann, Convoy, Co. Donegal.	7-2-1918	Labourer	8-8-1945
E/417040	GRANDON, Michael	Ballyroe, Carrigtoohill, Co. Cork.	20-4-1922	Farmer	8-8-1945
E/414858	GRANT, James	Bank Street, Templemore, Co. Tipperary.	26-11-1922	Student	8-8-1945
V/215036	GRANT, Joseph	Kinnagoe, Ballymangan, Buncrana, Co. Donegal.	15-5-1919	Labourer	8-8-1945
V/202960	GRANT, Joseph	Castleblunden, Co. Kilkenny.	19-3-1916	Labourer	22-3-1946
A/83495	GRANT, Martin	9 Georges Quay, Dublin.	8-6-1922	Mattress Maker	8-8-1945
209989	GRANT, Thomas	Mooncoin, Co. Kilkenny.	26-11-1918	Butcher	8-8-1945
E/404123	GRAY, Charles	29 Rockmount Street, Falls Road, Belfast.	29-9-1907	Part-time Fitter	8-8-1945
V/205698	GRAY, John	37 Rosary Rd., Maryland, Dublin.	23-4-1921	Labourer	8-8-1945
E/408224	GRAY, John	107 Seville Place, North Strand, Dublin.	7-5-1924	Office Boy	8-8-1945
E/425271	GRAY, Michael	Carnakelly, Ballinamuck, Co. Longford.	6-10-1917	Farm Labourer	8-8-1945
E/422698	GRAY, Michael	32 Legion Ave., Dundalk.	28-1-1916	Labourer	8-8-1945
E/431928	GRAY, Patrick	c/o Mrs. P. Kelly, Bridge St., Callan, Co. Kilkenny.	28-3-1921	Motor Driver	8-8-1945
A/83223	GRAYDON, Dominick	14 Henrietta St., Dublin.	10-5-1922	Labourer	8-8-1945
E/432981	GREALLY, John	15 Northumberland Ave., Dublin.	21-4-1922	Fitter's Apprentice	8-8-1945
77284	GREALY, Patrick	244 Clonard Rd., Crumlin, Dublin.	1-8-1920	Pumber	8-8-1945
A/79994	GREALY, Peter	Castlemaine St., Athlone.	22-7-1921	Carpenter	8-8-1945
V/204160	GREEN, Chris.	34 Vickery Street, Dublin.	2-5-1920	Labourer	8-8-1945
A/74970	GREEN, David	18 Harry Street, New Ross, Co. Wexford.	3-5-1917	Labourer	8-8-1945
E/422870	GREEN, James	c/o Peter Cassidy, Swanlinbar, Co. Cavan.	5-4-1921	Farm Labourer	8-8-1945
E/404021	GREEN, Kevin Charles	72 Mid. Abbey St., Dublin.	27-8-1921	Musician	8-8-1945
A/83055	GREENE, James	44 Cromwell Rd-, Ellesmere Port, Cheshire.	10-3-1922	Carpenter	8-8-1945
E/404589	GREENE, Noel	Ballygannon Cottages, Rathdrum, Co. Wicklow.	19-12-1922	Gardener	8-8-1945
E/404174	GREENE, Patrick	18 Stephen Street, Dublin.	8-9-1897	Motor Driver	8-8-1945

Army No.	Name.	Last Recorded Address.	Date of Birth.	Declared Occupation prior to enlistment in Defence Forces.	Date of Dismissal from Defence Forces.
E/425243	GREENE, William John	Kilmaglish, Knockdrim, Mullingar.	5-9-1924	Wood Worker	8-8-1945
E/434098	GREER, George	97 Lr. Dorset St., Dublin.	14-11-1920	Labourer	8-8-1945
V/208734	GREHAN, Michael	Massbrook, Boffenaun, Ballina.	15-12-1914	General Labourer	8-8-1945
E/408122	GREW, Dermot	Keenaghan, Moy, Co. Armagh.	3-10-1922	Bricklayer	8-8-1945
202001	GRIFFIN, Daniel	Ballymacquinn, Ardfert, Co. Kerry.	4-8-1914	Farm Labourer	8-8-1945
E/412557	GRIFFIN, Joseph	Ballyvoreen, Kildimo, Co. Limerick.	29-3-1921	None	8-8-1945
E/417027	GRIFFIN, Joseph P.	25 Hogan Ave., Killeely, Limerick.	26-3-1918	Salesman	8-8-1945
A/105508	GRIFFIN, Michael	100 Sarsfield Sq., Athlone.	27-2-1915	Labourer	8-8-1945
A/78156	GRIFFIN, Michael	Ballinasterring, Listowel.	21-7-1919	Student	8-8-1945
V/201215	GRIFFIN, Michael	28 Harbour View, Cobh.	8-2-1916	Labourer	8-8-1945
V/213059	GRIFFIN, Michael	Fernside Villas, Summerhill, Cork.	4-6-1922	Painter	8-8-1945
E/430502	GRIFFIN, Michael T.	107 Patrick St., Kilkenny.	13-8-1900	Clerk	8-8-1945
78189	GRIFFIN, Patrick	The Cottages, Castlerea, Co. Roscommon.	18-4-1915	Farm Labourer	8-8-1945
V/209757	GRIFFIN, Patrick	Ballynoe, Tallow, Co. Waterford.	11-6-1919	Builder's Labourer	8-8-1945
L/507402	GRIFFIN, Patrick	27 Broad Street, Limerick.	9-3-1927	Labourer	2-2-1946
79645	GRIMES, Charles	2 Seaview Ave., Church Road, Dublin.	30-9-1921	Labourer	8-8-1945
E/413848	GRIMES, John	Coonagh, Co. Limerick.	22-2-1910	Labourer	8-8-1945
V/204811	GRIMES, Patrick	4 O'Hanlon Pk., Dundalk.	22-2-1922	Labourer	8-8-1945
E/412972	GRIMES, Patrick	Orr Street, Kilmallock, Co. Limerick.	6-3-1921	Labourer	8-8-1945
77488	GRIMES, Thomas	Coonagh, Co. Limerick.	14-5-1915	Labourer	8-8-1945
E/433068	GRIMLEY, John	3 Walker Street, Armagh.	17-7-1901	Clerk	8-8-1945
E/432443	GRIMLEY, Vincent	Dublin Street, Monaghan.	18-12-1910	Grocer's Assistant	8-8-1945
E/402536	GROGAN, Thomas	4 North King St., Dublin.	16-10-1920	Boot Repairer	8-8-1945
L/507381	GUARE, John	Thonover, Knock, Co. Clare.	1-6-1925	Labourer	8-8-1945
E/411796	GUERIN, Stephen	Shallee, Kilnamona, Ennis.	5-11-1915	Labourer	8-8-1945
E/415937	GUIHAN, Michael	Dooks, Glenbeigh, Co. Kerry.	25-12-1915	Farm Labourer	8-8-1945
74507	GUIHEON, Michael	Blasket Mór, Co. Kerry.	15-11-1914	Farm Labourer	8-8-1945
E/435193	GUILFOYLE, Michael	Green Lane, Callan, Co. Kilkenny.	4-5-1923	Farm Labourer	8-8-1945
83833	GUINAN, Sean	38 Susanville Rd., Dublin.	2-3-1921	Lorry Driver	8-8-1945
83830	GUINEY, James	Brigade Lodge, Kilcullen, Co. Kildare.	28-2-1917	Waiter	8-8-1945
E/420474	GUMBLETON, Daniel	The Green Huts, Fahan, Co. Donegal.	13-2-1903	Able Seaman	8-8-1945
82120	GUNEEN, John	90 Mount Nebo Av., Cork.	16-1-1916	Labourer	8-8-1945
E/407120	GUNNING, James	Castletown, Rathmoylan, Co. Meath.	3-1-1922	Labourer	8-8-1945
E/409788	GUNNING, Joseph	19 Servia Street, Belfast.	31-10-1924	Gen. Labourer	8-8-1945
A/76474	GUTHRIE, Patrick	Ennistymon, Co. Clare.	16-3-1917	Labourer	8-8-1945
A/78292	GUY, Henry	Bunowen Beg, Ballyconnolly, Clifden, Galway.	10-8-1920	Farm Labourer	8-8-1945
V/207127	HACKETT, Denis	76 Eccles Street, Dublin.	28-6-1922	Labourer	8-8-1945
A/82819	HACKETT, Peter	6 Galmoy Road, Cabra, Dublin.	17-10-1922	Labourer	8-8-1945
A/71451	HADDOCK, Robert	Tullymangan Ctge., Cavan.	27-12-1910	Farm Labourer	8-8-1945
83463	HAFFEY, James	Shamrock Hotel, Monaghan.	23-2-1920	Labourer	8-8-1945
E/406317	HAFFORD, John	Green Lane, Drogheda.	18-1-1918	Labourer	8-8-1945
E/405183	HAGGANS, Christopher	25 Glenview Avenue, Drogheda.	25-12-1916	Farm Labourer	8-8-1945

Army No.	Name.	Last Recorded Address.	Date of Birth.	Declared Occupation prior to enlistment in Defence Forces.	Date of Dismissal from Defence Forces.
E/402015	HALLSSY, John	Bright's Lodging House, Summerhill, Dublin.	23-3-1918	Tradesman	8-8-1945
E/403460	HALES, Charles	11 Seville Terrace, North Strand, Dublin.	15-1-1911	Electrician	8-8-1945
E/433754	HALL, George	14 St. Cronan's Rd., Bray.	12-5-1907	Labourer	8-8-1945
V/211393	HALL, John	224 Clonard Rd., Crumlin, Dublin.	6-7-1922	Labourer	8-8-1945
E/434749	HALL, Patrick	8 Charleville Ave., North Strand, Dublin.	8-1-1922	Motor Assembler	5-12-1945
V/201770	HALLAHAN, Michael	St. Michael's Tce.,Sligo.	6-11-1920	Messenger	28-10-1945
A/76836	HALLAHAN, Patrick	297 Kilburn Ln., London.	4-5-1919	Messenger	8-8-1945
E/424569	HALLERON, Richard	Ballymanagh, Knockarilam P.O., Ballina, Co. Mayo.	12-1-1920	Motor Driver	8-8-1945
E/413254	HALLIGAN, Edward	Mooresfort, Lattin, Co. Tipperary.	22-5-1922	Farmer's son	8-8-1945
83801	HALLIGAN, Henry	16 Grenville St., Dublin.	21-11-1918	Labourer	8-8-1945
77619	HALLINAN, Edward	Milltown, Lisronagh, Clonmel.	28-8-1920	Labourer	8-8-1945
83132	HALLINAN, Patrick	Shanavine, Clonmel.	25-6-1913	Grocer's Assistant	8-8-1945
L/507169	HALLISSEY, Daniel	Patrick's Well, Clonmel.	15-4-1925	Messenger	8-8-1945
L/502789	HALPIN, Francis	45 Lismore Rd., Kimmage, Dublin.	26-2-1926	Turf Worker	27-8-1945
E/435069	HALPIN, Patrick	16 Keane's Rd., Waterford.	18-2-1923	Labourer	8-8-1945
E/404212	HAMILL, Peter	Carcullion, Hilltown, Co. Down.	22-12-1915	Bricklayer	8-8-1945
E/420183	HAMILTON, John	Sandyrow, Castlefin, Co. Donegal.	22-5-1922	Labourer	8-8-1945
210176	HAMILTON, John	17 Peter Street, Waterford.	10-5-1923	Messenger Boy	8-8-1945
V/211123	HAMILTON, Thomas	83 Cork Street, Dublin.	24-4-1922	None	8-8-1945
E/414280	HANAFIN, Christopher	Ballinbreanaght, Tralee.	27-5-1921	Labourer	8-8-1945
L/502908	HANAPHY, Walter	19 Grenville Street, Dublin.	2-9-1925	Box Maker	15-4-1946
E/432437	HANAWAY, Francis	Glasslough Street, Monaghan.	26-7-1919	Plumber	8-8-1945
E/405846	HAND, Michael	Copponagh, Bailieborough, Co. Cavan.	9-2-1923	Farm Labourer	8-8-1945
L/502407	HAND, Peter	Summerhill, Co. Meath.	2-6-1923	Farm Labourer	8-8-1945
V/207366	HAND, Peter J.	9 Church Ave., Glasnevin, Dublin.	12-2-1912	Storeman	8-8-1945
76128	HANLEY, John	Portain, Batterstown, Co. Meath.	1-1-1920	Labourer	8-8-1945
E/414353	HANLEY, John	Bartoose, Emly, Co. Tipperary.	3-8-1915	Labourer	8-8-1945
E/432628	HANLON, James	Caranure, Co. Cavan.	15-2-1900	Farm Labourer	8-8-1945
V/209957	HANLON, John	29 Daly's Terrace, Letterkenny.	5-12-1918	Labourer	8-8-1945
79431	HANLON, John	Cappagoland, Mount Bolas, Tullamore.	8-4-1921	Gardener	8-8-1945
V/206313	HANLON, Patrick	29 Wolfe Tone Street, Kilkenny.	6-7-1914	Labourer	8-8-1945
E/423078	HANLON, Patrick	18 Coleraine St., Dublin.	9-8-1913	None	8-8-1945
B/6012	HANLON, Patrick	Ballyrichard Road, Carrick-on-Suir.	15-2-1909	Bootmaker	8-8-1945
E/422699	HANLON, Peter	Ardtullimore, Carlingford, Co. Louth.	16-12-1917	Railway Porter	8-8-1945
E/454783	HANLON, Thomas	43 Dublin Road, Tullow, Co. Carlow.	11-11-1921	Motor Apprentice	8-8-1945
E/434869	HANLON, William	Crefogue, Enniscorthy, Co. Wexford.	24-2-1922	Motor Mechanic	8-8-1945
E/405094	HANNA, Henry J.	21 Dargle Road, Drumcondra, Dublin.	12-12-1918	Motor Driver	8-8-1945
79552	HANNA, Patrick	27 Bridge Street, Dundalk.	20-7-1921	Student	8-8-1945
E/400719	HANNAWAY, John	c/o Bonny Traynor, Market Street, Monaghan.	9-9-1913	Motor Driver	8-8-1945

Army No.	Name.	Last Recorded Address.	Date of Birth.	Declared Occupation prior to enlistment in Defence Forces.	Date of Dismissal from Defence Forces.
E/422071	HANNIGAN, Edward	Crilly, Pettigo, Co. Donegal.	26-9-1910	Joiner and Watchmaker	8-8-1945
77408	HANNON, James	Spruce Hill, Roscrea.	20-11-1919	Labourer	8-8-1945
E/412753	HANRAHAN, John	2 Court House Lane, Off Athlunkard St., Limerick.	4-5-1922	Labourer	8-8-1945
A/68843	HANRAHAN, Patrick	5 Hillgrove Place, Cork.	15-5-1908	Builders' Labourer	8-8-1945
77685	HANRAHAN, William	Luffaney, Mooncoin, Co. Kilkenny.	21-9-1914	Labourer	8-8-1945
A/73448	HANRATTY, Patrick	6 Priest's Lane, Drogheda.	22-9-1914	Labourer Farmer	8-8-1945
V/201633	HANRATTY, Peter	Drumleak South, Castle-blaney, Co. Monaghan.	4-5-1908	News Vendor	8-8-1945
79961	HARBISON, William	Ballyneilmore, Loup, Moneymore, Co. Derry.	15-2-1920	Motor Driver	8-8-1945
209614	HARDIMAN, Peter	3 Watling Street, Dublin.	24-6-1920	Labourer	8-8-1945
E/417986	HARDING, Nicholas	Glengoole, Newberming-ham, Thurles.	15-1-1924	Coal Miner	8-8-1945
76877	HARDY, Thomas	Mill View, Ennis.	2-2-1919	Labourer	8-8-1945
E/401459	HARGREAVES, Roger	10 Mountain View Terrace, Finglas, Co. Dublin.	14-9-1917	Clerk	8-8-1945
E/421828	HARKIN, Daniel	Greencastle, Moville, Co. Donegal.	16-8-1920	Joiner	8-8-1945
E/424281	HARKIN, James	Mullins, Donegal.	20-7-1922	General Labourer	8-8-1945
E/422765	HARKIN, John	Pucklish, Falcarragh, Co. Donegal.	13-1-1915	Labourer	14-9-1945
E/424925	HARKIN, John	Conlea, Ballyshannon, Co. Donegal.	15-4-1923	Farm Labourer	8-8-1945
E/421173	HARKIN, Patrick	c/o G. Devine, Lifford.	14-3-1900	Flax Rougher	8-8-1945
E/420570	HARKIN, William	c/o Mrs. McKenny, Green-castle, Moville, Co. Donegal.	12-2-1916	Carpenter	8-8-1945
E/423268	HARKINS, Thomas	105 Borne Street, Derry.	17-8-1922	Labourer	8-8-1945
L/502372	HARMON, Joseph	7 Halston Street, Dublin.	16-2-1925	Messenger	8-8-1945
76195	HARMON, Nicholas	Termonfeckin, Drogheda.	28-12-1919	Draper's Assistant	8-8-1945
E/414394	HARNETT, Laurence	Dromtrasna O'Brien, Abbeyfeale, Co. Limerick.	15-11-1916	Blacksmith	8-8-1945
E/403186	HAROLD, Laurence	5 Braithwaite St., Dublin.	15-8-1908	Labourer	8-8-1945
E/405862	HARRAN, Roy S.	St. Abbyn's, 13 Clarinda Park, Dun Laoghaire.	28-8-1922	Clerk	8-8-1945
L/502279	HARRIGAN, Edward	13 Henrietta St., Dublin.	13-5-1925	Messenger	8-8-1945
B/6008	HARRIGAN, James	St. Peter's Tce., Athlone.	1-12-1914	General Labourer	8-8-1945
A/72163	HARRIMAN, Patrick	1 Morgan Place, Dublin.	19-5-1909	Farm Labourer	8-8-1945
A/76166	HARRINGTON, Joseph	29 North Main St., Cork.	27-12-1919	Tailor	8-8-1945
E/406042	HARRIS, Christopher	34 Glen Road, Belfast.	1-2-1923	Butcher's Apprentice	8-8-1945
E/404023	HARRIS, Joseph	17 Congress Gardens, Sandycove, Co. Dublin.	19-10-1916	Labourer	8-8-1945
82673	HARRIS, Joseph	25 Castle Bks., Limerick.	28-2-1920	Labourer	8-8-1945
V/211464	HARRIS, Thomas	7 C. Block, Iveagh Bldgs., Patrick Street, Dublin.	9-12-1924	Messenger	8-8-1945
E/404890	HARRISON, Thomas	c/o Jas. Clerkin, High St., Monaghan.	31-12-1912	Labourer	8-8-1945
80347	HART, Arthur	18 Linenhall St., Dublin.	16-1-1922	Messenger	8-8-1945
80576	HARTE, Chas.	73 Dominick's Place, Waterford.	19-4-1921	Labourer	8-8-1945
V/200121	HARTE, Christopher	Knaggs Run, Victoria Pine, Sligo.	23-5-1920	Motor Driver	8-8-1945
E/420250	HARTE, John	21 St. Bridget's Terrace, Longford.	21-5-1922	Labourer	8-8-1945
E/423955	HARTE, Michael	Swanlinbar, Co. Cavan.	21-1-1922	Farm Labourer	8-8-1945

Army No.	Name.	Last Recorded Address.	Date of Birth.	Declared Occupation prior to enlistment in Defence Forces.	Date of Dismissal from Defence Forces.
L/502014	HARTE, Michael	46 Slievenamon Road, Crumlin, Dublin.	28-9-1924	Labourer	8-8-1945
204081	HARTE, Peter	Ballindown, Boyle, Co. Roscommon.	10-3-1910	Labourer	8-8-1945
A/79574	HARTE, Samuel	8 Sandyrow, Coalisland, Co. Tyrone.	24-5-1920	Labourer	8-8-1945
77686	HARTERY, Edward	5 New Cottages, Carrick-on-Suir.	24-7-1919	Labourer	8-8-1945
75847	HARTIGAN, James	Carrigeen, Croom, Co. Limerick.	13-6-1916	Farm Labourer	8-8-1945
85030	HARTMANN, Augustine	16 Synnott Place, Lower Dorset Street, Dublin.	13-11-1923	Heating Engineer	8-8-1945
V/209259	HARTNETT, Denis	Tournafulla, Newcastle West, Co. Limerick.	23-4-1921	Labourer	8-8-1945
V/209660	HARTNETT, John	64 Collins Avenue, Donnycarney, Dublin.	3-6-1922	Messenger Boy	8-8-1945
A/82286	HARTNETT, Matthew	8 Haig's Terrace, Tralee.	11-7-1922	Factory Worker	8-8-1945
L/506428	HARTNETT, William	336 Blarney Street, Cork.	5-5-1925	Labourer	8-8-1945
E/408022	HARTY, Henry	118 Fassaugh Road, Cabra, Dublin.	14-10-1923	Messenger Boy	8-8-1945
E/408618	HARTY, Patrick	7 Crostick Alley, Meath Street, Dublin.	7-10-1920	Farm Labourer	8-8-1945
A/77648	HARVEY, Neil	Glencoagh, Mt. Charles, Co. Donegal.	29-1-1915	Farmer	8-8-1945
E/404528	HASKINS, William	c/o Mrs. E. Brennan, Levitstown, Mageany, Athy.	30-1-1919	Porter	8-8-1945
E/423269	HASSON, James	16 Creggan Terrace, Derry.	8-5-1922	None	8-8-1945
78161	HASTINGS, Patrick	Shragh, Moyasta, Co. Clare.	9-3-1920	Farm Labourer	8-8-1945
B/6642	HATCHETT, Francis J.	c/o Mrs. Sweeney, Morristown Villas, Newbridge.	26-3-1913	Farm Labourer	8-8-1945
E/420185	HAUGHEY, Daniel	Hunterstown, Urney, Strabane.	19-11-1919	Farm Labourer	8-8-1945
E/433580	HAUGHEY, John	3 Thomas Street, Newry.	4-10-1905	Cook	8-8-1945
204415	HAUGHEY, Joseph	Jessing Halleson, Castlefin, Co. Donegal.	17-3-1914	Labourer	8-8-1945
78473	HAUGHEY, Kevin	3 Mary Street, Dundalk.	5-10-1920	Labourer	8-8-1945
E/420187	HAUGHEY, Thomas	Ringsend, Castlefin, Co. Donegal.	12-4-1922	Labourer	8-8-1945
V/203059	HAUHEY, Hugh	Clady Station, Co. Donegal.	12-11-1919	Labourer	8-8-1945
E/410582	HAWKINS, George	1 Ballymacthomas, Cork.	9-2-1915	Labourer	8-8-1945
A/57600	HAYDE, James	55 Connolly St., Kilkenny.	3-5-1905	Labourer	8-8-1945
L/506877	HAYDEN, Daniel	Main Street, Urlingford, Co. Kilkenny.	25-5-1925	Labourer	8-8-1945
E/408166	HAYDEN, James	14 Bride Road, Patrick Street, Dublin.	24-4-1916	Milk Deliverer	8-8-1945
E/434001	HAYDEN, John	87 Mount Tallant Avenue, Terenure, Dublin.	20-6-1922	Dairy Worker	8-8-1945
76415	HAYDEN, Thomas	181 Downpatrick Road, Crumlin, Dublin.	16-9-1919	Motor Engineering	8-8-1945
E/412891	HAYES, Edward	15 St. Columcille's Street, Island Field, Limerick.	11-7-1907	Shoe Maker	8-8-1945
E/409002	HAYES, Edward	Ballynockane, Ballymackey, Co. Tipperary.	3-6-1923	Farm Labourer	3-12-1945
E/434417	HAYES, Francis	4 Gt. Charles St., Dublin.	13-1-1900	Carpenter	8-8-1945
E/432165	HAYES, Francis	Annamult, Thomastown, Co. Kilkenny.	22-3-1922	Labourer	8-8-1945
F/412752	HAYES, Gerard	Clancy's Lane, William Street, Limerick.	21-2-1913	Labourer	8-8-1945
A/78197	HAYES, James	Kiltrusta, Strokestown, Co. Roscommon.	23-4-1920	Farm Labourer	8-8-1945
103898	HAYES, John	Holycross, Rathkeale, Co. Limerick.	9-9-1915	Labourer	8-8-1945

Army No.	Name.	Last Recorded Address.	Date of Birth.	Declared Occupation prior to enlistment in Defence Forces.	Date of Dismissal from Defence Forces.
E/415661	HAYES, John	Chapel Lane, Mallow, Co. Cork.	18-1-1922	Hairdresser	8-8-1945
E/408603	HAYES, Mervin	28 Lower Sean McDermott Street, Dublin.	13-4-1920	Painter	8-8-1945
A/77353	HAYES, Michael	3 Ahern's Row, Limerick.	24-7-1920	Labourer	8-8-1945
A/78421	HAYES, Michael	88 O'Hanlon Pk., Dundalk.	18-9-1920	General Labourer	8-8-1945
69661	HAYES, Michael	c/o Mr. J. Fleming, Claregate St., Kildare.	22-1-1907	Farm Labourer	8-8-1945
A/73130	HAYES, Patrick	3 Charlotte Street, Dublin.	27-4-1914	Labourer	8-8-1945
A/73648	HAYES, Patrick	71 Blenheim Gardens, London, W.2.	30-5-1915	Farm Labourer	8-8-1945
E/417122	HAYES, Patrick	27 Horgan's Bldgs., Cork.	12-9-1924	Waiter	8-8-1945
E/417321	HAYES, Patrick	5 Davis St., Dungarvan, Co. Waterford.	4-4-1923	Farm Labourer	30-1-1946
82367	HAYES, Patrick	27 Horgan's Bldgs., Cork.	24-9-1922	Waiter	8-8-1945
A/76119	HAYES, Robert	c/o Mrs. W. Flaherty, Lenamore, Ballylongford, Co. Kerry.	27-11-1916	Farm Labourer	8-8-1945
E/414899	HAYES, William J.	3 Mental Hospital Terrace, Limerick.	19-8-1922	Fireman	8-8-1945
E/416199	HAYTER, Terence	Lisselane, Clonakilty, Co. Cork.	6-5-1923	Farm Labourer	8-8-1945
E/404709	HEADLEY, Kevin	105 Sloan's St., Lurgan, Co. Armagh.	4-8-1921	Farm Labourer	8-8-1945
424187	HEAGNEY, Oliver	Clohan Glebe, Kiltoom, Athlone, Co. Roscommon.	18-7-1922	Labourer	1-7-1946
E/408696	HEALY, John	113 Ben Madigan Road, North Crumlin, Dublin.	23-6-1923	Labourer	8-8-1945
L/507363	HEALY, John	25 Cathedral Road, Gurranebraher, Cork.	19-4-1927	None	8-6-1946
V/204931	HEALY, John	6 Finbar's Avenue, Cork.	24-1-1917	Labourer	8-8-1945
E/432302	HEALY, John	Bracketsditch, Dungarvan, Thomastown, Co. Kilkenny.	15-8-1899	Farmer	8-8-1945
78989	HEALY, John	Curriheen, Glenbeigh, Co. Kerry.	31-8-1911	Labourer	8-8-1945
E/430536	HEALY, Joseph	44 Maudlin St., Kilkenny.	3-2-1922	Shop Boy	8-8-1945
E/410585	HEALY, Michael	11 Coleman's Lane, Cork.	5-10-1916	Labourer	8-8-1945
V/205357	HEALY, Sean	6 Warwick Tce., Ranelagh, Dublin.	11-7-1913	Motor Salesman	8-8-1945
E/402344	HEALY, Thomas	60 Corporation Place, Dublin.	19-6-1922	Labourer	8-8-1945
V/200226	HEAPHY, Thomas	Cork Hill, Youghal, Co. Cork.	25-4-1922	General Labourer	8-8-1945
73918	HEARNE, James	Ballyristeen, Bonmahon, Waterford.	12-5-1915	Agricultural Labourer	8-8-1945
V/208416	HEARTY, Coleman	c/o Hugh Casey, Hackballs Cross, Dundalk.	24-11-1921	Hairdresser	8-8-1945
73230	HEARTY, Michael	14 Russell's St., Coventry.	15-1-1911	Clerk	8-8-1945
E/404984	HEENAN, Kevin	46 Elm Rd., Donnycarney, Dublin.	29-12-1921	Joiner	8-8-1945
L/502522	HEERY, James	33 Fleming Road, Drumcondra, Dublin.	30-12-1925	Messenger	10-9-1945
78909	HEFFERNAN, Ed.	Garadee, Kilcock, Co. Kildare.	9-7-1920	Groom and Stable Boy	8-8-1945
V/202016	HEFFERNAN, James	Cronebane, Avoca, Co. Wicklow.	1-9-1912	Labourer	8-8-1945
E/404519	HEFFERNAN, Joseph	120 Lr. Rathmines Road, Dublin.	27-6-1918	Clerk	8-8-1945
E/433738	HEFFERNAN, Patrick	Ballyhernon, Castlecomer, Co. Kilkenny.	23-7-1923	Farm Labourer	8-8-1945
L/503320	HEFFERNAN, Vincent	4 Rosary Gardens, Dun Laoghaire.	18-7-1927	Fisherman	8-7-1946
E/433471	HEFFERNON, Daniel	16 Mary Street, Dublin.	30-1-1912	Shop Assistant	8-8-1945

Army No.	Name.	Last Recorded Address.	Date of Birth.	Declared Occupation prior to enlistment in Defence Forces.	Date of Dismissal from Defence Forces.
V/203057	HEGARTY, George	Moress, Inch, Buncrana, Co. Donegal.	14-8-1920	Farm Labourer	8-8-1945
E/421860	HEGARTY, Hugh	c/o P.O. Carndonagh, Co. Donegal.	30-6-1899	Labourer	8-8-1945
E/423200	HEGARTY, James	81 Lecky Road, Derry.	13-5-1913	Dock Labourer	8-8-1945
E/424963	HEGARTY, Michael	Derry, Rathcabban, Birr.	24-4-1923	Gen. Labourer	8-8-1945
E/420987	HEGARTY, Philip	Eloghbeg, Burnfoot, Co. Donegal.	21-10-1914	Labourer	8-8-1945
E/424713	HEGARTY, William	Grange, Ballymagorry, Strabane.	9-9-1921	Farm Labourer	8-8-1945
E/411800	HEHIR, Austin	c/o McCann's Lodging House. Mungret Street, Limerick.	23-1-1920	Labourer	8-8-1945
E/420939	HELLY, William	Ruanmore, Ardrahan, Co. Galway.	10-11-1911	Farmer	8-8-1945
L/503257	HEMPENSTALL, Robert	25 Sarsfield Street, Sallynoggin, Co. Dublin.	1-11-1927	Bricklayer's Apprentice	19-3-1946
84286	HEMSWORTH, John	22 Drumbane, Birr.	28-11-1922	Labourer	8-8-1945
E/422912	HENDERSON, Patrick	c/o Mgt. McClea, Bridgend P.O., Co. Donegal.	18-2-1922	Labourer	8-8-1945
E/400721	HENDERSON, William	88 Oban St., Portadown.	19-1-1920	Labourer	8-8-1945
V/204264	HENDRICK, Daniel	9 Marrowbone Ln., Dublin.	27-9-1921	Labourer	8-8-1945
E/407468	HENDRICK, John	30 O'Daly Road, Drumcondra, Dublin.	5-6-1923	Labourer	8-8-1945
E/438227	HENDRICKEN, Patrick	Brickfield Hse., Jamestown Road, Inchicore, Dublin.	8-4-1926	Porter	27-9-1945
E/408344	HENEBERY, Edward	8 Strathry Park, Belfast.	26-5-1924	Apprentice Hairdresser	8-8-1945
A/73726	HENEGHAN, George	Gibbstown, Navan.	4-1-1912	Farm Labourer	8-8-1945
E/437582	HENEGHAN, Patrick	Gibbstown, Navan.	3-10-1914	Labourer	8-8-1945
V/210064	HENNESSY, Charles	Cappalinan, Rathdowney, Leix.	26-9-1912	Labourer	8-8-1945
E/410531	HENNESSY, Daniel	201 Old Youghal Road, Cork.	19-8-1908	Operator	8-8-1945
E/433131	HENNESSY, John M.	19 Royal Terrace, West, Dun Laoghaire.	27-10-1920	Fisherman	8-8-1945
A/75711	HENNESSEY, Peter	142 Upper Dorset Street, Dublin.	26-7-1917	Labourer	8-8-1945
E/424896	HENNESSEY, Philip	Clonervy Poles P.O., Co. Cavan.	6-7-1916	Farm Labourer	8-8-1945
78548	HENNESSEY, Philip	15 Moore St., Rathdowney, Leix.	3-12-1920	Farm Labourer	8-8-1945
V/205130	HENNESSY, Stephen	2 Redford Cottages, Greystones, Co. Wicklow.	27-12-1920	Welder	8-8-1945
V/200230	HENNESSY, Terence	5 de Valera St., Youghal.	21-10-1921	School Boy	8-8-1945
E/432866	HENNESSY, William	108 Burke's Terrace, McCaffrey Estate, Mount Brown, Dublin.	16-11-1910	Clerk	8-8-1945
E/408160	HENRY, Francis	Derrytresk, Coalisland, Co. Tyrone.	19-10-1922	Gen. Labourer	8-8-1945
E/408845	HENRY, John J.	4 Linenhall Square, Newry.	10-6-1924	Student	8-8-1945
E/420409	HENRY, Michael	Court Devenish, Athlone.	3-6-1922	Shop Assistant	8-8-1945
E/402486	HENSEY, Christopher	38 St. Attracta Road, Cabra, Dublin.	24-7-1918	Motor Driver	8-8-1945
V/201343	HENSEY, Thomas	84 Treacy Park, Carrick-on-Suir.	1-10-1919	Labourer	8-8-1945
V/206014	HEPBURN, Thomas	Oakfield, Raphoe, Co. Donegal.	26-8-1918	Mason's Apprentice	8-8-1945
V/208955	HERAGHTY, John	Dooasken, Ballinful, Co. Sligo.	7-1-1912	Shoe Repairer	8-8-1945
76101	HERATY, Peter J.	Ballinalee, Edgeworthstown, Co. Longford.	2-8-1915	Medical Student	8-8-1945
83001	HERBERT, John	16 Ferguson Road, Drumcondra, Dublin.	30-11-1917	Labourer	8-8-1945
E/420765	HERRON, Joseph	Fintown, Co. Donegal.	12-9-1918	Farm Labourer	8-8-1945

Army No.	Name.	Last Recorded Address.	Date of Birth.	Declared Occupation prior to enlistment in Defence Forces.	Date of Dismissal from Defence Forces.
E/421174	HERRON, Thomas	Ballykerrigan, Cloghan, Co. Donegal.	26-12-1911	Motor Driver	8-8-1945
E/403018	HEUSTON, Connell	27 Tyrconnell Road, Inchicore, Dublin.	4-5-1912	Salesman	8-8-1945
E/402962	HEUSTON, Manus	27 Tyrconnell Road, Inchicore, Dublin.	5-1-1900	Bread Server	8-8-1945
205195	HEWITT, Joseph	20 Middle Gardiner Street, Dublin.	17-5-1921	Weaver	8-8-1945
77435	HEWITT, Matthew	Cannon, Cashel, Co. Tipperary.	24-4-1918	Farm Labourer	8-8-1945
E/433509	HEWITT, William	24 St. Joseph's Place, Dorset Street, Dublin.	18-10-1916	Welder's Improver	8-8-1945
E/406346	HEYDEN, John	34 Rugby Road, Ranelagh, Dublin.	13-10-1923	Labourer	8-8-1945
E/402466	HICKELY, Michael	9 Summerhill, Dublin.	26-2-1922	Painter	8-8-1945
76966	HICKEY, Michael	Ballyboyle, Clogheen, Co. Tipperary.	15-11-1919	Labourer	8-8-1945
E/411038	HICKEY, Myles	Mitchelstown, Co. Cork.	21-8-1916	Labourer	8-8-1945
E/424188	HICKEY, Patrick	5 Dillon St., Tullamore.	25-12-1922	Jobber Lad	8-8-1945
E/402050	HIGGINS, Edward	4 Mountainview, Harold's Cross, Dublin.	14-2-1917	Labourer	8-8-1945
V/203443	HIGGINS, Joseph	Killavalig, Kanturk, Co. Cork.	9-10-1916	Labourer	8-8-1945
A/79944	HIGGINS, Nicholas	Henry St., Roscommon.	4-6-1913	Labourer	8-8-1945
E/408727	HIGGINS, Patrick	Templeogue Cottages, Templeogue, Co. Dublin.	17-3-1924	Labourer	8-8-1945
77131	HIGGINS, Thomas	Castlelake, Cashel, Co. Tipperary.	24-12-1919	Labourer	8-8-1945
A/77882	HILL, Charles	Latt House, Cavan.	2-5-1919	Motor Mechanic	8-8-1945
E/417033	HILL, Kevin J.	St. Philomena's Villas, Crosshaven, Co. Cork.	9-10-1923	None	8-8-1945
V/205674	HILL, Michael	44 Bridgefoot St., Dublin.	24-11-1920	Tailor's Apprentice	8-8-1945
E/422026	HILL, Michael	2 Healy Tce., Tullamore.	26-7-1922	Factory Hand	8-8-1945
E/404094	HILL, Noel	7 Distillery Road, Dublin.	7-1-1922	Watchmaker's Improver	8-8-1945
A/68856	HILL, Peter	63 Carrow Road, North Crumlin, Dublin.	13-8-1909	Labourer	8-8-1945
A/73292	HILLARY, Andrew	5 Ranelagh Ave., Dublin.	17-6-1909	Labourer	8-8-1945
83951	HILLERY, Michael	5 Ward's Hill, Newmarket, Dublin.	25-6-1914	Labourer	8-8-1945
E/432231	HINCKS, James	Lisheen Row, Mallow, Co. Cork.	15-5-1921	Laboratory Assistant	8-8-1945
E/420480	HIRRELL, Michael	Maghermore, Clonmany, Co. Donegal.	8-12-1920	Labourer	8-8-1945
E/400645	HOBAN, Anthony	34 Peter Street, Dublin.	11-8-1902	Labourer	8-8-1945
80790	HODGKINS, Ernest	53 Lea Hill, London, E.10.	12-12-1921	Labourer	8-8-1945
E/400785	HOGAN, David	26D St. Joseph's Mansions, Killarney Street, Dublin.	12-12-1916	Labourer	8-8-1945
L/502519	HOGAN, Desmond	17 O'Brien's Place, Drumcondra, Dublin.	1-3-1926	Cycle Mechanic	25-10-1945
A/77213	HOGAN, Edward	33 Clarence Place, Dublin.	18-3-1920	Messenger	8-8-1945
74919	HOGAN, Francis	Corrovorin, Ennis.	4-1-1915	Labourer	8-8-1945
E/409015	HOGAN, James N.	20 Anna Villa, Ranelagh, Dublin.	6-1-1923	Labourer	8-8-1945
E/410335	HOGAN, Michael	7 Myles Street, Limerick.	18-9-1921	Labourer	8-8-1945
V/202962	HOGAN, Michael	Upr. Dillon St., Tipperary.	14-8-1922	Labourer	8-8-1945
L/506995	HOGAN, Patrick	31 St. Ann's Road, Gurranebraher, Cork.	26-11-1925	Labourer	8-8-1945
207931	HOGAN, Patrick	66 Ormond Market, Dublin.	17-11-1918	Labourer	8-8-1945
83806	HOGAN, Terence McSweeney	5 Chapel Street, Newry.	31-10-1920	Builder's Labourer	8-8-1945
E/412072	HOGAN, Thomas	Derry, Rathcobbin, Birr.	28-2-1912	Labourer	8-8-1945
200112	HOGAN, Thomas	9 Steeple View, Tralee.	24-1-1921	Driver's Helper	8-8-1945
E/423900	HOLLAND, Daniel	Rathmullen, Co. Donegal.	9-5-1916	Labourer	8-8-1945

Army No.	Name.	Last Recorded Address.	Date of Birth.	Declared Occupation prior to enlistment in Defence Forces.	Date of Dismissal from Defence Forces.
E/407261	HOLLAND, Henry J.	16 Brabazon Sq., Dublin.	30-9-1911	Tailor's Cutter	8-8-1945
73011	HOLLINSWORTH, Joseph	The Green, Rathnew, Co. Wicklow.	12-2-1910	Labourer	8-8-1945
E/421386	HOLMES, James	Hill Sixty, Ballinagh, Co. Cavan.	11-11-1920	Farm Labourer	8-8-1945
V/215198	HOLMES, Michael	Glengad, Pullathomas, Ballina.	27-7-1915	Farmer	8-8-1945
E/432161	HOLOHAN, Joseph	30 Pearse St., Kilkenny.	24-8-1908	Painter and Glazier	8-8-1945
E/408834	HOLT, Louis P.	8 Boyne Street, Westland Row, Dublin.	29-6-1923	Labourer	8-8-1945
E/421975	HONE, John	c/o D. McBride, Oldtown, Letterkenny.	9-5-1908	Labourer	8-8-1945
V/215185	HONE, Joseph	Meencarrigh, Ballybofey, Co. Donegal.	10-12-1918	Labourer	8-8-1945
E/420357	HOPPER, James	Friarstown, Dromahair, Co. Leitrim.	4-11-1909	Bricklayer	8-8-1945
A/74878	HORAN, Denis	12a Little Green Street, Dublin.	3-1-1912	Gen. Labourer	8-8-1945
A/75738	HORGAN, Edward	Knocknacaska, Abbey-dorney, Co. Kerry.	21-5-1919	Farm Labourer	8-8-1945
L/507602	HORGAN, Maurice	4 Church Rd., Ballinacurra, Midleton, Co. Cork.	3-7-1927	Labourer	8-8-1945
V/202519	HORNIBROOK, Abraham	7 Fitzgibbon Square, St. Mary's Road, Cork.	20-2-1919	Labourer	8-8-1945
E/411040	HORNIBROOK, John	198 Farranferris Avenue, Spangle Hill, Cork.	27-2-1910	Motor Driver	8-8-1945
E/414571	HOUGH, Michael	Church Rd., Cloughjordan, Co. Tipperary.	5-5-1917	Labourer	8-8-1945
E/422906	HOULIHAN, John W.	1 Little Water Street, Longford.	6-5-1918	Carpenter	8-8-1945
V/201245	HOULIHAN, Patrick	66 Ossory Park, Kilkenny.	7-3-1917	Labourer	8-8-1945
77685	HOURAHAN, William	Luffaney, Mooncoin, Kilkenny.	21-9-1917	Labourer	8-8-1945
E/415728	HOURIGAN, Jeremiah	14 New Prospect, Limerick.	10-4-1923	Fitter	8-8-1945
82702	HOURIGAN, John	Cromhill, Kilteely, Co. Limerick.	24-2-1918	Labourer	8-8-1945
E/436372	HOURIHANE, John	Ballyroe, Leap, Co. Cork.	9-3-1922	Farm Labourer	8-8-1945
E/420188	HOUSTON, Francis	Ballylass, Castlefin, Co. Donegal.	27-2-1922	Labourer	8-8-1945
E/434467	HOUSTON, Joseph	4 William Street, New Ross, Co. Wexford.	22-3-1922	Labourer	8-8-1945
E/420189	HOUSTON, William	Ballylass, Castlefin, Co. Donegal.	1-11-1918	Labourer	8-8-1945
L/501715	HOWARD, Kevin	4 Lr. Camden Pce., Dublin.	12-2-1924	Labourer	8-8-1945
77489	HOWARD, Michael	Shanbally, Cashel, Co. Tipperary.	26-1-1919	Labourer	8-8-1945
A/83360	HOWARD, Philip	8 Carysfort Road, Dalkey, Dublin.	10-10-1921	Messenger	8-8-1945
201510	HOWLEY, James	91 Phibsboro' Rd., Dublin.	23-7-1918	Student	8-8-1945
202060	HUBBOCK, John	Janeville Place, Athy.	10-12-1917	Moulder	8-8-1945
E/434865	HUDSON, Patrick	Monasterevan, Co. Kildare.	12-5-1920	Show-man	8-8-1945
84405	HUDSON, William	c/o Hudsons Amusements, Abbeyfair, Streete, Co. Westmeath.	15-6-1917	Amusement Caterer	8-8-1945
E/404906	HUGHES, Bernard	14 Donohue St., Inchicore, Dublin.	2-12-1922	Able Seaman	8-8-1945
A/75610	HUGHES, Charles	Castle View, Kells Road, Kilkenny.	13-4-1918	Waiter	8-8-1945
E/433098	HUGHES, Francis	Leppan, Castleshane, Co. Monaghan.	7-9-1923	Labourer	8-8-1945
81346	HUGHES, Gabriel	New Cottages, Derrybeg, Newry.	29-5-1924	Labourer	8-8-1945
E/404157	HUGHES, James	4 Chapel Street, Newry.	18-9-1921	Seaman	8-8-1945

Army No.	Name.	Last Recorded Address.	Date of Birth.	Declared Occupation prior to enlistment in Defence Forces.	Date of Dismissal from Defence Forces.
E/407767	HUGHES, James A.	Lisfancorney, Derryfubble, Dungannon, Co. Tyrone.	30-1-1919	Farm Labourer	8-8-1945
A/75872	HUGHES, James	1 Clancy Street, Fermoy, Co. Cork.	19-1-1919	Messenger Boy	8-8-1945
83822	HUGHES, Ignatius	148 Old Park Rd., Belfast.	19-11-1919	Factory Worker	8-8-1945
200610	HUGHES, John	15 Greenmount Lane, Dublin.	18-8-1920	Carpenter's Improver	8-8-1945
75781	HUGHES, Malachy	131 Foley Street, Dublin.	3-6-1918	Messenger	8-8-1945
78717	HUGHES, Michael	23 Smith's Villas, York Road, Dun Laoghaire.	3-1-1921	Fisherman	8-8-1945
E/409612	HUGHES, Owen	41 Servia Street, Belfast.	25-1-1925	Carter	8-8-1945
78996	HUGHES, Patrick	Dungannon Road, Coalislnd, Co. Tyrone.	7-12-1920	Labourer	8-8-1945
E/422769	HUGHES, Patrick E.	Meenanbary, Carrick, Co. Donegal.	26-8-1911	Packer and Motor Driver	8-8-1945
E/421976	HUGHES, William	Kinlette, Ballybofey, Co. Donegal.	13-7-1921	Labourer	8-8-1945
A/71542	HULSMAN, John	Barstown House, Batterstown, Co. Meath.	20-7-1911	Labourer	8-8-1945
A/109767	HUNT, Denis	Crosscannon, Killenaule, Co. Tipperary.	11-10-1915	Labourer	8-8-1945
A/83649	HUNT, Edward	Derrynalsha, Kilkelly, Co. Mayo.	1-2-1915	Motor Driver	8-8-1945
A/83605	HUNT, Francis	St. Coman's Castleknock, Co. Dublin.	12-6-1922	Welder	8-8-1945
E/405026	HUNT, John	Kilcool, Co. Wicklow.	24-5-1914	Carter	8-8-1945
B/83925	HUNT, Joseph	73 Comeragh Road, Drimnagh, Dublin.	6-2-1913	Clerk	8-8-1945
A/72949	HUNTER, James	Murlog, Ballinadrait, Lifford.	14-7-1912	Motor Driver	8-8-1945
209841	HUNTER, John	Ballybogan, Castlefin, Co. Donegal.	9-6-1918	Farm Labourer	8-8-1945
E/400226	HUNTER, William	13 Lambay Road, Drumcondra, Dublin.	21-11-1919	Labourer	8-8-1945
L/506930	HURLEY, John	49 Douglas Street, Cork.	24-11-1926	Messenger Boy	8-8-1945
A/75642	HURLEY, Richard	Blacklion, Greystones, Co. Wicklow.	19-2-1918	Gen. Labourer	8-8-1945
V/209758	HURLEY, William	Ballynoe, Tallow, Co. Waterford.	11-4-1921	Farm Labourer	8-8-1945
L/506991	HURLEY, William	74 Barnett Bldgs., Cork.	1-11-1926	Labourer	8-8-1945
E/408923	HUSSEY, William	30 Keogh Sq., Inchicore, Dublin.	4-10-1923	Cycle Mechanic	8-8-1945
E/432552	HUSTON, Thomas	12 White Church Row, Off Seville Place, Dublin.	1-4-1922	Labourer	8-8-1945
E/414676	HUTCHINSON, George	Old Road, Cahirciveen.	22-6-1911	Labourer	8-8-1945
E/407531	HUTCHINSON, James	Curry, Richhill, Co. Armagh.	7-3-1920	Machinist	8-8-1945
E/421091	HUTTON, Michael	Seaview, Fahan, Co. Donegal.	22-4-1921	Motor Driver	8-8-1945
E/421092	HUTTON, Peter	Seaview, Fahan, Co. Donegal.	15-3-1920	Motor Driver	8-8-1945
A/77252	HYLAND, Bart.	9 B Block, Iveagh Bldgs., Patrick Street, Dublin.	15-4-1920	Bookmaker	8-8-1945
A/83735	HYLAND, John	9 Gt. Longford St., Dublin.	3-12-1921	Messenger	8-8-1945
76221	HYLAND, John	72 Upper Prior's Nook, Cannon St., Waterford.	23-3-1919	Messenger Boy	8-8-1945
E/407390	HYLAND, John	Ballyack, Tralee.	25-12-1923	Milkman	8-8-1945
L/500591	HYLAND, Luke	73 Thatch Rd., Whitehall, Dublin.	3-10-1921	Labourer	8-8-1945
E/407490	HYLAND, Martin J.	37 St. Enda's Road, Terenure, Dublin.	1-6-1914	Shoe Repairer	8-8-1945
75615	HYLAND, Maurice	164 Ceannt's Fort, Kilmainham, Dublin.	3-5-1919	Butcher's Assistant	8-8-1945
E/403043	HYLAND, Michael	140 St. Michan's Flats, Mary's Lane, Dublin.	9-7-1922	Messenger Boy	8-8-1945

Army No.	Name.	Last Recorded Address.	Date of Birth.	Declared Occupation prior to enlistment in Defence Forces.	Date of Dismissal from Defence Forces.
E/402401	HYLAND, Stephen	24 Bargy Road, East Wall, Dublin.	11-6-1922	No occupation	8-8-1945
A/75229	HYLAND, Walter	248 North Galteemore Rd., Crumlin, Dublin.	8-9-1917	Labourer	8-8-1945
V/213240	HYNES, Edmond	14 Fr. Matthew Street, Tipperary,	6-10-1924	Messenger Boy	8-8-1945
A/79478	HYNES, Gerald	Singland, Ballysimon Rd., Limerick.	28-10-1916	Casual Labourer	8-8-1945
A/68080	HYNES, John	2 Glasses Lane, Athlone.	28-3-1906	Labourer	8-8-1945
E/420358	HYNES, Michael	Newmill, Ramelton, Co. Donegal.	23-6-1907	Seaman and Ship's Cook	8-8-1945
E/436220	INGRAM, George	Gowran, Co. Kilkenny.	23-7-1922	Farm Labourer	8-8-1945
E/409137	INGRAM, Seamus	19 Carnew Road, Aughrim Street, Dublin.	22-2-1924	Labourer	8-8-1945
83104	INGRAM, William	12 Carnew Street, Dublin.	14-3-1920	Hotel Porter	8-8-1945
E/423084	IVERS, George	80 Clonliffe Avenue, Ballybough, Dublin.	26-7-1922	Messenger	8-8-1945
85455	IRVINE, Gerard	56 Stanhope St., Belfast.	18-1-1927	Gen. Labourer	13-8-1946
E/422073	IRVINE, John	Main Street, Pettigo, Co. Donegal.	7-1-1921	Labourer	8-8-1945
E/421830	IRVINE, Joseph	Main Street, Ballyconnell, Co. Cavan.	11-9-1917	Shop Assistant	8-8-1945
79647	IRVINE, Kevin	Belfast Rd., Ballynahinch, Co. Down.	—-9-1921	Student	8-8-1945
E/416560	IRWIN, Edward	7 Glendalough Park, The Lough, Cork.	23-1-1924	Student	8-8-1945
E/422074	IRWIN, Thomas	Pettigo, Co. Donegal.	3-12-1920	Motor Driver	8-8-1945
E/437913	IVERS, John	305 A Block, Oliver Bond House, Dublin.	7-9-1923	General Labourer	9-9-1945
E/406957	JARDINE, Ernest A.	Church Road, Holywood, Belfast.	4-1-1913	Mechanical Engineer	8-8-1945
77650	JENNINGS, John	Killoville, Ballymote, Co. Sligo.	2-1-1920	Labourer	8-8-1945
77307	JENNINGS, Michael	Lough Mask Cottages, Ballinrobe, Co. Mayo.	6-9-1920	Labourer	8-8-1945
E/408643	JENNINGS, Robert	44 Upper Rutland Street, Dublin.	16-7-1923	Labourer	8-8-1945
E/431477	JONES, Alfred	21 Upper John Street, Wexford.	29-6-1913	Clerk	8-8-1945
E/402131	JONES, Gerald	1 Holles Street, Dublin.	1-7-1922	Plumber's Apprentice	8-8-1945
E/400869	JONES, John P.	1 Vincent Tce., Glasnevin, Dublin.	1-8-1905	Labourer	8-8-1945
E/403983	JONES, Patrick J.	32 Boat Street, Newry.	3-6-1921	Labourer	8-8-1945
E/422937	JONES, Peter	Blacklion, Co. Cavan.	7-6-1921	Farm Labourer	8-8-1945
E/422938	JONES, Thomas	Blacklion, Co. Cavan.	27-10-1920	Farm Labourer	8-8-1945
78910	JONES, William	12 Lower Bridge Street, Dublin.	25-3-1921	Messenger	8-8-1945
72997	JONES, William	3 Married Qrs., Plunkett Barracks, Curragh.	9-7-1908	Groom and Builder's Labourer	8-8-1945
E/433148	JOHNSON, William	Corrigumire, Bree, Co. Wexford.	5-4-1918	Labourer	8-8-1945
83311	JOHNSTON, James	Bradon, Clontibret, Co. Monaghan.	16-5-1922	Labourer	8-8-1945
E/432270	JOHNSTON, Joseph	65 Creggan Road, Derry.	19-4-1921	Shop Assistant	8-8-1945
B/3635	JOHNSTON, Patrick	Crebina, Laytown, Co. Meath.	10-5-1896	Labourer	8-8-1945
E/432627	JOHNSTONE, Edward	Wolfe Tone Street, Cavan.	25-5-1913	Saddler	8-8-1945
77293	JORDAN, Francis	4 Grattan Road, Galway.	21-10-1919	Pram Fitter	8-8-1945
E/402017	JORDAN, James	37B Corporation Place, Dublin.	24-9-1919	Labourer	8-8-1945
V/207767	JORDAN, James	4 French Villas, Grattan Road, Galway.	1-9-1921	Gen. Labourer	8-8-1945

Army No.	Name.	Last Recorded Address.	Date of Birth.	Declared Occupation prior to enlistment in Defence Forces.	Date of Dismissal from Defence Forces.
V/209765	JORDAN, Martin	Carrareagh, Bonniconlon, Ballina.	9-3-1917	Farm Labourer and Navvy	8-8-1845
E/414281	JOY, Martin	Bansha, Killorglin, Co. Kerry.	23-8-1922	Farmer	8-8-1945
V/207129	JOYCE, Arthur	55B Mercer House, Mercer Street, Dublin.	9-11-1919	Labourer	8-8-1945
E/421478	JOYCE, Christopher	133 Sarsfield Sq., Athlone.	15-1-1922	Labourer	8-8-1945
E/433474	JOYCE, Harold	16 Windale Road, Drumcondra, Dublin.	27-10-1921	Presser (Waterproofs)	8-8-1945
78102	JOYCE, James	Recess, Cashel, Co. Galway.	25-1-1920	Farm Labourer	8-8-1945
E/415963	JOYCE, James	Foxhall, Charleville, Co. Cork.	10-10-1922	Labourer	8-8-1945
72245	JOYCE, John	5 Cooldrinagh, Leixlip, Co. Kildare.	21-5-1912	Labourer	8-8-1945
84836	JOYCE, Martin	Illion West, Recess, Co. Galway.	15-7-1919	Farm Labourer	8-8-1945
V/208239	JOYCE, Martin	9 St. Mel's Tce., Athlone.	15-7-1921	Labourer	8-8-1945
E/423829	JOYCE, Michael	Shantallon, Hollymount, Co. Mayo.	27-9-1912	Labourer	8-8-1945
E/401000	JOYCE, Patrick	24 The Coombe, Dublin.	3-3-1907	Labourer	8-8-1945
V/207078	JOYCE, Patrick	247 Richmond Road, Dublin.	20-7-1922	Laundry Boy	8-8-1945
A/82579	JOYCE, Patrick	22 Roxboro Rd., Limerick.	6-6-1922	Labourer	8-8-1945
V/216815	JOYCE, Thomas	Ardnasilla, Oughterard, Co. Galway.	5-5-1922	Farmer	8-8-1945
E/420309	JOYCE, Thomas	9 St. Mel's Tce., Athlone.	28-4-1915	Gen. Labourer	8-8-1945
L/507290	KANE, Edward	8 James Street, Reeves Path, Limerick.	5-4-1926	Clerical and Labourer	20-3-1946
E/406843	KANE, Harold	7 Anderstown Gardens, Belfast.	12-5-1920	Labourer	8-8-1945
E/407832	KANE, John	233 Springfield Road, Belfast.	16-7-1920	Clerk	8-8-1945
V/206006	KANE, John James	Ruskey, Convoy, Co. Donegal.	28-1-1916	Labourer	8-8-1945
74190	KANE, John	Kilbride St., Tullamore.	2-7-1915	Barber	8-8-1945
E/407984	KANE, Michael	61 Brompton Pk., Ardoyne, Belfast.	15-8-1922	Tailor	8-8-1945
V/205361	KAVANAGH, Edward	33 Lr. Kevin St., Dublin.	22-5-1904	Labourer	8-8-1945
E/403263	KAVANAGH, Garret	13 St. Patrick's Square, Dalkey, Co. Dublin.	4-3-1909	Labourer	8-8-1945
E/407403	KAVANAGH, James	46 Lourdes Rd., Maryland, Dublin.	8-6-1923	Fish & Poultry Assistant	8-8-1945
V/211134	KAVANAGH, James	23 North Great George's Street, Dublin.	26-9-1910	Paper Warehouseman	8-8-1945
E/402280	KAVANAGH, James	17 Turner Cottages, Ballsbridge, Dublin.	13-7-1917	Labourer	8-8-1945
L/508411	KAVANAGH, James	Ballyboggan, Castlebride, Co. Wexford.	4-6-1924	Labourer	8-8-1945
E/400597	KAVANAGH, John	153 Ben Madigan Road, North Crumlin, Dublin.	27-10-1894	Labourer	8-8-1945
E/434271	KAVANAGH, Joseph	13 James Green, Kilkenny.	19-5-1920	Painter	8-8-1945
E/433189	KAVANAGH, Kevin	9 Upr. St. Joseph's Tce., Athy.	14-3-1921	Moulder	8-8-1945
E/404189	KAVANAGH, Matthew	18 Alberry Road, Sandycove, Dublin.	28-2-1910	Driver	8-8-1945
E/407965	KAVANAGH, Maurice	153 Ben Madigan Road, North Crumlin, Dublin.	24-3-1922	Labourer	8-8-1945
L/502807	KAVANAGH, Owen	23 Summerhill, Dublin.	20-6-1927	None	4-3-1946
E/405203	KAVANAGH, Patrick	32 Mercer House, Mercer Street, Dublin.	29-9-1914	Labourer	8-8-1945
E/408231	KAVANAGH, Patrick	42 Rita's Avenue, Gurranebraher, Cork.	29-3-1923	Plasterer	8-8-1945
E/433161	KAVANAGH, Patrick	2 Nelson Street, Athy.	1-7-1911	Barber	8-8-1945
L/500483	KAVANAGH, Patrick	Dublin Bridge, Mullingar.	17-7-1920	Labourer	8-8-1945

Army No.	Name.	Last Recorded Address.	Date of Birth.	Declared Occupation prior to enlistment in Defence Forces.	Date of Dismissal from Defence Forces.
80736	KAVANAGH, Paul	6 Lr. St. Joseph's Terrace, Athy.	28-1-1921	Labourer	8-8-1945
A/82301	KAVANAGH, Sean	O'Gorman's Square, Charleville, Co. Cork.	1-2-1922	Gen. Labourer	8-8-1945
78084	KAVANAGH, Timothy	132 Errigal Rd., Drimnagh, Dublin.	19-10-1922	Schoolboy	8-8-1945
E/405610	KAVANAGH, William	108 Caledon Road, East Road, Dublin.	29-1-1923	Messenger	8-8-1945
E/408267	KEALY, Christopher	24 Lr. Stephen St., Dublin.	8-7-1918	Labourer	8-8-1945
79567	KEALY, Thomas	Kiltown, Castlecomer, Co. Kilkenny.	23-12-1919	Miner	8-8-1945
E/433925	KEALY, Thomas	38 St. Bridget's Crescent, Muinebeag, Carlow.	20-2-1922	Carpenter	8-8-1945
E/425580	KEENA, Richard	Church St., Edgeworthstown, Co. Longford.	9-10-1925	Farm Labourer	29-10-1945
84652	KEANE, Colm	191 Griffith Ave., Dublin.	27-6-1921	Medical Student	8-8-1945
V/200423	KEANE, Coleman	Doirearta, Carraroe, Co. Galway.	7-5-1918	Farm Labourer	8-8-1945
V/204873	KEANE, Cornelius	10 Devonshire St., North, Cork.	8-1-1921	Labourer	8-8-1945
L/507851	KEANE, Edward	Oldtown, Hospital, Limerick.	14-5-1928	Labourer	12-8-1946
A/76291	KEANE, John	High Street, Kilrush, Co. Clare.	13-11-1919	Grocer's Assistant	16-11-1945
E/412761	KEANE, John	Railway Cottages, Rosbrien, Co. Limerick.	7-3-1911	Electrician	8-8-1945
E/423086	KEANE, Joseph	c/o T. Hudson, Glenardnee, Brittas, Co. Dublin.	28-7-1911	Plasterer	8-8-1945
209457	KEANE, Patrick	Balyclough, Rosbrien, Limerick.	14-4-1921	Labourer	8-8-1945
E/413930	KEANE, Thomas	37 Mitchell's Crescent, Tralee.	10-10-1913	Engineer	18-9-1945
75364	KEANE, William F.	6 Grattan St., Youghal, Co. Cork.	6-1-1910	Carriage Painter	8-8-1945
84403	KEANEY, Edward	Meenakilln, Ardara, Co. Donegal.	14-4-1921	Farm Labourer	8-8-1945
E/420362	KEANNY, Walter	Ardmoney, Glenfarne, Co. Leitrim.	22-8-1910	Gen. Labourer	8-8-1945
A/83852	KEARNEY, Noel	9 Killarney Avenue, North Strand, Dublin.	22-12-1921	Schoolboy	8-8-1945
E/406605	KEARNS, James	Rookley Hall, Dunleer, Co. Louth.	13-3-1922	Farm Labourer	8-8-1945
E/423364	KEARNS, James	Oakfield, Sligo.	8-7-1922	None	8-8-1945
E/403896	KEARNS, John	4 Bonham Street, Dublin.	28-1-1919	Labourer	8-8-1945
E/432077	KEARNS, Joseph	Knockanoran, Durrow, Co. Leix.	19-6-1922	Labourer	8-8-1945
E/408161	KEARNS, Michael	238 St. Attracta Road, Cabra, Dublin.	8-2-1923	Labourer	8-8-1945
A/75661	KEARNS, Michael	Gorey Hill, Gorey, Co. Wexford.	7-5-1918	Labourer	8-8-1945
E/403517	KEARNEY, Daniel	46 Chapel Hill, Lisburn.	28-12-1898	Boot and Shoe Operative	8-8-1945
E/401187	KEARNEY, Hugh	Urismanagh, Clonmany, Co. Donegal.	4-4-1903	Coat Maker	8-8-1945
E/408620	KEARNEY, James	52 Irish Quarters, Carrickfergus, Co. Antrim.	17-7-1921	Plumber	8-8-1945
84905	KEARNEY, John	Kilshanny, Co. Clare.	11-11-1926	Labourer	1-6-1946
78692	KEARNEY, Patrick	c/o St. Patrick's School, Upton, Co. Cork.	11-1-1921	Cook	8-8-1945
82609	KEARNEY, Thomas	11 Brunswick Place, London, S.E.19.	19-2-1922	Messenger	8-8-1945
E/422173	KEATING, Francis	c/o Mr. F. Walsh, Lake View Tce., Castleblaney, Co. Monaghan.	27-2-1915	Weaver	8-8-1945

Army No.	Name.	Last Recorded Address.	Date of Birth.	Declared Occupation prior to enlistment in Defence Forces.	Date of Dismissal from Defence Forces.
202654	KEATING, John	Grange, Kilmore, Co. Wexford.	28-5-1920	Labourer	8-8-1945
72950	KEATING, Joseph	19 Upper Dominick Street, Dublin.	28-4-1911	Labourer	8-8-1945
110743	KEATING, Leonard	Ballyvadley, Mullinahone, Co. Tipperary.	29-6-1916	Labourer	8-8-1945
83933	KEATING, Paul	c/o Mr. Caffrey, Raheny, Co. Dublin.	29-12-1922	Labourer	8-8-1945
E/432390	KEATING, Peter	5 North King St., Dublin.	18-7-1922	Labourer	8-8-1945
E/408413	KEAVY, Thomas	9 Rosary Road, Maryland, Dublin.	12-7-1923	Gen. Labourer	8-8-1945
84692	KEDDY, Cecil S.	Nevinstown, Cloghran, Co. Dublin.	4-1-1924	Gardener	8-8-1945
211396	KEEGAN, Andrew	13 Abbey Cottages, Upper Abbey Street, Dublin.	6-7-1922	Unemployed	8-8-1945
E/406743	KEEGAN, Francis	17 Emmet Buildings, Watling Street, Dublin.	20-6-1920	Labourer	8-8-1945
83062	KEEGAN, James	31 Cottage, Kilcool, Co. Wicklow.	8-3-1918	Labourer	8-8-1945
A/79334	KEEGAN, James	17 Emmett Buildings, James Street, Dublin.	26-7-1920	Labourer	8-8-1945
E/405504	KEEGAN, John J.	3 Ardee Road, Rathmines, Dublin.	9-4-1913	Cinema Operator	8-8-1945
V/201555	KEEGAN, Laurence	Mount Street, Claremorris, Co. Mayo.	—-11-1920	Labourer	8-8-1945
V/207095	KEEGAN, Michael	43 Stanaway Road, Kimmage, Dublin.	22-2-1922	Cold Storage Worker	8-8-1945
L/500182	KEEGAN, Patrick	17 Watling St., Buildings, Dublin.	25-10-1921	Labourer	8-8-1945
75425	KEEGAN, Thomas	Tielick, Abbeyshrule, Co. Longford.	5-6-1918	Labourer	8-8-1945
E/435434	KEEGAN, Thomas	Market Square, Newbridge, Co. Kildare.	3-3-1916	Chef	8-8-1945
L/502838	KEENA, Edward	8 Athboy Street, Trim.	1-1-1922	Farm Labourer	8-8-1945
E/422701	KEENAN, Daniel	44 James St., Bessbrook, Co. Armagh.	18-12-1901	Baker	8-8-1945
208814	KEENAN, Edward	52 North Great Georges Street, Dublin.	30-1-1920	Labourer	8-8-1945
E/420945	KEENAN, James	Kiltyrehar, Longford.	4-6-1916	Motor Driver	8-8-1945
E/404891	KEENAN, John	Cornahave, Killbrone P.O., Emyvale, Co. Monaghan.	12-10-1922	Farm Labourer	8-8-1945
E/422174	KEENAN, Owen	Cornahave, Killbrone, P.O., Emyvale, Co. Monaghan.	19-4-1921	Farmer	8-8-1945
E/423202	KEENAN, Patrick	8 St. Columba's Street, Derry.	16-12-1922	Hotel Messenger Boy	8-8-1945
E/422027	KEENAN, Philip	Main St., Swanlinbar, Co. Cavan.	13-12-1920	Farmer	8-8-1945
E/430089	KEHOE, George	2 Toll House Street, New Ross, Co. Wexford.	10-11-1916	Labourer	8-8-1945
E/435535	KEHOE, James	Donanore, Old Ross, Co. Wexford.	28-5-1914	Farm Labourer	8-8-1945
E/400390	KEHOE, Joseph	Derrypark, Baltinglass, Co. Wicklow.	21-2-1922	Labourer	8-8-1945
E/421692	KEIGHRAN, Frank	West Gardens, Sligo.	18-3-1922	Barber's Apprentice	8-8-1945
E/425331	KEIGHREY, Joseph	Tulrush, Ballinasloe, Co. Galway.	2-3-1920	Farm Labourer	9-8-1945

Army No.	Name.	Last Recorded Address.	Date of Birth.	Declared Occupation prior to enlistment in Defence Forces.	Date of Dismissal from Defence Forces.
V/211283	KELCH, Michael	2 Lr. Erne Place, Pearse Street, Dublin.	9-6-1922	Boot Repairer	8-8-1945
E/407635	KELLEHER, Arnold	213 Newvale, Shankill, Co. Co. Dublin.	15-2-1923	Labourer	8-8-1945
A/77165	KELLEHER, Chris.	26 Neagle's Tce., Kilrush, Co. Clare.	25-5-1919	Labourer	8-8-1945
69885	KELLEHER, John B.	Clash, Little Island, Co. Cork.	16-8-1918	Motor Engineer	8-8-1945
108660	KELLIHER, William	Irremore, Lixnaw, Co. Kerry.	26-2-1916	Farmer	8-8-1945
V/211143	KELLS, Ernest	4 Baggot Court, Baggot Street, Dublin.	28-2-1922	None	8-8-1945
E/405772	KELLY, Andrew	106 Thatch Rd., Whitehall, Dublin.	9-9-1907	Motor Driver	8-8-1945
83308	KELLY, Christopher	42 Kilfenora Road, Kimmage, Dublin.	6-5-1921	None	8-8-1945
V/211462	KELLY, Christopher	126 Walsh Road, Drumcondra, Dublin.	12-6-1922	Woodworker	8-8-1945
E/432965	KELLY, Christopher	6 Buckgrave, Booterstown, Co. Dublin.	13-8-1922	Milk Server	8-8-1945
E/435878	KELLY, Christopher	Rathfield, Newbridge, Co. Kildare.	10-10-1923	Farm Labourer	29-12-1945
V/403610	KELLY, Cornelius	24 Lower Gardiner Street, Dublin.	27-5-1919	Motor Driver	8-8-1945
E/420771	KELLY, Edward	Magheracorn, Convoy, Co. Donegal.	5-6-1921	Carpenter	8-8-1945
A/80552	KELLY, Edward	Kilrush, Kilcullen, Co. Kildare.	5-5-1922	Farm Labourer	8-8-1945
E/407277	KELLY, Edward	13 Frederick Street, Bessbrook, Co. Armagh.	31-3-1908	Carpenter	8-8-1945
E/433482	KELLY, Edward	24 Lower Gardiner Street, Dublin.	25-8-1914	Upholsterer	8-8-1945
V/208633	KELLY, Edward	Craighdoo, Convoy, Co. Donegal.	22-10-1916	Farm Labourer	8-8-1945
E/408336	KELLY, Edward J.	Connolly Street, Nenagh, Co. Tipperary.	21-1-1924	Labourer	8-8-1945
E/403518	KELLY, Fabian	51a Pearse Street, Dublin.	19-1-1919	Spring Maker	8-8-1945
E/400724	KELLY, Francis	c/o Robert Cullen, Dawson Street, Monaghan.	10-8-1913	Labourer	8-8-1945
70490	KELLY, Henry	c/o Glendenning, 4 Emily Place, Glasgow.	18-3-1911	Labourer	8-8-1945
V/209123	KELLY, Hugh	Graffy, Castlefin, Co. Donegal.	22-1-1919	Apprentice Carpenter	8-8-1945
V/208634	KELLY, Hugh	Tiernish, Castlefin, Co. Donegal.	15-4-1916	Labourer	8-8-1945
E/406515	KELLY, James	4 Lr. Rutland St., Dublin.	6-5-1923	None	8-8-1945
75114	KELLY, James	Lisbush, Mageany, Co. Kildare.	1-1-1917	Labourer	8-8-1945
E/424182	KELLY, James	St. Columbcille Terrace, Granard, Co. Longford.	10-12-1922	Labourer	8-8-1945
E/421152	KELLY, James	Connolly Street, Ballina, Co. Mayo.	23-4-1922	Labourer	8-8-1945
E/432465	KELLY, James	c/o Mrs. McCabe, Dublin Street, Monaghan.	28-11-1909	Lorry Driver	8-8-1945
L/500535	KELLY, James	17 Sarsfield Street, Sallynoggin, Dun Laoghaire.	4-10-1917	Labourer	8-8-1945
72276	KELLY, James	51 Marrowbone Lane, Dublin.	3-9-1913	Labourer	8-8-1945
74095	KELLY, James	33 Ossory Park, Kilkenny.	19-8-1911	Builder's Helper —Labourer	8-8-1945
208807	KELLY, James	3 McGovern's Cottages, Windy Arbour, Co. Dublin.	17-8-1921	Labourer	8-8-1945
E/408241	KELLY, John	c/o John Doherty, Carrigans, Letterkenny,	2-5-1922	Labourer	8-8-1945

Army No.	Name.	Last Recorded Address.	Date of Birth.	Declared Occupation prior to enlistment in Defence Forces.	Date of Dismissal from Defence Forces.
V/201451	KELLY, John	4 Buckingham St., Dublin.	10-4-1901	Butcher	8-8-1945
E/425346	KELLY, John	Lenan, Clonmany, Co. Donegal.	3-8-1920	Farmer	8-8-1945
E/424256	KELLY, John	29 Scrabby Road, Granard, Co. Longford.	12-12-1922	Labourer	8-8-1945
V/205302	KELLY, John	Spa, Ballingarry, Co. Limerick.	4-7-1920	Labourer	8-8-1945
E/437993	KELLY, John	70 Durham Street, Belfast.	9-7-1925	Apprentice Joiner	8-8-1945
209749	KELLY, John	2 Castle Bks., Limerick.	17-6-1922	Messenger Boy	8-8-1945
V/403984	KELLY, Joseph	57 Ceelar Ave., Belfast.	13-9-1915	Clerk	8-8-1945
A/83251	KELLY, Joseph	306 "A" Block, Marrowbone Lane, Dublin.	25-3-1921	Labourer	8-8-1945
E/411806	KELLY, Joseph	2 Sheep's Street, Off Mary Street, Limerick.	17-3-1921	Labourer	8-8-1945
E/407199	KELLY, Joseph	13 Frederick Street, Bessbrook, Co. Armagh.	10-12-1909	Butcher	8-8-1945
83191	KELLY, Joseph	Toberbonny, Cloghran, Co. Dublin.	3-2-1921	Farm Labourer	8-8-1945
E/424156	KELLY, Josh.	4 Ardee Terrace, Sligo.	17-10-1922	Telephone Operator	8-8-1945
78399	KELLY, Kevin	Sportsmanshall, Dundalk.	11-2-1921	Messenger	8-8-1945
65794	KELLY, Kieran	2 Main St., Templetuohy, Templemore.	4-11-1904	Labourer	8-8-1945
A/73977	KELLY, Matthew	Sherwood Park, Kilbride, Tullow, Co. Carlow.	2-4-1913	Farm Labourer	8-8-1945
V/209290	KELLY, Maurice	Coolewest, Athea, Co. Limerick.	9-12-1910	Labourer	8-8-1945
E/409407	KELLY, Michael	Coolarty, Edgeworthstown, Co. Longford.	26-9-1923	Motor Driver	8-8-1945
E/421519	KELLY, Michael	c/o P. Kerrigan, Navaney Street, Ballybofey, Co. Donegal.	30-5-1919	Clerk	8-8-1945
E/425290	KELLY, Michael	9 Cathedral View, Mullingar.	16-11-1924	Porter	8-8-1945
E/412764	KELLY, Michael	4 Meatmarket Lane, Mary Street, Limerick.	13-1-1921	None	8-8-1945
E/433391	KELLY, Michael	34B Liberty Hall, Railway Street, Dublin.	9-10-1921	Baker	8-8-1945
E/423251	KELLY, Michael	Skeaghmore, Rathconrath, Co. Westmeath.	26-8-1922	Motor Mechanic	8-8-1945
A/73096	KELLY, Michael	18 Cloyne Road, Crumlin, Dublin.	22-12-1911	Labourer	8-8-1945
L/501903	KELLY, Michael	8 Albert Place, Charlemont Street, Dublin.	28-10-1924	Messenger	8-8-1945
E/437945	KELLY, Patrick	Springfield, Mullingar.	12-3-1920	Motor Driver	8-8-1945
83230	KELLY, Patrick	11 Park Terrace, Francis Street, Dublin.	24-5-1922	Labourer	8-8-1945
75924	KELLY, Patrick	Ballinakeel, Leckanuan P.O., Co. Leitrim.	12-2-1918	Farm Labourer	8-8-1945
E/407764	KELLY, Patrick	15 Queen Street, Dublin.	14-1-1922	Cook	8-8-1945
A/73239	KELLY, Patrick	26 Summerhill, Dublin.	18-2-1914	Boot-maker	8-8-1945
79856	KELLY, Patrick	Naas Road, Ballymore-Eustace, Co. Kildare.	2-10-1921	Labourer	8-8-1945
E/429678	KELLY, Patrick	14 Connolly Terrace, Bohermore, Co. Galway.	21-1-1924	Labourer (Shop Messenger)	8-8-1945
E/422176	KELLY, Patrick	Killyfudly, Newbliss, Co. Monaghan.	5-9-1922	Labourer	8-8-1945
E/431779	KELLY, Patrick	Cullen, Knockcroghery, Co. Roscommon.	6-8-1916	Welder and Fitter	8-8-1945
E/412576	KELLY, Patrick	6 Sumner Street, Limerick.	26-7-1917	Labourer	8-8-1945
A/110321	KELLY, Patrick	c/o Mrs. O'Brien, 548 Ballymanny, Kildare.	6-6-1913	Quarry Worker	8-8-1945
E/422874	KELLY, Patrick	c/o Patrick Logan, Burnfoot, Co. Donegal.	11-4-1922	Labourer	8-8-1945

Army No.	Name.	Last Recorded Address.	Date of Birth.	Declared Occupation prior to enlistment in Defence Forces.	Date of Dismissal from Defence Forces.
E/408880	KELLY, Patrick	4 Sunbury Gardens, Dartry Road, Dublin.	21-12-1923	Student	8-8-1945
76419	KELLY, Patrick	30 Marlboro St., Dublin.	15-7-1919	Messenger	8-8-1945
L/500050	KELLY, Patrick	13 Chancery House, Charles Street, West, Dublin.	16-11-1919	Motor Driver	8-8-1945
A/72826	KELLY, Peter	15 Upr. Clanbrassil Street, Dublin.	25-4-1913	Labourer	8-8-1945
E/402635	KELLY, Richard	3 Eugene Street, Cork St., Dublin.	5-6-1922	None	8-8-1945
E/435333	KELLY, Richard	5 Hanover Street, Carlow.	21-10-1922	Labourer	8-8-1945
A/83504	KELLY, Stephen	301 Joy Street, Ringsend, Dublin.	17-6-1922	Labourer	8-8-1945
E/400447	KELLY, Thomas W.	54 Grove Park, Rathmines, Dublin.	27-2-1916	Motor Driver	8-8-1945
E/401651	KELLY, Thomas	158 Townsend St., Dublin.	9-2-1908	Labourer	8-8-1945
E/408517	KELLY, Thomas	27 Fishamble St., Dublin.	12-12-1923	Baker's Helper	2-9-1945
203987	KELLY, Thomas	Carrigarila, Erril, Leix.	20-3-1914	Farm Labourer	8-8-1945
A/113067	KELLY, Vincent	Sallybank, Ballykelly, Derry.	9-1-1916	Farm Labourer	8-8-1945
A/83412	KELLY, Vincent	Carnin, Ballyjamesduff, Co. Cavan.	24-1-1922	Farm Labourer	8-8-1945
E/405420	KELLY, Vincent	5 McDonald's Terrace, Dundalk.	29-6-1920	Electrical Engineer	8-8-1945
83299	KELLY, William J.	5 Annally Road, Cabra, Dublin.	18-1-1922	Labourer	8-8-1945
E/407406	KELLY, William	Corbans Lane, Naas.	8-1-1924	Gardener	8-8-1945
E/421644	KELLY, William	Clohmucker, Keenagh, Co. Longford.	4-7-1921	Labourer	8-8-1945
E/434751	KELLY, William	51 Shelmalier, Rd., Church Road, Dublin.	5-4-1922	Student	8-8-1945
E/433035	KELLY, William	4 Temple Bar, Dublin.	29-6-1921	Iron Worker	8-8-1945
79319	KELLY, William	1 Railway Tce., Drogheda.	23-7-1917	Coach Body Builder	8-8-1945
80544	KEMP, William	McGowan's Terrace, Brownstown, Co. Kildare.	9-11-1913	Stable-Hand	8-8-1945
L/507516	KENEALLY, Peter	12 Old Weigh House Lane, Cork.	26-6-1927	Messenger	8-8-1945
A/76061	KENEFICK, James	Loughane, Ladysbridge, Co. Cork.	14-1-1915	Farm Labourer	8-8-1945
E/402544	KENNA, Peter	79 Stanaway Rd., Crumlin, Dublin.	25-4-1922	Labourer	8-8-1945
77331	KENNEALLY, Patrick	Mountain Barracks, Mitchelstown, Co. Cork.	20-7-1920	Farm Labourer	8-8-1945
V/205441	KENNEDY, Andrew	48 Georges Avenue, Blackrock, Co. Dublin.	26-4-1922	Page-Boy	8-8-1945
83413	KENNEDY, Brendan	Clonardon, Garlow Cross, Navan.	1-11-1921	Labourer	8-8-1945
E/415560	KENNEDY, Bryan	4 Greenville Tce., Tralee.	13-9-1920	Carpenter	8-8-1945
E/421331	KENNEDY, Charles	Main Street, Ballybofey, Co. Donegal.	12-8-1909	Plasterer	8-8-1945
A/74435	KENNEDY, Edward	c/o Mrs. Finn, Eyrefield Cottage, Newbridge, Co. Kildare.	12-8-1911	Clerk	8-8-1945
E/404672	KENNEDY, Francis	4 East James St., Dublin.	5-4-1921	Sheet Metal Worker	8-8-1945
E/415859	KENNEDY, Francis	1 Treacy Villas, Cashel, Co. Tipperary.	11-3-1923	Labourer	8-8-1945
E/422468	KENNEDY, James	c/o R. Mulholland, Glenfin Street, Ballybofey, Co. Donegal.	15-1-1922	Labourer	8-8-1945
A/83973	KENNEDY, James	39 Emmett Square, Williamstown, Co. Dublin.	9-10-1922	Van Boy	8-8-1945
A/79872	KENNEDY, James	143 Up. Dorset St., Dublin.	3-2-1921	Messenger	8-8-1945
E/404742	KENNEDY, Thomas	27 Summer Place, Summerhill, Dublin.	30-8-1921	Labourer	8-8-1945

Army No.	Name.	Last Recorded Address.	Date of Birth.	Declared Occupation prior to enlistment in Defence Forces.	Date of Dismissal from Defence Forces.
A/78194	KENNEDY, Thomas	Riverstown, Birr.	31-1-1920	Farm Labourer	8-8-1945
E/433727	KENNEDY, Thomas	7 Thomas Ave., Waterford.	1-8-1917	Labourer	8-8-1945
208478	KENNEDY, Vincent	1 Bride Road, Dublin.	16-6-1916	Labourer	8-8-1945
E/423713	KENNEDY, William	Ardfarna, Bundoran, Co. Donegal.	17-6-1913	Labourer	8-8-1945
78730	KENNY, Augustine	13 St. Bridget's Cottages, Clondalkin, Co. Dublin.	21-5-1917	Electric Welder	8-8-1945
E/407782	KENNY, Chris.	10 Old Court Park, Boghall, Bray.	18-2-1924	Labourer	8-8-1945
L/502794	KENNY, Denis	5 Parnell Street, Sally-noggin, Co. Dublin.	18-2-1926	Gardener	8-8-1945
A/84776	KENNY, James	105 St. Declan's Road, Marino, Dublin.	5-1-1923	General Labourer	8-8-1945
E/409128	KENNY, John	105 St. Declan's Road, Marino, Dublin.	13-9-1924	None	8-8-1945
83415	KENNY, John	Christianstown, Duffy's Cross, Ardee, Co. Louth.	1-2-1921	Labourer	8-8-1945
E/415096	KENNY, John	11 St. Bridget's Road, Gurranebraher, Cork.	13-10-1922	Labourer	8-8-1945
V/208434	KENNY, Joseph	Station View, Castlerea, Co. Roscommon.	14-6-1910	Mechanic	8-8-1945
83033	KENNY, Joseph	Toorard, Headford, Co. Galway.	16-1-1917	Barman	8-8-1945
73472	KENNY, Michael	268 City Road, London, E.C.1.	5-7-1910	Fitter and Turner	8-8-1945
81827	KENNY, Michael	64 High Road, Thomond-gate, Limerick.	30-12-1925	Gen. Labourer	25-2-1946
E/422745	KENNY, Patrick	248 Cottage, Enniscrone, Co. Sligo.	2-4-1919	Farm Labourer	25-1-1946
20,3004	KENNY, Patrick	44 Eire Street, Gorey, Co. Wexford.	20-5-1922	Labourer	8-8-1945
L/508931	KENNY, Patrick	Riverstown, Birr.	25-2-1925	Farm Labourer	19-1-1946
E/124385	KENNY, Peter	Curraboy, Athlone.	30-11-1922	Factory Worker, Motor Driver	8-8-1945
L/507491	KENNY, Peter	158 St. Munchin's Street, Island Field, Limerick.	17-8-1927	Labourer	17-5-1946
E/403863	KENNY, Richard	Shaughmore, Avoca, Co. Wicklow.	2-8-1920	Labourer	8-8-1945
E/498066	KENNY, Terence	Dromintee, Newry, Co. Down.	12-2-1923	General Dealer	8-8-1945
V/200635	KENNY, Thomas	40 Lambay Rd., Glasnevin, Dublin.	20-2-1920	Fitter's Apprentice	8-8-1945
A/74282	KENNY, Thomas	120 Lr. Clanbrassil Street, Dublin.	10-9-1910	Electrician and Builder's Labourer	8-8-1945
E/123347	KEOGH, Christopher	Thomastown, Killucan, Co. Westmeath.	4-9-1922	Farm Labourer	8-8-1945
A/60875	KEOGH, James	Lisnalea, Turraroan, Co. Kilkenny.	27-11-1904	Labourer	8-8-1945
E/400404	KEOGH, John	10 Charleville Mall, North Strand, Dublin.	14-2-1904	Bus Driver	8-8-1945
E/402607	KEOGH, John	30 Findlater Street, Glasthule, Dun Laoghaire.	24-12-1897	Electrician	8-8-1945
E/432546	KEOGH, John	12 Upr. Buckingham St., Dublin.	9-9-1922	Labourer	8-8-1945
E/404743	KEOGH, Michael	1 Gaelic Street, North Strand, Dublin.	29-10-1919	Electrician Apprentice	8-8-1945
84398	KEOGH, Nicholas	16 Parnell Tce., Mullingar.	13-9-1915	Labourer	8-8-1945
A/70435	KEOGH, Patrick	302 Cashel Road, Crumlin, Dublin.	30-3-1911	Grocer's Assistant	8-8-1945
L/508120	KEOGH, Paul	Barrack St., Tullamore.	13-3-1922	Labourer	8-8-1945
E/435471	KEOGH, Thomas	13 Garden Lane, Francis Street, Dublin.	5-2-1920	Builder's Labourer	8-8-1945
E/425368	KEOHANE, Donald	Lislea, Ballinalee, Co. Longford.	25-3-1923	Farm Labourer	8-8-1945

Army No.	Name.	Last Recorded Address.	Date of Birth.	Declared Occupation prior to enlistment in Defence Forces.	Date of Dismissal from Defence Forces.
E/423203	KEOWN, Donald	c/o Cyril McGriskin, Kiltyclogher, Co. Leitrim.	19-8-1922	Farm Labourer	8-8-1945
E/423204	KEOWN, Patrick	c/o Cyril McGriskin, Kiltyclogher, Co. Leitrim.	15-8-1921	Labourer	8-8-1945
E/415940	KERINS, John	5 Cathedral Place, Cobh.	3-6-1916	Labourer	8-8-1945
E/403197	KERNA, Francis	Benburb, Co. Tyrone.	10-1-1915	Bricklayer	8-8-1945
83612	KERR, Arthur	211 North Circular Road, Dublin.	19-1-1920	Assembler	8-8-1945
A/75769	KERR, Edward	18 Bantry Street, Belfast.	22-11-1920	Butcher	8-8-1945
E/432814	KERR, John	32 Belton Park Avenue, Donnycarney, Co. Dublin.	19-9-1916	Terrazzo Polisher	8-8-1945
E/422505	KERR, Laurence	1 Rockfield Terrace, Buncrana, Co. Donegal.	17-3-1903	Labourer	8-8-1945
A/73704	KERRIGAN, James	George's Street, Sligo.	12-9-1914	Telegraph Messenger	8-8-1945
V/201475	KERRIGAN, Kevin	36 Lord Edward St., Sligo.	5-6-1920	Labourer	8-8-1945
208431	KERRIGAN, Patrick	Cloontytown, Castlegar, Co. Sligo.	1-8-1921	Labourer	8-8-1945
V/208668	KERRIGAN, Thomas	Sharaigh, Bunnahowen, Co. Mayo.	15-8-1914	Labourer	8-8-1945
A/72070	KERRY, Patrick	50 O'Moore Place, Portlaoighise.	7-3-1911	Labourer	8-8-1945
V/211281	KERSTING, Patrick	2 Nicholas Street, Dublin.	8-4-1922	Labourer	8-8-1945
204454	KERTON, George	6 St. Ignatius Road, Drumcondra, Dublin.	8-3-1922	Cabinet Maker	8-8-1945
E/435842	KERVICK, Joseph	17 Ozanam St., Waterford.	10-1-1924	Stable Boy	8-8-1945
L/508663	KERWICK, James	17 Rothe Tce., Kilkenny.	8-12-1923	Wool Spinner	8-8-1945
E/420836	KETTERICK, Martin	Lr. Chapel St., Castlebar.	7-7-1910	Tractor Driver	8-8-1945
E/416289	KIDNEY, Edward	c/o Mrs. Byrne, Lr Grange, Waterford.	1-6-1923	Lorry Helper	8-8-1945
E/435293	KIELY, Andrew	Carrigrea Lodge, Kilrossanty, Waterford.	5-10-1916	Labourer	8-8-1945
E/416753	KIELY, James	Killishall, Cappagh, Co. Waterford.	14-3-1917	Lorry Driver and Builder	8-8-1945
80810	KIELY, James	Glendalligen, Killrosanty, Waterford.	4-12-1916	Labourer	8-8-1945
81649	KIELY, John	28 High Street, Limerick.	3-6-1923	Builder's Labourer	8-8-1945
L/507691	KIELY, Patrick	8 Derheen, Thurles.	13-3-1926	Farm Labourer	4-8-1946
E/423090	KIELY, Peter	The Diamond, Glenties, Co. Donegal.	18-8-1922	Student	8-8-1945
E/432492	KIERNAN, James	Tycusker, Co. Cavan.	10-2-1905	Butcher	8-8-1945
79776	KIERNAN, John Jos.	5 Echlin Street, James's Street, Dublin.	9-11-1921	Steel Polisher	8-8-1945
80601	KIERNAN, Louis	6 St. Fintan's Terrace, Cabra, Dublin.	13-4-1922	None	8-8-1945
A/82664	KILEY, John	67 Garrymore, Clonmel.	3-7-1921	Labourer	8-8-1945
E/433479	KILLEEN, James	Ballygavin, Hilltown, Co. Down.	13-11-1917	Motor Mechanic	8-8-1945
E/423901	KILLIAN, James	Killashee, Co. Longford.	28-10-1916	Shop Assistant	8-8-1945
A/76029	KILROY, John	Abbey Road Cottages, Athlone.	22-2-1919	Woollen Mill Helper	8-8-1945
E/405954	KIMBERLEY, John	172 Lr. Rathmines Road, Dublin.	30-9-1913	House Painter	8-8-1945
E/425340	KILMARTIN, James	Munakill, Manorhamilton, Co. Leitrim.	23-2-1924	Farmer	8-8-1945
E/406909	KILSHAW, Stephen	32 Yellow Rd., Whitehall, Dublin.	28-1-1923	Messenger	8-8-1945
L/503649	KINAHAN, Peter	32 Haddington Road, Dublin.	20-8-1926	Bottle Blower	8-8-1945
E/420085	KINEAID, Bartholomew	Clogher Tang, Ballymahon, Co. Westmeath.	28-10-1921	Farm Labourer	8-8-1945
E/413853	KING, Alphonsus	60 Clare Street, Limerick.	26-10-1919	Labourer	8-8-1945

Army No.	Name.	Last Recorded Address.	Date of Birth.	Declared Occupation prior to enlistment in Defence Forces.	Date of Dismissal from Defence Forces.
E/424775	KING, Christopher	c/o J. Lally, Cregmore, Clare-Galway, Co. Galway.	13-8-1923	Farm Labourer	8-8-1945
79065	KING, Desmond	Priest Lane, Carrick-on-Shannon.	30-2-1920	Farm Labourer	8-8-1945
V/207765	KING, John	5 Grattan Terrace, Fair Hill, Galway.	3-5-1918	Labourer	8-8-1945
A/83548	KING, John	29 Sarsfield Street, Sally-noggin, Dun Laoghaire.	16-5-1922	Tailor	8-8-1945
E/401332	KING, Joseph	3 Pools Terrace, Dolphin's Barn, Dublin.	21-12-1920	Shoe Repairs	8-8-1945
E/423447	KING, Michael	Knockmartin, Longford.	4-9-1922	Farm Labourer	8-8-1945
E/422370	KINIRY, Patrick	Caherlag, Glanmire, Co. Cork.	9-2-1906	Clerk	8-8-1945
E/407418	KINNEMONT, Adrian	42 Ballinteer Gardens, Dundrum, Co. Dublin.	4-7-1923	Student	8-8-1945
E/404458	KINSELLA, Andrew ...	3 Irish St., Enniscorthy, Co. Wexford.	21-9-1912	Wireless Operator	8-8-1945
205918	KINSELLA, James	Lady's Island, Broadway, Co. Wexford.	27-10-1915	Motor Driver	8-8-1945
A/79351	KINSELLA, Patrick	22 Clonliffe Ave., Dublin.	18-6-1921	None	8-8-1945
E/422876	KINSELLA, Patrick	c/o Mrs. McLoughlin, St. Mures, Fahan, Co. Donegal.	1-3-1921	Labourer	8-8-1945
72556	KINSELLA, Patrick	214 B Block, St. Audeon's House, Bridge Street, Dublin.	9-4-1913	Labourer	8-8-1945
E/417364	KIRBY, Patrick	Main Street, Midleton, Co. Cork.	12-2-1923	Student	8-8-1945
E/404342	KIRKWOOD, John	21 Manor Street, Dublin.	8-4-1917	Carpenter	8-8-1945
79559	KIRWAN, Laurence P.	Garrantemple, Knockloftry, Clonmel.	21-8-1918	Motor Driver	8-8-1945
E/411190	KIRWAN, Patrick	30 River Street, Clonmel.	5-12-1921	Factory Worker	8-8-1945
E/407123	KITSON, William	133 Durham St., Belfast.	18-4-1918	Lorry Driver	8-8-1945
E/403304	KNEAFSEY, Ambrose	49 Oakley Road, Ranelagh, Dublin.	11-3-1895	Commercial Traveller	8-8-1945
E/406019	KNELL, Leonard	Farmyard, Castlebelling-ham, Co. Louth.	13-3-1922	Labourer	8-8-1945
E/402449	KNIBB, Ernest D.	201 South Circular Road, Dublin.	11-12-1917	Clerk	8-8-1945
E/405378	KNIGHT, William G.	27 O'Donnell Gardens, Dun Laoghaire.	21-4-1917	Accountant's Clerk	8-8-1945
E/403391	KNOTT, John	32 Pembroke Cottages, Ringsend, Dublin.	24-3-1912	Driver	8-8-1945
E/416564	KURLIN, Thomas	Rathpeak, Mallow Road, Blarney, Co. Cork.	30-12-1918	Plasterer	8-8-1945
V/211398	LACEY, James	72 Cabra Drive, Dublin.	21-2-1922	None	11-1-1946
208236	LACEY, James	14 Michael St., Kilkenny.	20-12-1917	Butcher's Assistant	8-8-1945
E/435318	LACEY, Patrick	80 Wolfe Tone Villas, Wexford.	9-3-1921	General Labourer	13-10-1945
E/420682	LACKEY, Martin	Ballyloughan, Co. Galway.	9-7-1921	General Labourer	8-8-1945
V/200213	LACKEY, Patrick	6 Troyley Park, Ballina.	22-4-1922	Labourer	8-8-1945
208926	LAFFAN, Patrick	187 Keogh Square, Inchicore, Dublin.	17-9-1921	Labourer	8-8-1945
V/208636	LAFFERTY, Cornelius	Cashel, Carndonagh, Co. Donegal.	——6-1914	Labourer	8-8-1945
V/206282	LAFFERTY, Edward	Mill St., Urney, Clady, Strabane, Tyrone.	14-12-1919	Fisherman	8-8-1945
E/423273	LAFFERTY, John	111 Lecky Road, Derry.	20-7-1922	Labourer	8-8-1945
E/405280	LAHIFF, Francis	71 Sundrive Road, Kimmage, Dublin.	27-8-1922	Driver	8-8-1945
72612	LAHIFF, Peter	12 Castle Street, Dublin.	23-8-1909	Labourer	8-8-1945

Army No.	Name.	Last Recorded Address.	Date of Birth.	Declared Occupation prior to enlistment in Defence Forces.	Date of Dismissal from Defence Forces.
E/407382	LALLY, Thomas	14 North Great Georges Street, Dublin.	23-7-1922	Labourer	8-8-1945
E/436060	LALOR, James	12 O'Connell Street, Clara, Offaly.	23-5-1924	Textile Worker	8-8-1945
206867	LAMB, John	17 Green Street, Dublin.	28-7-1921	Labourer	8-8-1945
V/211446	LAMBE, Francis	18 Hendrick St., Dublin.	29-6-1922	None	8-8-1945
E/406343	LAMBE, Joseph C.	7B East Arran St., Dublin.	25-6-1923	Brush Maker	8-8-1945
L/506940	LAMBE, William	Carrigmore Lodge, Cobh, Co. Cork.	10-4-1926	Gardener	8-8-1945
201893	LAMBERT, Michael	Hannin's Cottages, Tipperary.	4-10-1920	Farmer	8-8-1945
L/507755	LANDY, Patrick	Shankill, Newtown, Kilmacthomas, Co. Waterford.	12-9-1927	Labourer	20-1-1946
E/417903	LANE, Benjamin	Glenakell, North Rockchapel, Co. Cork.	15-6-1918	Motor Driver	8-8-1945
82950	LANE, Edmond	Knockeeacurrig, Kiskean, Boherbee, Co. Cork.	18-2-1922	Labourer	8-8-1945
83036	LANE, Gerard	Poulnafany, Athenry, Co. Galway.	20-1-1917	Lorry Driver	8-8-1945
E/414343	LANE, Michael J.	20 Connolly Terrace Newcastlewest, Co. Limerick.	1-5-1916	Aero Engineer	8-8-1945
82125	LANE, Patrick	6 Beaumont Avenue, Ballintemple, Co. Cork.	2-5-1919	Machinist	8-8-1945
77569	LANE, Thomas	Monteagle, Brosna, Co. Kerry.	21-8-1919	Farm Labourer	8-8-1945
A/67801	LANE, Timothy	11 More Street, Cork.	8-6-1906	Labourer	8-8-1945
L/500928	LANE, William	1 Pearse House, Pearse Street, Dublin.	15-3-1923	Messenger	8-8-1945
80718	LANGAN, Michael	Mount Carmel, Fr. Griffin Road, Galway.	17-8-1919	Butcher	8-8-1945
E/422816	LANIGAN, James	Moran's Terrace, Ballyhaunis, Co. Mayo.	22-1-1918	Labourer	8-8-1945
80626	LANIGAN, James	Lawcus, Stonyford, Co. Kilkenny.	21-6-1920	Motor Driver	8-8-1945
69476	LANIGAN, Peter	83 Bangor Road, Crumlin, Dublin.	25-6-1908	Messenger	8-8-1945
E/433075	LAPPIN, Joseph	The Cottages, Smithboro, Co. Monaghan.	1-3-1922	Messenger Boy	8-8-1945
E/408334	LAPPIN, Patrick J.	Rockcorry, Co. Monaghan.	3-3-1923	Labourer	8-8-1945
209117	LARKIN, Andrew	Ballyduff, Kilmeadon, Co. Waterford.	30-5-1922	Gardener	8-8-1945
L/507988	LARKIN, Christopher	21 Knockalcon, Nenagh.	24-12-1925	Labourer	9-8-1946
V/217124	LARKIN, John	50 Smith's Villas, York Road, Dun Laoghaire.	25-11-1921	Porter	8-8-1945
A/75102	LARNER, John	47 Annamoe Park, N.C.Rd., Dublin.	16-1-1917	Messenger Boy	8-8-1945
80715	LAUNCHPAUP, Ed.	Narraghmore, Ballytore, Co. Kildare.	23-10-1919	Labourer	8-8-1945
V/207226	LAVERTY, Henry	Ternaskea, Castleblaney, Co. Monaghan.	5-6-1910	Farm Labourer	8-8-1945
81282	LAVERTY, Joseph	16 Hughes Park, Dundalk.	2-8-1919	Labourer	30-9-1945
E/434684	LAVERY, Francis	46 Grosvenor Sq., Dublin.	7-2-1916	Butcher's Apprentice	8-8-1945
E/405814	LAVERY, Richard	103 Phibsboro' Road, N.C.Rd., Dublin.	20-2-1920	Motor Driver	8-8-1945
76999	LAWLER, James	8 Dunville Avenue, Ranelagh, Dublin.	21-8-1918	Labourer	8-8-1945
A/83855	LAWLOR, Ambrose	6 Rosary Gardens, Dun Laoghaire.	5-1-1922	None	8-8-1945
L/503299	LAWLOR, James	91 Keogh Sq., Inchicore, Dublin.	24-2-1928	Milk Boy	28-3-1946
V/200910	LAWLOR, Patrick	Tombeagh, Hacketstown, Co. Carlow.	3-11-1920	Labourer	8-8-1945
E/406190	LAWLOR, Peter	9 Parnell Terrace, Arklow.	13-2-1913	Motor Driver	8-8-1945

Army No.	Name.	Last Recorded Address.	Date of Birth.	Declared Occupation prior to enlistment in Defence Forces.	Date of Dismissal from Defence Forces.
V/204877	LAWLOR, William	Craigue, Lr., Killenaule, Thurles.	29-6-1920	Labourer	8-8-1945
A/102656	LAWLOR, William	243 Wigan Road, Ashton-in-Makerfield, Lancs.	7-1-1916	Labourer	8-8-1945
205791	LAWLESS, Hubert	41 Eden Villas, Sandycove, Co. Dublin.	12-6-1921	Messenger Boy	8-8-1945
E/403203	LAWRENCE, Peter	9 Vincent Street, Berkeley Road, Dublin.	26-2-1908	Shopkeeper	8-8-1945
A/10728	LEACY, John	Curraghmore, Ramsgrange, Wexford.	6-4-1915	Farm Labourer	8-8-1945
A/73693	LEAHY, Denis	Bohermacrusha, Holycross, Co. Tipperary.	5-5-1915	Labourer	8-8-1945
E/410393	LEAHY, John	Farmons, Waterville, Killarney.	27-4-1922	Labourer	8-8-1945
V/214048	LEAHY, Martin	14 St. Michael's Avenue, Tipperary.	7-10-1921	Labourer	8-8-1945
E/407586	LEAHY, Michael	Glenbane, Lattin, Co. Tipperary.	16-1-1919	Labourer	8-8-1945
E/407377	LEAHY, Patrick	Bedford, Listowel.	30-5-1921	Steel Worker	8-8-1945
E/435771	LEAHY, Patrick	9 Park View Tce., Cahir, Co. Tipperary.	12-3-1915	Motor Driver	8-8-1945
E/420364	LEATHAM, John	Railway Terrace, Ballinamore, Co. Leitrim.	16-5-1896	General Labourer	8-8-1945
V/215164	LEAVY, Thomas	Cloghan, Abbeystrule, Co. Longford.	11-8-1925	General Labourer	8-8-1945
78086	LECKY, James	11 Bucket Street, Mallow.	7-5-1923	Technical Student	8-8-1945
E/424578	LECKY, William	Carrickmacross, Newtown-cunningham, Co. Donegal.	16-3-1920	Labourer	8-8-1945
E/405349	LEDDY, James	10 Connolly Ave., Navan.	19-2-1922	Boiler Man	8-8-1945
L/501396	LEDEBOER, Brendan	2 Arnott Street, S.C.Rd., Dublin.	13-5-1923	Shorthand Typist	8-8-1945
L/507279	LEE, Anthony	17 Bachelor's Quay, Cork.	27-7-1926	Labourer	8-8-1945
78418	LEE, Francis	4 Magee's Court, Off Charlotte St., Dublin.	1-7-1919	General Labourer	8-8-1945
V/209552	LEE, John	2 Lake View Tce., Cavan.	10-1-1912	Labourer	8-8-1945
L/501229	LEE, John	2 Church Lane, Kevin St., Dublin.	11-11-1923	Labourer	8-8-1945
E/409158	LEE, John J.	50 New Street, Dublin.	11-11-1924	Marble Polisher	8-8-1945
V/201548	LEE, John	Rathasker Road, Naas.	15-10-1912	Labourer	8-8-1945
A/76086	LEE, Michael	Gortnaskagh, Manor-hamilton, Co. Leitrim.	18-5-1919	Labourer	8-8-1945
E/422181	LEE, Patrick	St. Bridget's Tce., Cavan.	4-2-1919	Butcher	8-8-1945
E/421308	LEE, Patrick	Deerpark, Manor-hamilton, Co. Leitrim.	12-3-1910	Builder's Labourer	8-8-1945
V/209708	LEE, Philip	21 Belton Park Avenue, Donnycarney, Dublin.	16-7-1920	Shop Boy	8-8-1945
E/406560	LEEPER, Ignatius J.	26 Linenhall St., Dublin.	19-2-1920	Tailor	8-8-1945
75019	LEIGH, William	Belan, Moone, Co. Kildare.	14-10-1917	Farm Labourer	8-8-1945
A/79507	LENEGHAN, John	Innisbiggle, Achill, Co. Mayo.	7-8-1920	General Labourer	8-8-1945
E/421871	LENEGHAN, Patrick	Ballintogher, Co. Sligo.	26-3-1914	Labourer	8-8-1945
E/406613	LENNON, Daniel	67 Kilmarey Street, Newry.	6-7-1920	Joiner and Cabinet Maker	8-8-1945
E/403930	LENNON, Francis	3 Fairfield Street, Belfast.	11-7-1893	Barman	8-8-1945
79412	LENNON, Francis G.	3 Fairfield Street, Belfast.	17-12-1920	Grocer's Assistant	8-8-1945
E/409987	LENNON, James S.	56 Iris Drive, Belfast.	16-7-1923	Motor Driver	8-8-1945
74289	LENNON, John	Strand Street, Athlone.	21-9-1910	Mill Worker (Yarn Twister)	8-8-1945
E/408027	LENNON, Michael	Drumever, Ballymackney, Co. Monaghan.	1-5-1923	Farm Labourer	8-8-1945
V/204812	LENNON, Patrick	16 Hughes Park, Dundalk.	10-3-1921	Labourer	8-8-1945
E/434421	LENNON, Patrick Joseph	13 Commons St., Dublin.	14-11-1922	Messenger Boy	

Army No.	Name.	Last Recorded Address.	Date of Birth.	Declared Occupation prior to enlistment in Defence Forces.	Date of Dismissal from Defence Forces.
E/421154	LENNOX, Donald	Pearse Street, Ballina.	18-4-1922	Labourer	8-8-1945
E/409254	LENNOX, George	34 Carman's Hall, Francis Street, Dublin.	20-7-1924	Carpenter	8-8-1945
E/420913	LEONARD, James	c/o Jas. McGuire, Rooe, Gortahill P.O., Blacklion, Co. Cavan.	5-11-1913	General Labourer	8-8-1945
E/408664	LEONARD, Patrick J.	69 Eskdale Gardens, Crumlin Road, Belfast.	3-6-1924	Labourer	8-8-1945
E/408744	LEONARD, Peter C.	3 Bleach Cottages, Athy, Co. Kildare.	14-11-1923	Labourer	8-8-1945
E/422877	LEONARD, Peter	Castlequarters, Fahan, Co. Donegal.	8-4-1911	Lorry Driver	8-8-1945
V/202538	LETTICE, Christopher	3 Mount Carmel Road, Greenmount, Cork.	26-5-1922	Labourer	8-8-1945
V/206460	LEVEY, John	47 Lr. Kevin St., Dublin.	14-11-1919	General Labourer	8-8-1945
78464	LEVEY, Michael	5 Church Lane, Kevin Street, Dublin.	28-12-1920	Messenger	8-8-1945
E/403350	LEWIS, James	34 Summerhill, Dublin.	23-7-1907	Electrician	8-8-1945
202456	LEWIS, Patrick	15 High Street, Wexford.	13-5-1920	Labourer	8-8-1945
E/423274	LIDDY, James	17 Crettan Terrace, Derry.	4-12-1921	Labourer	8-8-1945
E/409912	LIGGETT, Daniel	121 Brompton Pk., Balfast.	1-8-1923	General Labourer	8-8-1945
E/409911	LIGGETT, Patrick	121 Brompton Pk., Belfast.	14-2-1925	Labourer	8-8-1945
L/503422	LINDSAY, David	53 Ballybough Road, Dublin.	12-5-1927	Builders Labourer	4-7-1946
A/79721	LINDSAY, Patrick	Hugginstown, New Ross, Co. Wexford.	2-3-1921	Farm Labourer	8-8-1945
E/421221	LINDSAY, Thomas	c/o Meldrums, Castle St., Sligo.	12-8-1921	Shop Assistant	8-8-1945
E/408903	LINEHAN, John	Carrig, Mallow, Co. Cork.	17-12-1922	Farm Labourer	8-8-1945
75340	LINEHAN, John	Aglish, Ballyhar, Co. Kerry.	29-8-1918	Farm Labourer	8-8-1945
V/201946	LINEHAN, Joseph	Ballyburden, Ballincollig, Co. Cork.	11-3-1912	Labourer	8-8-1945
L/509045	LINEHAN, Peter	No. 1 Millgrove Ln., Cork.	3-3-1926	Farm Labourer	8-8-1945
E/433594	LINSDAY, Richard	28 Middle Third, Killester, Dublin.	13-8-1922	None	8-8-1945
L/507512	LITTICE, Timothy	33 Mount Carmel Road, Greenmount, Cork.	21-3-1927	Shoemaker	19-2-1946
204087	LITTLE, Bernard	Killylard, Belturbet, Co. Cavan.	16-8-1910	Labourer	8-8-1945
E/435867	LITTLE, James	6 College Street, Cavan.	21-7-1923	Stable Boy	8-8-1945
L/501240	LITTLE, Thomas	42 Moore Street, Dublin.	21-7-1924	Fitter	8-8-1945
E/420313	LOCKE, Christopher	28 Connaught St., Athlone.	25-11-1918	Hotel Waiter	8-8-1945
L/502821	LOFTUS, Gerard	25 Grenville St., Dublin.	1-1-1927	Labourer	14-2-1946
E/404733	LOGAN, Alexander	11 Island Bawn Drive, Belfast.	16-4-1908	Paviour	8-8-1945
E/421175	LOGAN, Daniel	Meenboge, Ballybofey, Co. Donegal.	5-8-1918	Bricklayer	8-8-1945
E/424267	LOGHAN, John	Rice Hill, Cavan.	13-1-1919	Farm Labourer	8-8-1945
E/421978	LOGUE, Arthur	84 Bishop Street, Derry.	25-8-1916	Electrician	8-8-1945
85514	LOGUE, Hugh Peter	Main Street, Ballybofey, Co. Donegal.	16-4-1926	Motor Driver	3-2-1946
E/414491	LONERGAN, David J.	Ardnacrusha, Co. Limerick.	19-7-1922	Labourer	8-8-1945
75139	LONERGAN, James	7 Clonmore Av., Boherbee, Tralee.	30-11-1917	Messenger Boy	8-8-1945
E/414572	LONERGAN, John	Oola, Co. Limerick.	20-2-1911	Labourer	17-3-1946
E/415424	LONERGAN, Joseph	23 Albert Street, Clonmel.	21-3-1921	Painter's Assistant	8-8-1945
E/416015	LONERGAN, Patrick	Newtownadin, Cahir, Co. Tipperary.	17-3-1923	Labourer	8-8-1945
A/77688	LONERGAN, Peter	Ard Muire, Carrick-on-Suir.	10-6-1920	Labourer	8-8-1945

Army No.	Name.	Last Recorded Address.	Date of Birth.	Declared Occupation prior to enlistment in Defence Forces.	Date of Dismissal from Defence Forces.
77570	LONG, Daniel	37 Warren's Lane, Cork.	13-10-1916	General Labourer	8-8-1945
L/506088	LONG, Gerard	37 Warren's Lane, Cork.	19-2-1923	Labourer	8-8-1945
B/423206	LONG, George	5 St. Columb's Wells, Derry.	17-3-1920	Labourer	8-8-1945
E/402042	LONG, James	74 Leighlin Road, Crumlin, Dublin.	29-7-1917	Plasterer	8-8-1945
75942	LONG, John	New Road, Kilworth, Fermoy, Cork.	15-8-1915	Farm Labourer	8-8-1945
E/411730	LONG, Timothy	1 Garvey's Range, Off Broad Street, Limerick.	22-2-1911	Labourer	8-8-1945
203611	LONG, William	21 Bengal Tce., Limerick.	11-4-1914	Builder's Labourer	8-8-1945
A/73411	LOUGHLIN, Josh.	Stratford-on-Slaney, Co. Wicklow.	18-12-1913	Labourer	8-8-1945
E/423749	LOUGHLIN, Patrick	Carlough, Drumshambo, Co. Leitrim.	15-6-1922	Labourer	8-8-1945
79789	LOUGHRAN, James	Dreamore, Dungannon, Co. Tyrone.	28-10-1921	Labourer	8-8-1945
E/437555	LOUGHRAN, Michael	Listamlet, Moy, Co. Tyrone.	29-11-1920	General Labourer	8-8-1945
E/409939	LOUGHRAN, Thomas	37 Annamond St., Belfast.	18-5-1925	Builder's Labourer	8-8-1945
81360	LOUGHREY, John J.	112 S.C.Rd., Kilmainham, Dublin.	31-8-1926	Student	13-4-1946
E/422293	LOUGHREY, Patrick	Drumhaggard, Burnfoot, Co. Donegal.	29-10-1908	Labourer	8-8-1945
E/421856	LOUGHREY, Patrick	Ballysheedy, Gort, Co. Galway.	13-3-1921	Drainsman	8-8-1945
78772	LOUTHE, William	Downstown, Duleek, Co. Meath.	5-12-1921	Farm Labourer	8-8-1945
E/430830	LOWE, Patrick	St. Patrick's Terrace, Clara, Offaly.	15-4-1922	Labourer	8-8-1945
E/404597	LOWE, Richard P.	Ballinascorney, Tallaght, Co. Dublin.	19-6-1911	Grocer and Publican	8-8-1945
211146	LOWERY, Thomas	99 Eden Villas, Glasthule, Co. Dublin.	8-6-1922	Laundry Messenger	8-8-1945
L/503306	LUBY, Brendan	73 Lr. Clanbrassil Street, Dublin.	8-9-1927	General Labourer	28-3-1946
E/413110	LUCEY, Denis	Model Village, Tower, St. Ann's Hill, Co. Cork.	23-8-1919	Factory Worker	8-8-1945
V/201598	LUCEY, James	Two Mile Bridge, Clonmel.	31-7-1917	Labourer	8-8-1945
V/213118	LUCEY, Patrick	Tanyard, Lackabawn, Millstreet, Co. Cork.	15-3-1920	Labourer	24-12-1945
82126	LUCEY, Victor	31 Roche's Buildings, Cork.	7-12-1921	Labourer	8-8-1945
E/404560	LUNDY, James G. O.	188 West Lane, Salford, Manchester.	18-4-1921	Shop Assistant	8-8-1945
84125	LUNNERY, Patrick	Scotstown, Ballyconnell, Co. Cavan.	7-4-1919	Farm Labourer	8-8-1945
A/84133	LUNNY, James	Drumilly, Derrylin, Co. Fermanagh.	4-4-1921	Farm Labourer	8-8-1945
E/420282	LYDON, Charles	Creagh Road, Ballinrobe, Co. Mayo.	10-6-1914	Labourer	8-8-1945
E/407621	LYDON, Ernest	25 Pembroke Street, Irishtown, Dublin.	31-3-1918	Skilled Labourer	8-8-1945
E/413748	LYDON, Peter	3 James' Street, Tralee.	19-7-1919	Clerk	8-8-1945
E/423207	LYNCH, Alexander	42 St. Colum's Wells, Derry.	9-10-1919	Labourer	8-8-1945
V/205745	LYNCH, Augustine	64 Mountjoy Sq., Dublin.	20-1-1922	Messenger	8-8-1945
E/423742	LYNCH, Bernard	Carrowkeel, Ballyforan, Co. Roscommon.	10-1-1922	Labourer	8-8-1945
77787	LYNCH, Christopher	Carrigaholt, Co. Clare.	25-5-1919	Labourer	8-8-1945
L/506897	LYNCH, Daniel	7 Cobh Street, Cork.	2-5-1926	Cook's Helper	8-8-1945

Army No.	Name.	Last Recorded Address.	Date of Birth.	Declared Occupation prior to enlistment in Defence Forces.	Date of Dismissal from Defence Forces.
E/403898	LYNCH, Henry	30 Post Office Street, Warrenpoint, Newry.	7-7-1916	Lorry Driver	8-8-1945
207294	LYNCH, Henry	17 St. Joseph's Terrace, Sligo.	16-3-1916	Builder's Labourer	8-8-1945
E/408529	LYNCH, Hugh P.	12 Holmdene Gardens, Belfast.	1-1-1924	Dock Labourer	8-8-1945
A/75057	LYNCH, James	6 Spenser Street, S.C.Rd., Dublin.	29-1-1917	Farm Labourer & Basket Maker	8-8-1945
A/82414	LYNCH, James	Southern Rd., Smithwick, Staffordshire.	15-1-1923	Student	8-8-1945
E/421647	LYNCH, James	Curray, Aclare, Co. Sligo.	21-9-1921	Labourer	8-8-1945
E/416915	LYNCH, James	3 Glover's Place, Carey's Road, Limerick.	1-7-1924	Grocer's Assistant	8-8-1945
A/69617	LYNCH, John	5 Irish Street, Drogheda.	25-10-1909	Fisherman	8-8-1945
83551	LYNCH, John	15 Eustace Street, Dublin.	16-5-1922	Messenger	8-8-1945
E/413129	LYNCH, John	c/o Mrs. Price, James St., Cork.	14-8-1909	Labourer	8-8-1945
77964	LYNCH, John	Drumsally, Cappamore, Co. Limerick.	21-5-1920	Labourer	8-8-1945
E/430649	LYNCH, John	31 North Cumberland Street, Dublin.	30-5-1920	Labourer	20-9-1945
204916	LYNCH, John	Ballyporeen, Douglas, Co. Co. Cork.	19-5-1910	Labourer	8-8-1945
V/204686	LYNCH, Joseph	21 Tarmon Cottages, Boyle, Co. Roscommon.	8-1-1920	General Labourer	8-8-1945
E/422184	LYNCH, Joseph	c/o Andy Carran, Grainin, Toulett, Co. Donegal.	10-5-1920	Labourer	8-8-1945
E/403649	LYNCH, Joseph	31 North Cumberland Street, Dublin.	30-5-1925	Labourer	20-9-1945
83802	LYNCH, Joseph	Newtownvillas, Kilbroney, Rostrevor, Co. Down.	27-4-1922	Labourer	8-8-1945
V/205327	LYNCH, Kevin	13R Pearse House, Dublin.	30-3-1921	Labourer	8-8-1945
E/194694	LYNCH, Luke	49 St. Attracta Road, Cabra, Dublin.	19-9-1906	Steel Erector	8-8-1945
75631	LYNCH, Martin	18 Greenway Road, Runcorn, Cheshire.	29-4-1919	Student	8-8-1945
L/507343	LYNCH, Matthew	28 Mungret St., Limerick.	20-2-1927	Labourer	8-8-1945
83260	LYNCH, Michael	165 Kildare Rd., Crumlin, Dublin.	18-9-1920	Labourer	8-8-1945
75649	LYNCH, Owen	Clonsilla, Lisduff, Kells.	10-8-1914	Farm Labourer	8-8-1945
A/75625	LYNCH, Patrick Desmond	Moneen, Castlebar.	25-2-1920	Messenger Boy	4-2-1946
78549	LYNCH, Patrick	c/o Mr. J. O'Sullivan, Emmet St., Birr, Offaly.	2-3-1921	Tailor	8-8-1945
L/503083	LYNCH, Patrick	57 St. Edward's Terrace, Sligo.	17-3-1928	Labourer	13-2-1946
201483	LYNCH, Patrick	6 New Street, Off Quay Street, Sligo.	3-8-1915	Motor Driver	8-8-1945
E/414780	LYNCH, Richard	Barry's Court, Carrigtwohill, Co. Cork.	7-10-1916	Motor Driver	8-8-1945
76674	LYNCH, Stephen	Liscarol, Feakle, Co. Clare.	26-12-1917	Labourer	8-8-1945
E/412903	LYNCH, Thomas	O'Shea's Garage, Newcastle West, Co. Limerick.	2-7-1913	Motor Mechanic	8-8-1945
E/436646	LYNCH, Thomas	28 'E' Block, Oliver Bond House, Bridgefoot Street, Dublin.	13-4-1924	General Labourer	6-12-1945
E/417723	LYNCH, William	22 Red Abbey Street, Cork.	31-12-1917	Lorry Driver	8-8-1945
E/434230	LYNCH, William	Piltown, Kinsalebeg, Youghal.	5-10-1922	Farm Labourer	8-8-1945
V/200122	LYNOTT, Patrick	57 St. Joseph's Terrace, Sligo.	20-3-1919	Labourer	8-8-1945
A/84202	LYNSKEY, Martin	Woodquay, Galway.	4-4-1918	Truck Driver	8-8-1945
V/215203	LYONS, Augustine	Main Street, Castlerea, Co. Roscommon.	12-5-1922	Labourer	8-8-1945
V/205721	LYONS, John	3 H Block, Corporation Buildings, Dublin.	2-11-1921	Messenger Boy	8-8-1945

Army No.	Name.	Last Recorded Address.	Date of Birth.	Declared Occupation prior to enlistment in Defence Forces.	Date of Dismissal from Defence Forces.
E/431407	LYONS, John	23 Esmonde Street, Gorey, Co. Wexford.	7-4-1922	Labourer	8-8-1945
E/416326	LYONS, John C.	62 Madden's Buildings, Cork.	14-12-1923	Messenger Boy	8-8-1945
A/75905	LYONS, Michael F.	14 Galtymore Drive, North Crumlin, Dublin.	24-7-1916	Motor Driver	11-8-1945
A/75166	LYONS, Patrick	7 Townsend Rd., Southall, Middlesex.	26-4-1916	Labourer	8-8-1945
E/420311	LYONS, Patrick	67 Sarsfield Sq., Athlone.	11-10-1919	Woollen Worker	8-8-1945
200980	LYONS, Patrick Joseph	11 Castle Barracks, Limerick.	4-7-1915	Porter (Tailor's Shop)	8-8-1945
E/424066	LYONS, Thomas	Terigg, Kilkelly, Co. Mayo.	21-11-1915	Labourer	8-8-1945
A/73196	LYONS, Thomas	14 Hill House, High Street, Limerick.	8-5-1914	Mechanic	8-8-1945
E/404886	LYTTLE, Frank	Drummons, Selloo, Scotstown, Co. Monaghan.	18-10-1922	Labourer	8-8-1945
V/210173	McALEAVEY, Peter	29 O'Hanlon's Park, Dundalk.	10-1-1920	Slater	8-8-1945
204831	McALEEMAN, Gerald	c/o M. Fagan, North Commons, Carlingford, Co. Louth.	25-6-1910	Labourer	8-8-1945
E/404108	McALERNON, Patrick	Tullydagan, Lurgan.	22-4-1920	Farm Labourer	8-8-1945
E/405187	McALINDEN, Hugh	14 Waring Street, Lurgan.	22-10-1918	Fowl Dealer	8-8-1945
E/434583	MacALINDEN, Patrick	Gurteen, Ballacolla, Leix.	6-1-1922	Barman	8-8-1945
E/424929	McALISTER, Joseph	Burnfoot, Co. Donegal.	15-1-1915	Labourer	8-8-1945
E/406237	McALEESE, Joseph	54 Grove Park, Dublin.	19-1-1914	Clerk	8-8-1945
E/422263	McALLEN, Martin	Killenena, Cahir, Feakle, Co. Clare.	28-3-1918	Mechanic and Motor Driver	8-8-1945
A/83901	McALLISTER, James	Altananum, Aughafatten, Co. Antrim.	28-3-1921	Farming	8-8-1945
E/438238	McALLISTER, William	9 St. James's Drive, Belfast.	30-9-1923	Fitter	8-8-1945
E/422079	McALYNN, Joseph	c/o O. McGoldrick, Crilly, Pettigo, Co. Donegal.	15-12-1905	Labourer	8-8-1945
A/76757	McANANEY, John	Sandymill, Ballindrait, Co. Donegal.	4-4-1910	Labourer	8-8-1945
209975	McANAW, Charles	Meengrove, Stranorlar, Co. Donegal.	1-3-1915	Clerk	8-8-1945
V/215199	McANDREW, Patrick	Glengad, Pullathomas, Ballina.	17-3-1917	Farmer	8-8-1945
E/422470	McANEE, George	c/o P. Kerrigan, Navaney Street, Ballybofey, Co. Donegal.	9-6-1917	Cinema Attendant	8-8-1945
78721	McARDLE, Hugh	Danenaire, Monaghan.	23-2-1921	Factory Worker	8-8-1945
210063	McARDLE, James	Woodhill, Dunleer, Co. Louth.	23-3-1913	Motor Driver	8-8-1945
E/422199	McARDLE, Malachy	c/o J. Murray, Main St., Castleblaney, Co. Monaghan.	5-11-1917	Labourer	8-8-1945
206179	McARDLE, Michael	c/o Mr. P. Carey, Park Street, Dundalk.	4-12-1916	Shoemaker	8-8-1945
E/403625	McARDLE, Patrick	44 Water Street, Newry.	4-7-1906	Labourer	8-8-1945
81293	McAREAVEY, Francis	21 Whiterock Dr., Belfast.	28-8-1926	Butcher	23-9-1945
E/405407	McAREAVEY, Harry	1 William St., Drogheda.	21-7-1920	Butcher	8-8-1945
E/423210	McATEER, Daniel	76 William Street, Derry.	15-12-1911	Barman	8-8-1945
E/408808	McATEER, Thomas	Ballycuby, Randalstown, Co. Antrim.	13-12-1922	Lorry Driver	8-8-1945
E/437524	McAULEY, Francis	32 Scotch Street, Belfast.	11-10-1924	Painter's Apprentice	8-8-1945
79791	McAULEY, James	12 Campbell's Tce., Belfast.	18-4-1918	Labourer	8-8-1945
E/409972	McAULEY, Robert	12 Lady Street, Belfast.	22-1-1924	Apprentice Turner	8-8-1945
82169	McAULIFFE, William	1 House 5B Collins Bks., Cork.	12-6-1922	School Boy	8-8-1945

Army No.	Name.	Last Recorded Address.	Date of Birth.	Declared Occupation prior to enlistment in Defence Forces.	Date of Dismissal from Defence Forces.
A/77653	McBREARTY, Francis	Classeygowan, St. Johnstown, Co. Donegal.	29-8-1920	Labourer	8-8-1945
E/420378	McBRIDE, Hugh	Lanagarveagh, Downings, Co. Donegal.	18-6-1921	Apprentice Tailor	8-8-1945
E/421874	McBRIDE, John	Middletown, Derrybeg, Lifford.	6-11-1921	Labourer	8-8-1945
F./406484	McBRIDE, Patrick L.	Glenmacoffer, Gortin, Co. Tyrone.	11-3-1920	Farm Labourer	8-8-1945
E/406408	McBRIDE, Thomas B.	Perry Street, Dungannon, Co. Tyrone.	6-1-1922	Shoe Machinist	8-8-1945
F./406548	McBRYAN, Arthur	33 Dartmouth Road, Ranelagh, Dublin.	21-4-1923	Cook	8-8-1945
E/437505	McBURNEY, Gerard	56 Durham Street, Belfast.	23-6-1925	Apprentice Cloth Cutter	8-8-1945
A/72262	McCABE, Alistair	23 Grosvenor Square, Rathmines, Dublin.	21-12-1919	None	8-8-1945
E/437507	McCABE, Alexander	26 Grosvenor Pce., Belfast.	4-9-1924	General Labourer	8-8-1945
E/400730	McCABE, James	Glasslough St., Monaghan.	17-8-1911	Labourer	8-8-1945
E/401695	McCABE, James	404 Mourne Rd., Crumlin, Dublin.	13-4-1921	Labourer	8-8-1945
A/76945	McCABE, John	Walshestown, Bally-murphy, Co. Carlow.	10-7-1918	Labourer	8-8-1945
A/76277	McCABE, Laurence	9 Brabazon Row, The Coombe, Dublin.	27-1-1917	Labourer	8-8-1945
V/204288	McCABE, Michael	90 Pembroke Cottages, Donnybrook, Dublin.	10-7-1910	Labourer, Garage Work	8-8-1945
V/205625	McCABE, Thomas	2 Mount Sion Road, Cork.	5-10-1921	Messenger Boy	8-8-1945
E/423958	McCAFFREY, Philip	Castle Balfour, Lisnakea, Co. Fermanagh.	11-11-1922	Farm Labourer	22-8-1945
200127	McCAFFERTY, Edward	Brew, Drumkeen, Co. Donegal.	23-9-1920	Motor Driver	8-8-1945
E/425088	McCAFFERTY, Patrick	Middlebrook, Pettigo, Co. Donegal.	25-11-1921	Labourer (Mechanic)	8-8-1945
E/432729	McCAFFERTY, William	2 Church Street, Cootehill, Co. Cavan.	20-8-1908	French Polisher	8-8-1945
E/423610	McCAFFREY, Brian	Gowlan, Blacklion, Co. Cavan.	19-1-1918	Labourer	8-8-1945
E/422036	McCAFFREY, Charles	O'Neill's Park, Clones.	11-6-1907	Groom	8-8-1945
V/206592	McCAFFREY, Christopher	14 Dixon Place, Limerick.	5-8-1920	Electrical Student	8-8-1945
E/422037	McCAFFREY, Conor	The Diamond, Belturbet, Co. Cavan.	6-10-1920	Labourer	8-8-1945
E/403752	McCAFFREY, Desmond	104 Kickham Road, Inchicore, Dublin.	25-8-1922	Upholsterer	8-8-1945
E/424356	McCAFFREY, Patrick	Stratone, Derrygonnelly, Enniskillen.	20-8-1921	Farmer	8-8-1945
E/422039	McCAFFREY, Thomas	The Diamond, Belturbet, Co. Cavan.	17-3-1920	Labourer	8-8-1945
E/423279	McCALLIAN, Daniel	8 Creggan, Terrace, Derry.	6-4-1919	Labourer	8-8-1945
E/418026	McCALLIAN, Desmond	Branch Rd., Ballyna-groarty, Co. Derry.	2-4-1926	Apprentice Foundry Moulder	8-8-1945
E/423211	McCALLION, James	5 Cross Street, Rosemount, Derry.	28-6-1921	Labourer	8-8-1945
E/424690	McCALLION, Patrick	Kildrum, Carrigans, Co. Donegal.	12-5-1923	Labourer	8-8-1945
E/422471	McCALLION, Patrick	c/o R. Mulholland, Glenfin Street, Ballybofey, Co. Donegal.	18-7-1922	Labourer	8-8-1945
83838	McCALLUM, James	35 Elmfield Street, Belfast.	26-8-1915	Farmer	8-8-1945
E/421679	McCANN, Denis	Allendara, Woodford, Co. Galway.	8-3-1922	Farm Labourer	8-8-1945
73133	McCANN, Henry	72 Church Street, Cookstown, Co. Tyrone.	25-7-1911	Motor Mechanic	8-8-1945

Army No.	Name.	Last Recorded Address.	Date of Birth.	Declared Occupation prior to enlistment in Defence Forces.	Date of Dismissal from Defence Forces.
E/409555	McCANN, John	34 Lady Street, Belfast.	9-8-1923	Mill Worker	8-8-1945
E/406247	McCANN, Laurence	65 Lucan Street, Falls Road, Belfast.	14-3-1901	Motor Driver	8-8-1945
E/407351	McCANN, Michael	2 James's Terrace, James's Street, Dublin.	23-7-1920	Window Cleaner	8-8-1945
E/437693	McCANN, Patrick E.	71 Albert Street, Belfast.	5-9-1925	Labourer	8-8-1945
E/407452	McCANN, Patrick	Dun Muire, Sutton, Co. Dublin.	13-1-1921	Barman	8-8-1945
V/205739	McCANN, Patrick	9 Charlemont St., Dublin.	14-3-1919	Porter	8-8-1945
E/432384	McCANN, Peter	14 North Portland Row, Dublin.	1-7-1921	Butcher	8-8-1945
E/422040	McCARNEY, Terence	Fermanagh Street, Clones.	2-8-1921	Labourer	8-8-1945
E/404713	McCARROLL, Frank	Seaview House, Wicklow.	29-6-1922	Student	8-8-1945
E/432439	McCARROLL, Michael	Carga, Clogher, Co. Tyrone	24-1-1910	Insurance Agent	8-8-1945
E/437519	McCARRON, David	38 Peel Street, Belfast.	16-4-1925	Slater's Helper	8-8-1945
A/84126	McCARRON, Philip	c/o Mr. J. Blake, Slieve Russell, Ballyconnell, Co. Cavan.	13-11-1919	Farm Labourer	8-8-1945
A/84120	McCARRY, Stephen	Tullinmoil, Dowra, Co. Cavan.	25-12-1918	Labourer	8-8-1945
E/413481	McCARTHY, Alfred	44 Evergreen Street, Cork.	23-7-1902	Mill Worker	8-8-1945
79777	McCARTHY, Denis	Cooleagh, Ballynure, Thurles	13-6-1919	Farm Labourer	8-8-1945
E/411826	McCARTHY, James	Waggoon, Tulla, Co. Clare.	17-6-1921	Student	8-8-1945
E/410595	McCARTHY, Jeremiah	34 Henry Street, Kenmare, Co. Kerry.	21-5-1919	Solicitor's Clerk	8-8-1945
V/213199	McCARTHY, Jeremiah	Fawnmore, Kilcrohane, Bantry, Co. Cork.	24-7-1921	Farmer	8-8-1945
79417	McCARTHY, John	31 Cathedral Walk, Cork.	24-5-1921	Messenger	8-8-1945
V/209636	McCARTHY, John	Greenville, Listowel, Co. Kerry.	5-7-1922	Farm Labourer	8-8-1945
E/414347	McCARTHY, John C.	Croghtamore Gardens, Pouladuff Road, Cork.	3-12-1921	Barman	8-8-1945
E/415235	McCARTHY, John	66 Friars Road, Turner's Cross, Cork.	17-10-1922	Machinist	8-8-1945
V/203898	McCARTHY, John	11 Hill Grove Lane, Cork.	12-2-1922	Messenger Boy	8-8-1945
E/434761	McCARTHY, John	7 Spring Garden Passage, North Strand, Dublin.	24-4-1922	Labourer	8-8-1945
V/204919	McCARTHY, Joseph	20 Step Lane, Shandon Road, Cork.	27-10-1919	Labourer	8-8-1945
E/410274	McCARTHY, Maurice	Camp, Castleisland, Co. Kerry.	18-1-1922	Farmer	8-8-1945
A/74024	McCARTHY, Michael	81 Eversley Avenue, Bernehurst, Kent.	19-6-1914	Labourer	8-8-1945
E/433336	McCARTHY, Michael	15 George's Place, Dublin.	16-7-1918	None	8-8-1945
V/202968	McCARTHY, Michael	43 St. Michael's Avenue, Tipperary.	4-2-1914	Labourer	8-8-1945
E/415721	McCARTHY, Michael	7 Church Avenue, Cork.	2-4-1923	Labourer	8-8-1945
E/411452	McCARTHY, Patrick	3 O'Mara's Cottages, Tipperary.	7-8-1908	Labourer	8-8-1945
82016	McCARTHY, Patrick	Kilbrogan Hill, Bandon, Co. Cork.	1-8-1914	Farm Labourer	8-8-1945
L/502311	McCARTHY, Patrick	19 Iveagh Trust Buildings, Dublin.	9-1-1925	Factory Hand	8-8-1945
A/78236	McCARTHY, Sean	Union Buildings, Boyle.	28-2-1921	Labourer	8-8-1945
E/404596	McCARTHY, Thomas	22 North Circular Road, Dublin.	29-6-1902	Self Employed	8-8-1945
E/400796	McCARTHY, William	20 East Road, Dublin.	15-8-1921	Farm Labourer	8-8-1945
A/79598	McCARTHY, William	77 Gurranebraher Avenue, Cork.	17-2-1921	Boot Maker	8-8-1945
E/422298	McCARTNEY, George	5 Foster's Terrace, Moville, Co. Donegal.	8-3-1920	Labourer	8-8-1945
E/424020	McCAUL, Bernard	23 Fermanagh St., Clones.	3-7-1917	Motor Driver	8-8-1945
L/500627	McCAUL, Bernard	2 Hogan's Place, Dublin.	28-1-1921	Capstan Operator	8-8-1945

Army No.	Name.	Last Recorded Address.	Date of Birth.	Declared Occupation prior to enlistment in Defence Forces.	Date of Dismissal from Defence Forces.
E/403968	McCAUL, Nicholas	32 St. Clare's Av., Newry.	31-10-1921	Shop-boy	8-8-1945
E/433339	McCAUL, Patrick	14 Belmont Park, Donnybrook, Dublin.	14-7-1912	Carpenter	8-8-1945
E/422914	McCAWLEY, James	c/o J. Devlin, Bridge End P.O., Co. Donegal. .	5-4-1922	Clerk	8-8-1945
E/422514	McCAULEY, James	c/o Cyril McGrisken, Kilty-clogher, Co. Leitrim.	29-10-1920	Blacksmith	8-8-1945
V/203081	McCAULEY, William	Bredagh, Glin, Moville, Co. Donegal.	19-10-1914	Joiner Apprentice	8-8-1945
E/422880	McCAULEY, William	Tooban, Burnfoot, Co. Donegal.	27-8-1922	Messenger Boy	8-8-1945
83854	McCLELLAND, Edward	40 St. Nicholas Avenue, Dundalk.	10-6-1917	Gardener	8-8-1945
E/404213	McCLELLAND, James E.	8 St. Patrick's Avenue, Newry.	10-10-1921	Builder	8-8-1945
E/423212	McCLEMENTS, William	13 Osborne, Street, Rosemount, Derry.	4-11-1921	Labourer	8-8-1945
E/421747	McCLOSKEY, Frank	c/o John Devlin, Bridgend, Co. Donegal.	25-12-1921	Labourer	8-8-1945
L/502080	McCLUSKEY, George	5 Liberty House, Railway Street, Dublin.	23-8-1929	Labourer	8-8-1945
E/405575	McCLUSKEY, James	Derrynshesco, Knockatallon, Monaghan.	17-6-1916	Labourer	8-8-1945
E/409916	McCLUSKEY, Joseph	10 State Street, Belfast.	5-2-1925	Painter's Apprentice	8-8-1945
E/423959	McCOLE, Daniel	Carrowhugh, Moville, Co. Donegal.	6-4-1914	Plasterer	8-8-1945
84144	McCOLGAN, Hugh	Ballindrait, Lifford.	27-4-1919	Motor Mechanic	8-8-1945
E/425128	McCOLGAN, John	29 Longtower, St., Derry.	24-4-1924	Messenger Boy	8-8-1945
E/421982	McCOLGAN, Patrick	Gurtnagrace, Castlefin, Co. Donegal.	16-10-1913	Farm Labourer	8-9-1945
E/404727	McCONNELL, Brian	36 Galtymore Road, Crumlin, Dublin.	25-3-1918	Motor Driver	8-8-1945
E/423653	McCONNELL, Hugh	Furnaceland, Swanlinbar, Co. Cavan.	15-11-1913	Motor Driver and Mechanic	8-8-1945
E/400118	McCONNELL, Patrick	Larkfield Farm, Clondalkin, Co. Dublin.	15-7-1913	None	8-8-1945
E/422472	McCOOL, Albert	c/o J. McGarrigle, Coney Barrow Road, Lifford.	26-7-1922	Cycle Mechanic	8-8-1945
A/79050	McCOOL, Alexander	16 Moore Street, Derry.	2-4-1921	Labourer	8-8-1945
206288	McCOOL, Barry	Garsheey, Bogan, Co. Donegal.	4-12-1919	Labourer	8-8-1945
E/423282	McCOOL, David	23 Creggan Street, Derry.	17-3-1921	Lorry Driver	8-8-1945
V/207188	McCOOL, Eugene	13 Hamilton Street, Derry.	18-4-1917	Labourer	8-8-1945
E/425412	McCOOL, John	15 Elmwood Street, Derry.	6-4-1925	Barman	8-8-1945
E/420997	McCOOL, William	Bridgend, Co. Donegal.	2-9-1910	Lorry Driver	8-8-1945
E/423369	McCORMACK, Brien	Drumasooey, Riverstown, Co. Sligo.	12-8-1913	Farmer	8-8-1945
E/422747	McCORMACK, Edward	5 St. Patrick's Tce., Cavan.	13-7-1914	Egg Packer	8-8-1945
E/402147	McCORMACK, John	38 Waterford St., Dublin.	1-1-1915	News Vendor	8-8-1945
80779	McCORMACK, Joseph	Ballyquarry, Kilkenny.	28-5-1918	Carter	8-8-1945
83042	McCORMACK, Patrick	8 Windsor Terrace, Portobello, Dublin.	17-9-1912	Labourer	8-8-1945
83147	McCORMACK, Patrick	14 Stafford Street, Dublin.	26-2-1922	Labourer	8-8-1945
80345	McCORMACK, Samuel	Argrey, Ballindrait, Co. Donegal.	1-11-1921	Farm Labourer	8-8-1945
E/408123	McCORMACK, Stephen	Coragh, Loughgall, Co. Armagh.	22-9-1921	Labourer	8-8-1945
E/400395	McCORMACK, Thomas	5 Kiltalown, Jobstown, Co. Dublin.	30-6-1911	Wireless Operator	8-8-1945
A/83166	McCORMACK, Thomas	1 Hanbury Lane, Meath Street, Dublin.	3-6-1922	Messenger	8-8-1945
E/437853	McCORRY, Brendan	Bannfort, Lurgan.	6-5-1925	Farmer	8-8-1945
E/405441	McCORRY, William	59 Upper Coombe, Dublin.	12-1-1917	Photographer	8-8-1945

Army No.	Name.	Last Recorded Address.	Date of Birth.	Declared Occupation prior to enlistment in Defence Forces.	Date of Dismissal from Defence Forces.
E/437520	McCOTTER, Patrick	36 Irwin Street, Belfast.	20-1-1925	General Labourer	8-8-1945
E/437404	McCOURT, James	40 Institution Place, Belfast.	2-12-1924	General Labourer	8-8-1945
E/422882	McCOURT, Jeremiah	Burnfoot Village, Co. Donegal.	22-10-1915	Labourer	8-8-1945
E/423283	McCOURT, John	97 Lecky Road, Derry.	29-10-1917	Polisher	8-8-1945
E/422203	McCOURT, John	Elaghbeg, Burnfoot, Co. Donegal.	12-9-1912	Labourer	8-8-1945
E/409598	McCOY, Daniel	8 Majorca Street, Belfast.	25-9-1923	Machinist	8-8-1945
E/408253	McCOY, Frederick	123 South Circular Road, Dolphin's Barn, Dublin.	11-2-1922	Solicitor's Clerk	8-8-1945
78412	McCOY, John	30 Springfield, Mullingar.	27-3-1920	Cook's Assistant	8-8-1945
E/403995	McCOY, William	Roseville, Douglas Road, Cork.	4-4-1909	Production Supervisor	8-8-1945
E/408700	McCREADY, Thomas	31 Fort Street, Belfast.	15-12-1923	Labourer	8-8-1945
E/409520	McCRORY, Francis	15 Upr. Mount St., Dublin.	16-2-1923	General Labourer	8-8-1945
V/210249	McCROSSAN, Laurence	Porthall, Lifford, Co. Donegal.	20-5-1921	Farm Labourer	8-8-1945
E/424920	McCROSSAN, Liam	Townpark, Raphoe, Co. Donegal.	18-2-1923	Farm Labourer	8-8-1945
E/421983	McCROSSAN, Patrick	Carrigans, Co. Donegal.	26-4-1918	Plasterer	8-8-1945
E/423284	McCROSSIN, Joseph	Main Street, Irvinestown, Co. Fermanagh.	6-9-1922	Labourer	8-8-1945
A/740251	McCRYSTAL, R.	Moate, Co. Westmeath.	4-4-1915	Packer	8-8-1945
E/425167	McCULLAGH, Alfred	c/o J. Boles, The Curragh, Letterkenny.	14-10-1909	Motor Mechanic	8-8-1945
E/420529	McCULLAGH, Edward	4 St. John's Terrace, Sligo.	7-7-1904	Labourer	8-8-1945
E/404764	McCULLAGH, Patrick	106 Marlborough Street, Dublin.	11-4-1906	Motor Driver	8-8-1945
E/436643	McCULLAGH, Peter J.	108 Belham Street, Belfast.	3-1-1926	Student	1-10-1945
E/437931	McCULLAGH, Richard	2 Kilwood Street, Belfast.	19-7-1925	Apprentice to Aircraft Fitter	8-8-1945
E/422042	McCULLION, Gerald	Willowbrook House, Ballyshannon, Co. Donegal.	3-12-1920	Farm Labourer	8-8-1945
B/3370	McCULLOUGH, James	37 Upper Gardiner Street, Dublin.	28-2-1909	Labourer	8-8-1945
A/84056	McCUSKER, John	Lr. McCurtin St., Clones.	27-7-1918	Barman	8-8-1945
E/422043	McCUSKER, Vincent	McCurtin Street, Clones.	21-1-1918	Quarry Labourer	8-8-1945
E/421524	McDAID, Arthur	The Cottages, Lifford.	18-9-1921	Apprentice Barber	8-8-1945
A/84140	McDAID, Charles	Urrisnanagh, Clonmany, Co. Donegal.	17-4-1918	Labourer	8-8-1945
E/424921	McDAID, James	Beltony, Raphoe, Co. Donegal.	15-10-1918	Farm Labourer	8-8-1945
209127	McDAID, James	Killogs, Inver, Co. Donegal.	11-7-1921	Labourer	8-8-1945
E/422345	McDAID, John	Druminin, Brunagh, New Mills, Letterkenny.	10-6-1921	Labourer	8-8-1945
79770	McDAID, Patrick	76 Foxes Corner, Derry.	4-11-1920	Butcher	8-8-1945
79495	McDERMOTT, James	261 Simonside Terrace, Heaton, Newcastle-on-Tyne.	30-12-1920	Carpenter	8-8-1945
V/201467	McDERMOTT, John	13 St. Anne's Tce., Sligo.	1-5-1914	Labourer	8-8-1945
77517	McDERMOTT, John	Ballinarvey, Granard.	11-7-1920	Labourer	8-8-1945
E/414696	McDERMOTT, John	c/o Patrick Heffernan, Muregasty Cottages, Tipperary.	15-6-1910	Mechanic	8-8-1945
A/73160	McDERMOTT, John	Ballynoe, Co. Galway.	8-5-1910	Storeman	8-8-1945
E/423997	McDERMOTT, John	Pollymount, Scramogue, Co. Roscommon.	4-7-1922	Farm Labourer	8-8-1945
E/404989	McDERMOTT, Maurice	10A Cuffe Street, Dublin.	9-1-1919	Motor Driver	8-8-1945
E/421001	McDERMOTT, Patrick	Crossconnell, Co. Donegal.	25-3-1920	Farmer	8-8-1945

Army No.	Name.	Last Recorded Address.	Date of Birth.	Declared Occupation prior to enlistment in Defence Forces.	Date of Dismissal from Defence Forces.
E/401952	McDONAGH, Francis	37A Corporation Buildings, Foley Street, Dublin.	21-8-1921	Bootmaker	8-8-1945
79866	McDONAGH, James	13 St. Mel's Terrace, Athlone.	20-1-1921	Labourer	8-8-1945
E/423285	McDONAGH, James	Bridge Street, Irvinestown, Co. Fermanagh.	27-4-1921	Labourer	8-8-1945
E/424319	McDONAGH, James	Cloonagh, Cloughboley P.O., Co. Sligo.	11-6-1922	Tinsmith	8-8-1945
E/429634	McDONAGH, John	Indreabhain, Co. Galway.	7-1-1919	Farm Labourer	8-8-1945
E/423998	McDONAGH, John	9 St. Anne's Tce., Athlone.	1-6-1920	Tinsmith	8-8-1945
E/433340	McDONAGH, Laurence	4 Echlin Street, off James's Street, Dublin.	29-4-1920	Acetylene Burner	8-8-1945
E/429561	McDONAGH, Michael	Letterkeane, Maam Cross, Co. Galway.	11-2-1907	Motor Driver	8-8-1945
E/424745	McDONAGH, Patrick	West Rock, Ballyshannon, Co. Donegal.	1-3-1921	Labourer	8-8-1945
A/84804	McDONAGH, Patrick	Doirindarae Tir na Fiadh, Lettermore, Co. Galway.	14-2-1921	Farm Labourer	8-8-1945
L/502106	McDONAGH, Patrick	Fair Hill, Dundalk.	15-8-1923	Tinsmith	8-8-1945
L/506994	McDONAGH, Patrick	Church Rd., Borrisokane, Co. Tipperary.	4-7-1923	Labourer	8-8-1945
E/424047	McDONAGH, Patrick	Cloonagh, Cloughboley, Co. Sligo.	6-11-1920	Tinsmith	8-8-1945
206866	McDONAGH, Patrick	4 Upper Dominick Street, Dublin.	3-6-1922	Messenger Boy	8-8-1945
E/423311	McDONAGH, Sargent	Bohermore, Galway.	5-11-1920	Labourer	8-8-1945
E/438279	McDONAGH, William	Ballyvary, Foxford, Co. Mayo.	11-6-1926	General Labourer	9-8-1945
V/215237	McDONALD, Alexander	Porthall, Lifford.	1-1-1919	Labourer	8-8-1945
79921	McDONALD, Benjamin	26 Upr. Dorset St., Dublin.	4-5-1920	Farm Labourer	8-8-1945
V/207770	McDONALD, Colm	Green Gardens, Fair Hill, Galway.	28-3-1921	Messenger Boy	8-8-1945
A/77822	McDONALD, Edward	Ballygarran, Gusserane, Co. Wexford.	25-3-1918	Farm Labourer	8-8-1945
A/83555	McDONALD, Joseph	119 St. Mary's Rd., Church Road, Dublin.	3-8-1921	Bootmaker	14-8-1945
V/206562	McDONALD, Joseph	3 Kelly's Row, Dorset St., Dublin.	25-10-1919	Cobbler	8-8-1945
69275	McDONALD, Joseph	33 Hardwick St., Dublin.	9-4-1908	Grocer's Porter	8-8-1945
A/76817	McDONALD, Joseph F.	46 O'Donnell's Gds., Glasthule, Dun Laoghaire.	28-9-1919	Motor Mechanic	8-8-1945
E/423110	McDONALD, Kevin	46 O'Donnell Gardens, Sandycove, Co. Dublin.	6-6-1922	Gardener	8-8-1945
E/402082	McDONALD, Matthew	4 Thomas Court, Thomas Street, Dublin.	16-11-1921	Messenger	8-8-1945
209141	McDONALD, Michael	Rosehouse, Borris, Co. Carlow.	12-5-1921	Labourer	8-8-1945
V/215174	McDONALD, Patrick	Porthall, Lifford.	13-3-1915	Gen. Labourer	8-8-1945
E/421750	McDONALD, Patrick	c/o Bridgend P.O., Co. Donegal.	23-2-1921	Labourer	8-8-1945
E/424661	McDONNELL, Bernard	Clover Terrace, Ballaghaderreen, Co. Roscommon.	12-12-1922	Farm Labourer	8-8-1945
E/401232	McDONNELL, Denis	133 Rialto Cotts., Dublin.	18-9-1902	Motor Driver	8-8-1945
E/400139	McDONNELL, George	22 Lower Dominick Street, Dublin.	8-7-1911	Tailor's Presser	8-8-1945
A/80697	McDONNELL, James	268 Maynooth Road, Celbridge, Co. Kildare.	23-3-1923	Lorry Driver	8-8-1945
A/74167	McDONNELL, James	11 Whitehorse Hill, Chatham, Kent.	1-4-1916	Electrical Engineer	8-8-1945
V/209114	McDONNELL, Jeremiah	Ballinluska, Crosshaven, Co. Cork.	24-5-1922	Farm Labourer	8-8-1945
E/414968	McDONNELL, Patrick	6 Walsh's Lane, Edward Street, Limerick.	22-7-1918	Messenger Boy	8-8-1945
E/402262	McDONNELL, Philip	65D Corporation Place, Dublin.	30-4-1921	Labourer	8-8-1945

Army No.	Name.	Last Recorded Address.	Date of Birth.	Declared Occupation prior to enlistment in Defence Forces.	Date of Dismissal from Defence Forces.
E/409854	McDONNELL, Randal	Kilmore, Glenaraffe, Co. Antrim.	11-12-1921	Veterinary Student	8-8-1945
E/400795	McDONNELL, Terence	3 Dowling's Court, Townsend Street, Dublin.	21-5-1916	Labourer	8-8-1945
E/407248	McDOWELL, James	21 Little Denmark Street, Dublin.	7-6-1913	Motor Driver	8-8-1945
215037	McDOWELL, William	c/o J. Robinson, Inch Island, Buncrana, Co. Donegal.	5-12-1915	Shoemaker	8-8-1945
E/425423	McELENEY, Edward	Tullagh, Glenmooney, Co. Donegal.	18-12-1916	Labourer and Fisherman	8-8-1945
E/423871	McELHINNEY, Michael	Muff, Co. Donegal.	16-4-1917	Lorry Driver	8-8-1945
E/420919	McELHINNEY, Thomas	Dromore, Raphoe, Co. Donegal.	7-5-1900	Labourer	8-8-1945
77149	McELLIGOTT, John	Bridge Street, Listowel.	15-1-1920	Student	8-8-1945
80711	McELROY, Brendan	63 Brian Avenue, Marino, Dublin.	21-1-1921	Apprentice (Armature Winding)	8-8-1945
210113	McELROY, James	26 Cannyburrow Road, Lifford.	16-10-1921	Farm Labourer	8-8-1945
E/405576	McELROY, Thomas	87 Thomas Street, Dublin.	29-4-1913	Boot Repairer	8-8-1945
A/72737	McENEANEY, Gerard	Gurteen, Innsheen, Co. Monaghan.	6-8-1913	Mill Hand	8-8-1945
E/400490	McEVATT, Matthew	19 Upper Sean McDermott Street, Dublin.	15-8-1920	Bootmaker	8-8-1945
E/435258	McEVOY, Edward	Rossligham, Portlaoighise, Leix.	25-7-1923	Labourer	8-8-1945
V/207384	McEVOY, Michael	154 Caledon Road, Dublin.	27-3-1922	Farm Labourer	8-8-1945
80078	McEVOY, Patrick	101 St. Attracta Road, Dublin.	21-8-1914	Motor Driver	8-8-1945
E/432528	McEVOY, Thomas	48A Patrick Street, Dublin.	2-8-1921	Labourer	8-8-1945
A/79414	McEVOY, Vincent	Ballynagreehan, Co. Down.	1-1-1919	Farm Labourer	8-8-1945
E/406446	McEVOY, William	54 Donnellan Avenue, Mount Brown, Dublin.	9-3-1919	Electrician's Improver	8-8-1945
V/206294	McFADDEN, Bernard	Dunmore, Carrigans, Co. Donegal.	1-11-1920	Labourer	8-8-1945
E/421488	McFADDEN, Charles	Carrigart, Co. Donegal.	7-10-1919	Student	8-8-1945
79053	McFADDEN, Daniel	14 Moore Street, Derry.	8-6-1919	Labourer	8-8-1945
209940	McFADDEN, Michael	Derryreeh, Falcarragh, Co. Donegal.	22-11-1918	Labourer	8-8-1945
E/438044	McFARLAND, James	192 Beake Avenue, Radford, Coventry.	13-4-1926	Labourer	11-10-1945
E/421841	McFARLAND, Joseph	c/o P. O'Doherty, Bridge Street, Carndonagh, Co. Donegal.	2-12-1918	Fowl Plucker	8-8-1945
E/422044	McGAHAN, George	Main Street, Ballyconnell, Co. Cavan.	5-3-1922	Gen. Labourer	8-8-1945
E/407528	McGAHAN, Hugh	Ballsmill, Silverbridge, Co. Armagh.	22-12-1918	Farm Labourer	8-8-1945
L/502950	McGANN, Joseph	144 Annamoe Dr., Dublin.	4-10-1927	Painter's Helper	8-8-1945
E/436034	McGARR, John	Jigginstown, Caragh Road, Naas.	12-9-1921	Farm Labourer	28-11-1945
E/425191	McGARRIGLE, Celestine	5 Bowling Green, Strabane, Co. Tyrone.	22-4-1922	Baker	8-8-1945
E/422347	McGARRIGLE, Patrick	c/o Mrs. Deeney, Burnfoot, Co. Donegal.	31-3-1915	Cook	8-8-1945
E/422474	McGARRIGLE, Thomas	Coneyborough Rd., Lifford.	11-2-1917	Joiner	8-8-1945
E/421985	McGARRITY, Joseph	Beragh, Co. Tyrone.	12-5-1918	Motor Driver	8-8-1945
E/421131	McGARRY, Edward	13 Mount Bulbin Terrace, Sligo.	10-2-1916	Labourer	8-8-1945
E/423462	McGARRY, Francis	2 Hyde Terrace, Mohill, Co. Leitrim.	5-10-1915	Motor Driver	8-8-1945
E/430680	McGARRY, Michael	12 High Street, Birr.	18-7-1911	Labourer	8-8-1945
75112	McGARRY, Patrick	Moorpark Street, Birr.	14-9-1915	Bottler	8-8-1945

Army No.	Name.	Last Recorded Address.	Date of Birth.	Declared Occupation prior to enlistment in Defence Forces.	Date of Dismissal from Defence Forces.
E/400361	McGARVEY, Patrick	Iveagh House, Bride Street, Dublin.	17-1-1914	Labourer	8-8-1945
208897	McGAUGHEY, Michael	Meeting House, Raphoe, Co. Donegal.	23-4-1921	Labourer	8-8-1945
A/84368	McGEE, Dominick	6 Kingston Terrace, Carrick-on-Shannon.	2-7-1924	Farm Labourer	8-8-1945
E/423287	McGEE, Henry	123 Bogside, Derry.	30-10-1921	Motor Driver	8-8-1945
E/421987	McGEE, John	Fern, Castlefin, Co. Donegal.	18-12-1912	Motor Driver and Painter	8-8-1945
E/424443	McGEE, William	Attymachugh, Foxford, Co. Mayo.	8-6-1915	Farm Labourer	8-8-1945
A/71118	McGEE, William	Water Street, Longford.	31-12-1911	Labourer	8-8-1945
E/422884	McGEEHAN, Anthony	Mill Brae, Buncrana, Co. Donegal.	15-1-1920	Draper	8-8-1945
E/423676	McGEEHAN, Hugh	Glenkeeragh, Newmills P.O., Co. Donegal.	9-11-1919	Labourer	8-8-1945
E/404802	McGEOWN, Edward	18 Clareville, Rd., Dublin.	29-9-1922	None	8-8-1945
E/408983	McGEOWN, John	Shankill Street, Lurgan.	14-2-1924	Barman	8-8-1945
E/421529	McGERIGAL, Bernard	c/o P.O., Newtowncunningham, Co. Donegal.	3-3-1918	Labourer	8-8-1945
V/209207	McGILL, Bernard	Scadaman, Ardara, Co. Donegal.	9-6-1918	Farmer	8-8-1945
V/209206	McGILL, John	Scadaman, Ardara, Co. Donegal.	20-5-1918	Farmer	8-8-1945
V/205358	McGILLIVANEY, Hugh	6 Coleraine Street, Dublin.	2-3-1920	Labourer	8-8-1945
E/416546	McGILLYCUDDY, Denis	Coolroe, Killorglin, Co. Kerry.	27-1-1924	Student	8-8-1945
E/420591	McGINLEY, Alexander	Woodside, Carndonagh, Co. Donegal.	15-7-1905	Tinsmith	8-8-1945
E/420384	McGINLEY, Alexander	Clarkellymore, Kilmacrenan, Lifford.	12-10-1917	Tinsmith	8-8-1945
E/422775	McGINLEY, Brian	Meenamore, East, Fintown, Co. Donegal.	19-11-1915	Labourer	8-8-1945
208896	McGINLEY, Dennis	Meeting House Street, Raphoe, Co. Donegal.	1-4-1917	Tinsmith	8-8-1945
84281	McGINLEY, James	Drumbury, Lifford.	21-9-1921	Labourer	8-8-1945
E/425151	McGINLEY, John	Towneylea P.O., Drumkeerin, Co. Leitrim.	4-6-1921	Labourer	8-8-1945
E/423214	McGINLEY, John	77 Irish Street, Waterside, Derry.	7-6-1922	Labourer	8-8-1945
209919	McGINLEY, Patrick	Church Street, Raphoe, Co. Donegal.	18-8-1916	Labourer	8-8-1945
E/425296	McGINLEY, Simon	Cleenagh, Ballymangan, Buncrana, Co. Donegal.	15-4-1924	Farm Labourer	8-8-1945
E/421861	McGINLEY, Simon	Woodside, Carndonagh, Co. Donegal.	3-1-1903	Labourer	8-8-1945
E/422083	McGINN, Bernard	Crilly, Pettigo, Co. Donegal.	25-2-1919	Farmer	8-8-1945
E/420785	McGINTY, Joseph	Townagorm, Barnesmore, Co. Donegal.	26-9-1911	Motor Mechanic	8-8-1945
V/200814	McGINTY, Joseph	Asylum Rd., Letterkenny.	5-11-1919	Labourer	8-8-1945
E/420201	McGINTY, Patrick	Glenamguin, Knockbock, Letterkenny.	9-12-1918	Labourer	8-8-1945
V/206272	McGINTY, Patrick	Camamuggagh, Letterkenny.	24-8-1921	Labourer	8-8-1945
E/404239	McGINTY, Peter	Kilpie Terrace, Coalisland, Co. Tyrone.	18-5-1912	Motor Driver	8-8-1945
80313	McGIRR, John F.	15 Robert St., Waterside, Derry.	23-6-1919	Waiter	8-8-1945
E/416806	McGIVERN, James A.	Railway Cottages, Dundalk Road, Carrickmacross.	7-8-1923	Machinist	8-8-1945
E/438292	McGLADE, James	25 Dingle Road, Cabra West, Dublin.	13-9-1916	Plumber	1-10-1945
207193	McGLINCHEY, James	Newtownhamilton, Co. Armagh.	18-10-1915	Cook	8-8-1945

Army No.	Name.	Last Recorded Address.	Date of Birth.	Declared Occupation prior to enlistment in Defence Forces.	Date of Dismissal from Defence Forces.
207190	McGLINCHEY, Michael	Quigley's Island, Lifford.	17-11-1917	Labourer	8-8-1945
E/421990	McGLINCHEY, Patrick	c/o P. McHugh, Cronalaghy, Ballybofey, Co. Donegal.	8-6-1922	Lorry Driver	8-8-1945
E/420302	McGLINCHY, Michael	Dunmore, Carrigans, Co. Donegal.	23-4-1904	Farm Labourer	8-8-1945
E/422516	McGLOIN, James	Laughty Bar, Kiltyclogher, Co. Leitrim.	8-2-1922	Farm Labourer	8-8-1945
V/209414	McGLOIN, Patrick	Castlegal, Grellegh, Co. Sligo.	22-5-1915	Farmer	8-8-1945
208894	McGOLDRICK, Patrick	Porthall, Lifford.	8-6-1920	Labourer	8-8-1945
V/210069	McGONAGLE, Michael	Meenadreen, Glencolumbcille, Co. Donegal.	17-4-1918	Farmer	8-8-1945
E/438291	McGONNELL, Terence	25 Ramona Avenue, Strandtown, Belfast.	1-2-1923	Aircraft Inspector	8-8-1945
V/215092	McGOVERN, Francis	Knockmore, Bawnboy, Co. Cavan.	27-11-1914	Farm Labourer	8-8-1945
E/433105	McGOVERN, James	c/o Mr. Thomas Carroll, Lappin, Castleshane, Co. Monaghan.	3-11-1919	Labourer	8-8-1945
E/400049	McGOVERN, John	56 Bellview Buildings, Thomas Court, Dublin.	28-7-1904	Packer	8-8-1945
E/405676	McGOVERN, Michael	2M Pearse House, Pearse Street, Dublin.	26-2-1918	Motor Driver	8-8-1945
A/76948	McGOVERN, Michael	Ashville, Collon, Co. Louth.	1-9-1917	Farm Labourer	8-8-1945
L/421928	McGOVERN, Peter	Mooneensaureen, Glangevlin, Co. Cavan.	15-5-1906	Farmer	8-8-1945
109571	McGOVERN, Thomas	Glangevlin, Co. Cavan.	7-5-1910	Farmer	8-8-1945
E/422349	McGOWAN, Anthony	c/o McIvors, Burnfoot, Co. Donegal.	4-9-1920	Labourer	8-8-1945
E/423613	McGOWAN, Henry	Toam, Blacklion, Co. Cavan.	15-7-1919	Labourer	8-8-1945
E/422477	McGOWAN, James	c/o Mrs. Armstrong, Stranorlar, Co. Donegal.	19-12-1915	Labourer	8-8-1945
V/201054	McGOWAN, James	Cummins House, Suncroft, Kildare.	7-12-1920	Labourer	8-8-1945
206283	McGOWAN, John J.	12 Moore Street, Off Bishop Street, Derry.	18-9-1920	Mason	8-8-1945
E/422475	McGOWAN, Joseph	c/o Mrs. Armstrong, Stranorlar, Co. Donegal.	26-2-1922	Labourer	8-8-1945
V/209717	McGOWAN, Michael	80 St. Patrick's Park, Carrick-on-Shannon.	21-5-1921	General Labourer	8-8-1945
E/424178	McGOWAN, Patrick	Raheelin, Kiltyclogher, Co. Leitrim.	8-9-1922	Labourer	8-8-1945
E/423436	McGOWAN, Patrick	Kinlough, Co. Leitrim.	3-3-1922	Labourer	8-8-1945
E/425267	McGOWAN, Patrick	42 Healy Terrace, Ballina, Co. Mayo.	4-7-1924	General Labourer	8-8-1945
E/421876	McGOWAN, Patrick	Cloonagh, Cloughboley, Co. Sligo.	4-3-1914	Labourer	8-8-1945
76104	McGOWRAN, Patrick	11 F Block, 58 Benburb Street, Dublin.	17-11-1919	Tailor	8-8-1945
V/206018	McGOWAN, Thomas	Dreenan, Ballybofey, Co. Donegal.	23-7-1915	Labourer	8-8-1945
E/422885	McGRADE, John James	Slieverussell, Ballyconnell, Co. Cavan.	3-6-1919	Mason	8-8-1945
E/436628	McGRANAGHAN, John	26 Nelson Street, Derry.	30-6-1925	Lorry Driver	8-8-1945
A/83781	McGRATH, Andrew	227 St. Attracta Road, Dublin.	9-3-1922	Mechanic	8-8-1945
77415	McGRATH, Christopher	42 St. Michael's Avenue, Tipperary.	21-12-1919	Farmer	8-8-1945
E/409941	McGRATH, Edward	Creenagh, Coalisland, Co. Tyrone.	2-12-1924	Labourer	8-8-1945
E/405950	McGRATH, Hugh	8 Marine Road, Dun Laoghaire.	16-9-1922	Barman	8-8-1945

Army No.	Name.	Last Recorded Address.	Date of Birth.	Declared Occupation prior to enlistment in Defence Forces.	Date of Dismissal from Defence Forces.
E/411669	McGRATH, Jeremiah	Gurrane, Fermoy.	29-6-1921	Labourer	8-8-1945
E/402409	McGRATH, John	157 Clonmacnoise Road, Kimmage, Dublin.	3-12-1921	None	8-8-1945
V/206178	McGRATH, John	Church Road, Haggardstown, Co. Louth.	9-11-1920	Labourer	8-8-1945
E/404383	McGRATH, John	Avondale Hall, Carysfort Avenue, Blackrock, Co. Dublin.	29-3-1908	Coach Painter	8-8-1945
202992	McGRATH, John	Mulrankin, Bridgetown, Wexford.	3-9-1918	Blacksmith	8-8-1945
E/424049	McGRATH, Kevin	Carr, Arva, Co. Cavan.	6-9-1922	Farm Labourer	8-8-1945
E/402767	McGRATH, Laurence	82 Kilfenora Rd., Crumlin, Dublin.	20-6-1922	Labourer	8-8-1945
E/411004	McGRATH, Patrick	Arywell, Fedamore, Co. Limerick.	4-2-1921	Labourer	8-8-1945
L/503223	McGRATH, Patrick	13 St. Cronin's Rd., Bray.	24-3-1928	Messenger	2-4-1946
77823	McGRATH, Patrick	Cloone, Kilmoganny, Co. Kilkenny.	22-6-1920	Farm Labourer	8-8-1945
E/431835	McGRATH, Patrick	Ballybricken, Waterford.	24-1-1914	General Labourer	8-8-1945
E/413444	McGRATH, Robert	31 Cashel Road, Clonmel.	3-8-1907	Lorry Driver	8-8-1945
E/429670	McGRATH, Timothy	Bodyke, Co. Clare.	20-10-1917	Shop Assistant	8-8-1945
A/80454	McGRATH, William	Collosmulton, Cappoquin, Co. Waterford.	29-8-1920	Farm Labourer	8-8-1945
E/422774	McGREALY, Bernard	c/o J. Gallagher, Baltony, Gortahork, Co. Donegal.	11-9-1919	Barman	8-8-1945
L/501801	McGREER, Kevin	24 Stradbrook Park, Blackrock, Co. Dublin.	24-6-1921	Gardener	8-8-1945
E/402913	McGREGOR, George	8 Meathville Terrace, Long Lane, Dublin.	17-12-1919	Telephone Installer Improver	8-8-1945
V/215023	McGROARTY, Thomas	Bank Terrace, Ramelton, Co. Donegal.	24-5-1920	Labourer	8-8-1945
A/79069	McGROARTY, Thomas	13 St. Eunan's Terrace, Letterkenny.	1-11-1918	Labourer	8-8-1945
E/405438	McGROGAN, Austin	56 Dawson Street, Dublin.	16-5-1920	Sheet Metal Worker	8-8-1945
404855	McGROGAN, Robert	10 St. Patrick's Sq., Bray.	8-6-1922	Labourer	8-8-1945
E/425155	McGRATTY, Francis	2 Irish Green Street, Derry.	20-2-1924	Labourer	8-8-1945
E/421489	McGROTTY, Edward	Church Street, Ramelton, Co. Donegal.	3-2-1907	Motor Driver and Mechanic	8-8-1945
E/420683	McGUINN, Christopher	Merchant's Road, Galway.	14-10-1919	Printer	8-8-1945
E/438025	McGUINNESS, Edward	31 John Martin Gardens, Newry.	13-12-1925	Labourer	8-8-1945
E/406320	McGUINNESS, Francis	30 Trinity Gardens, Drogheda.	3-8-1922	Labourer	8-8-1945
81829	McGUINNESS, Henry	6 Wilson Street, Belfast.	28-12-1921	General Labourer	16-11-1945
E/438071	McGUINNESS, James	34 Iona Crescent, Dublin.	17-2-1920	Turf Inspector	8-8-1945
A/79225	McGUINNESS, John	86 Devenish Road, Kimmage, Dublin.	12-6-1919	Clerk	8-8-1945
A/84102	McGUINNESS, John	5 Watergate, Custume Barracks, Athlone.	19-7-1918	Shop Assistant	8-8-1945
A/83559	McGUINNESS, Kevin	87 Devenish Road, Kimmage, Dublin.	28-5-1922	Clerk	8-8-1945
E/423288	McGUINNESS, Michael	3 Osborne Street, Rosemount, Derry.	15-8-1922	Labourer	8-8-1945
A/78344	McGUINNESS, Owen	13 Temple Lane, Ranelagh, Dublin.	7-1-1920	Messenger	8-8-1945
E/423312	MacGUINNESS, Patrick	97 Stransfield St., Belfast.	13-6-1914	Skilled Labourer	8-8-1945
E/408574	McGUINNESS, Patk. John	111 Slievemore Road, Crumlin, Dublin.	18-2-1924	Apprentice Motor Mechanic	8-8-1945
E/424725	McGUUINNESS, Timothy	Fortview House, Mohill, Co. Leitrim.	13-3-1910	Bank Official	8-8-1945

Army No.	Name.	Last Recorded Address.	Date of Birth.	Declared Occupation prior to enlistment in Defence Forces.	Date of Dismissal from Defence Forces.
E/421490	McGUIRE, James	Lettergonnel, Ballinalee, Co. Longford.	9-1-1918	Farm Labourer	8-8-1945
E/422341	McGUIRE, James Patrick	c/o Bridgend P.O., Co. Donegal.	20-10-1921	Labourer	8-8-1945
E/423794	McGUIRE, John	Moran's Terrace, Ballyhaunis, Co. Mayo.	29-4-1922	Labourer	8-8-1945
E/401436	McGUIRE, Michael	11 Lennox Street, Dublin.	24-2-1908	Labourer	8-8-1945
L/502739	McGUIRE, William	24 Hyde Park, Dundalk.	11-2-1927	Labourer	8-8-1945
83234	McGUIRK, Andrew	10 Lower Sandwith Street, Dublin.	2-8-1917	Labourer	8-8-1945
E/407693	McGUIRK, John	Edenderry, Benburb, Co. Armagh.	28-1-1924	Farm Labourer	8-8-1945
A/83881	McGUIRK, Joseph	87 Rosetta Park, Belfast.	18-5-1915	Clerk	8-8-1945
83853	McGUIRK, Robert	Hillcrest, Wellington Road, Dungannon, Co. Tyrone.	28-5-1922	Motor Mechanic	8-8-1945
E/424357	McGULLION, John	Cornmore, Kiltyclogher, Co.Leitrim.	20-7-1919	Farm Labourer	8-8-1945
E/422886	McGURK, John	c/o William Hegarty, Cloghabeg, Burnfoot, Co. Donegal.	11-10-1910	Labourer	8-8-1945
V/209866	McGUSKER, Leo T.	2 Moore Terrace, Dundalk.	28-11-1914	Grocer's Assistant	8-8-1945
215096	McHUGH, Francis	c/o Miss McGoldrick, Main Street, Swanlinbar, Co. Cavan.	14-5-1914	Farmer	8-8-1945
V/206025	McHUGH, James	Gortiher, Killygordon, Co. Donegal.	23-12-1915	Farm Labourer	8-8-1945
80103	McHUGH, John	Killeter Road, Castlederg, Co. Tyrone.	4-10-1920	Motor Driver	8-8-1945
A/73071	McHUGH, John	64 Father Paul Murphy St., Edenderry, Offaly.	28-8-1914	Farm Labourer	1-9-1945
60730	McHUGH, John	Gortnagrace, Castlefin, Co. Donegal.	1-7-1904	Labourer	8-8-1945
V/208895	McHUGH, Patrick	Porthall, Lifford.	17-3-1919	Motor Mechanic and Driver	8-8-1945
E/401078	McHUGH, Thomas J.	91 Lower Gardiner Street, Dublin.	30-10-1905	Hairdresser	8-8-1945
V/203096	McHUGH, Thomas	Scadaman, Ardara, Co. Donegal.	9-3-1920	Farmer	8-8-1945
83898	McILDUFF, James	36 English Street, Belfast.	15-2-1915	Labourer	8-8-1945
E/422821	McILMURRAY, James	42 Lower Gardiner Street, Dublin.	27-7-1908	Press Printer	8-8-1945
E/407124	McINERNEY, Joseph	Quin, Co. Clare.	8-6-1922	Labourer	8-8-1945
75382	McINERNEY, John	10 Lanesbury, Street, Greenock, Scotland.	24-5-1918	Stable Boy	8-8-1945
L/507271	McINERNEY, Michael	14 Shelbourne Avenue, Limerick.	1-2-1925	Labourer	13-2-1946
E/416581	McINERNEY, Patrick	13 Vizes Fields, Limerick.	15-8-1923	Labourer	8-8-1945
E/421337	McINTYRE, George	Seaview, Fahan, Co. Donegal.	22-6-1920	Butcher	8-8-1945
E/425328	McIVOR, James	Falcarragh Park, Ballyshannon, Co. Donegal.	24-7-1924	Laundry Worker	8-8-1945
E/421530	McIVOR, Patrick	Carndonagh, Co. Donegal.	10-7-1920	Labourer	8-8-1945
E/421133	McKAY, John	Kilraine Upper, Glenties, Co. Donegal.	18-12-1916	Steel Worker	8-8-1945
E/402627	McKEAN, Gerald	c/o James Swift, Dublin Street, Monaghan.	9-7-1922	Labourer	8-8-1945
E/432659	McKEANE, David	c/o J. Swift, Dublin Street, Monaghan.	20-5-1920	Labourer	8-8-1945
E/408612	McKEATING, Edward	115 Prompton Pk., Belfast.	2-9-1924	Aircraft Rivetter	8-8-1945
E/420203	McKEE, Henry	Cloughfin, Castlefin, Co. Donegal.	16-10-1901	Labourer	8-8-1945
83835	McKEE, Seán	38 Beechfield Ave., Belfast.	15-6-1922	Welder	8-8-1945
83859	McKEE, Thomas	12 Prestwick Park, Belfast.	2-2-1921	Motor Mechanic	8-8-1945
E/409333	McKEEVER, John	39 Milford Street, Belfast.	17-3-1924	Clerk	8-8-1945

85

Army No.	Name.	Last Recorded Address.	Date of Birth.	Declared Occupation prior to enlistment in Defence Forces.	Date of Dismissal from Defence Forces.
E/423289	McKEEVER, Liam	4 Brook St. Ave., Derry.	2-6-1922	Labourer	8-8-1945
L/500841	McKEEVER, Patrick J.	Tullyneskeogh, Carrick-macross.	13-3-1921	Farm Labourer	8-8-1945
E/421843	MacKELL, Thomas	Main Street, Longford.	21-3-1913	Storeman	8-8-1945
E/402341	McKENNA, Charles	21 Ellesmere Ave., Dublin.	15-3-1909	Engineer	8-8-1945
E/423113	McKENNA, Charles	176 P Block, Oliver Bond House, Bridgefoot Street, Dublin.	1-10-1904	Labourer	8-8-1945
203741	McKENNA, Denis	57 Clonmore Ave., Tralee.	24-1-1917	Tile Maker	8-8-1945
E/408734	McKENNA, Francis	Carrickroe, Emyvale, Co. Monaghan.	24-4-1923	Labourer	8-8-1945
E/422046	McKENNA, James	The Diamond, Clones.	4-6-1921	Farm Labourer	8-8-1945
71652	McKENNA, James	2 Sheridan's Lane, Bray.	14-5-1919	Labourer	8-8-1945
77945	McKENNA, James	Scotstown, Co. Monaghan.	28-9-1917	Farm Labourer	8-8-1945
A/83718	McKENNA, John	Turners Hill, Kingscourt, Co. Cavan.	8-7-1919	Storeman	8-8-1945
206462	McKENNA, Joseph	3 Lulham St., Balbriggan, Dublin.	6-2-1918	Motor Driver	8-8-1945
E/404556	McKENNA, Luke	Bragan, Carrickroe, Emyvale, Co. Monaghan.	10-3-1922	Motor Driver	8-8-1945
84476	McKENNA, Patrick	72 Caravogue Villas, Sligo.	29-12-1925	Farm Labourer	8-8-1945
E/421751	McKENNA, Patrick J.	Muff, Lifford.	5-5-1916	Shop Assistant	8-8-1945
E/406654	McKENNA, Peter	Emyvale, Co. Monaghan.	12-6-1922	Weaver	8-8-1945
V/206131	McKENNA, Thomas	Courtbane, Sheilogh, Dundalk.	20-3-1920	Tailor	8-8-1945
E/409056	McKENZIE, J.	8 Ross Street, Belfast.	7-7-1924	Oiler	8-8-1945
E/417018	McKENZIE, Timothy	9 Horgan's Buildings, Cork	5-8-1924	Painter	8-8-1945
E/422217	McKEOWN, Francis	Creighan, Cavan.	11-7-1910	Motor Mechanic	8-8-1945
E/408931	McKEOWN, John	Lisdoo Road, Dundalk.	10-5-1915	General Labourer	8-8-1945
E/405577	McKEOWN, Joseph	Muckno St., Castleblaney, Co. Monaghan.	8-11-1916	Lorry Driver	8-8-1945
E/424112	McKINNEY, Francis	Main Street, Moville, Co. Donegal.	8-12-1917	Labourer	8-8-1945
E/404639	McKINNEY, Laurence	Iveagh House, Bride Street, Dublin.	14-8-1914	Clerk	8-8-1945
E/423290	McKINNEY, Michael	6 Orchard Lane, Derry.	22-7-1922	Labourer	8-8-1945
E/425123	McKINNEY, William	5 Moore Street, Derry.	2-6-1923	Apprentice Carpenter	8-8-1945
68484	McLAVERTY, Manus	280 New Flats, Kevin Street, Dublin.	8-5-1906	Labourer	8-8-1945
E/404491	McLAUGHLIN, Andrew	39 Lower Baggot Street, Dublin.	28-3-1917	Insurance Agent	8-8-1945
E/421006	McLAUGHLIN, Charles	Inch Level, Burtonport, Co. Donegal.	19-2-1920	Labourer	8-8-1945
A/72042	McLAUGHLIN, Thomas	John Street, Killaloe, Co. Clare.	26-1-1911	Labourer	8-8-1945
E/404335	McLAUGHLIN, William	59 Sprinfield Rd., Belfast.	12-7-1911	Insurance Agent	8-8-1945
V/207951	McLEAN, Peter	10 Shamrock Villas, Dublin.	8-5-1921	Labourer	8-8-1945
61010	McLEAVEY, James	5 Market Street, Dundalk.	1-1-1906	Slater	8-8-1945
V/200620	McLOONE, Bernard	9 Gartan Avenue, Lindsay Road, Dublin.	10-7-1914	Salesman	8-8-1945
V/210146	McLOUGHLIN, Andrew	Cashel, Linsfort P.O., Co. Donegal.	5-3-1920	Farmer	8-8-1945
E/437518	McLOUGHLIN, Bernard	28 Irwin Street, Belfast.	12-7-1925	General Labourer	8-8-1945
E/421752	McLOUGHLIN, Bernard	19 Cable Street, Derry.	20-9-1905	Labourer	8-8-1945
A/73226	McLOUGHLIN, Denis	2 Drimnagh Cottages, Crumlin, Dublin.	30-8-1914	Labourer	8-8-1945
E/405147	McLOUGHLIN, Desmond	23 Lawless Terrace, Balbriggan, Co. Dublin.	25-11-1922	Factory Worker	8-8-1945
E/425154	McLOUGHLIN, Edward	7 Irish Green Street, Limavady, Co. Derry.	9-9-1921	Labourer	8-8-1945

Army No.	Name.	Last Recorded Address.	Date of Birth.	Declared Occupation prior to enlistment in Defence Forces.	Date of Dismissal from Defence Forces.
84044	McLOUGHLIN, Edward	Ballymagan, Buncrana, Co. Donegal.	16-10-1918	Clerk	8-8-1945
E/400732	McLOUGHLIN, Francis	c/o John O'Gorman, Market St., Monaghan.	8-11-1919	Motor Driver	8-8-1945
E/423291	McLOUGHLIN, George	60 Griffin Rd., Rosemount, Derry.	28-2-1922	Labourer	8-8-1945
80384	McLOUGHLIN, Henry	Drummor, Buncrana, Co. Donegal.	23-6-1921	Labourer and Cycle Mechanic	8-8-1945
A/73198	McLOUGHLIN, James	10 Gardiner Place, Dublin.	25-4-1914	Labourer	8-8-1945
E/414198	McLOUGHLIN, John	Ballynash, Foynes, Co. Limerick.	17-7-1915	Butcher	8-8-1945
206279	McLOUGHLIN, John	Bridge, Castlefin, Co. Donegal.	9-11-1918	Labourer	8-8-1945
E/421059	McLOUGHLIN, Joseph	Massinass, Creeslough, Co. Donegal.	13-6-1922	Labourer	8-8-1945
A/83665	McLOUGHLIN, Joseph	172 Keeper Road, Drimnagh, Dublin.	6-4-1922	None	8-8-1945
E/415591	McLOUGHLIN, Joseph	13 Mountain View, Tipperary.	27-7-1922	Labourer	8-8-1945
A/75886	McLOUGHLIN, Patrick	4 Westend Terrace, Derry.	6-5-1916	Labourer	8-8-1945
V/215038	McLOUGHLIN, Patrick	Kinnogue, Ballymangan, Buncrana.	9-4-1919	Motor Driver	8-8-1945
E/423307	McLOUGHLIN, Patrick	60 Griffin Rd., Rosemount, Derry.	18-3-1921	Labourer	8-8-1945
E/421359	McLOUGHLIN, Peter	10 Benbulbin Tce., Sligo.	24-3-1922	Builder's Labourer	8-8-1945
E/414197	McLOUGHLIN, Richard	35 St. Michael's Avenue, Tipperary.	15-4-1912	Labourer	8-8-1945
111082	McLOUGHLIN, Robert	3 Garryowen, Limerick.	2-12-1916	Wireless Apprentice	8-8-1945
A/82635	McLOUGHLIN, Thomas	Drumbane, Thurles, Co. Tipperary.	9-6-1920	Labourer	8-8-1945
A/78945	McLOUGHLIN, Thomas	6 Kilworth Road, North Crumlin, Dublin.	7-6-1920	Brass Polisher	8-8-1945
E/422104	McLOUGHLIN, William	Derryhereff, Cashelmore, Co. Donegal.	29-1-1918	Dental Mechanic	8-8-1945
79633	McLOUGHLIN, William	Lifford.	1-5-1920	Labourer	8-8-1945
E/423116	McMAHON, Christopher	7 Lower Dominick Street, Dublin.	12-12-1921	Messenger	8-8-1945
E/432436	McMAHON, Francis	Lisleitrim, Braddox, Monaghan.	4-9-1917	Labourer	8-8-1945
A/76818	McMAHON, George	45 O'Hanlon Park, Dundalk.	22-1-1914	Labourer	8-8-1945
V/214122	McMAHON, James	Cooltomin, Shanagolden, Co. Limerick.	28-5-1920	Labourer	8-8-1945
E/408874	McMAHON, John J.	Tunker, Belturbet, Co. Cavan.	22-8-1915	Parachute Packer	8-8-1945
A/73707	McMAHON, John	2 Grattan Street, Cork.	4-7-1914	Labourer	8-8-1945
E/406013	McMAHON, Michael	99 St. Nicholas Avenue, Dundalk.	14-11-1915	Carpenter's and Builder's Apprentice	8-8-1945
E/406538	McMAHON, Michael	John Mitchell St., Newry.	1-12-1919	Cinema Attendant	8-8-1945
E/434495	McMAHON, Owen	Shanganagh, Grove, Ballybrack, Co. Dublin.	21-11-1910	Gardener	8-8-1945
76016	McMAHON, Patrick	Dirreen, Athea, Co. Limerick.	17-3-1918	Farm Labourer	8-8-1945
E/423115	McMAHON, Patrick Joseph	60 Up. Edward St., Newry.	23-3-1921	Motor Driver	8-8-1945
E/405410	McMAHON, Peter	Garleygobban, Ballymackney, Co. Louth.	3-6-1918	Carpenter	8-8-1945
E/409901	McMAHON, Samuel	64 McDonnell St., Belfast.	7-9-1924	General Labourer	8-8-1945
E/406024	McMAHON, William	9 La Salle Tce., Dundalk.	7-9-1916	Motor Driver	8-8-1945

Army No.	Name.	Last Recorded Address.	Date of Birth.	Declared Occupation prior to enlistment in Defence Forces.	Date of Dismissal from Defence Forces.
E/403754	McMANUS, Brendan	Dunaval, Kilkeel, Co. Down.	2-12-1922	Driver	8-8-1945
E/423339	McMANUS, Ernest	Coolorkin, Boho, Co. Fermanagh.	31-8-1911	Farm Labourer	8-8-1945
V/202389	McMANUS, Gerard	9 Thomas Street, Dundalk.	17-4-1920	Student	8-8-1945
E/422048	McMANUS, James	O'Neill Park, Clones.	31-7-1922	Farmer	8-8-1945
79034	McMANUS, John	Lurgankeel, Kilcurry, Dundalk.	24-6-1920	Farm Labourer	8-8-1945
E/422049	McMANUS, Joseph	The Diamond, Belturbet, Co. Cavan.	18-3-1922	Creamery Worker	8-8-1945
E/424018	McMANUS, Joseph	Ardnanure, Drum, Athlone.	18-6-1914	Farmer	8-8-1945
E/421932	McMANUS, Joseph	Stranamort, Blacklion, Co. Cavan.	9-1-1922	Barman	8-8-1945
E/407824	McMANUS, Michael	5 Henrietta Street, Dublin.	3-7-1923	Messenger	8-8-1945
E/423654	McMANUS, Patrick	O'Neill Park, Clones.	17-3-1900	Salesman	8-8-1945
V/202316	McMANUS, Stephen	6 Harmony Lane, Sligo.	25-12-1914	Labourer	8-8-1945
A/83177	McMANUS, William	11 Fleming Road, Drumcondra, Dublin.	4-5-1922	Messenger	8-8-1945
E/434923	McMASTER, James	Skeogh, Callan, Co. Kilkenny.	6-1-1923	General Labourer	8-8-1945
E/422269	McMENAMIN, Michael	Pettigo, Co. Donegal.	1-12-1917	Joiner	8-8-1945
E/437770	McMEWHIRTER, Robert	Castleroche, Dundalk.	19-10-1913	Farm Labourer	8-8-1945
E/424149	McMONAGLE, James	Breenagh, Newmills, Lifford.	27-2-1913	Plasterer's Helper	8-8-1945
71362	McMORROUGH, Jeremiah	15 Nore Terrace, Kilkenny.	27-8-1916	Labourer	8-8-1945
E/403628	McMORROUGH, Patrick	15 Nore Terrace, Kilkenny.	15-2-1915	Hotel Book-keeper	8-8-1945
E/422050	McMULKIN, Philip	Three Mile House, Monaghan.	17-10-1916	Farm Labourer	8-8-1945
A/83829	McMULLEN, Malachy	Kernon, Gilford, Co. Down.	14-3-1917	Shop Assistant	8-8-1945
A/76552	McMORROUGH, Edward	15 Maudlin St., Kilkenny.	1-2-1920	Butcher's Helper	8-8-1945
A/76222	McMORROUGH, James	15 Rose Terrace, Kilkenny.	13-1-1920	Factory Worker	8-8-1945
E/408637	McMULLEN, John	121 Cullingtree Road, Belfast.	24-1-1924	Shop Assistant	8-8-1945
V/209231	McMULLAN, Thomas	30 Eden Quay, Dublin.	12-8-1917	Labourer	8-8-1945
E/437747	McNALLY, Anthony	Corballis Cottage, Donabate, Co. Dublin.	10-12-1915	Ship Stoker	8-8-1945
E/409811	McNALLY, Columba	31 Lr. English St., Armagh.	3-3-1923	Bricklayer	8-8-1945
E/408214	McNALLY, Peter	Chapel Street, Cookstown, Co. Tyrone.	21-8-1921	Gardener	8-8-1945
V/203185	McNAMARA, Christopher	8 Jones Place, Mungret Street, Limerick.	17-8-1912	None	8-8-1945
A/78157	McNAMARA, James	Cullinagh, Crusheen, Co. Clare.	12-7-1919	Farm Labourer	8-8-1945
82444	McNAMARA, John F.	5 Annmount, Friars Walk, Cork.	24-2-1921	Motor Car Upholsterer	8-8-1945
V/209870	McNAMARA, John	2 Old Market Place, Cork.	5-7-1919	Labourer	8-8-1945
E/414232	McNAMARA, Joseph	Annacotty, Lisnagry, Co. Limerick.	20-6-1920	Railway Porter	8-8-1945
E/416382	McNAMARA, Martin	32 Davitt's St., Tipperary.	7-12-1923	Labourer	8-8-1945
E/417204	McNAMARA, Michael	81 St. Munchin's Street, Island Field, Limerick.	2-10-1920	Labourer	8-8-1945
E/413535	McNAMARA, Nicholas	17 Keane Street, Killalea, Limerick.	8-2-1922	None	8-8-1945
E/412213	McNAMARA, William	11 Oliver Plunkett Street, Clonmel.	21-5-1922	Plumber's Assistant	8-8-1945
E/404344	McNAMEE, Francis	34 Ashfield Rd., Ranelagh, Dublin.	20-7-1915	Masseur, Chiropodist	8-8-1945
E/424714	McNAMEE, James	Milltown, Burnbennett, Strabane.	16-12-1922	Farm Labourer	8-8-1945
E/406049	McNAMEE, William	99 Islandbridge, Dublin.	7-2-1910	Steel Fixer	8-8-1945
E/406331	McNEE, Thomas	Culloville, Dundalk.	4-8-1921	Labourer	8-8-1945

Army No.	Name.	Last Recorded Address.	Date of Birth.	Declared Occupation prior to enlistment in Defence Forces.	Date of Dismissal from Defence Forces.
E/406693	McNELIS, Bernard	Tychaney, Ballygawley, Co. Tyrone.	15-12-1917	Labourer	8-8-1945
E/406501	McNIFF, Hugh	Carrabo, Blacklion, Co. Cavan.	23-10-1920	Labourer	8-8-1945
E/425364	McNULTY, John	The Diamond, Raphoe, Co. Donegal.	15-1-1921	Shop Assistant	8-8-1945
V/200261	McNULTY, Patrick	Humbert Street, Ballina.	24-10-1910	Builder's Labourer	8-8-1945
E/403565	McNULTY, Thomas	90 Dunluce Road, Clontarf, Dublin.	26-6-1916	Tailor	8-8-1945
E/402890	McPARLAND, Edward	c/o John Smith, Dublin Street, Monaghan.	9-8-1912	Aircraft Fitter	8-8-1945
E/406653	McPARLAND, Kevin	Ancurk, Newtownhamilton, Co. Armagh.	16-7-1921	Farm Labourer	8-8-1945
E/421132	McPARTLAND, Thomas	Abbey Street, Sligo.	19-10-1918	Messenger Boy	8-8-1945
E/433609	McPHILLIPS, Joseph	Lake View Terrace, Bailieboro', Co. Cavan.	6-4-1922	Labourer	8-8-1945
E/407578	McQUAID, Eamon	4 Beechmount St., Belfast.	18-8-1923	Labourer	8-8-1945
E/423560	McQUAID, James	c/o Mrs. Keenan, Ballina-muck, Co. Longford.	11-12-1919	Farm Labourer	8-8-1945
E/422223	McQUAID, James	Killylis, Dungannon. Co. Tyrone.	2-5-1917	Labourer	8-8-1945
E/406473	McQUILLAN, Daniel J.	Duke Street, Ballymena, Co. Antrim.	14-10-1906	Clerical Worker	8-8-1945
E/407585	McRORY, Patrick J.	Ballymagilly, Cookstown, Co. Tyrone.	14-7-1913	Farmer	8-8-1945
E/420209	McSORLEY, George	Churchtown, Carrigans, Co. Donegal.	15-12-1916	Labourer	8-8-1945
E/421994	McSORLEY, Patrick	Churchtown, Carrigans, Co. Donegal.	25-5-1914	Labourer	8-8-1945
E/438002	McSTRAVICK, John	Woodlong House, Springfield Rd., Belfast.	6-5-1922	Motor Driver	8-8-1945
E/400809	McSWEENEY, Alexander	111 Rialto Ctgs., Dublin.	3-1-1921	Film Operator	8-8-1945
E/415855	McSWEENEY, James	5 Upper John Street, Cork.	11-8-1907	Labourer	8-8-1945
E/422612	McSWEGAN, Joseph	Albert Terrace, Lifford.	5-2-1909	Barber	8-8-1945
E/424040	McTIGUE, Joseph	Kilkelly, Castlebar, Co. Mayo.	6-11-1920	Farmer	8-8-1945
E/433614	McVEAGH, John	Scrag Road, Donovan Road, Kilkeel, Co. Down.	12-1-1919	Lorry Driver and Fitter	8-8-1945
E/421492	McVEIGH, Michael	Annagh, Tourlestrane, Co. Sligo.	28-5-1918	Farmer	8-8-1945
E/432435	McVEIGH, Patrick	Glaslough St., Monaghan.	2-4-1919	Motor Driver	8-8-1945
E/436645	McWILLIAMS, Francis	10 Cupar Street, Belfast.	6-12-1923	General Labourer	17-11-1945
76182	MACK, John	Canal Road, Johnstown, Co. Kilkenny.	9-2-1918	Farm Labourer	8-8-1945
E/432354	MACKEN, Patrick	c/o John Marry, Main St., Castleblayney, Co. Monaghan.	28-2-1894	Painter	8-8-1945
E/423386	MACKEN, Thomas Gerard	The Mall. Westport, Co. Mayo.	3-7-1922	Mechanic	8-8-1945
E/437610	MACKIN, George	5 St. Brigid's Avenue, North Strand, Dublin.	28-9-1924	Labourer	8-8-1945
E/406309	MACKIN, Nicholas	Tullinavall, Ballyhanna, Co. Armagh.	30-4-1919	Farmer	8-8-1945
E/410044	MADDEN, David	11 Fort Street, Cork.	11-8-1921	Garage Hand	8-8-1945
E/400481	MADDEN, Francis	6 North Gloucester Place, Dublin.	11-11-1921	Boot Repairer	8-8-1945
E/409998	MADDEN, Hugh G.	46 Iris Drive, Belfast.	14-10-1924	Painter	8-8-1945
E/408648	MADDEN, James	26 Eccles Street, Dublin.	20-11-1920	General Labourer	8-8-1945
108243	MADDEN, John	New Park, Kilkenny.	18-7-1917	Labourer	8-8-1945
E/420522	MADDEN, Michael	Brackernagh, Ballinasloe.	2-9-1912	Clerk	8-8-1945
E/424191	MADDEN, Michael	Ballagh, Kilrooskey, Co. Roscommon.	21-8-1922	Metal Worker	8-8-1945

Army No.	Name.	Last Recorded Address.	Date of Birth.	Declared Occupation prior to enlistment in Defence Forces.	Date of Dismissal from Defence Forces.
E/404128	MADINE, Robert	65 Lr. Mount St., Dublin.	14-7-1919	Motor Driver	8-8-1945
E/423208	MAGEE, Bernard Joseph	c/o Cyril McGrisken, Kiltyclogher, Co. Leitrim.	18-11-1920	Farm Labourer	8-8-1945
E/422187	MAGEE, Charles	54 Perrose Hill, Armagh.	4-6-1922	Labourer	8-8-1945
E/425170	MAGEE, Harry	Grahamstand, Castlefin, Co. Donegal.	8-8-1923	Farm Labourer	8-8-1945
78766	MAGEE, Thomas	Main Street, Carrigans, Co. Donegal.	28-2-1919	Labourer	8-8-1945
E/434490	MAGENNIS, Arthur G.	22 Little Denmark Street, Dublin.	26-10-1913	Clerk and Store Keeper	8-8-1945
E/407451	MAGENNIS, John	4 St. John's Terrace, Newcastle, Co. Down.	17-10-1915	Store Keeper	8-8-1945
E/423892	MAGUIRE, Bernard	Kiltyclogher, Co. Leitrim.	6-8-1922	Farm Labourer	8-8-1945
78438	MAGUIRE, David	8 Taylor's Lane, Dublin.	2-1-1921	Tailor	8-8-1945
E/421835	MAGUIRE, Desmond J.	Main Street, Ballyconnell, Co. Cavan.	25-4-1922	Shop Assistant	8-8-1945
E/424203	MAGUIRE, Edward	Clonooney, Drumulty, Co. Cavan.	22-8-1913	Farm Labourer	8-8-1945
E/422029	MAGUIRE, Hugh	Three Mile House, Monaghan.	26-5-1920	Farm Labourer	8-8-1945
E/406375	MAGUIRE, Hugo	Annaveagh, Scotstown, Co. Monaghan.	8-9-1922	Mechanic	8-8-1945
E/400150	MAGUIRE, James	31 J Block, Pearse House, Dublin.	28-11-1905	Motor Driver	8-8-1945
E/405442	MAGUIRE, James	59 Upper Coombe Street, Dublin.	24-2-1916	Storeman and Packer	8-8-1945
E/422030	MAGUIRE, James	Fermanagh Street, Clones, Co. Monaghan.	30-12-1912	Farmer	8-8-1945
E/423549	MAGUIRE, John	Swanlinbar, Co. Cavan.	31-3-1919	Motor Mechanic	8-8-1945
E/425396	MAGUIRE, John	c/o Mrs. Kerrigan, O'Connell St., Athlone.	17-4-1924	Tailor	8-8-1945
V/206422	MAGUIRE, Joseph	2 James Connolly Street, Cavan.	29-10-1919	Repairer	8-8-1945
V/207426	MAGUIRE, Joseph	Balscaddin, Delahasey, Co. Dublin.	18-3-1921	Farm Labourer	8-8-1945
E/421834	MAGUIRE, Joseph	Main Street, Ballyconnell, Co. Cavan.	14-3-1916	Shop Assistant	8-8-1945
E/430725	MAGUIRE, Joseph	c/o Kilroys, High Street, Tullamore.	8-9-1917	Motor Driver	8-8-1945
E/408401	MAGUIRE, Michael	Kilcrutten, Lisnaskea, Co. Fermanagh.	29-7-1924	Farmer	8-8-1945
83700	MAGUIRE, Noel	63 Haddington Road, Dublin.	22-12-1922	Van Boy	8-8-1945
E/403820	MAGUIRE, Patrick	119 Upper Dorset Street, Dublin.	9-2-1921	Motor Driver	8-8-1945
E/422508	MAGUIRE, Philip	c/o J. McGuillan, Tullyinchy, Kiltyclogher, Co. Leitrim.	1-11-1915	Farmer	8-8-1945
83947	MAGUIRE, Richard	64 Kickham Road, Inchicore, Dublin.	7-3-1922	Labourer	8-8-1945
V/202257	MAGUIRE, Terence	Church View, Kells.	27-10-1920	Labourer	8-8-1945
E/400359	MAHER, Denis	29 Golden Lane, Dublin.	19-1-1912	Labourer	8-8-1945
E/406986	MAHER, Francis J.	Oldcourt, Blessington, Co. Wicklow.	7-5-1922	Farmer	8-8-1945
E/437948	MAHER, Henry D.	Sans Souci Cottage, Convent Road, Bray.	17-4-1925	General Labourer	8-8-1945
E/405124	MAHER, James	17 North Great George's Street, Dublin.	17-4-1917	Painter	8-8-1945
E/421100	MAHER, James	Rathgarrett, Tyrrellspass, Mullingar.	11-7-1900	Labourer	18-11-1945
84705	MAHER, John	54 Durrow Rd., Kimmage, Dublin.	24-11-1923	Factory Hand	8-8-1945
E/408503	MAHER, John J.	Greenwood, Hallstown, Co. Kilkenny.	27-10-1924	General Labourer	8-8-1945
E/406577	MAHER, Kevin	246 Cashel Road, Crumlin, Dublin.	20-7-1921	Labourer	8-8-1945

Army No.	Name.	Last Recorded Address.	Date of Birth.	Declared Occupation prior to enlistment in Defence Forces.	Date of Dismissal from Defence Forces.
E/400558	MAHER, Patrick	8 Hardwicke Place, Dublin.	30-3-1920	Fitter	8-8-1945
74922	MAHER, Philip	7 Cove Street, Cork.	17-8-1918	Messenger	8-8-1945
A/73440	MAHER, Timothy	Moore Street, Cappamore, Co. Limerick.	14-3-1914	General Labourer	8-8-1945
E/409870	MAHON, John	9 Prospect Rd., Glasnevin, Dublin.	25-3-1925	Clerk	8-8-1945
E/424089	MAHON, John	c/o Mrs. O'Donoghue, Railway View, Galway.	16-12-1921	Farm Labourer	8-8-1945
E/437517	MAHON, Michael	21 Wolfe Tone St., Dublin.	28-8-1925	Pork Butcher's Apprentice	4-2-1946
E/403525	MAHON, Patrick	32 Ormond Square, Dublin.	15-3-1919	Cycle Assembler	8-8-1945
L/503012	MAHON, Patrick	112 Slievemore Road, North Crumlin, Dublin.	7-4-1928	Van Boy	12-4-1946
A/76240	MAHON, Thomas	4 Churchtown, Rathgar, Dublin.	13-12-1919	Welder's Assistant	8-8-1945
V/213167	MAHONEY, Maurice	Ballydonoghue, Lisselton, Co. Kerry.	20-8-1912	Labourer	8-8-1945
E/417201	MAHONEY, Seamus	Gallows Fields, Tralee.	12-7-1921	Barman	8-8-1945
A/57646	MAHONY, Richard	66 Great Western Road, London, W.2.	16-9-1905	Shoemaker	8-8-1945
E/423869	MAILEY, Thomas	Muff, Co. Donegal.	27-1-1918	Farmer	8-8-1945
E/434520	MALLON, Brendan J.	8 Shamrock Cottages, North Strand, Dublin.	8-2-1922	None	8-8-1945
E/403562	MALLON, Patrick	Tullnacrow, Castleblayney, Co. Monaghan.	8-10-1922	None	8-8-1945
79820	MALONE, Aloysius	Cootehill, Boyle, Co. Roscommon.	31-1-1918	Labourer	28-11-1945
84053	MALONE, Christopher	9 St. Bridget's Avenue, Island Field, Limerick.	31-5-1921	General Labourer	8-8-1945
L/503198	MALONE, Francis	35 Yellow Road, Whitehall, Dublin.	2-2-1928	Messenger	26-1-1946
L/502050	MALONE, Jeremiah	52 Bolton Street, Dublin.	22-1-1925	None	8-8-1945
68359	MALONE, John	315 Mayfield, Cork.	5-3-1909	Labourer	8-8-1945
L/501955	MALONE, John J.	Newtown, Tallaght, Co. Dublin.	29-7-1922	Farm Labourer	8-8-1945
E/403038	MALONE, John	7 Stephen's Place, Off Lr. Mount Street, Dublin.	25-1-1922	Messenger	8-8-1945
E/433352	MALONEY, James	28 Upper Ormond Quay, Dublin.	12-1-1894	Labourer	8-8-1945
71201	MALONEY, John	3 Brown Street, Belfast.	8-7-1910	Barber	8-8-1945
E/424056	MALONEY, Patrick	Creaghmore, Ballinasloe.	15-3-1922	Labourer	8-8-1945
E/403046	MALONEY, Thomas	114 Galtymore Road, Crumlin, Dublin.	6-9-1922	Motor Driver	8-8-1945
83717	MANGAN, Christopher	51 Donnycarney Road, Dublin.	7-8-1922	Labourer	8-8-1945
V/205725	MANGAN, James	11 Great Longford Street, Dublin.	—-2-1922	Carter	8-8-1945
80997	MANGAN, Justin	8 Grey Homes, Curragh, Co. Kildare.	2-1-1925	Student	8-8-1945
E/401960	MANGAN, William	11 Great Longford Street, Dublin.	7-1-1919	Labourer	8-8-1945
78221	MANNING, Eamonn	69 Mount Prospect Avenue, Dublin.	23-9-1913	Commercial Traveller	8-8-1945
E/400792	MANNING, Edward	150 Keogh Sq., Inchicore, Dublin.	20-4-1922	Labourer	8-8-1945
A/82368	MANNION, Patrick	20 Gurranebraher Road, Cork.	20-12-1922	Painter	8-8-1945
E/436037	MANSFIELD Michael J.	64 Upper Prior's Knock, Waterford.	2-5-1922	Gen. Labourer	8-8-1945
E/407455	MANSFIELD, William	Ballycorus House, Enniskerry, Co. Wicklow.	9-11-1923	Van-man	8-8-1945
206529	MARCHETTI, Joseph	30 Charlotte St., Dublin.	14-5-1922	Ice-cream Vendor	8-8-1945
E/413779	MARKHAM, Michael	53 Hammon's Place, Charleville, Co. Cork.	1-12-1921	None	8-8-1945

Army No.	Name.	Last Recorded Address.	Date of Birth.	Declared Occupation prior to enlistment in Defence Forces.	Date of Dismissal from Defence Forces.
V/209274	MARKS, Michael	Ballagan, Greenore, Co. Louth.	3-1-1922	Farmer	8-8-1945
V/207123	MARKS, Robert	71 Charlemont St., Dublin.	30-9-1919	Carpenter Improver	8-8-1945
E/405417	MARLEY, James	Kilsoran, Castlebellingham, Co. Louth.	6-10-1922	Labourer	8-8-1945
E/404801	MARRY, Michael	Castlebellingham, Co. Louth.	3-11-1913	Shop Assistant	8-8-1945
205777	MARSHALL, Charles	Werburgh Street, Dublin.	27-6-1917	Labourer	8-8-1945
A/68302	MARSHALL, David	10 High Street, Dublin.	1-8-1905	Machine Feeder	8-8-1945
V/209663	MARSHALL, John	Kilscaron, Scartaglin, Co. Kerry.	14-3-1912	Labourer	12-10-1945
L/500601	MARSHALL, Patrick	15 Grey Square, Meath Street, Dublin.	24-8-1920	Labourer	8-8-1945
E/408339	MARTIN, Anthony	52 North Great Charles Street, Dublin.	13-1-1919	Labourer	8-8-1945
E/422191	MARTIN, Daniel	c/o Mrs. McLean, Bridgend, Co. Donegal.	7-4-1917	Motor Driver	8-8-1945
V/204396	MARTIN, Francis	Kilmacoo, Athlone.	21-9-1921	Farm Labourer	8-8-1945
E/420585	MARTIN, James	Lisdiligney, Killimor, Co. Galway.	27-7-1911	Saw Mill Hand	8-8-1945
A/110981	MARTIN, James	Munachee, Arthurstown, Co. Wexford.	4-12-1915	Farm Labourer	8-8-1945
E/403562	MARTIN, John	17 New Street, Dublin.	19-3-1922	Sheet Metal Worker	8-8-1945
A/80760	MARTIN, John	Raheen, Adamstown, Co. Wexford.	21-11-1919	Gen. Labourer	8-8-1945
A/77511	MARTIN, Joseph	47 O'Molloy St., Tullamore	31-3-1920	Labourer	8-8-1945
E/421521	MARTIN, Manus Bernard	c/o J. Kirwan, P.O., Newtowncunningham, Co. Donegal.	7-12-1919	Labourer	8-8-1945
83236	MARTIN, Patrick	123 St. Jarlath's Road, Cabra, Dublin.	20-5-1922	Labourer	8-8-1945
E/423856	MARTIN, Patrick	Liscooley, Castlefin, Co. Donegal.	15-6-1919	Labourer	8-8-1945
V/201293	MARTIN, Thomas	Abbey Street, Kilkenny.	14-4-1921	Labourer	8-8-1945
78150	MARTIN, Thomas	Careen, Tourmakeady, Co. Mayo.	23-9-1920	Farm Labourer	8-8-1945
102800	MARTIN, William	Mullabaun, Carrickmacross, Co. Monaghan.	17-3-1915	Farm Labourer	8-8-1945
A/71165	MARUM, James	55 Green St., Portlaoighise.	12-2-1911	Labourer	8-8-1945
206534	MASON, Francis	42 Temple Bldgs., Dublin.	11-10-1915	Motor Driver	8-8-1945
E/407564	MASON, Patrick	63 Ballinteer Cottages, Dundrum, Co. Dublin.	12-11-1923	Electrician	8-8-1945
204556	MASON, William	42 Temple Buildings, Broadstone, Dublin.	13-8-1921	Wire Worker	8-8-1945
V/210130	MASTERSON, Christopher	42 Mount Drummond Ave., Harold's Cross, Dublin.	16-10-1921	Labourer	8-8-1945
78213	MASTERSON, Gerard	Dromard, Moyne, Co. Longford.	20-9-1919	Barber	8-8-1945
E/401226	MASTERSON, James M.	6 St. Patrick's Terrace, North King St., Dublin.	30-7-1919	Mechanical Engineer	8-8-1945
E/402108	MASTERSON, John	5 Mary's Abbey, Dublin.	29-4-1921	Grocer's Porter	8-8-1945
E/437603	MATEER, Joseph	20 Sultan Street, Belfast.	18-8-1925	Builder's Labourer	8-8-1945
E/404920	MATTHEW, Charles	14 Kinahan Street, Dublin.	9-2-1919	Dairyman	8-8-1945
A/79335	MATTHEWS, Charles	154 Stanaway Road, Crumlin, Dublin.	3-10-1918	None	8-8-1945
V/209933	MATTHEWS, Eamon	Killeevan, Newbliss, Co. Monaghan.	10-2-1923	Gen. Labourer	8-8-1945
E/400679	MATTHEWS, James	Killeevan, Newbliss, Co. Monaghan.	10-3-1921	Labourer	8-8-1945
E/409976	MATTHEWS, Patrick J.	62 Estoral Park, Crumlin Road, Belfast.	6-2-1925	Fitter	8-8-1945

Army No.	Name.	Last Recorded Address.	Date of Birth.	Declared Occupation prior to enlistment in Defence Forces.	Date of Dismissal from Defence Forces.
E/409321	MATTHEWS, Seán	5 Stratford Gardens, Ardoyne, Belfast.	19-2-1921	Student	8-8-1945
E/425142	MAXWELL, Edward	58 Wellington St., Derry.	8-11-1923	Motor Driver	8-8-1945
L/508796	MAXWELL, Patrick	14 St. Eunan's Terrace, Letterkenny.	6-1-1926	Blacksmith	8-8-1945
E/402451	MAY, Bernard	3 Lr. Rutland St., Dubiln.	26-10-1906	Labourer	8-8-1945
A/78466	MAY, Christopher	24 Slievemore Road, Crumlin, Dublin.	29-11-1920	Messenger	8-8-1945
E/433341	MAY, Denis	31 Mountjoy Sq., Dublin.	26-4-1922	Messenger	8-8-1945
205705	MAY, Francis	Men's Hostel, Peter Street, Dublin.	27-4-1901	Fitter	8-8-1945
E/404648	MAY, John	6 Gardiner's Lane, Dublin.	5-5-1915	Shoemaker	8-8-1945
V/205110	MAY, William	5 Lady Ann Lane, Dublin.	19-9-1918	Motor Driver	8-8-1945
A/83240	MAYCOCK, John	14 McCabe's Villas, Booterstown, Co. Dublin.	25-2-1922	Labourer	8-8-1945
E/408396	MEADE, Patrick	Tankardstown, Sherwin's Cross, Kilmallock, Co. Limerick.	1-9-1923	Farm Labourer	8-8-1945
E/438388	MEADE, Thomas	49 Bargy Road, East Wall, Dublin.	9-11-1925	Baker	11-2-1946
V/211402	MEAGHER, David	9 Charlemont Mall, Dublin.	12-11-1918	Labourer	8-8-1945
E/414298	MEAGHER, William R.	38 Castle Street, Nenagh.	20-7-1911	Journalist	8-8-1945
78898	MEANEY, Michael	7 Little Michael Street, Waterford.	27-9-1920	Deck Boy	8-8-1945
209724	MEANEY, Stephen	19 Arundel Sq., Waterford.	13-2-1922	Labourer	8-8-1945
A/75169	MEANEY, William	Grangemore, Kilcullen, Co. Kildare.	20-3-1918	None	8-8-1945
77312	MEARS, Kevin	St. Brigid's Terrace, Ballinamore, Co. Leitrim.	24-3-1920	Helper on Lorry	8-8-1945
68247	MEEDE, Thomas	496 North Circular Road, Dublin.	13-7-1908	Labourer	8-8-1945
A/76276	MEEGAN, Leo	17 Lake View, Muncho Street, Castleblayney, Co. Monaghan.	18-2-1918	Egg Packer	8-8-1945
77894	MEEHAN, Bernard	Lisnagree, Poyntzpass, Co. Armagh.	18-7-1911	Farmer	8-8-1945
B/78760	MEEHAN, Edward	9 Malvern Terrace, Derry.	14-8-1918	Shop Assistant	8-8-1945
A/111637	MEEHAN, James	Kilcoman East, Rathkeale, Co. Limerick.	1-3-1916	Farm Labourer	8-8-1945
E/424142	MEEHAN, James P.	Kevinsfort, Sligo.	9-1-1918	Farm Hand	8-8-1945
A/84531	MEEHAN, Michael	Paceland, Dunboyne, Co. Meath.	6-9-1922	Labourer	8-8-1945
E/422295	MEEHAN, William	Drumhaggard, Muff, Co. Donegal.	16-6-1919	Labourer	8-8-1945
A/77512	MELIA, Thomas	Fore, Castlepollard, Co. Westmeath.	19-3-1919	Labourer	8-8-1945
E/420288	MELLETT, Martin	Demesne Cottages Ballinrobe, Co. Mayo.	7-3-1918	Labourer	8-8-1945
E/434775	MENEHAN, Patrick	Ballykelly, Monasterevan, Co. Kildare.	18-12-1919	Labourer	8-8-1945
84889	MEREDITH, James	120 Kildare Road, Crumlin, Dublin.	13-2-1924	Shop Assistant	13-3-1946
E/433966	MERRINS, James	Ballyrae, Grange, Mullen, Athy.	2-10-1921	Farm Labourer	8-8-1945
E/405052	MILEY, Michael	3 New Street, Dublin.	3-8-1915	Fruit Dealer	8-8-1945
E/403655	MILLANE, John	85 St. Declan Road, Clontarf, Dublin.	31-7-1917	Teacher	8-8-1945
208638	MILLER, James	New Buildings, Pier Head Road, Derry.	23-5-1914	Labourer	8-8-1945
E/406286	MILLER, John	43 Neehan Street, Newry.	25-2-1919	House Painter	8-8-1945
V/208714	MILLETT, William	27 St. Patrick's Terrace, Athlone.	20-10-1912	Piecer, Woollen Mills	8-8-1945
E/421244	MILLS, James	Goola, Glenmany, Ballina.	5-1-1915	Skilled Labourer	8-8-1945
83652	MILLS, Owen	28 Seatown, Dundalk.	27-8-1919	Lorry Driver	8-8-1945

Army No.	Name.	Last Recorded Address.	Date of Birth.	Declared Occupation prior to enlistment in Defence Forces.	Date of Dismissal from Defence Forces.
E/412905	MINIHAN, Patrick	20 D Road, Killeely, Limerick.	3-3-1903	Labourer	8-8-1945
E/437597	MITCHELL, Charles	9 Golden Vale, Inchicore, Dublin.	15-9-1914	Motor Driver	8-8-1945
E/425256	MITCHELL, Denis	Doorish, Newtowncunningham, Co. Donegal.	31-1-1924	Labourer	8-8-1945
L/502550	MITCHELL, John	90 Pembroke Rd., Dublin.	4-10-1925	Bus Attendant	8-8-1945
E/422296	MITCHELL, Martin	11 Orchard Route, Derry.	3-10-1916	Metal Dresser	8-8-1945
77313	MOFFAT, Thomas	Abbey Street, Ballinrobe.	22-1-1920	Labourer	8-8-1945
E/413805	MOFFATT, Michael	Broghill, Charleville, Co. Cork.	20-7-1912	Labourer	8-8-1945
V/215123	MOFFITT, Charles	Cottages, Dunfanaghy, Co. Donegal.	21-5-1912	Motor Driver	8-8-1945
84107	MOGAN, Patrick	Moy, Kinvara, Co. Galway.	6-11-1921	Motor Driver	8-8-1945
E/405136	MOHAN, Patrick	51 St. Attracta Road, Dublin.	26-2-1921	Seaman	8-8-1945
A/73141	MOHAN, Patrick	37 Ossory Park, Kilkenny.	9-11-1912	Messenger Boy	8-8-1945
E/405526	MOLLOY, Daniel	134 Lismore Road, Kimmage, Dublin.	20-6-1922	Messenger	8-8-1945
73488	MOLLOY, David	Limerick Road, Roscrea.	8-12-1913	Labourer	8-8-1945
E/406304	MOLLOY, James A.	Cornascribe, Portadown.	27-6-1919	Lorry Driver's Assistant	8-8-1945
E/422958	MOLLOY, John	Grany, Inver, Co. Donegal.	13-1-1916	Labourer	8-8-1945
A/77689	MOLLOY, John	Limerick Road, Roscrea.	14-5-1920	General Labourer	8-8-1945
B/79711	MOLLOY, Kevin	Sheenhills, Roscrea.	4-9-1921	Farm Labourer	8-8-1945
E/434989	MOLLOY, Michael Joseph	Esker, Jenkinstown, Co. Kilkenny.	27-9-1923	Farm Labourer	8-8-1945
A/80066	MOLLOY, Michael	Rathvilly, Co. Carlow.	7-9-1917	Motor Driver	8-8-1945
E/407171	MOLLOY, Patrick	3 Grenville Street, Dublin.	28-6-1923	Van Boy	8-8-1945
A/79336	MOLLOY, Patrick J.	c/o Mrs. Kelly, Newbridge, Co. Kildare.	19-1-1920	Labourer	8-8-1945
112698	MOLLOY, Peter	Bohereen, Ennis.	9-6-1917	Labourer	8-8-1945
V/217214	MOLLOY, Richard	6 Rutland Cottages, Lr. Rutland Street, Dublin.	8-7-1926	Lift Boy	24-5-1946
E/421176	MOLLOY, Tobias	c/o J. McGee, Sandy Row, Castlefin, Co. Donegal.	7-1-1919	Labourer	8-8-1945
V/203069	MOLLOY, Willam	Drimore, Glencolumcille, Co. Donegal.	4-1-1921	Farmer	8-8-1945
E/409109	MOLONEY, Christopher	14 St. Declan's Terrace, Marino, Dublin.	24-12-1910	Carpenter and Joiner	8-8-1945
E/407700	MOLONEY, Christopher	33 Lord Edward Street, Ballina, Co. Mayo.	9-2-1920	Motor Driver and Fitter	8-8-1945
E/408439	MOLONEY, James	34 Beresford St., Dublin.	7-4-1926	General Labourer	17-9-1945
A/82886	MOLONEY, Martin	5 St. John's Sq., Limerick.	21-8-1922	Messenger Boy	8-8-1945
V/204958	MOLONEY, Martin	5 St. John's Sq., Limerick.	20-6-1921	Messenger Boy	8-8-1945
L/507472	MOLONEY, Michael	3 White's Cottages, Grattan St., Limerick.	15-8-1927	Labourer	17-3-1946
V/208967	MOLONEY, Michael	Abbeylands, Rathkeale, Co. Limerick.	8-8-1921	Labourer	8-8-1945
78585	MOLONEY, Patrick	18 Lavitt Lane, Cork.	21-10-1920	Labourer	8-8-1945
A/63182	MOLONEY, Patrick	31 Queen Street, Dublin.	19-12-1905	Labourer	8-8-1945
L/507401	MOLONEY, Thomas	2 Bell Tavern Lane, Broad Street, Limerick.	8-7-1927	Labourer	3-3-1946
V/207254	MOLOUGHNEY, James	4 Ikerrin Road, Thurles.	18-8-1922	Labourer	8-8-1945
80580	MOLYNEAUX, Martin	4 Offaly Street, Tullamore.	6-7-1919	Hair Dresser	8-8-1945
V/200637	MONAGHAN, Albert	1 Cameron Square, Kilmainham, Dublin.	1-11-1918	Labourer	8-8-1945
E/423276	MONAGHAN, Andrew	Drumharvey, Irvinestown, Co. Fermanagh.	22-8-1919	Labourer	8-8-1945
E/401840	MONAGHAN, Daniel	Rath Cottage, Danespark, Clontarf, Dublin.	5-11-1914	Messenger	8-8-1945
A/83554	MONAGHAN, Desmond	1 North Road, Finglas, Dublin.	13-7-1922	Farm Labourer	8-8-1945

Army No.	Name.	Last Recorded Address.	Date of Birth.	Declared Occupation prior to enlistment in Defence Forces.	Date of Dismissal from Defence Forces.
E/422032	MONAGHAN, James	Main Street, Swanlinbar, Co. Cavan.	18-11-1917	Farmer	8-8-1945
L/508109	MONAGHAN, James	Mears Court, Mullingar.	18-11-1923	Labourer	8-8-1945
79780	MONAGHAN, Joseph	Tatinalee, Brookboro, Co. Fermanagh.	7-9-1913	Farm Labourer	8-8-1945
E/422268	MONAGHAN, Michael	Tower, Pettigo, Co. Donegal.	22-6-1904	Labourer	8-8-1945
E/421744	MONAGHAN, Terence	West End, Buncrana, Co. Donegal.	1-12-1921	Motor Driver	8-8-1945
E/438242	MONAGHAN, William	Bartons Cottages, Castletown, Dundalk.	26-5-1926	Weaver	8-8-1945
E/432968	MONGEY, Desmond	141 Phibsboro' Road, Dublin.	1-3-1921	Cabinet Maker	8-8-1945
V/206665	MONKS, William	70 Durrow Road, Crumlin, Dublin.	16-11-1920	Chimney Cleaner	8-8-1945
A/78217	MONTGOMERY, Cecil	Carriglass, Co. Longford.	23-10-1921	Farm Labourer	8-8-1945
E/406265	MONTGOMERY, John J.	34 Mill Lane, Larne.	17-5-1917	Machine Operator	8-8-1945
A/79489	MONTGOMERY, Patrick	c/o Mrs. McGrath, Main Street, Cappoquin.	14-6-1918	General Labourer	8-8-1945
V/202704	MONTGOMERY, Robert	82 Garavogue Villas, Sligo.	18-12-1920	Labourer	8-8-1945
77985	MOODY, James C.	Moylisha, Clonegal, Co. Carlow.	23-12-1919	Page Boy	8-8-1945
L/503435	MOONEY, Christopher	16 Eden Villas, Sandycove, Dublin.	28-7-1927	Milk Server	23-7-1946
A/73605	MOONEY, Daniel	7 Swilly Tce., Buncrana, Co. Donegal.	22-1-1915	Farm Labourer	8-8-1945
E/408394	MOONEY, Hugh	130 Mourne Road, Crumlin, Dublin.	17-3-1923	Messenger	8-8-1945
208779	MOONEY, Hugh	Baldonnel, Clondalkin, Co. Dublin.	12-8-1920	Lorry Driver's Assistant	8-8-1945
A/41296	MOONEY, James	5 Wolfe Tone St., Cavan.	29-10-1905	Labourer	8-8-1945
E/402024	MOONEY, John	21 Garden Lane, Francis Street, Dublin.	20-2-1920	Labourer	8-8-1945
E/408393	MOONEY, John	130 Mourne Road, Crumlin, Dublin.	6-4-1921	Shop Assistant	8-8-1945
V/205792	MOONEY, Joseph	9 Crosthwaite Park, Dun Laoghaire.	22-7-1921	Unemployed	8-8-1945
A/73788	MOONEY, Joseph	Caherconlish, Co. Limerick.	21-10-1915	Labourer	8-8-1945
77844	MOONEY, Laurence	Fenagh, Bagenalstown, Co. Carlow.	16-1-1920	Labourer	8-8-1945
E/402549	MOONEY, Michael	8 Lower Pembroke Street, Dublin.	11-1-1921	House Porter	8-8-1945
A/83326	MOONEY, Patrick C.	2 James Connolly Square, Bray.	8-12-1920	Messenger	8-8-1945
E/433605	MOONEY, Robert	2 Russell Avenue, Dublin.	17-10-1921	Telephone Engineer	8-8-1945
L/502767	MOONEY, Stephen	35 Pimlico, Dublin.	12-5-1927	Messenger	15-4-1946
E/407584	MOONEY, Terence	Lissen, Cookstown, Co. Tyrone.	12-8-1917	Farm Labourer	8-8-1945
E/405100	MOORE, Henry	22 Pearse Square, Dublin.	24-3-1922	Labourer	8-8-1945
E/424771	MOORE, James	Wood Quay, Galway.	2-4-1921	Electrician	8-8-1945
217170	MOORE, James	Ballintra, Co. Donegal.	23-3-1926	None	8-8-1945
E/415533	MOORE, John P. J.	30 Daly Ave., Janesboro', Limerick.	28-12-1922	Cinema Attendant	8-8-1945
V/217116	MOORE, John	48 New Grange Road, Cabra, Dublin.	9-2-1922	Coach Builder	8-8-1945
83804	MOORE, John	62 Charlotte Street, Warrenpoint, Co. Down.	7-4-1922	Schoolboy	8-8-1945
E/431297	MOORE, Martin	21 William Street, Clonmel.	8-12-1921	Labourer	8-8-1945
A/72650	MOORE, Martin	Carnmore, Oranmore, Co. Galway.	30-7-1911	Farmer	8-8-1945
79908	MOORE, Michael	17 Long Tower St., Derry.	19-1-1922	Waiter	8-8-1945
V/200393	MOORE, Owen	Baltrasna, Mullingar.	11-10-1917	Labourer	8-8-1945
83135	MOORE, Patrick	9 Peter Street, Dublin.	22-4-1922	Messenger Boy	8-8-1945

Army No.	Name.	Last Recorded Address.	Date of Birth.	Declared Occupation prior to enlistment in Defence Forces.	Date of Dismissal from Defence Forces.
E/434914	MOORE, Patrick	8 Maudlin St., Kilkenny.	27-7-1922	General Labourer	8-8-1945
E/425597	MOORE, Thomas	4 Bridge Street, Derry.	2-2-1926	Bread Server	8-8-1945
E/408563	MOORE, William Patrick	318 Ballybough House, Ballybough, Dublin.	16-12-1921	Motor Driver	8-8-1945
E/407341	MOORELAND, Patrick	52 Malcolmson St., Belfast.	11-12-1923	Farm Labourer	8-8-1945
V/205947	MORAHAN, Sean	Louisburgh, Co. Mayo.	15-11-1918	Student	8-8-1945
E/408970	MORAN, Dermot	7 Laurence Place, Dundalk.	12-8-1924	Butcher's Apprentice	8-8-1945
A/65504	MORAN, Edward	Carragawn, Carrick-on-Suir, Co. Tipperary.	11-5-1908	Labourer	8-8-1945
E/407307	MORAN, John P.	82 Downpatrick Road, Crumlin, Dublin.	9-6-1923	Messenger	8-8-1945
E/423738	MORAN, Joseph	49 Frawley Park, Ballina, Co. Mayo.	3-2-1922	Labourer	8-8-1945
E/406531	MORAN, Michael	56 Devenish Road, Kimmage, Dublin.	12-4-1922	Labourer	8-8-1945
L/509029	MORAN, Michael	27 O'Moore's Place, Portlaoighise.	8-9-1926	Farm Labourer	3-3-1946
E/400083	MORAN, Michael	106 Downpatrick Road, Crumlin, Dublin.	12-4-1922	Motor Mechanic	8-8-1945
E/422400	MORAN, Michael	6 McBride's Terrace, West-port, Co. Mayo.	16-8-1912	Labourer	8-8-1945
E/414116	MORAN, Noel	5 Downes Square, Wolfe Tone Street, Limerick.	16-7-1922	Labourer	8-8-1945
E/430570	MORAN, Patrick	26 O'Moore Place, Portlaoighise	11-5-1909	Motor Driver	8-8-1945
204002	MORAN, Patrick	Clonmoyle, Mullingar.	31-7-1920	Farm Labourer	8-8-1945
E/422879	MORAN, Robert	St. Mura's, Fahan, Co. Donegal.	25-7-1919	Labourer	8-8-1945
E/432535	MORAN, Thomas	125 Carrow Road, Crumlin, Dublin.	24-9-1920	Driver and Van Boy	8-8-1945
L/500019	MORAN, Thomas	22 Dowth Road, Cabra, Dublin.	5-5-1922	Labourer	8-8-1945
A/75210	MORAN, William	Tullanrone, Listowel.	19-12-1917	Labourer	8-8-1945
83897	MORGAN, Daniel	Drumsesk Road, Rostrevor, Co. Down.	25-5-1921	Labourer	8-8-1945
78423	MORGAN, James	6 Campbell Park, Ardee, Co. Louth.	23-1-1915	General Labourer	8-8-1945
E/411820	MORGAN, James	3 Rines Street, Sandsmill, Limerick.	7-7-1922	Labourer	8-8-1945
E/401644	MORGAN, Timothy	11 Gardiner's Pce., Dublin.	7-1-1915	Carter	8-8-1945
E/415206	MORIARTY, Thomas	Gurtacurrane, Annascaul, Co. Kerry.	17-8-1913	Farming	8-8-1945
E/410404	MORONEY, Richard	3 White Heart, Enniskillen.	11-7-1919	Labourer	8-8-1945
E/433354	MORRIN, George	23 Farranboley Cottages, Dundrum, Co. Dublin.	15-9-1913	Hairdresser	8-8-1945
V/208196	MORRIS, Bernard	Coronagh, Virginia, Co. Cavan.	17-9-1918	Lorry Driver	8-8-1945
E/434797	MORRIS, John	8 Collery Tce., Tullamore.	2-10-1920	Lorry Driver	8-8-1945
A/83150	MORRIS, Laurence	77 Durrow Rd., Kimmage, Dublin.	28-12-1921	Labourer	8-8-1945
E/405007	MORRISON, William	14 Wolfe Tone Sq., North, Bray.	21-6-1922	Electrician	8-8-1945
V/200639	MORRISSEY, Francis	1 Virginia Terrace, Seville Place, Dublin.	7-11-1918	Fitter	8-8-1945
79019	MORRISSEY, James	Monard, Co. Tipperary.	15-4-1921	Farm Labourer	8-8-1945
V/200727	MORRISSEY, Peter	Lisheen, Ballynacally, Ennis.	29-6-1919	Labourer	8-8-1945
A/82743	MORRISSEY, Thomas	Mantlehill, Golden, Co. Tipperary.	27-3-1922	Labourer	8-8-1945
A/78997	MORRISSEY, William	18 Boulavogue Road, East Wall, Dublin.	2-2-1921	Butcher	8-8-1945
E/425409	MORROW, James	Killegar, Killeshandra, Co. Cavan.	19-5-1923	Truck Driver	8-8-1945

Army No.	Name.	Last Recorded Address.	Date of Birth.	Declared Occupation prior to enlistment in Defence Forces.	Date of Dismissal from Defence Forces.
V/201720	MORTON, William	4 Henrietta Street, Dublin.	17-8-1919	Labourer	8-8-1945
E/421981	MOSS, John	Castlefin, Co. Donegal.	8-5-1920	Labourer	8-8-1945
A/78586	MOTHERWAY, Thomas	Ballybutler, Ladysbridge, Cork.	14-4-1918	Farm Labourer	8-8-1945
E/424422	MOYLAND, Thomas	Rathwilloncloon, Tubber, Co. Galway.	23-11-1918	Farm Labourer	8-8-1945
78998	MOYNES, James	51 Arbour Hill, Dublin.	1-9-1920	Vanman	8-8-1945
E/431603	MOYNEY, James	Church St., Rathdowney, Co. Leix.	26-12-1911	Farm Labourer	8-8-1945
E/411923	MOYNIHAN, Patrick	Clasheens, Killarney.	28-12-1911	Labourer	8-8-1945
E/433276	MULALLY, John	Dunamaggen, Thomas-town, Co. Kilkenny.	4-1-1920	Farm Labourer	8-8-1945
E/401011	MULCAHY, John	Iveagh House, Bride Street, Dublin.	3-3-1909	Carpenter	8-8-1945
E/403315	MULCAHY, John J.	Iveagh House, Bride Street, Dublin.	29-10-1894	Civil Servant	8-8-1945
76296	MULCAHY, John	50 Harrison's Place, Charleville, Cork.	4-6-1918	Labourer	8-8-1945
80406	MULCAHY, John	Newcastle, Co. Galway.	10-9-1916	Painter	8-8-1945
E/434823	MULCAHY, Patrick	32 Prior's Knock, Waterford.	29-6-1912	None	8-8-1945
E/433043	MULCAHY, Patrick	28 Tolka Road, Ballybough, Dublin.	27-3-1920	Labourer	8-8-1945
77014	MULCAHY, Thomas	Chapel Street, Clogheen, Co. Tipperary.	17-11-1919	Messenger	8-8-1945
E/420994	MULDOON, Joseph	Kilmere, Loughrea, Co. Galway.	29-5-1921	General Labourer	8-8-1945
E/401484	MULDOON, Patrick	Kilfaharon, Emyvale, Co. Monaghan.	12-12-1919	Labourer	8-8-1945
79377	MULDOON, Peter	Brookdale, Upr. Glasheen Road, Cork.	18-4-1921	Barman	8-8-1945
A/111926	MULHALL, John	23 Powell Park, Dundalk.	22-12-1916	Labourer	8-8-1945
E/401157	MULHALL, Patrick J.	7 Knocknaree Road, Crumlin, Dublin.	2-6-1902	Chef	8-8-1945
V/201249	MULHALL, William	Willsgrove, Athy.	3-4-1921	Labourer	8-8-1945
E/422343	MULHERN, Anthony	Bruminin, Brunagh, New Villas, Letterkenny.	11-3-1922	Labourer	8-8-1945
A/78391	MULHERN, Arthur	Aughlish, Feeney, Co. Donegal.	22-3-1918	Labourer	8-8-1945
78358	MULHERN, James	Aughlish, Feeney, Co. Derry.	19-7-1920	Farm Labourer	8-8-1945
E/420366	MULHERN, Peter	Camross, Ballymote, Co. Sligo.	21-5-1922	Labourer	8-8-1945
E/404154	MULHOLLAND, John	Ballybeg, Ahoghill, Co. Leitrim.	22-8-1913	Millworker	8-8-1945
E/404749	MULHOLLAND, Patk. J.	36 Lr. Buckingham Street, Dublin.	17-5-1919	Carpenter's Helper	8-8-1945
E/405821	MULHOLLAND, Terence	90 Annamoe Drive, Cabra, Dublin.	9-8-1921	Cabinet Maker	8-8-1945
109884	MULKERRINS, Joseph	Myenish, Carna, Co. Galway.	13-9-1915	Labourer	8-8-1945
A/112053	MULKERRINS, Patrick	Myenish, Carna, Co. Galway.	12-5-1916	Farm Labourer	8-8-1945
A/113238	MULLALLY, Joseph	Turnpike, Moate, Co. Westmeath.	16-12-1915	General Labourer	8-8-1945
E/400728	MULLAN, George	Market Street, Monaghan.	22-5-1918	Plasterer	8-8-1945
E/421177	MULLAN, Patrick	c/o E. Cranford, Raws, Castlefin, Co. Donegal.	28-4-1911	Cycle Mechanic	8-8-1945
V/207452	MULLAN, Patrick J.	637 Alexandra Parade, Glasgow.	15-8-1919	Student	8-8-1945
80332	MULLANE, Donald	6 St. Joseph's Street, Limerick.	17-5-1917	Labourer	8-8-1945
A/75621	MULLANE, John	25 Slattery's Avenue, Cork.	15-8-1917	Labourer	8-8-1945
V/201403	MULLANE, Joseph	6 St. Joseph's Terrace, Limerick.	29-6-1920	Draper's Assistant	8-8-1945

Army No.	Name.	Last Recorded Address.	Date of Birth.	Declared Occupation prior to enlistment in Defence Forces.	Date of Dismissal from Defence Forces.
79307	MULLANEY, Gerald	76 Errigal Road, Dublin.	12-1-1921	None	8-8-1945
E/424110	MULLEADY, Anthony	3 Termon Cottages, Boyle, Co. Roscommon.	12-6-1921	Labourer	8-8-1945
E/421178	MULLEN, Daniel	Drumban, Castlefin, Co. Donegal.	4-4-1919	Labourer	8-8-1945
V/209974	MULLEN, John	Garra, Linsfort P.O., Buncrana, Co. Donegal.	19-2-1922	General Labourer	8-8-1945
E/429624	MULLEN, Michael	Uadamact, Inishmore, Aran, Co. Galway.	16-9-1919	Farm Labourer	8-8-1945
83125	MULLEN, Patrick	Kilmore Road, Artane, Dublin.	31-10-1921	Labourer	8-8-1945
V/200033	MULLIGAN, Christopher	6 Mount Brown, Dublin.	18-11-1920	Bootmaker's Apprentice	8-8-1945
205033	MULLIGAN, Hugh	Sunbeam Terrace, Clones, Co. Monaghan.	20-9-1920	Farm Labourer	8-8-1945
E/424268	MULLIGAN, Matthew	Main Street, Ballyconnell, Co. Cavan.	10-1-1916	Labourer	8-8-1945
E/425371	MULLIGAN, Patrick	Glasslough St., Monaghan.	17-3-1924	Shoemaker	8-8-1945
V/201315	MULLINS, Eugene	Faggott Hill, Blarney Road, Cork.	6-12-1918	Labourer	8-8-1945
E/405113	MULLINS, John	60 Ben Madigan Road, Crumlin, Dublin.	2-2-1922	Electrician	8-8-1945
E/413280	MULLINS, John	61 St. Patrick's Avenue, Tipperary.	25-5-1921	Clerk	8-8-1945
100536	MULLINS, Patrick	11 Annally Road, Cabra, Dublin.	7-10-1914	Labourer	8-8-1945
E/422901	MULLOY, Patrick	Curryanne, Swinford, Co. Mayo.	1-11-1911	Labourer	8-8-1945
L/507502	MULQUEEN, Bernard	28 St. Munchin's Street, Island Field, Limerick.	15-6-1927	Labourer	13-5-1946
E/411823	MULQUEEN, Christopher	2 St. Patrick's Avenue, Island Field, Limerick.	27-10-1918	Barman	8-8-1945
V/204434	MULREADY, William	88 Clonliffe Ave., Dublin.	25-10-1917	Mechanic	8-8-1945
E/429675	MULROE, Patrick	Cloughbrook Upper, Clonbur, Co. Galway.	10-4-1908	Farmer	8-8-1945
A/78184	MULRY, Martin	14 St. Kiernan's Terrace, Athlone.	22-7-1921	Weaver	8-8-1945
75771	MULRYAN, John	Rockfield, Athenry, Co. Galway.	25-2-1917	Labourer	8-8-1945
L/503059	MULVANEY, George	139 Leighlin Road, Crumlin, Dublin.	31-7-1927	Messenger Boy	30-1-1946
L/503191	MULVEY, Christopher	285 " C " Block, Oliver Bond House, Usher's Quay, Dublin.	10-12-1927	Vanman	25-3-1946
E/421199	MULVEY, Denis	Riverview Hse., Almonnies, Omagh, Co. Tyrone.	11-3-1902	General Labourer	8-8-1945
207828	MULVEY, Nicholas	18 St. Bridget's Terrace, Dargle Road, Bray.	3-9-1917	Labourer	8-8-1945
E/416692	MULVIHILL, Daniel	65 Evergreen Street, Cork.	8-9-1922	Barman	8-8-1945
E/404064	MUMBLEY, James	63 Bridgefoot St., Dublin.	19-10-1919	Shoe Repairer	8-8-1945
E/406266	MURNIHAN, Anthony	73 Ranelagh, Dublin.	4-11-1913	Motor Driver and Mechanic	8-8-1945
V/205144	MURPHY, Arthur	162 Downpatrick Road, Crumlin, Dublin.	3-8-1920	Labourer	8-8-1945
E/405805	MURPHY, Brendan	153 Kilworth Road, Crumlin, Dublin.	2-3-1923	Labourer	8-8-1945
A/72216	MURPHY, Christopher	14 Upper Exchange Street, Dublin.	19-6-1911	Labourer	8-8-1945
E/409091	MURPHY, Christopher	132 Church Road, East Wall, Dublin.	24-3-1924	Tailor	8-8-1945
A/81692	MURPHY, Christopher	84 Gurranabraher Avenue, Cork.	31-12-1923	Labourer	8-8-1945
E/414293	MURPHY, Cornelius	Broghall, Charleville, Co. Cork.	25-5-1922	Farm Labourer	8-8-1945

Army No.	Name.	Last Recorded Address.	Date of Birth.	Declared Occupation prior to enlistment in Defence Forces.	Date of Dismissal from Defence Forces.
E/410182	MURPHY, Daniel	3 Hegarty's Lane, Off Blarney Street, Cork.	22-6-1910	Labourer	8-8-1945
A/80301	MURPHY, Daniel	Churchtown, Buttevant, Co. Cork.	7-1-1922	Labourer	8-8-1945
E/415006	MURPHY, Denis	10 Henry Street, Cork.	20-6-1920	Labourer	8-8-1945
V/207179	MURPHY, Donald	Gould's Square, Cove Street, Cork.	20-5-1922	General Labourer	8-8-1945
E/409848	MURPHY, Edward	24 Park View St., Belfast.	5-12-1924	Butcher's Apprentice	8-8-1945
V/215034	MURPHY, Edward	Chryslakeel, Burnfoot, Co. Donegal.	6-8-1916	Labourer	8-8-1945
L/507514	MURPHY, Eugene	28 Moville Tce., Turner's Cross, Cork.	16-5-1927	None	10-2-1946
E/404679	MURPHY, George	19 Temple Rd., Blackrock, Co. Dublin.	18-3-1917	Licensed Vintner and Grocer	8-8-1945
E/413688	MURPHY, Gerald	Lyrecrompane, Listowel, Co. Kerry.	28-3-1892	Rivetter	8-8-1945
V/200073	MURPHY, Henry	30 Wolfe Tone Street, Kilkenny.	5-6-1918	Electrical Linesman	8-8-1945
217199	MURPHY, Henry	132 Church Road, East Wall, Dublin.	28-5-1926	General Labourer	3-1-1946
85164	MURPHY, James	18 Old Court Park, Bray.	1-9-1921	General Labourer	8-8-1945
E/404418	MURPHY, James	66 Lower Wellington St., Dublin.	27-5-1909	Builder's Labourer	8-8-1945
V/205531	MURPHY, James	Henry Street, Castleblayney, Co. Monaghan.	22-2-1922	Labourer	8-8-1945
E/412684	MURPHY, James S.	Cork Hill, Youghal.	2-7-1922	Student	8-8-1945
E/433811	MURPHY, James	Rose Cottage, Taghmon, Co. Wexford.	29-8-1916	Carpenter	8-8-1945
200090	MURPHY, James	9 Linen Hall St., Dublin.	2-3-1914	Labourer	8-8-1945
83841	MURPHY, John	10 Mill Street, Newry.	4-2-1922	Railway Porter	8-8-1945
82050	MURPHY, John	22 Mitchell's Ave., Tralee.	19-9-1919	Shoemaker's Assistant	8-8-1945
82440	MURPHY, John	c/o M. Leary, Carhue, Coachford, Co. Cork.	10-12-1922	Labourer	8-8-1945
L/506093	MURPHY, John	7 Bunker's Hill, St. Mary's Road, Cork.	2-1-1922	Cleaner	8-8-1945
E/432975	MURPHY, John	55 Pimlico, Dublin.	13-7-1922	Labourer	8-8-1945
A/77715	MURPHY, John	86 Douglas Street, Cork.	1-3-1926	Builder's Labourer	25-10-1945
L/502290	MURPHY, John	15 L Block, Oliver Bond House, Bridgefoot Street, Dublin.	15-2-1926	Upholsterer	8-8-1945
76107	MURPHY, John	Chairhayse, Abbeyfeale, Co. Limerick.	19-4-1919	Farm Labourer	8-8-1945
E/409174	MURPHY, Joseph	285 Farranboley Cottages, Windy Arbour, Co. Dublin.	3-7-1923	Motor Driver	8-8-1945
E/411920	MURPHY, Joseph	51 McCurtain's Buildings, Cork.	20-10-1920	Labourer	8-8-1945
A/70864	MURPHY, Joseph	Rathvilly, Co. Carlow.	19-6-1911	Carpenter	8-8-1945
A/75701	MURPHY, Joseph	116 Kilberry Terrace, Spangle Hill, Cork.	14-12-1918	Bootmaker	8-8-1945
75271	MURPHY, Leo	c/o Mrs. Whelan, 21 Webster Rd., Liverpool.	29-12-1917	Farm Labourer	8-8-1945
E/402210	MURPHY, Michael	24 North Charles Street, Dublin.	7-5-1920	Labourer	8-8-1945
E/402721	MURPHY, Michael	6E Pearse House, Pearse Street, Dublin.	19-10-1900	Labourer	8-8-1945
E/402259	MURPHY, Michael	12 Fleming Road, Drumcondra, Dublin.	9-5-1920	Labourer	8-8-1945
76702	MURPHY, Michael	Bruree, Co. Limerick.	23-1-1919	Labourer	8-8-1945
E/405979	MURPHY, Michael	11 Blackhall Pde., Dublin.	29-11-1914	Motor Driver	8-8-1945

Army No.	Name.	Last Recorded Address.	Date of Birth.	Declared Occupation prior to enlistment in Defence Forces.	Date of Dismissal from Defence Forces.
V/204283	MURPHY, Michael	1 Westmoreland Park, Ranelagh, Dublin	26-5-1922	Labourer	8-8-1945
A/83970	MURPHY, Michael	18 Braithwaite St., Dublin.	24-8-1922	Van Driver	8-8-1945
E/413360	MURPHY, Michael	New Street, Buttevant, Co. Cork.	19-2-1903	Labourer	8-8-1945
E/416132	MURPHY, Michael	West End, Mill Street, Co. Cork.	9-10-1919	Seaman	8-8-1945
V/203932	MURPHY, Michael	37 Templeacre Avenue, Gurranebraher, Cork.	28-10-1921	Messenger	8-8-1945
A/80822	MURPHY, Nicholas	Priest's Terrace, Convent Hill, Waterford.	30-5-1922	Newsboy	8-8-1945
E/413361	MURPHY, Oliver	13 Charlemont Terrace, Wellington Road, Cork.	29-5-1920	Seaman	8-8-1945
A/75592	MURPHY, Patrick	Termonfeckin, Drogheda.	11-6-1917	Carpenter	8-8-1945
E/407304	MURPHY, Patrick	10 Kilfenora Road, Kimmage, Dublin.	30-10-1923	Dairy Boy	8-8-1945
E/420151	MURPHY, Patrick	Knocknagur, Miltown, Co. Galway.	12-5-1908	Builder's Labourer and Waiter	8-8-1945
E/422033	MURPHY, Patrick	Coolnalone, Clones.	22-5-1911	Labourer	8-8-1945
77558	MURPHY, Patrick	Knockanode, Avoca, Co. Wicklow.	3-1-1920	Farm Labourer	8-8-1945
81705	MURPHY, Patrick	5 Smith's Rd., Charleville, Co. Cork.	13-12-1924	Labourer	8-8-1945
A/82062	MURPHY, Patrick	27 Gould Street, Cork.	4-7-1922	Bookmaker	8-8-1945
E/433959	MURPHY, Patrick	Convent Lane, Athy.	17-1-1918	Foundry Worker	8-8-1945
E/432718	MURPHY, Patrick J.	Garden House, Bailieboro, Co. Cavan.	14-7-1921	Tailor	8-8-1945
80486	MURPHY, Patrick	38 J.K.L. Place, New Ross.	5-11-1921	Porter	8-8-1945
E/413010	MURPHY, Peter	Ballinakill, Kilmeady, Co. Limerick.	29-6-1922	Labourer	8-8-1945
V/203129	MURPHY, Peter	43 Emmett Tce., Navan.	14-6-1919	Upholsterer	8-8-1945
E/423957	MURPHY, Philip	Swanlinbar, Co. Cavan.	28-8-1922	Improver Electrician	8-8-1945
E/437543	MURPHY, Robert	Ballinamore, Redcross, Co. Wicklow.	22-7-1919	Farm Labourer	3-2-1946
E/415506	MURPHY, Stephen	6 Denmark St., Limerick.	27-12-1921	Shop Assistant	8-8-1945
A/84664	MURPHY, Terence	The Quay, Graiguena-managh, Co. Kilkenny.	12-12-1923	Labourer	8-8-1945
E/400482	MURPHY, Thomas	14D St. Joseph's Mansions, Killarney Street, Dublin.	15-3-1915	Labourer	8-8-1945
75514	MURPHY, Thomas	St. Anne's Tallaght, Co. Dublin.	7-2-1919	Farm Labourer	8-8-1945
83553	MURPHY, Thomas	3 Upper Sean McDermott Street, Dublin.	24-11-1918	Labourer	8-8-1945
83108	MURPHY, Thomas	55 Lr. Wellington Street, Dublin.	30-9-1921	Labourer	8-8-1945
E/414156	MURPHY, Thomas	Mountain View, Tipperary.	17-11-1921	Student	8-8-1945
E/434521	MURPHY, Thomas	13 Melvin Road, Terenure, Dublin.	26-1-1903	Labourer	8-8-1945
80889	MURPHY, Thomas F.	39 Barrack St., Waterford.	29-1-1923	Ship's Steward	8-8-1945
107505	MURPHY, Thomas	17 Maddenstown Terrace. Curragh Camp.	2-3-1916	Blacksmith	8-8-1945
207623	MURPHY, Thomas	Lakemount, Ballyglass, Co. Mayo.	9-10-1916	Porter	8-8-1945
E/413757	MURPHY, Timothy	Carrigdown, Listowel.	15-4-1919	Lorry Driver	8-8-1945
85714	MURPHY, William	59 St. Michael's Avenue, Tipperary.	5-7-1926	Labourer	12-8-1946
E/408843	MURPHY, William	24 Grosvenor Rd., Dublin.	22-3-1919	Sailor and Rigger	8-8-1945
E/434689	MURPHY, William	31 Union St., Portadown.	24-2-1922	None	8-8-1945
E/408977	MURRAY, Arthur	26 Nelson Street, Dublin.	4-2-1909	Motor Engineer	8-8-1945
E/417543	MURRAY, Denis	80 Oliver Plunkett Street, Cork.	4-1-1909	Fitter	8-8-1945
205672	MURRAY, Francis	1 James's Street, Dublin.	2-5-1909	None	8-8-1945

Army No.	Name.	Last Recorded Address.	Date of Birth.	Declared Occupation prior to enlistment in Defence Forces.	Date of Dismissal from Defence Forces.
83635	MURRAY, Frederick	9 H Block, Arbour Hill Barracks, Dublin.	24-2-1921	Film Operator	8-8-1945
A/79954	MURRAY, Hugh	79 Eden Villas, Glasthule, Co. Dublin.	23-5-1921	General Labourer	8-8-1945
E/425408	MURRAY, James	Rosegarland, Magherafelt, Co. Derry.	30-4-1924	Motor Driver	8-8-1945
E/423105	MURRAY, James	28C Aldboro House, Killarney Street, Dublin.	22-10-1921	Labourer	8-8-1945
E/405010	MURRAY, John J.	137 Leighlin Road, Crumlin, Dublin.	17-8-1922	Golf Caddie	8-8-1945
A/71030	MURRAY, John	7 Hardwicke Pce., Dublin.	12-2-1910	Grocer's Porter	8-8-1945
E/406213	MURRAY, John	35 Rialto Cttgs., Dublin.	28-4-1923	Painter's Apprentice	8-8-1945
V/211165	MURRAY, Joseph	126 Tolka Rd., Ballybough, Dublin.	23-2-1922	Labourer	8-8-1945
E/422034	MURRAY, Michael	Milltown, Co. Monaghan.	19-11-1920	Labourer	8-8-1945
83908	MURRAY, Patrick	6 Fulham Rd., Balbriggan, Co. Dublin.	9-1-1921	Textile Worker	8-8-1945
A/79607	MURRAY, Patrick	12 Ballybough Road, Kilkenny.	4-5-1921	Motor Driver	8-8-1945
77716	MURRAY, Richard	51 McCurtain's Buildings., Cork.	19-7-1918	General Labourer	8-8-1945
72644	MURRAY, Robert	14 Connolly St., Athlone.	6-2-1915	Labourer	8-8-1945
83873	MURRAY, Sean	Killaughey, Lurgan.	7-3-1921	Clerk	8-8-1945
79499	MURRAY, Sean	58 Bangor Road, Crumlin, Dublin.	13-12-1920	None	8-8-1945
E/434492	MURRAY, Sean	Ferguson Road, Drumcondra, Dublin.	26-5-1922	Messenger	8-8-1945
A/76298	MURRAY, Senan	Tamon, Lisdeen, Kilkee, Co. Clare.	21-11-1919	Farm Labourer	8-8-1945
E/423887	MURRAY, Thomas	Cara Street, Clones.	15-6-1915	Labourer	8-8-1945
E/412145	MURRAY, Thomas	24 Old Youghal Road, Mayfield, Cork.	10-1-1914	Machinist	8-8-1945
78475	MURRAY, Thomas	39 Emmett Tce, Navan.	10-3-1920	Messenger	8-8-1945
E/414895	MURRAY, William	36 Evergreen Road, Cork.	4-9-1922	Metal Worker	8-8-1945
E/433781	MURRY, Sylvester	14 Wolfe Tone Street, Kilkenny.	1-5-1912	Waiter	8-8-1945
E/438184	MURTAGH, Bernard	55 Harty Place, Dublin.	18-5-1926	Apprentice Welder	8-8-1945
E/400556	MURTAGH, James	18 Dunne Street, Dublin.	4-4-1916	Labourer	8-8-1945
E/405709	MURTAGH, James	15 Ashworth Place, Harold's Cross, Dublin.	18-2-1902	Driver	8-8-1945
E/434511	MURTAGH, James	Carrigeen, Boyle, Co. Roscommon.	28-12-1907	Clerk	8-8-1945
E/404651	MURTAGH, John	15 Hill Street, Dublin.	27-5-1919	Labourer	8-8-1945
L/503352	MURTAGH, Joseph	17 Dorset Avenue, Dorset Street, Dublin.	11-10-1928	Messenger	4-5-1946
201637	MURTAGH, Patrick	Henry St., Castleblayney, Co. Monaghan.	22-4-1915	Farm Labourer	8-8-1945
A/73431	MURTAGH, Peter	Long Lane, Dublin.	22-9-1913	Cabinet Maker	8-8-1945
81451	MURTAGH, William	5 Hardiman's Row, Drumcondra, Dublin.	25-7-1927	Messenger	16-5-1946
207538	MUSKETT, Joseph	28 Assumption Rd., Cork.	23-2-1916	Shop Assistant	8-8-1945
E/402387	MYERS, Bernard	21 Youngfield Road, Crumlin, Dublin.	21-4-1922	Messenger	8-8-1945
E/434149	MYLER, James	31 Peter Street, Waterford.	12-10-1922	Shoemaker	8-8-1945
A/78900	MYLER, Patrick	15 Prussia Street, Dublin.	27-1-1919	Labourer	8-8-1945
E/414839	MYRES, Maurice	249 Cathedral Rd., Cork.	6-1-1917	Labourer	8-8-1945
V/208316	NAGLE, Albert	Corhuduff, Kilshanny, Co. Clare.	6-4-1921	Farmer	8-8-1945
E/410195	NAGLE, John	14 Devonshire Street, Cork.	25-4-1899	Labourer	8-8-1945
E/422887	NASH, Edward	c/o Michael McHale, Muff, Co. Donegal.	6-10-1921	Labourer	8-8-1945
E/422352	NASH, John	2 Speer's Ln., Letterkenny.	18-12-1913	Labourer	8-8-1945

Army No.	Name.	Last Recorded Address.	Date of Birth.	Declared Occupation prior to enlistment in Defence Forces.	Date of Dismissal from Defence Forces.
E/421010	NASH, Patrick	2 Cottage Row, Letterkenny.	3-3-1920	Labourer	8-8-1945
77921	NASH, Patrick	5 Glenbrook Tce., Derry.	2-3-1916	Dock Labourer	8-8-1945
E/425144	NASH, Thomas	8 Gallagher's Sq., Derry.	27-7-1924	Labourer	8-8-1945
E/416218	NAUGHTON, Benjamin	137 Brendan's Rd., Cork.	29-9-1923	Foundry Worker	8-8-1945
75663	NAUGHTON, Peter	4 Smithfield Tce., Dublin.	10-2-1917	Labourer	8-8-1945
77481	NEABE, Edward W.	21 Culmcille Street, Islandfield, Limerick.	16-6-1920	Labourer	8-8-1945
E/422051	NEESON, Patrick	Corroe Street, Clones.	14-11-1918	Lorry Helper	8-8-1945
E/431653	NEILUS, William	Factory Ln., Portlaoighise.	14-4-1921	Labourer	8-8-1945
79816	NELIGAN, Denis	Brosna, Co. Kerry.	11-9-1920	Labourer	8-8-1945
V/205895	NELIS, Joseph	Moylough, Co. Kildare.	3-7-1914	Gardener	8-8-1945
72980	NESTOR, Patrick	67 New Road, Thomond Gate, Limerick.	25-1-1913	General Labourer	8-8-1945
78229	NEVIN, Dominick	Shannon Road, Portumna.	2-8-1921	Farm Labourer	8-8-1945
E/408386	NICHOLL, Francis J.	25 Benbulbin Road, Crumlin, Dublin.	30-4-1924	Messenger	8-8-1945
E/423219	NICHOLL, Michael	54 Fountain Hill, Waterside, Derry.	7-10-1917	Labourer	17-9-1945
E/404577	NICHOLSON, John	Castle Hill, Carlingford, Co. Louth.	28-6-1916	Driver	8-8-1945
E/433370	NICHOLSON, Patrick	38 Our Lady's Road, Maryland, Dublin.	3-4-1922	Sheet Metal Worker	8-8-1945
E/400279	NIX, Robert	62 Cabra Road, Dublin.	24-6-1892	Farmer	8-8-1945
E/408289	NOCTOR, Patrick	15 Clonfert Road, Kimmage, Dublin.	14-5-1912	Labourer	8-8-1945
A/81553	NOLAN, Benjamin	Brosna, Co. Kerry.	9-2-1923	Shoemaker	8-8-1945
77071	NOLAN, Edward	Conoboro Road, Rathdowney, Leix.	10-3-1917	Labourer	8-8-1945
E/406254	NOLAN, James	8 Redcow Lane, North King Street, Dublin.	18-9-1919	Messenger	8-8-1945
E/436110	NOLAN, Jeremiah	882 Rathfield, Newbridge, Co. Kildare.	25-8-1917	Motor Driver	8-8-1945
V/201728	NOLAN, John	24 Knockree Road, Crumlin, Dublin.	1-12-1919	Bootmaker's Apprentice	8-8-1945
83179	NOLAN, John	55 Bangor Rd., Crumlin, Dublin.	25-7-1921	Mechanic's Apprentice	8-8-1945
75529	NOLAN, Joseph	Barrack Street, Dundalk.	23-12-1919	Farm Labourer	8-8-1945
E/422224	NOLAN, Patrick	Craig House, Rosses Point, Co. Sligo.	17-3-1905	Garden Labourer	8-8-1945
E/433367	NOLAN, Patrick	5 Phoenix St., Inchicore, Dublin.	22-11-1913	Labourer	8-8-1945
E/414390	NOLAN, Patrick	Station House, Glanworth, Co. Cork.	21-4-1922	Messenger Boy	8-8-1945
E/423802	NOLAN, Thomas	Edgeworthstown, Co. Longford.	8-7-1921	Labourer	8-8-1945
A/71503	NOLAN, Thomas	1 Thomas Davis Street, Dublin.	27-3-1910	Labourer	8-8-1945
80489	NOLAN, William	Clonhamon, Ferns, Co. Wexford.	5-4-1922	General Labourer	8-8-1945
E/411132	NOONAN, Denis	32 Reid's Square, Cork.	20-7-1917	Motor Driver	8-8-1945
79693	NOONAN, Patrick	2 Thomas Street, Fermoy.	24-4-1917	Porter	8-8-1945
V/209394	NOONAN, Timothy	Homeville, Blackrock, Cork.	23-5-1910	Motor Driver	8-8-1945
V/200007	NOONAN, William	13 Bachelor's Quay, Cork.	3-9-1920	Messenger Boy	8-8-1945
E/425233	NOONE, James	Barrack Hill, Westport, Co. Mayo.	14-3-1924	Shoemaker	8-8-1945
210237	NORRIS, Lawrence	3 Keating's Terrace, Dungarvan, Co. Waterford.	12-5-1922	Motor Driver	8-8-1945
E/406227	NORTHEY, Ernest	12 St. Patrick's Sq., Bray.	2-12-1919	Baker	8-8-1945
L/502953	NOTARO, Mark	159 M Block, Oliver Bond House, Bridgefoot Street, Dublin.	5-2-1927	Cook	8-8-1945
E/415816	NUGENT, Patrick	Kilreedy, Tubber, Co. Clare.	2-2-1919	Farmer	8-8-1945

Army No.	Name.	Last Recorded Address.	Date of Birth.	Declared Occupation prior to enlistment in Defence Forces.	Date of Dismissal from Defence Forces.
72197	NUGENT, Thomas	Burnfoot, Co. Donegal.	22-2-1914	Labourer	8-8-1945
E/424150	NUGENT, Walter	Coneyboro Road, Lifford.	27-2-1907	Bus Driver	8-8-1945
84011	NULTY, Michael	Carrickboy, Mostrim, Co. Longford.	18-9-1920	Labourer	8-8-1945
E/424166	OATES, James	Cartubber, Carrick-on-Shannon.	15-11-1922	Labourer	8-8-1945
74216	O'BOYLE, Vincent	11 Iveagh Drive, Falls Road, Belfast.	20-9-1914	Clerk	8-8-1945
E/435749	O'BRIEN, Andrew	1 Drumgoold, Enniscorthy, Co. Wexford.	15-7-1922	Labourer	8-8-1945
E/410797	O'BRIEN, Cecil	3 High Street, Limerick.	31-10-1920	Labourer	8-8-1945
E/412219	O'BRIEN, Christopher	34 Cashel Road, Clonmel.	29-11-1917	Skilled Labourer	8-8-1945
79555	O'BRIEN, Christopher	32 Golden Bridge Avenue, Dublin.	29-6-1916	Universal Grinder	8-8-1945
E/404937	O'BRIEN, Cornelius	11 St. Alban's Rd., Dublin.	1-10-1921	Shoemaker	8-8-1945
E/431236	O'BRIEN, Daniel	61 Longmore, Dungarvan, Co. Waterford.	3-10-1919	Labourer	8-8-1945
E/435002	O'BRIEN, Daniel	58 Ossory Park, Kilkenny.	9-2-1918	Farm Labourer	8-8-1945
L/506863	O'BRIEN, David	106 Mount Nebo Avenue, Gurranebraher, Cork.	19-8-1926	Messenger Boy	8-8-1945
E/400011	O'BRIEN, Denis	35B Pearse House, Hanover Street, Dublin.	22-3-1905	Labourer	8-8-1945
76684	O'BRIEN, Denis	Newcastlewest, Co. Limerick.	18-12-1919	Labourer	8-8-1945
L/506513	O'BRIEN, Denis	106 Mount Nebo Avenue, Gurranebraher, Cork.	19-12-1924	Messenger Boy	8-8-1945
V/206182	O'BRIEN, Edward	9 Arbour Terrace, Arbour Hill, Dublin.	22-2-1921	Labourer	8-8-1945
V/210058	O'BRIEN, Edward	64 New Rd., Thomondgate, Limerick.	11-9-1914	Labourer	8-8-1945
E/431880	O'BRIEN, Edward	Wolfe Tone Villas, Wexford.	27-2-1919	Labourer	8-8-1945
E/406535	O'BRIEN, Edward	22 Old Camden St., Dublin.	27-5-1923	Mechanic Apprentice	8-8-1945
E/408281	O'BRIEN, Francis	Tankardstown, Ratoath, Co. Meath.	1-5-1923	Farm Labourer	8-8-1945
E/407799	O'BRIEN, Gerard	41 Beechill Avenue, Donnybrook, Dublin.	23-10-1923	Messenger	8-8-1945
V/200528	O'BRIEN, Henry	8 Castle Bks., Limerick.	1-12-1921	Messenger Boy	8-8-1945
E/411006	O'BRIEN, James	Moneygale, Offaly.	5-2-1922	Labourer	8-8-1945
E/406122	O'BRIEN, James	107 Joy Street, Belfast.	28-2-1923	Joiner (Apprentice)	8-8-1945
E/414439	O'BRIEN, James	11 Mitchell's Road, Boherbee, Tralee.	15-4-1915	Labourer	8-8-1945
A/82362	O'BRIEN, James	Percival Street, Kanturk, Co. Cork.	25-7-1922	Carrier	8-8-1945
A/78827	O'BRIEN, James	The Racks, Carrick-on-Suir, Co. Tipperary.	27-4-1915	Butcher	8-8-1945
79556	O'BRIEN, James	115 E Block, Iveagh Buildings, New Bride Street, Dublin.	11-10-1914	Motor Driver	8-8-1945
L/507467	O'BRIEN, John	8 Anderson's Court, Carey's Road, Limerick.	26-12-1926	Labourer	30-6-1946
V/210147	O'BRIEN, John	Corkey, Manorcunningham, Co. Donegal.	12-10-1921	Labourer	8-8-1945
E/416454	O'BRIEN, John	Duagh, Listowel.	15-8-1922	Labourer	8-8-1945
V/205187	O'BRIEN, John	20 Island Street, Dublin.	10-7-1910	Labourer	8-8-1945
E/424818	O'BRIEN, John Chris.	Ratheney, Peterswell, Gort, Co. Galway.	26-4-1915	Farm Labourer	8-8-1945
V/207388	O'BRIEN, Joseph	5 Camden Court, Camden Street, Dublin.	30-2-1921	Messenger Boy	8-8-1945
E/407388	O'BRIEN, Joseph	Fair Hill, Dundalk.	22-8-1919	Farm Labourer	8-8-1945
82995	O'BRIEN, Joseph	30 Geraldine St., Dublin.	10-11-1919	Labourer	8-8-1945

Army No.	Name.	Last Recorded Address.	Date of Birth.	Declared Occupation prior to enlistment in Defence Forces.	Date of Dismissal from Defence Forces.
E/423642	O'BRIEN, Joseph	Broad Road, Arvagh, Co. Cavan.	8-8-1908	Blacksmith	8-8-1945
75459	O'BRIEN, Joseph	4 Hanover Street, Coombe, Dublin.	17-3-1918	Labourer	8-8-1945
E/402414	O'BRIEN, Kevin	31 Charlemont St., Dublin.	10-10-1921	Labourer	8-8-1945
V/204633	O'BRIEN, Leslie	Croydon Cottages, Philipsburgh Avenue, Dublin.	14-3-1922	Shoemaker	8-8-1945
E/407294	O'BRIEN, Mark	55 O'Byrne Road, Bray.	12-12-1923	Student	8-8-1945
V/211282	O'BRIEN, Martin	St. Anne's, North Brunswick St., Dublin.	22-7-1917	Butcher	8-8-1945
A/80650	O'BRIEN, Martin	Ballylemon, Castlecomer, Co. Kilkenny.	7-7-1918	Blacksmith	8-8-1945
A/76550	O'BRIEN, Martin	36 Townsend St., Dublin.	12-1-1920	Messenger	8-8-1945
79113	O'BRIEN, Martin	14 Hogan Place, Dublin.	27-3-1921	Labourer	8-8-1945
75302	O'BRIEN, Maurice	Pyke Road, Fermoy.	26-7-1916	Farm Labourer	8-8-1945
A/80396	O'BRIEN, Michael	10 H Block, Arbour Hill Barracks, Dublin.	17-10-1921	Cinema Operator	8-8-1945
B/5875	O'BRIEN, Michael	10 Gravel Walk, Clonmel.	12-5-1911	Farm Labourer	8-8-1945
E/416548	O'BRIEN, Michael	Duagh, Listowel.	27-10-1922	Labourer	8-8-1945
L/506248	O'BRIEN, Michael	Clonmore, Tralee.	20-6-1924	Labourer	8-8-1945
E/424115	O'BRIEN, Michael	O'Brien Street, Tullamore.	16-4-1916	Builder's Labourer	8-8-1945
205133	O'BRIEN, Michael	12 Lower Dominick Street, Dublin.	30-11-1917	Helper on Motor Lorry	8-8-1945
E/412662	O'BRIEN, Patrick	Hill View Cottage, Stillorgan, Co. Dublin.	13-6-1922	Messenger	8-8-1945
78991	O'BRIEN, Patrick	11 Clonliffe Avenue, Ballybough, Dublin.	25-3-1921	Presser	8-8-1945
V/201565	O'BRIEN, Patrick	14 St. Edward's Terrace, Sligo.	12-7-1918	Labourer	8-8-1945
E/415791	O'BRIEN, Patrick	11 Glenview Terrace, Dillon's Cross, Cork.	4-7-1922	Bicycle Mechanic	8-8-1945
E/416918	O'BRIEN, Patrick	13 Military Road, Cork.	6-9-1912	Gardener	8-8-1945
A/70506	O'BRIEN, Patrick	C Block, Military Barracks, Newbridge, Co. Kildare.	26-8-1911	Grocer's Assistant	8-8-1945
V/209687	O'BRIEN, Patrick	42 Doyle's Road, Turner's Cross, Cork.	28-11-1922	Factory Worker	8-8-1945
V/200888	O'BRIEN, Patrick J.	23 Kells Road, Kilkenny.	19-3-1912	Labourer	8-8-1945
L/507934	O'BRIEN, Peter	101 St. Joseph's Park, Nenagh.	1-9-1928	Labourer	28-2-1946
E/412488	O'BRIEN, Peter	3 St. Peter Avenue, Cork.	29-6-1917	Storeman	8-8-1945
201658	O'BRIEN, Pierce	94 Ballytruckle, Waterford.	7-7-1917	Farm Labourer	8-8-1945
L/500590	O'BRIEN, Reginald	15 Prussia Street, Dublin.	26-11-1922	Labourer	8-8-1945
E/430434	O'BRIEN, Richard	Old Kilcullen, Co. Kildare.	27-10-1914	Labourer	8-8-1945
A/60063	O'BRIEN, Richard	86 St. Michael's Avenue, Tipperary.	15-10-1903	Farrier	8-8-1945
L/506249	O'BRIEN, Richard	Duagh, Listowel.	12-7-1917	Labourer	8-8-1945
V/207002	O'BRIEN, Stephen	Millers March, Waterford.	3-5-1922	Messenger	8-8-1945
V/214169	O'BRIEN, Stephen	Brookville, Co. Tipperary.	20-6-1923	Labourer	5-2-1946
77852	O'BRIEN, Thomas	42 Doyle's Road, Turner's Cross, Cork.	4-5-1920	Baker	8-8-1945
2656	O'BRIEN, Thomas	78 St. Nicholas Avenue, Castletown, Dundalk.	21-7-1904	Labourer	8-8-1945
E/414902	O'BRIEN, Thomas	24 Prospect Villas, Limerick.	12-1-1923	Clerk	8-8-1945
A/82788	O'BRIEN, Thomas	34 Cashel Road, Clonmel.	24-7-1920	Labourer	8-8-1945
V/205815	O'BRIEN, Thomas	Old Chapel St., Mooncoin, Co. Kilkenny.	9-8-1909	Fisherman	3-2-1946
E/409462	O'BRIEN, Vincent	15 Glasthule Buildings, Glasthule, Co. Dublin.	14-5-1923	Carpenter	8-8-1945
L/507400	O'BRIEN, William	1 Benson's Lane, Mungret Street, Limerick.	26-3-1925	Labourer	29-4-1946
E/432151	O'BRIEN, William	43 Connolly St., Kilkenny.	5-4-1922	Labourer	8-8-1945
V/202914	O'BROIN, Miceal	63 Iveagh Gardens, Crumlin, Dublin.	31-12-1916	Pawn Broker's Assistant	8-8-1945

Army No.	Name.	Last Recorded Address.	Date of Birth.	Declared Occupation prior to enlistment in Defence Forces.	Date of Dismissal from Defence Forces.
E/434535	O'BYRNE, James	10 Dublin Rd., Stillorgan, Co. Dublin.	7-5-1905	Clerk	8-8-1945
E/435048	O'BYRNE, Patrick	Garrangreine, Borrisoleigh, Co. Tipperary.	1-10-1922	Farm Labourer	8-8-1945
L/502506	O'BYRNE, Peter	42 Restoration Lane, Adelaide Road, Dublin.	8-8-1925	Labourer	8-8-1945
84842	O'CADHAIN, Peter	Pairc a Doire, Tourmakeady, Co. Mayo.	27-1-1921	Farm Worker	8-8-1945
E/417788	O'CALLAGHAN, Edward A.	6 Kilbrogan St., Bandon, Co. Cork.	13-6-1910	Tailor	8-8-1945
V/201676	O'CALLAGHAN, Edward	13 Fair Street, Mallow, Co. Cork.	10-2-1916	Motor Driver	8-8-1945
L/506892	O'CALLAGHAN, Eugene	5 Upper Castle St., Cork.	27-7-1926	Van Boy	7-4-1946
E/405524	O'CALLAGHAN, James	28 Hanbury Lane, Meath Street, Dublin.	3-5-1922	Messenger	8-8-1945
A/76050	O'CALLAGHAN, James	17 George's Place, Temple Street, Dublin.	4-9-1919	Blacksmith's Helper	8-8-1945
78697	O'CALLAGHAN, Jeremiah	Dirha West, Listowel, Co. Kerry.	28-4-1920	Butcher	8-8-1945
V/201527	O'CALLAGHAN, John	34 Fitzgibbon St., Dublin.	21-1-1907	Bus Driver	8-8-1945
A/75940	O'CALLAGHAN, Michael	Raheen Cottage, Ballybawn, Leix.	15-5-1913	Farm Labourer	8-8-1945
E/412009	O'CALLAGHAN, Michael J.	5 Green's Quay, Youghal, Co. Cork.	13-5-1918	Mason's Improver	8-8-1945
79740	O'CALLAGHAN, Michael	Rath, Churchtown, Mallow, Co. Cork.	4-5-1913	Labourer	8-8-1945
E/407900	O'CALLAGHAN, Patrick	Tyross, Ballybrolly, Armagh.	25-12-1923	Labourer	8-8-1945
A/70609	O'CALLAGHAN, Patrick	11 Millmount Terrace, Milltown, Dublin.	17-3-1909	Bus Conductor	8-8-1945
83809	O'CALLAGHAN, Terence	7 Hyde Terrace, Newry.	12-1-1914	Lorry Driver	8-8-1945
L/506764	O'CALLAGHAN, William	36 Peacock Lane, Cork.	4-12-1925	Messenger	8-8-1945
A/82777	O'CARROLL, Christopher	Ballybehy, Abbeyfeale, Co. Limerick.	15-12-1919	Labourer	8-8-1945
L/500228	O'CARROLL, Denis	173 James's Street, Dublin.	13-10-1922	Van Boy	8-8-1945
E/410855	O'CARROLL, James	Bridge St, Ballylongford, Co. Kerry.	29-11-1920	Student	8-8-1945
E/401584	O'CARROLL, Michael	Boynagh, Cottage, Kingscourt, Co. Cavan.	6-12-1901	Commercial Traveller	8-8-1945
A/78154	O'CATHAIN, Seán	Ballinglen, Dunquin, Co. Kerry.	24-4-1914	Labourer	8-8-1945
E/416315	O'CONNELL, Charles	24 Upper Friar's Road, Turner's Cross, Cork.	21-9-1923	Architect's Assistant	8-8-1945
E/411059	O'CONNELL, Daniel	11 Red Abbey Place, Mary Street, Cork.	15-11-1908	Labourer	8-8-1945
V/209664	O'CONNELL, Daniel	Slievedara, Ballyduff, Tralee.	14-7-1918	Farmer	8-8-1945
E/435291	O'CONNELL, Mitchell	18 Ballybough Street, Kilkenny.	7-5-1922	Shoemaker	8-8-1945
A/83653	O'CONNELL, Patrick	6 Hollyfield Buildings, Rathmines, Dublin.	16-6-1922	None	8-8-1945
79147	O'CONNELL, Patrick	Brideswell Street, Athlone.	1-3-1921	Hair Dresser	8-8-1945
A/111645	O'CONNOR, Bernard	Knockavagh, Rathvilly, Co. Carlow.	27-11-1916	Labourer	8-8-1945
75429	O'CONNOR, Daniel	Farranakilla, Castlegregory, Co. Kerry.	16-9-1918	Farm Labourer	8-8-1945
V/201383	O'CONNOR, Denis	Maiden Street, Newcastle West, Co. Limerick.	1-5-1921	Labourer	8-8-1945
E/416755	O'CONNOR, Edmond	Bank Place, Tipperary.	4-8-1917	Commercial Traveller	8-8-1945
A/78671	O'CONNOR, Edward	Brickfield, Kilmallock, Co. Limerick.	10-1-1921	Farm Labourer	8-8-1945
78861	O'CONNOR, Gerald	7 River Lane, Sand Mall, Limerick.	23-9-1920	General Labourer	8-8-1945
A/76900	O'CONNOR, Gerard	38 Connolly Villas, Ennis.	10-1-1920	Labourer	8-8-1945

Army No.	Name.	Last Recorded Address.	Date of Birth.	Declared Occupation prior to enlistment in Defence Forces.	Date of Dismissal from Defence Forces.
A/78616	O'CONNOR, James	Oldtown Station, Letterkenny, Co. Donegal.	31-1-1921	Farm Labourer	8-8-1945
E/401845	O'CONNOR, James	34 Peter Street, Dublin.	20-6-1900	Tailor	8-8-1945
V/208403	O'CONNOR, John	St. Raphael's Terrace, Fr. Griffin Road, Galway.	30-12-1919	Carpenter	8-8-1945
E/425070	O'CONNOR, John	Lavally, Ballintogher, Co. Sligo.	25-3-1923	Labourer	8-8-1945
E/415359	O'CONNOR, John	Aughacasla, Castlegregory, Co. Kerry.	5-6-1915	Machine Operator	8-8-1945
203403	O'CONNOR, John	Behenaugh, Knocknagoshel, Co. Kerry.	—-12-1912	Labourer	8-8-1945
E/404043	O'CONNOR, John	59 Carlingford Parade, Grand Canal, Dublin.	12-5-1915	Labourer	8-8-1945
E/409269	O'CONNOR, John	2 Matthew Terrace, Blackrock, Co. Dublin.	8-6-1924	Dairyman	8-8-1945
V/200500	O'CONNOR, Joseph	Drogheda Road, Duleek, Co. Meath.	12-6-1918	Farm Labourer	8-8-1945
79198	O'CONNOR, Martin	Main Street, Coalisland, Co. Tyrone.	21-6-1920	Labourer	8-8-1945
E/433675	O'CONNOR, Matthew	13 Patrick's Place, Enniscorthy.	12-2-1921	Draper's Clerk	8-8-1945
V/202517	O'CONNOR, Michael	Kilmainham, Kells.	14-5-1917	Labourer	8-8-1945
V/209532	O'CONNOR, Patrick	4 Armagh Road, Crumlin, Dublin.	22-7-1922	Labourer	8-8-1945
E/425018	O'CONNOR, Patrick	c/o Mrs. Rooney, Main St., Castlerea, Co. Roscommon.	17-3-1910	Blacksmith	8-8-1945
E/434038	O'CONNOR, Patrick	38 Jervis Street, Dublin.	24-5-1916	Labourer	8-8-1945
E/424158	O'CONNOR, Patrick	The Mall, Tuam, Co. Galway.	6-1-1920	Butcher	8-8-1945
A/73052	O'CONNOR, Peter	Rathnew, Co. Wicklow.	7-3-1913	Labourer	8-8-1945
E/405483	O'CONNOR, Philip	17 St. Attracta Road, Cabra, Dublin.	17-4-1922	Cutter	8-8-1945
E/414835	O'CONNOR, Richard	Church, Glin, Co. Limerick.	29-11-1922	Labourer	8-8-1945
E/406712	O'CONNOR, Richard	50 Lambay Road, Drumcondra, Dublin.	19-5-1923	Labourer	8-8-1945
E/401753	O'CONNOR, Thomas	283 St. Attracta Road, Cabra, Dublin.	6-7-1921	Labourer	8-10-1945
V/205991	O'CONNOR, Thomas	c/o Patrick Maloney, Main Street, Hospital, Co. Limerick.	16-12-1913	Labourer	8-8-1945
A/75699	O'CONNOR, Thomas	John Street, Dingle, Co. Kerry.	25-1-1916	General Labourer	8-8-1945
78462	O'CONNOR, Thomas	Ballyeagh, Ballybunion, Co. Kerry.	17-8-1915	Barman	8-8-1945
E/408082	O'CONNOR, Thomas	Baymore Road, Drogheda.	4-10-1913	Labourer	8-8-1945
E/401571	O'CONNOR, William	15 East James's Street, Dublin.	8-12-1918	Packer	8-8-1945
E/403427	O'CONNOR, William	26 Leo Street, Dublin.	31-3-1906	Phone Operator	8-8-1945
77781	O'DEA, Martin	Springfield, Ballacolla, Leix.	29-8-1920	Farm Labourer	8-8-1945
V/203231	O'DEA, Thomas	The Hill, Knocklong, Co. Limerick.	9-10-1920	Labourer	8-8-1945
E/420468	O'DOHERTY, Eamon	c/o M. Hegarty, Bridge End, Co. Donegal.	1-4-1896	Cook	8-8-1945
E/403244	O'DOHERTY, James	5 Stanaway Road, Kimmage, Dublin.	2-3-1919	Hairdresser	8-8-1945
E/421995	O'DOHERTY, James	c/o Patrick Kelly, Castlefin, Co. Donegal.	12-4-1912	Motor Driver	8-8-1945
84142	O'DOHERTY, Michael	19 Edenmore Street, Derry.	22-9-1921	Student	8-8-1945
V/215121	O'DONNELL, Arthur	Dunfanaghy, Co. Donegal.	28-2-1920	Motor Driver	8-8-1945
V/203781	O'DONNELL, Charles	Main Street, Glenties, Co. Donegal.	19-9-1920	Machinist Hosiery Factory	8-8-1945
A/84254	O'DONNELL, Daniel	Ruskey, Convoy, Co. Donegal.	21-8-1917	Gen. Labourer	8-8-1945

Army No.	Name.	Last Recorded Address.	Date of Birth.	Declared Occupation prior to enlistment in Defence Forces.	Date of Dismissal from Defence Forces.
74172	O'DONNELL, Daniel	Liscannor, Co. Clare.	29-4-1915	Fisherman	8-8-1945
79568	O'DONNELL, Edward	11 Wolfe Tone Street, Kilkenny.	2-9-1921	Labourer	8-8-1945
E/422353	O'DONNELL, Hugh	c/o Mrs. Harrison, Ture, Donegal.	23-12-1914	Labourer	8-8-1945
E/423220	O'DONNELL, James	4 Strabane Road, Waterside, Derry.	26-10-1921	Labourer	8-8-1945
E/406249	O'DONNELL, James	Main Street, Coalisland, Co. Tyrone.	30-4-1919	Bricklayer	8-8-1945
113182	O'DONNELL, James	Liscannor, Co. Clare.	21-10-1917	Farm Labourer	8-8-1945
E/421879	O'DONNELL, James	Magheraclogher, Derrybeg, Co. Donegal.	13-2-1921	Labourer	8-8-1945
V/215261	O'DONNELL, John	Dunfanaghy, Co. Donegal.	25-2-1924	Shop Assistant	8-8-1945
E/402586	O'DONNELL, John	10 Malpas Place, New St., Dublin.	2-11-1910	Labourer	8-8-1945
E/403987	O'DONNELL, John	Carrick Hill, Portmarnock, Dublin.	18-12-1905	Commercial Clerk	8-8-1945
79682	O'DONNELL, Joseph	130 Strand Street, Derry.	22-5-1920	Student	8-8-1945
84490	O'DONNELL, Michael	Sleadrin, Buncrana, Co. Donegal.	18-9-1925	Lorry Driver	8-8-1945
E/41555	O'DONNELL, Michael	Ballygrennan, Convent Rd., Bruff, Co. Limerick.	16-2-1923	Farm Labourer	8-8-1945
E/421501	O'DONNELL, Patrick	Boughtofudd, Ballaghaderreen.	27-7-1913	Bricklayer	8-8-1945
E/414234	O'DONNELL, Patrick	Ballygrennan, Bruff, Co. Limerick.	10-1-1920	Trapper	8-8-1945
A/68558	O'DONNELL, Patrick	3 Hatch Street Lane, Dublin.	6-1-1904	Motor Driver	8-8-1945
E/407212	O'DONNELL, Patrick J.	2 Homeville, Rathmines, Dublin.	16-4-1923	Labourer	8-8-1945
76357	O'DONNELL, Peter	Kincasslagh, Co. Donegal.	19-5-1921	Shop Assistant	8-8-1945
A/84301	O'DONNELL, Thomas	Moyras, Carna, Co. Galway.	16-7-1916	Farmer	8-8-1945
V/201311	O'DONNELL, Thomas	Broghill, Charleville, Co. Cork.	23-1-1919	Labourer	8-8-1945
A/75978	O'DONOGHUE, Daniel	Camas Road, Cashel, Co. Tipperary.	27-2-1919	Barber's Assistant	8-8-1945
V/201276	O'DONOGHUE, Daniel	Toorath, Fountain, Ennis.	6-5-1919	None	8-8-1945
E/414565	O'DONOGHUE, Edward	8 Hegarty's Square, Blarney Street, Cork.	17-6-1921	Bookmaker	8-8-1945
V/209871	O'DONOGHUE, Edward	3 Benson Place, Mungret Street, Limerick.	20-1-1920	Labourer	8-8-1945
77262	O'DONOGHUE, James	Bohernabreena, Tallaght, Co. Dublin.	3-9-1919	Quarry Worker	8-8-1945
80333	O'DONOGHUE, James	9 Grosvenor Sq., Dublin.	19-12-1921	Plumber's Assistant	8-8-1945
78730	O'DONOGHUE, Michael	31 Carmel Hall, Francis Street, Dublin.	21-2-1921	Shoemaker	8-8-1945
E/412635	O'DONOGHUE, Michael	Benson's Row, Mungret Street, Limerick.	2-6-1918	Labourer	8-8-1945
85603	O'DONOGHUE, Thomas J.	Killatly, Ballyhooley, Co. Cork.	30-5-1925	Farm Labourer	17-8-1946
E/410552	O'DONOGHUE, William	1 Shaws Alley, Barrack Street, Cork.	18-12-1921	Labourer	8-8-1945
V/201487	O'DONOGHUE, William	81 North King St., Dublin.	11-4-1915	Bus Conductor	8-8-1945
E/423018	O'DONOVAN, Charles	10 Upper Mountpleasant Avenue, Dublin.	7-7-1922	Draper's Apprentice	8-8-1945
E/407362	O'DONOVAN, Timothy	68 Old Kilmainham, Dublin.	26-1-1915	Driver	8-8-1945
A/83734	O'DOWD, Patrick	Brawn Bog, Bansha, Co. Tipperary.	25-8-1920	Labourer	8-8-1945
E/412154	O'DRISCOLL, Cornelius	Ballymore, Cobh.	15-4-1919	Cycle Mechanic	8-8-1945
E/413025	O'DRISCOLL, William	4 Newgate Place, Nicholas Street, Limerick.	29-8-1920	Mill Hand	8-8-1945
78131	O'DUILLEAN, Micheál	Killearney, Aran, Co. Galway.	24-9-1919	Student	8-8-1945

Army No.	Name.	Last Recorded Address.	Date of Birth.	Declared Occupation prior to enlistment in Defence Forces.	Date of Dismissal from Defence Forces.
77418	O'DWYER, Edmond	Knockane, Doolis, Pallasgreen, Co. Limerick.	—5-1919	Farmer	8-8-1945
V/204960	O'DWYER, Gerald	47 Wolfe Tone Street, Limerick.	20-6-1921	Messenger Boy	8-8-1945
82289	O'DWYER, Richard	5 Kirkwood Villas, Cobh.	25-3-1922	Mechanic and Motor Driver	8-8-1945
E/400984	O'FAOLAIN, Eamon	41 Upper Mount Street, Dublin.	21-3-1894	Storekeeper	8-8-1945
E/408128	O'FARRELL, Sean	22 Crostwaithe Park, Dun Laoghaire.	18-12-1923	Shop Assistant	8-8-1945
V/206415	O'FARRELL, Vincent	7 North Wall, Dublin.	25-4-1922	Sailor	8-8-1945
507640	O'FLAHERTY, Michael	50 O'Rahilly Tce., Tralee.	11-2-1921	Labourer	5-5-1946
E/429615	O'FLANAGAN, Anthony	Tullindaly Road, Tuam, Co. Galway.	14-7-1922	Hotel Boots	8-8-1945
64324	O'FLYNN, Cornelius	5A Fownes Street, Dublin.	14-8-1904	Labourer	8-8-1945
83738	O'FLYNN, Patrick	46 Hawthorn St., Belfast.	13-2-1922	Painter	8-8-1945
84122	O'FRIGHILL, Tomás	Derrybeg, Co. Donegal.	25-10-1914	Labourer	8-8-1945
E/406875	O'GLESBY, Thomas	40 Hardwicke St., Dublin.	7-8-1922	Motor Driver	8-8-1945
E/412918	O'GORMAN, Christopher	60 Back Clare Street, Limerick.	11-3-1922	Labourer	8-8-1945
78345	O'GORMAN, Henry M.	9 St. Mary's Street, Dun Laoghaire.	28-10-1920	Golf Caddie	8-8-1945
85438	O'GORMAN, Joseph	112 St. Joseph's Terrace, Sligo.	19-6-1927	Labourer	7-5-1946
A/112340	O'GORMAN, Patrick	58 Ard Muire, Carrick-on-Suir, Co. Tipperary.	17-11-1918	Labourer	8-8-1945
L/502073	O'GORMAN, Patrick	63 Bridgefoot St., Dublin.	17-3-1925	None	8-8-1945
E/414440	O'GORMAN, Thomas	111 Roche's Buildings, Cork.	9-4-1922	Foundry Hand	8-8-1945
V/202981	O'GRADY, John	12 Wolfe Tone Street, Kilkenny.	14-2-1919	Labourer	8-8-1945
84283	O'GRADY, John	3 Clownmore, Mullingar.	26-3-1923	Labourer	8-8-1945
A/82495	O'GRADY, Patrick	17 Connolly's Villas, Ennis.	18-2-1923	Messenger Boy	8-8-1945
V/202634	O'GRADY, Thomas	Kilmanmanagh, Collooney, Co. Sligo.	10-1-1917	Motor Driver	8-8-1945
A/78802	O'GRADY, William	Westcourt, Callan, Co. Kilkenny.	26-1-1921	Farm Labourer	8-8-1945
E/429674	O'GREALLY, Dudley	Kilbracken, Rossmuck, Co. Galway.	15-5-1913	Labourer	8-8-1945
E/408847	O'HAGAN, James	Lurgaveagh, Ballyardle, Kilhill, Down.	24-9-1924	Tractor Driver	8-8-1945
E/404982	O'HAGAN, Patrick	2 Iveagh Terrace, Cork Street, Dublin.	19-6-1922	Labourer	8-8-1945
E/422888	O'HAGAN, Sean	Burnfoot, Co. Donegal.	11-7-1922	Builder's Helper	8-8-1945
E/411840	O'HALLORAN, Joseph	129 St. Munchin's Place, Island Field, Limerick.	18-8-1920	Labourer	8-8-1945
E/412802	O'HALLORAN, Joseph	3 Nolan's Cottages, Mary Street, Limerick.	28-2-1916	Waiter	8-8-1945
E/438089	O'HALLORAN, Peter	51 Bow Lane, Dublin.	27-4-1926	General Labourer	26-8-1945
E/432780	O'HALLORAN, Richard	O'Connell's Place, Waterford.	23-5-1916	Waiter	8-8-1945
83010	O'HANLON, John	65 Paul Street, Dublin.	23-8-1921	Messenger	8-8-1945
V/208892	O'HANLON, Patrick	Saltpass, Rathmullan, Co. Donegal.	2-11-1919	Labourer	8-8-1945
L/502855	O'HANLON, Stephen	33 Fleming Road, Drumcondra, Dublin.	8-11-1926	Messenger	1-7-1946
E/434000	O'HANLON, William	2 Harbour St., Tullamore.	22-6-1906	Motor Driver	8-8-1945
E/405450	O'HARA, Arthur	Church St., Clara, Offaly.	29-4-1920	Medical Student	8-8-1945
E/423779	O'HARA, Arthur	Mail Coach Road, Sligo.	22-11-1919	Machine Hand	8-8-1945
E/421572	O'HARA, James	Camderry, East Bars, Glenfarne, Co. Leitrim.	23-10-1922	Student	8-8-1945
84235	O'HARA, Michael	Drumlish, Co. Longford.	4-6-1916	Shop Assistant	8-8-1945

Army No.	Name.	Last Recorded Address.	Date of Birth.	Declared Occupation prior to enlistment in Defence Forces.	Date of Dismissal from Defence Forces.
200263	O'HARA, Michael	Farrnew, Ballina, Co. Mayo.	25-3-1915	Labourer	8-8-1945
A/72939	O'HARA, Patrick	4 Greenfield Terrace, Cove Street, Cork.	25-8-1910	Labourer	8-8-1945
E/434793	O'HARA, Patrick	Collinstown, Clara, Offaly.	18-11-1914	Labourer	8-8-1945
E/405109	O'HARA, Sean	117 Harold's Cross Cottages, Dublin.	17-12-1922	Telephone Operator	8-8-1945
E/436026	O'HARA, Thomas	Maxtown, Callan, Co. Kilkenny.	25-7-1922	Labourer	8-8-1945
E/404217	O'HARE, Harry	Hilltown, Newry.	20-11-1916	Driver	8-8-1945
E/422228	O'HARE, Kevin	c/o E. Waters, Main St., Castleblayney, Co. Monaghan.	16-1-1921	None	8-8-1945
83910	O'HARE, James	16 Caulfield Place, Newry.	14-1-1922	Labourer	8-8-1945
E/406802	O'HARE, John	John Street, Rathfriland, Co. Down.	7-3-1920	Shop Assistant	8-8-1945
V/211636	O'HARE, Thomas	Donoghmore, Kilkerly, Co. Louth.	23-10-1923	Farm Labourer	8-8-1945
E/433779	O'HERLIHY, Patrick	28 Wolfe Tone Street, Kilkenny.	3-9-1916	Blacksmith	8-8-1945
E/424961	O'KANE, William	Glack, Limavady, Co. Derry.	4-8-1918	Labourer	8-8-1945
E/407391	O'KEEFFE, Albert	3 Bellview Terrace, Military Road, Cork.	27-11-1923	Tailor	8-8-1945
79535	O'KEEFFE, Charles	40 Roche's Buildings, Cork	26-12-1919	Butcher's Assistant	8-8-1945
A/70768	O'KEEFFE, Denis	53 Patrick Street, Dublin.	6-11-1911	Labourer	8-8-1945
82810	O'KEEFFE, James	Knockroe, Kilteely, Co. Limerick.	20-8-1913	Farmer	8-8-1945
A/82019	O'KEEFFE, John	40 Roche's Buildings, Cork	8-4-1918	Labourer	8-8-1945
V/204752	O'KEEFFE, Martin	110 Oliver Plunkett Street, Island Field, Limerick.	8-8-1919	None	8-8-1945
A/53076	O'KEEFFE, Patrick	Ardrahan, Kanturk, Co. Cork.	3-11-1904	Labourer	8-8-1945
80414	O'KEEFFE, Patrick	5 Mescander St., Waterford	9-3-1922	Messenger Boy	8-8-1945
V/211172	O'KEEFFE, Sean	2 Camac Park, Bluebell, Inchicore, Dublin.	12-9-1921	Mill Worker	8-8-1945
A/101229	O'KEEFFE, Walter	Pembrokestown, Butlerstown, Co. Waterford.	1-11-1913	Farm Labourer	8-8-1945
V/203744	O'KEEFFE, William	c/o Miss G. Rowe, 26 Doddridge Street, Liverpool.	13-8-1920	Waiter	8-8-1945
200208	O'KEEFFE, William	12 Usher's Island, Dublin.	25-4-1921	Hosiery Trimmer	8-8-1945
L/502438	O'KELLY, Anthony	Carriglea Park, Dun Laoghaire.	16-4-1926	Stable Boy	8-8-1945
78672	O'KELLY, Thomas Joseph	Fairfield, Kilmallock, Co. Limerick.	22-1-1921	Casual Labourer	8-8-1945
A/78195	O'LAOID, Sean	Derrygimlagh, Clifden, Co. Galway.	10-11-1918	Farm Labourer	8-8-1945
E/431128	O'LEARY, Aiden	Monart East, Enniscorthy, Co. Wexford.	21-5-1922	Farm Labourer	12-1-1946
E/414811	O'LEARY, Daniel	66 Horgan's Bldgs., Cork.	11-11-1922	Barman	8-8-1945
75288	O'LEARY, Denis	14 Crescent Street, London, W.2.	1-5-1918	Labourer	8-8-1945
E/411934	O'LEARY, Francis	Coachford, Co. Cork.	28-4-1900	Motor Mechanic	8-8-1945
E/416551	O'LEARY, Humphrey	Kilcoe, Aughadown, Skibbereen, Co. Cork.	12-12-1920	Farmer	8-8-1945
E/435752	O'LEARY, Joseph Morgan	Church View, Lomgarron, Ballycarney, Ferns, Co. Wexford.	7-2-1921	Farm Labourer	8-8-1945
77718	O'LEARY, Michael	6 Haig Gardens, Boreenmoira, Cork.	24-2-1920	Messenger	8-8-1945
69029	O'LEARY, Mortimer	4 Merrypole Lane, Blarney Street, Cork.	5-11-1908	Labourer	8-8-1945

Army No.	Name.	Last Recorded Address.	Date of Birth.	Declared Occupation prior to enlistment in Defence Forces.	Date of Dismissal from Defence Forces.
E/405042	O'LEARY, Nicholas	19 Blessington St., Dublin.	16-3-1907	Clerk	8-8-1945
E/416845	O'LEARY, Patrick	Ballinablaun, Glen, Killarney.	1-2-1915	Labourer	8-8-1945
L/500566	O'LEARY, Seamus	Shandon Cottages, Dundrum, Dublin.	3-3-1923	Labourer	8-8-1945
E/404714	O'LENNY, Henry	44 Main St., Rathfarnham, Co. Dublin.	10-8-1919	Telephone Worker	8-8-1945
E/422084	OLIVER, John	Main Street, Pettigo, Co. Donegal.	11-1-1919	Labourer	8-8-1945
E/423294	OLIVER, Thomas	Bridge St., Irvinestown, Co. Fermanagh.	8-10-1921	Labourer	8-8-1945
E/423295	OLIVER, Thomas	Main Street, Irvinestown, Co. Fermanagh.	22-5-1922	Lorry Driver	8-8-1945
A/84605	O'LOUGHLIN, Bartle	Warrenstown, Dunboyne, Co. Meath.	28-9-1921	Labourer	10-9-1945
V/207308	O'LOUGHLIN, Hugh	170 McCaffrey's Estate, Mount Brown, Dublin.	5-3-1909	Fitter's Apprentice	8-8-1945
E/408000	O'LOUGHLIN, John	37 Lambay Road, Glasnevin, Dublin.	8-4-1921	Shoemaker	8-8-1945
V/209469	O'LOUGHLIN, John	Rusbane, Kilmanora, Co. Clare.	—-2-1910	Farm Labourer	8-8-1945
A/79317	O'LOUGHLIN, Mortimer	28 Athenry Road, Tuam, Co. Galway.	23-9-1920	Student	8-8-1945
E/412019	O'LOUGHLIN, Peter	2 St. Finbar's Place, Cork.	3-11-1916	Lorry Driver	8-8-1945
V/205896	O'LOUGHLIN, Thomas	Figgneirt, Raphoe, Co. Donegal.	23-2-1905	Labourer	8-8-1945
L/502636	O'MAHONEY, Cecil	Charbury Lodge, Booterstown Ave.,Blackrock, Co. Dublin.	14-10-1926	None	15-4-1946
L/507259	O'MAHONEY, Jeremiah	2 Ballydaheen, Mallow, Co. Cork.	26-1-1926	Labourer	24-1-1946
A/82097	O'MAHONEY, John	Boolard, Charleville, Co. Cork.	10-2-1912	Labourer	8-8-1945
A/69110	O'MAHONEY, Michael	14 St. Finbar's Ave., Cork.	29-1-1911	Labourer	8-8-1945
E/410867	O'MAHONY, Daniel	15 St. Anthony's Road, Gurranebraher, Cork.	17-8-1907	Labourer	8-8-1945
80136	O'MAHONY, John	College View, Mungret, Co. Limerick.	27-4-1921	Gardener	8-8-1945
E/414891	O'MAHONY, John	47 Gurranebraher Road, Cork.	1-11-1922	Shop Assistant	8-8-1945
76081	O'MAHONY, John	655 White Avenue, Kildare.	27-4-1920	Cinema Attendant	8-8-1945
76212	O'MAHONY, Patrick	Kilcree, Aherla, Co. Cork.	26-4-1918	Farm Labourer	8-8-1945
74673	O'MAITHNIN, Michael	Turlough, Rosmuck, Co. Galway.	6-9-1917	Farm Labourer	8-8-1945
74798	O'MALLEY, Bartley	Fuarglass, Ballyconnelly, Clifden, Co. Galway.	2-10-1919	Farmer	8-8-1945
V/217086	O'MALLEY, Denis	Market Street, Cootehill, Co. Cavan.	18-9-1916	Butcher	8-8-1945
E/413457	O'MALLEY, Eugene	11 Lower Gerald Griffin Street, Limerick.	24-2-1918	Shop Assistant	8-8-1945
E/420239	O'MALLEY, John	Cainfowler, Belmullet, Co. Mayo.	26-5-1918	Seaman	8-8-1945
E/420240	O'MALLEY, Martin	Cainfowler, Belmullet, Co. Mayo.	25-12-1922	Seaman	8-8-1945
V/203761	O'MALLEY, Martin	Beal-an-Daingin, Connemara, Co. Galway.	14-3-1911	Farm Labourer	8-8-1945
E/434423	O'MARA, James	24 Tram Terrace, Terenure, Dublin.	25-3-1921	Messenger	8-8-1945
E/423126	O'MARA, John	50 Eccles Street, Dublin.	6-8-1905	Porter	8-8-1945
77256	O'MEARA, Daniel	46 Railway View, Roscrea.	27-7-1920	Labourer	8-8-1945
A/73706	O'MEARA, Denis	40 Railway View, Roscrea.	11-7-1911	Motor Mechanic	8-8-1945
E/414611	O MEARA, William	Upper Ballingarry, Thurles.	4-10-1911	Labourer	8-8-1945
E/414165	O MEARA, William	Copper, Ballincurry, Thurles.	12-8-1921	Labourer	8-8-1945

Army No.	Name.	Last Recorded Address.	Date of Birth.	Declared Occupation prior to enlistment in Defence Forces.	Date of Dismissal from Defence Forces.
E/438000	O'NEILL, Charles	11 Brabazon St., Dublin.	10-5-1925	General Labourer	8-8-1945
A/109280	O'NEILL, Charles	46 Lacey Av., Templemore, Co. Tipperary.	25-12-1915	Labourer	8-8-1945
205511	O'NEILL, Cornelius	200 Old Youghal Road, Cork.	15-8-1910	Fitter Driver	8-8-1945
75487	O'NEILL, Daniel	122 Farrenferris Av., Cork.	6-2-1919	Tailor	8-8-1945
E/408879	O'NEILL, Desmond	309 Clontarf Rd., Dublin.	22-2-1923	Clerk	8-8-1945
A/79438	O'NEILL, Desmond	19 Charleville Avenue, Ballybough, Dublin.	1-8-1921	General Labourer	8-8-1945
E/407481	O'NEILL, Donald	17 Margaret Street, Cork.	29-1-1920	Carpenter	8-8-1945
L/500363	O'NEILL, Edward	49 Kickham Rd., Inchicore, Dublin.	31-9-1922	Labourer	8-8-1945
L/503303	O'NEILL, Edward	206 Keogh St, Inchciore, Dublin.	23-7-1927	Farm Labourer	27-3-1946
E/404748	O'NEILL, Francis	35 Tralee Street, Belfast.	16-7-1922	Clerk	8-8-1945
79760	O'NEILL, Francis	11 Linfield Street, Dungannon, Co. Tyrone.	9-8-1913	Labourer	8-8-1945
E/422354	O'NEILL, Gerald	Burnfoot, Co. Donegal.	27-7-1921	Farm Labourer	8-8-1945
E/407639	O'NEILL, Hugh	Kilmascally, Stewartstown, Co. Tyrone.	7-7-1923	Labourer	8-8-1945
V/211543	O'NEILL, Hugh	21 Lr. Leeson St., Dublin.	25-8-1921	Engineer	8-8-1945
E/417214	O'NEILL, Hugh	3 Cathedral Road, Gurranebraher, Cork.	6-5-1924	Messenger Boy	8-8-1945
E/408137	O'NEILL, James	Annaghmore, Coalisland, Co. Tyrone.	3-5-1924	General Labourer	8-8-1945
78792	O'NEILL, Jeremiah	Market Street, Cahir, Co. Tipperary.	9-1-1919	Shoemaker	8-8-1945
V/209965	O'NEILL, John	Cloone Railway Station, Creeslough, Co. Donegal.	20-2-1921	Motor Mechanic Apprentice	8-8-1945
E/435510	O'NEILL, John	Scarenwalsh, Enniscorthy.	12-5-1919	Motor Mechanic	8-8-1945
E/435508	O'NEILL, John	Gorey Road, Gorey.	12-5-1919	Motor Mechanic	8-8-1945
E/422355	O'NEILL, John	c/o Mrs. McIvors, Burnfoot, Co. Donegal.	24-3-1918	Labourer	8-8-1945
110778	O'NEILL, John	Mill Street, Callan, Co. Kilkenny.	12-8-1916	Farm Labourer	8-8-1945
68905	O'NEILL, John	91 Cavendish St., Belfast.	10-4-1911	Mechanic	8-8-1945
L/502043	O'NEILL, John	6 Queen Street, Dublin.	31-12-1924	None	8-8-1945
78734	O'NEILL, John	23 O'Neill's Park, Clones, Co. Monaghan.	10-3-1921	Groom	8-8-1945
203347	O'NEILL, Joseph	c/o W. Daly, Kylegrove, Portlaoighise.	23-4-1920	None	8-8-1945
84622	O'NEILL, Michael Joseph	28 Dobbyn Street, Armagh.	21-5-1917	Clerk	8-8-1945
V/213072	O'NEILL, Owen	Ballinvroling, Timoleague, Co. Cork.	7-6-1920	Carpenter	8-8-1945
E/406492	O'NEILL, Owen Roe	36 Ravesdale Mansions, Harringay Park, Crouch End, London.	17-4-1922	Labourer	8-8-1945
E/422719	O'NEILL, Patrick	c/o Mrs. McSorley, Braugham St., Dundalk.	17-6-1922	Student	8-8-1945
E/420056	O'NEILL, Patrick	New Antrim Street, Castlebar, Co. Mayo.	17-3-1922	Tailor	8-8-1945
A/82688	O'NEILL, Patrick	Garrison, Pallasgreen, Co. Limerick.	20-3-1920	Labourer	8-8-1945
E/400379	O'NEILL, Patrick	Carnew, Co. Wicklow.	3-8-1920	Labourer	8-8-1945
V/201214	O'NEILL, Peter	26 Connolly Street, Cobh.	11-10-1917	Labourer	8-8-1945
77913	O'NEILL, Phelim	Stewartstown Road, Coalisland, Co. Tyrone.	5-9-1920	Labourer	8-8-1945
79057	O'NEILL, Robert Owen	Main Street, Dungiven, Co. Derry.	19-7-1916	Labourer	8-8-1945
76352	O'NEILL, Sean T.	15 Dufferin Ave., Dublin.	20-10-1921	Student	8-8-1945
79744	O'NEILL, Thomas	Tarbert, Co. Kerry.	7-10-1920	Labourer	8-8-1945
E/431143	O'NEILL, Thomas	7 Irish Street, Enniscorthy.	1-2-1922	Motor Driver	8-8-1945
418163	O'NEILL, Walter	6 Windsor Terrace, St. Luke's, Cork.	2-1-1926	Radio Engineer	23-7-1946

Army No.	Name.	Last Recorded Address.	Date of Birth.	Declared Occupation prior to enlistment in Defence Forces.	Date of Dismissal from Defence Forces.
76228	O'NEILL, Wilfrid	6 Dromard Rd., Drimnagh, Dublin.	15-4-1919	Shoemaker	8-8-1945
E/416233	O'NEILL, William	New Street, Cahirciveen, Co. Kerry.	17-9-1916	Labourer	8-8-1945
77811	O'NEILL, William	Anahorish, Castledawson, Co. Kerry.	1-7-1917	Dredger	8-8-1945
A/78286	O'NIAD, Colm	Turlough, Rosmuck, Co. Galway.	6-7-1919	Farm Labourer	8-8-1945
78095	O'REGAN, John	Keelogue, Killeshin, Co. Carlow.	15-11-1922	None	8-8-1945
E/431317	O'REGAN, John	69 Maudlin St., Kilkenny.	16-4-1919	Shoemaker	8-8-1945
E/435573	O'REGAN, Patrick	30 Dean Street, Kilkenny.	24-1-1923	Cook	8-8-1945
83423	O'REILLY, Christopher	Tallon's Row, Athboy, Co. Meath.	25-12-1920	Clerk	8-8-1945
81483	O'REILLY, Christopher	12 Linenhall St., Dublin.	29-12-1919	General Labourer	1-4-1946
84642	O'REILLY, Gerald	17 McSweeney Street, Dundalk.	6-7-1916	Motor Driver	8-8-1945
E/406601	O'REILLY, John	31 Smithfield, Dublin.	13-6-1923	Upholsterer's Apprentice	8-8-1945
V/200623	O'REILLY, John J.	24 Munster Street, Dublin.	2-9-1914	Salesman	8-8-1945
E/425508	O'REILLY, Joseph	Boylehill, Lisnaskea,, Co. Fermanagh.	7-4-1924	Farmer	8-8-1945
E/420057	O'REILLY, Joseph	10 St. Peter's Terrace, Athlone.	27-5-1908	Butcher	8-8-1945
E/408616	O'REILLY, Michael	Painstown, Donadee, Co. Kildare.	5-4-1923	Gardener	8-8-1945
L/507415	O'REILLY, Michael	Ballyglass, Parteen, Co. Clare.	8-6-1927	Gardener	23-5-1946
L/502428	O'REILLY, Peter	24C Greek Street, Dublin.	5-5-1926	Messenger	8-8-1945
78723	O'REILLY, Thomas	25 Fairvew Strand, Dublin.	19-8-1918	Carpenter	8-8-1945
A/75470	O'REILLY, Thomas	81 Bride Street, Dublin.	17-11-1918	Labourer	8-8-1945
E/422480	O'REILLY, Thomas	c/o P. McLoughlin, Castle Street, Carndonagh, Co. Donegal.	11-7-1918	Clerk	8-8-1945
E/431902	ORGAN, William	Ballybonogue, Kilmacthomas, Co. Waterford.	26-9-1921	Labourer	8-8-1945
E/404691	O'RIORDAN, Eugene	72 Galtymore Park, Drimnagh, Dublin.	7-4-1916	Fitter	8-8-1945
A/72778	O'ROURKE, Joseph	Ballyshannon, Kilcullen, Co. Kildare.	11-1-1914	Labourer	8-8-1945
E/408561	O'ROURKE, Eamon	171 Clontarf Road, Dublin.	1-12-1920	Timber Merchant	8-8-1945
A/75194	O'ROURKE, John	10 Francis Street, Dublin.	19-2-1914	Builder's Labourer	8-8-1945
56672	O'ROURKE, John	Killasonna, Lismacaffrey, Streete, Co. Westmeath.	21-1-1898	Labourer	8-8-1945
A/70780	O'ROURKE, Michael	11 Waggett's Lane, Cork.	16-12-1910	Labourer	8-8-1945
83702	O'ROURKE, Michael	7 O'Carolan Road, Dublin.	14-1-1924	Electrical Engineering	8-8-1945
79441	O'ROURKE, Sean	6 Upr. Jane Place, Dublin.	3-2-1921	Labourer	8-8-1945
E/408469	O'ROURKE, William J.	35 Oulton Street, Belfast.	20-9-1922	News Vendor	8-8-1945
E/404933	ORR, James	28 North Great George's Street, Dublin.	12-7-1919	Painter	8-8-1945
E/405618	ORR, James	16 Mackin Street, Dublin.	6-7-1922	Labourer	8-8-1945
79803	OSBORNE, Harry	18 Colinview St., Belfast.	17-11-1921	Labourer	8-8-1945
E/409227	OSBORNE, Henry	Camlough, Newry, Co. Down.	17-11-1921	Clerk	8-8-1945
A/73274	O'SHAUGHNESSY, Michael	Room 9, Strand Barracks, Limerick.	13-6-1914	Labourer	8-8-1945
A/78738	O'SHEA, Denis	Limagilla, Ballypar, Co. Kerry.	21-7-1920	Farm Labourer	8-8-1945
76375	O'SHEA, Florence	West Village, Ballincollig, Co. Cork.	24-8-1921	Student	8-8-1945
E/437706	O'SHEA, George	Feigh Mane, Valentia Island, Co. Kerry.	1-4-1922	Labourer	8-8-1945

Army No.	Name.	Last Recorded Address.	Date of Birth.	Declared Occupation prior to enlistment in Defence Forces.	Date of Dismissal from Defence Forces.
71416	O'SHEA, Gerald	Main Street, Castleconnell, Co. Limerick.	6-6-1904	Carpenter	8-8-1945
E/404134	O'SHEA, James	35 Royal Canal Bank, Phibsboro', Dublin.	28-12-1905	Labourer	8-8-1945
E/417454	O'SHEA, James	80 Hill View, Carrickbeg, Carrick-on-Suir.	15-11-1923	Motor Driver	8-8-1945
69326	O'SHEA, James	67 Mount Eden Road, Gurranebraher, Cork.	19-1-1909	Labourer	8-8-1945
A/82706	O'SHEA, Jeremiah	Longstone, Cullen, Co. Tipperary.	7-12-1917	Labourer	8-8-1945
E/416857	O'SHEA, John	Wonderhill, Kilteely, Co. Limerick.	14-8-1923	Labourer	8-8-1945
A/76088	O'SHEA, Martin	Clarefield, Lisdeen, Kilkee, Co. Clare.	6-1-1919	Farm Labourer	8-8-1945
79519	O'SHEA, Martin	Ballyheagan, Borris, Co. Carlow.	4-9-1914	Barman	8-8-1945
A/110400	O'SHEA, Patrick	19 Cathal Brugha Place, Dungarvan, Co. Waterford.	13-4-1918	Farm Labourer	8-8-1945
E/43592	O'SULLIVAN, Andrew	Rathcrogue, Co. Carlow.	3-9-1920	Labourer	8-8-1945
76640	O'SULLIVAN, Bartholomew	311 Blarney Street, Cork.	10-5-1919	Messenger Boy	8-8-1945
E/412692	O'SULLIVAN, Cornelius	11 Smith's Street, Cork.	22-1-1917	Labourer	8-8-1945
70395	O'SULLIVAN, Denis	Station Road, Millstreet, Co. Cork.	15-2-1921	Labourer	8-8-1945
75234	O'SULLIVAN, Denis	1 Winchester Street, London, S.W.1.	29-3-1918	Labourer	8-8-1945
L/507403	O'SULLIVAN, Donal	17 McSweeney's Villas, Cork.	23-5-1927	Messenger	22-5-1946
V/209047	O'SULLIVAN, James	Monastery Lane, Ennistymon, Co. Clare.	5-4-1921	Labourer	8-8-1945
E/417725	O'SULLIVAN, James	Franstown, Watergrasshill, Co. Cork.	12-9-1917	Labourer	8-8-1945
82588	O'SULLIVAN, James	Killaready, Newcastle West, Co. Limerick.	14-2-1922	Labourer	8-8-1945
71130	O'SULLIVAN, James	15 Ariel Road, West Hampstead, Paddington, London.	23-1-1915	Labourer	8-8-1945
V/208253	O'SULLIVAN, Jeremiah	13 Castle St., Waterford.	8-6-1913	Labourer	8-8-1945
A/57681	O'SULLIVAN, John	27 Mary Street, Cork.	2-8-1904	Labourer	8-8-1945
L/500863	O'SULLIVAN, John	Iveagh Buildings, Bride Street, Dublin.	1-6-1917	Farm Labourer	8-8-1945
L/507328	O'SULLIVAN, John	17 McSweeney's Villas, Cork.	7-3-1927	Cobbler	5-5-1946
E/413545	O'SULLIVAN, Maurice	20 Keane Street, Killalee, Co. Limerick.	16-6-1913	Labourer	8-8-1945
E/415100	O'SULLIVAN, Patrick	Ballynoe Upper, Kilfinane, Co. Limerick.	15-9-1920	Labourer	8-8-1945
82358	O'SULLIVAN, Patrick	c/o O'Malley, Tarnons, Waterville, Co. Kerry.	21-2-1920	Plumber	8-8-1945
V/201279	O'SULLIVAN, Patrick	Cragleigh, Ennis.	—-1-1918	Farm Labourer	8-8-1945
82206	O'SULLIVAN, Patrick	90 Gurranebraher Avenue, Cork.	16-12-1921	Tailor	8-8-1945
E/411068	O'SULLIVAN, Peter	5 Gillahugh Cottages, Forth Street, Cork.	25-8-1914	Labourer	8-8-1945
E/408722	O'SULLIVAN, Sean P.	295 Griffith Ave., Dublin.	24-5-1921	Mechanical Student	8-8-1945
E/434538	O'SULLIVAN, Thomas	158 Walsh Road, Drumcondra, Dublin.	14-6-1918	Fitter	8-8-1945
L/506455	O'SULLIVAN, Thomas	Rosbrien, Co. Limerick.	17-7-1924	Messenger	8-8-1945
V/203005	O'SULLIVAN, Thomas	7 Kickham St., Kilkenny.	5-11-1919	Labourer	8-8-1945
67938	O'SULLIVAN, Timothy	40 New Road, Gorey, Co. Wexford.	9-6-1907	Farm Labourer	8-8-1945
83372	O'SULLIVAN, Timothy	Cousane, Kealkil, Bantry, Co. Cork.	29-4-1916	Barman	8-8-1945

Army No.	Name.	Last Recorded Address.	Date of Birth.	Declared Occupation prior to enlistment in Defence Forces.	Date of Dismissal from Defence Forces.
V/206383	O'SULLIVAN, William	8 Hallen's Abbey, Gt. Wm. O'Brien Street, Cork.	12-4-1922	Messenger Boy	8-8-1945
E/406507	O'TOOLE, Edward	24 Bolton Street, Dublin.	31-7-1919	Bus Conductor	8-8-1945
83783	O'TOOLE, James	10 Summerhill, Dublin.	23-4-1922	Labourer	8-8-1945
E/432189	O'TOOLE, James	Blackmiller Hill, Kildare.	7-7-1918	Groom	8-8-1945
E/402554	O'TOOLE, Luke	12 Albert Place, Inchicore, Dublin.	22-2-1914	Labourer	8-8-1945
73518	O'TOOLE, Patrick	16 Bailey New Street, Waterford.	21-1-1913	Labourer	8-8-1945
E/406801	O'TOOLE, Sean	205 Keogh Square, Inchicore, Dublin.	20-9-1920	Labourer	8-8-1945
206482	OWENS, Edward	29 Oaklands Park, Dublin.	3-7-1922	Labourer	8-8-1945
V/210097	OWENS, John	Dunaldron, Monaghan.	25-10-1921	Labourer	10-9-1945
79909	OWENS, Michael	42 Spencer's Road, Derry.	16-7-1920	Porter	8-8-1945
E/421757	OWENS, Thomas	Bridgend P.O., Co. Donegal.	4-2-1914	Labourer	8-8-1945
76364	PAGE, Patrick	Tully West, Kildare.	7-7-1921	Schoolboy	8-8-1945
83220	PARES, Ralph	29 Palmerston Rd., Dublin.	10-12-1918	Clerk	8-8-1945
E/436642	PARKER, Vincent	27 Cyprus Street, Belfast.	6-9-1925	Welder's Assistant	8-8-1945
V/200123	PARKES, Michael	Barroe, Sligo.	15-11-1915	Labourer and Clerk	8-8-1945
V/204011	PARKINSON, John	Manorcunningham, Co. Donegal.	7-6-1910	Farm Labourer	8-8-1945
E/402805	PARLE, Christopher	22 Ave Maria Road, Maryland, Dublin.	25-3-1921	Wireless Operator	8-8-1945
L/508920	PARLE, John	Ramsgrange, Co. Wexford.	27-5-1925	Farm Labourer	8-8-1945
208285	PARSONS, Frank	21 St. David's Terrace, N.C.Rd., Dublin.	7-5-1920	Carpenter	8-8-1945
E/422890	PATTERSON, Joseph	c/o Mrs. McLoughlin, St. Muras Terrace, Fahan, Co. Donegal.	15-3-1912	Motor Driver	8-8-1945
209550	PATTERSON, Robert	Braddox, Clontibret, Co. Monaghan.	29-6-1911	Motor Cycle Mechanic and Driver	8-8-1945
E/411844	PEARL, John	Turkenna, Flagmount, Feakle, Co. Clare.	23-3-1917	Labourer	8-8-1945
E/431154	PEMBROKE, Patrick	33 St. John's Villas, Enniscorthy, Co. Wexford.	23-7-1920	Moulder	8-8-1945
A/83316	PENDER, Thomas	Ballymooney, Arklow, Co. Wicklow.	5-6-1921	Labourer	8-8-1945
E/400944	PENDER, William	41 Kilfenora Road, Kimmage, Dublin.	15-8-1904	Labourer	8-8-1945
80750	PENNY, Peter	14 Foyle Road, Fairview, Dublin.	27-7-1922	Student	8-8-1945
A/71417	PENROSE, Joseph	11 Gardiner St., Dublin.	1-9-1912	Labourer	8-8-1945
A/74155	PHELAN, Edmond	6 William's Park, Rathmines, Dublin.	21-11-1909	Wireless Operator	8-8-1945
E/434591	PHELAN, Edward A.	45 Ard na Greine, Waterford.	25-6-1908	Labourer	8-8-1945
E/431927	PHELAN, James	53 Waterford Road, Kilkenny.	2-12-1919	Labourer	8-8-1945
A/80669	PHELAN, Joseph	Adelphia Hotel, Bray.	19-3-1922	None	20-10-1945
A/70536	PHELAN, Maurice	5 Annesley Bridge Road, Fairview, Dublin.	16-9-1911	Labourer	8-8-1945
79899	PHELAN, Peter	Maryboro Rd., Mountrath, Co. Leix.	21-1-1921	Farm Labourer	8-8-1945
E/401750	PHELAN, Thomas	12 Upper Stephen Street, Dublin.	6-6-1920	Labourer	8-8-1945
V/210132	PHILLIPS, Francis	334 Mourne Road, Crumlin, Dublin.	17-8-1921	Labourer	8-8-1945
78378	PHILLIPS, James	Ballinstraw, Glenbrian, Enniscorthy.	13-4-1920	Farm Labourer	8-8-1945
V/203556	PHILLIPS, Kevin	59 Up. Cary Rd., Limerick.	4-2-1920	Body Builder	8-8-1945
E/431751	PHILLIPS, Thomas	Inch, Ballytore, Co. Kildare.	7-6-1915	Motor Driver	8-8-1945

Army No.	Name.	Last Recorded Address.	Date of Birth.	Declared Occupation prior to enlistment in Defence Forces.	Date of Dismissal from Defence Forces.
E/434766	PIERCE, Francis	17 Reilly's Avenue, Dolphin's Barn, Dublin.	23-11-1910	Carpenter	8-8-1945
A/79620	PIERSE, Gerald	Coolkeragh, Listowel.	28-4-1916	Labourer	8-8-1945
E/411269	PIGGOTT, William	Orr Street, Kilmallock, Co. Limerick.	8-9-1918	Labourer	8-8-1945
E/406356	PILSON, Robert	43 Upr. Sean McDermott Street, Dublin.	5-10-1923	Lorry Driver's Helper	8-8-1945
E/404636	PLACE, James	29 Phoenix Street, Inchicore, Dublin.	10-10-1922	Van Helper	8-8-1945
E/405023	PLANT, Joseph	4 Merry Meeting, Rathnew, Co. Wicklow.	23-6-1922	Labourer	8-8-1945
208622	PLUMMER, James	62 Bishop Street, Derry.	25-4-1911	Labourer	8-8-1945
A/73355	PLUNKETT, Oliver	22 Upr. Dorset St., Dublin.	11-8-1914	Labourer	8-8-1945
V/203752	PORTER, Aloysius	Main Street, Lifford.	19-10-1917	Farm Labourer	8-8-1945
V/217094	PORTER, Michael	Conary Lower, Avoca, Co. Wicklow.	9-2-1921	Farm Labourer	8-8-1945
E/421758	PORTER, Michael	Maghrintine, Buncrana, Co. Donegal.	8-10-1922	Labourer	8-8-1945
75419	PORTER, Richard	Old Grange, Monasterevan, Co. Kildare.	14-10-1913	Labourer	8-8-1945
E/423221	PORTER, William	10 Deanery Place, Derry.	9-6-1920	Labourer	8-8-1945
L/502560	POWELL, Christopher	12 Canning Place, Oriel Street, Dublin.	9-9-1926	None	8-8-1945
E/400738	POWELL, Malachy	c/o Frank Kerr, Park Street, Monaghan.	16-11-1919	Motor Driver	8-8-1945
201258	POWELL, Patrick	14 Owenroe Tce., Cavan.	20-3-1921	Motor Engineer	8-8-1945
E/409845	POWER, Aidan	St. Joseph's Rd., Carlow.	22-11-1921	Clerk	8-8-1945
103756	POWER, David	27 Dungarvan Road, Clonmel.	24-12-1913	Motor Engineer	8-8-1945
V/208240	POWER, John	Main Street, Ballymahon, Co. Longford.	20-3-1920	Farm Labourer	8-8-1945
79102	POWER, John	Ballyheelan P.O., Ballymarry Co. Cavan.	9-1-1916	Farm Labourer	8-8-1945
E/408960	POWER, Joseph	320 Cashel Rd., Kimmage, Dublin.	16-5-1924	Dairy Hand	8-8-1945
E/405664	POWER, Michael	c/o Mrs. Simpson, 34 Castle Street, Waterford.	15-12-1899	Motor Mechanic	8-8-1945
V/202974	POWER, Patrick	The Level, Carrick-on-Suir.	15-1-1921	Labourer	8-8-1945
84296	POWER, Patrick	Barradlay, Carraroe, Co. Galway.	24-1-1922	Farmer's Boy	8-8-1945
E/410355	POWER, Richard	Long Lane, Carrick-on-Suir.	3-2-1899	Motor Driver	8-8-1945
E/421772	POWER, Samuel	c/o Molloy's, Finner Road, Bundoran, Co. Donegal.	1-3-1913	General Labourer	8-8-1945
A/74253	POWER, William	108 Dominick Place, Gracedieu Rd., Waterford.	16-8-1916	Labourer	8-8-1945
A/54700	PRENDERGAST, Patrick	Ullard, Borris, Co. Carlow.	30-11-1899	Labourer	8-8-1945
L/503091	PRESTON, Peter	21 "B" Block, St. Joseph's Mansions, Killarney St., Dublin.	25-2-1928	Messenger Boy	29-3-1946
L/503212	PRICE, James	3 "C" Block, St. Joseph's Mansions, Killarney St., Dublin.	23-5-1927	General Labourer	25-3-1946
77919	PRICE, John	Main Street, Moate, Co. Westmeath.	3-5-1918	Labourer	8-8-1945
E/412030	PRICE, Joseph	Thomas Street, Mitchelstown, Co. Cork.	9-11-1914	Painter	8-8-1945
L/507382	PRICE, Michael	15 Eaton's Cottages, Tipperary.	3-9-1925	Labourer	8-8-1945
V/200819	PRICE, Patrick	Barrack Road, Buncrana, Co. Donegal.	30-11-1919	Labourer	8-8-1945
L/507370	PRICE, Patrick	15 Eaton's Cottages, Tipperary.	23-8-1924	Labourer	8-8-1945
202833	PRICE, Thomas	184 Keogh Square, Inchicore, Dublin.	1-2-1920	Labourer	8-8-1945

Army No.	Name.	Last Recorded Address.	Date of Birth.	Declared Occupation prior to enlistment in Defence Forces.	Date of Dismissal from Defence Forces.
E/421997	PRICE, William	17 Brien Street, Tullamore.	26-8-1914	Labourer	8-8-1945
E/405703	PRINDERVILLE, Garrett F.	93 South Circular Road, Dublin.	30-9-1920	Motor Driver	8-8-1945
L/503307	PROUDFOOT, Christopher	13B St. Michan's House, Greek Street, Dublin.	1-5-1922	Messenger	28-3-1946
E/402848	PURCELL, James	31 Mill Road, Milltown, Co. Dublin.	8-6-1922	Van Driver	8-8-1945
E/412230	PURCELL, James	Upperchurch, Thurles.	15-11-1916	Farmer	8-8-1945
A/759088	PURCELL, John	11 Upper. Stephen Street, Dublin.	16-1-1921	Van Boy	8-8-1945
81941	PURCELL, John	Carron, Limerick Junction, Co. Tipperary.	22-4-1920	Plasterer	8-8-1945
V/204789	PURCELL, Thomas	Ballyrichard Road, Carrick-on-Suir.	24-7-1920	Labourer	8-8-1945
E/423222	PURCELL, William	81 Irish Street, Waterside, Derry.	2-2-1919	Newspaper Vendor	8-8-1945
E/405973	PURDUE, John	61 Bridgefoot St., Dublin.	13-2-1923	None	8-8-1945
L/501820	PURDUE, Thomas	252 St. Attracta Road, Dublin.	20-2-1925	Messenger	8-8-1945
E/407951	PURDUE, William	252 St. Attracta Road, Dublin.	17-1-1921	Labourer	8-8-1945
E/437951	PURDY, John	15 Kilworth Rd., Crumlin, Dublin.	16-4-1924	General Labourer	8-8-1945
74782	PURTILL, Patrick	Rockmount, Ennis, Co. Clare.	2-9-1919	Farm Labourer	8-8-1945
A/84222	PYNE, Michael	Cashelragh, New Mills, Lifford.	25-8-1921	Grocer's Assistant	8-8-1945
V/217008	QUEALLY, John	Loughinney, Barna, Co. Kilkenny.	30-8-1916	Labourer	8-8-1945
E/424930	QUIGG, Nial	c/o Mrs. Murray, Lismonaghan, Letterkenny.	28-5-1916	Lorry Driver and Mechanic	8-8-1945
85329	QUIGG, Patrick	Tawney Cross, Co. Derry.	3-10-1926	Greaser	18-4-1946
E/422357	QUIGLEY, John	c/o John Shiel, Craightown, Fahan, Co. Donegal.	28-11-1921	Joiner	8-8-1945
E/422236	QUIGLEY, John	129 Creggan Road, Derry.	3-2-1922	Painter	8-8-1945
E/432956	QUIGLEY, John	27 View Street, Dublin.	14-6-1920	Labourer	8-8-1945
V/201281	QUIGLEY, Michael	Killaloe, Co. Clare.	19-9-1919	Baker	8-8-1945
E/420131	QUIGLEY, Patrick	Glenfin Street, Ballybofey, Co. Donegal.	17-3-1913	Motor Mechanic and Driver	8-8-1945
E/422403	QUIGLEY, Patrick	Cluid, Ballymote, Co. Sligo.	13-3-1914	Bricklayer	8-8-1945
A/77072	QUINLAN, Patrick	Glenveigh, Holycross, Thurles.	13-9-1917	Labourer	8-8-1945
E/434786	QUINLAN, William Joseph	64 Church Street, Clara, Offaly.	20-5-1914	Motor Driver	8-8-1945
E/403972	QUINN, Desmond	5 River Street, Newry.	10-4-1922	Baker	8-8-1945
E/407627	QUINN, Edward	11A Cross Kevin Street, Dublin.	8-5-1915	Domestic Porter	8-8-1945
A/82552	QUINN, Edward	Ballingrue, Kildorrery, Co. Cork.	30-9-1921	Labourer	8-8-1945
A/79947	QUINN, Edward	Templeathea, Athea, Co. Limerick.	13-9-1916	Labourer	8-8-1945
E/406546	QUINN, Gerald	Kingarve, Dungannon, Co. Tyrone.	2-11-1921	Labourer	8-8-1945
209285	QUINN, Hugh	6 Lakeview Terrace, Cavan.	1-10-1921	Labourer	8-8-1945
E/423965	QUINN, James	Bonada, Tourlestrane, Ballymote, Co. Sligo.	2-4-1917	Labourer	8-8-1945
E/414846	QUINN, James	Ballyblake, Grange, Kilmallock, Co. Limerick.	6-10-1922	Labourer	8-8-1945
E/413976	QUINN, John	Newfoundland, Kilfrest, Hospital, Co. Limerick.	30-4-1909	Farmer	8-8-1945
V/209899	QUINN, Joseph	Ballylea, Gort, Co. Galway.	9-4-1919	Plasterer	8-8-1945
E/433183	QUINN, Joseph	Curraghavanra, Banagher, Co. Tipperary.	9-6-1913	Time Keeper	8-8-1945

Army No.	Name.	Last Recorded Address.	Date of Birth.	Declared Occupation prior to enlistment in Defence Forces.	Date of Dismissal from Defence Forces.
A/77426	QUINN, Joseph	Clasheaquirk, Bansha, Co. Tipperary.	19-3-1919	Farmer	8-8-1945
V/207031	QUINN, Joseph	Coole West, Athea, Co. Limerick.	22-2-1916	Motor Driver	8-8-1945
L/507476	QUINN, Patrick	6 Kerwick Lane, Lr. Gerald Griffin Street, Limerick.	2-2-1927	Boot Repairer	4-3-1946
77478	QUINN, Patrick	Templeathea, Athea, Co. Limerick.	2-3-1919	Labourer	8-8-1945
E/400393	QUINN, Patrick	Kilcool, Co. Wicklow.	15-1-1922	Labourer	8-8-1945
77657	QUINN, Patrick	110 Bogside, Derry.	3-11-1919	Labourer	8-8-1945
79753	QUINN, Philip	James St., Mitchelstown, Co. Cork.	4-7-1913	Electric Wiring	8-8-1945
E/430144	QUINN, Thomas	85 Irish St., Enniscorthy, Co. Wexford.	13-9-1914	Labourer	8-8-1945
E/421422	QUINN, William	34 St. Bridget's Place, Sligo.	19-12-1916	General Labourer	8-8-1945
E/435666	QUIRKE, Thomas	Ballycondra, Co. Kilkenny.	4-9-1923	Labourer	8-8-1945
A/75696	RADFORD, Michael	Newberry Stores, Mallow, Co. Cork.	1-7-1917	Labourer	8-8-1945
E/415479	RADFORD, Patrick	5 Drawbridge Street, Cork.	11-11-1922	Timber Cutter	8-8-1945
E/422659	RAFFERTY, Francis	44 O'Hanlon Pk., Dundalk.	7-8-1906	Labourer	8-8-1945
E/409332	RAFFERTY, Gerard	20 Frere Street, Belfast.	24-8-1924	Apprentice Iron Moulder	8-8-1945
A/72449	RAFFERTY, John	24 St. Patrick's Terrace, Mullingar.	3-12-1911	General Labourer	8-8-1945
B/3180	RAFFERTY, Peter	6 The Coombe, Dublin.	4-12-1900	Butcher	8-8-1945
B/3759	RAFTER, James	12 Crowe Street, Dublin.	8-6-1922	Medical Apprentice	8-8-1945
E/421206	RAFTERY, Patrick	Jubilee St., Ballinasloe, Co. Galway.	3-9-1895	Labourer	8-8-1945
A/82391	RAHILLY, John	Lismore, Newmarket, Co. Cork.	8-12-1919	Labourer	8-8-1945
V/209976	RAMSEY, Charles	Porthall, Lifford.	19-11-1919	Hotel Boots	8-8-1945
V/208898	RAMSEY, Patrick	Porthall, Lifford.	7-8-1917	Labourer	8-8-1945
L/502667	RAY, James	12 Fishamble St., Dublin.	30-11-1926	Messenger	8-8-1945
L/507539	RAY, Joseph	26 St. Joseph's Park, Nenagh.	26-10-1926	Labourer	8-8-1945
E/411847	RAY, Martin	11 Walsh's Lane, Off Edward Street, Limerick.	8-12-1921	Labourer	8-8-1945
E/416572	REA, Patrick	8 Horgan's Bldgs., Cork.	25-10-1920	Motor Driver	8-8-1945
E/421289	REA, Patrick William	c/o Shearan, West End, Bundoran, Co. Donegal.	12-1-1915	Carpenter	8-8-1945
E/434426	REDDY, Joseph	2 Clarke Cottages, Stoneybatter, Dublin.	3-11-1915	Grocer's Porter	8-8-1945
74956	REDDY, Patrick	1 Blackhall Sq., Mullingar.	2-10-1914	Hotel Waiter	8-8-1945
E/435803	REDMOND, Edward	75 Wolfe Tone Villas, Wexford.	23-3-1920	Labourer	8-8-1945
V/211077	REDMOND, Harry	27 Dean's Grange, Blackrock, Co. Dublin.	22-2-1922	Labourer	8-8-1945
E/402851	REDMOND, John	5 Carlton Road, Marino, Dublin.	5-12-1922	Butcher	8-8-1945
E/408552	REDMOND, John	Coolnahinch, Gorey, Co. Wexford.	27-11-1919	Trimmer	8-8-1945
E/431159	REDMOND, Patrick	32 Irish St., Enniscorthy.	2-10-1921	Labourer	8-8-1945
L/503322	REDMOND, Peter	73 Marlboro' St., Dublin.	14-7-1928	Railway Porter	3-5-1946
V/210021	REDMOND, William	2 Marlboro' Place, Marlboro' St., Dublin.	27-8-1922	Messenger	8-8-1945
L/508507	REDMOND, William	Millgrove, Brockanagh, Rathangan, Co. Kildare.	29-9-1924	Labourer	8-8-1945
205386	REEVES, Kevin	3 Patrick Street, Mullingar.	22-7-1919	Student	8-8-1945
A/78408	REGAN, Michael	338 Blarney Street, Cork.	15-3-1920	Labourer	8-8-1945
E/404101	REID, Albert	23 Blessington St., Dublin.	25-3-1900	Aircraft Rigger	8-8-1945
83977	REID, Christopher	33 George's St., Drogheda.	15-6-1922	Clerk	8-8-1945
E/414309	REID, James	2 Friary Gardens, Friar's Walk, Cork.	8-11-1914	Labourer	8-8-1945

Army No.	Name.	Last Recorded Address.	Date of Birth.	Declared Occupation prior to enlistment in Defence Forces.	Date of Dismissal from Defence Forces.
E/406937	REID, John	15 Lambay Road, Glasnevin, Dublin.	4-12-1922	Messenger Boy	8-8-1945
206651	REID, Patrick	185 Crumlin Rd., Dublin.	4-10-1909	Foreman Carpenter	8-8-1945
E/432372	REID, Patrick	14 Whitworth Street, Oriel Street, Dublin.	10-4-1922	Labourer	8-8-1945
103410	REIDY, John	Rossduff, Co. Waterford.	16-6-1911	Farm Labourer	8-8-1945
79446	REILLY, Christopher	19 St. Mel's Tce., Athlone.	9-1-1921	Twister, Woollen Mills	8-8-1945
A/71773	REILLY, Francis	6 Jervis Street, Dublin.	16-6-1909	Labourer	8-8-1945
E/423519	REILLY, James	Church Street, Edgeworthstown, Co. Longford.	1-10-1910	Electric Plater	8-8-1945
V/204208	REILLY, James	57 Lismore Road, Kimmage, Dublin.	20-2-1920	Labourer	8-8-1945
E/406610	REILLY, James	190 Pearse Park, Drogheda.	25-10-1922	None	8-8-1945
E/407164	REILLY, James	Newtownbutler, Co. Fermanagh.	15-10-1911	Farmer	8-8-1945
E/423967	REILLY, John	Swanlinbar, Co. Cavan.	6-1-1922	Farm Labourer	8-8-1945
V/502555	REILLY, John	57 Lismore Road, Kimmage, Dublin.	25-4-1925	Labourer	8-8-1945
V/211192	REILLY, Michael	21A Corporation Bldgs., Nicholas St., Dublin.	23-7-1919	Painter and Decorator	8-8-1945
E/409690	REILLY, Michael	24 Phoenix St., Smithfield, Dublin.	24-8-1921	Labourer	8-8-1945
E/408006	REILLY, Patrick	Derryatt, Lisnaskea, Co. Fermanagh.	22-9-1922	Farm Worker	8-8-1945
E/407167	REILLY, Thomas E.	Drumgrole, Ballybay, Co. Monaghan.	26-1-1923	Labourer	8-8-1945
A/79804	REILLY, William	Falyses Lane, Birr, Offaly.	27-1-1921	Farm Labourer	8-8-1945
75011	RENNIE, John	18 Haig's Gardens, Boreenmanna Rd., Cork.	27-8-1913	Assistant Chef	8-8-1945
V/502954	REVILLE, Andrew	24K Pearse House, Hanover St., Dublin.	12-10-1927	General Labourer	8-8-1945
E/202991	REVILLE, Philip.	Tomhaggard, Co. Wexford.	25-12-1920	Labourer	8-8-1945
V/503005	REYNOLDS, Andrew	49 "A" Block, Marshalsea Barracks, Off Thomas Street, Dublin.	30-4-1928	Messenger	27-11-1945
77548	REYNOLDS, Edward	14 George's Place, Dublin.	2-5-1919	Labourer	8-8-1945
V/200458	REYNOLDS, Michael	Kilfahoron, Emyvale, Co. Monaghan.	21-2-1921	Farm Labourer	8-8-1945
E/408304	REYNOLDS, Michael	87 Park Cottages, Ringsend, Dublin.	28-1-1922	General Labourer	8-8-1945
V/215206	REYNOLDS, Patrick	Kill, Kilnaleck, Co. Cavan.	8-2-1915	Shop Assistant	8-8-1945
A/61773	RICE, James	53 Carnlough, Road, West Cabra, Dublin.	25-9-1906	Labourer	8-8-1945
E/405482	RICE, Patrick	7 Eden Villas, Sandycove, Co. Dublin.	13-8-1922	Messenger Boy	8-8-1945
V/501345	RICE, Vincent	225 Oliver Bond House, Bridgefoot St., Dublin.	25-6-1923	Tailor	8-8-1945
76058	RICKARD, Michael	107 St. Brigid's Parade, Clara, Offaly.	9-3-1919	Labourer	8-8-1945
E/405315	RICKERLY, Joseph	25 Pembroke Cottages, Donnybrook, Dublin.	13-9-1922	Labourer	8-8-1945
E/424503	RIDGE, John	Upper Camas, Costello P.O., Co. Galway.	25-8-1918	Farm Labourer	8-8-1945
V/506494	RIORDAN, Patrick	6 Millfield Cottages, Mallow Road, Cork.	15-8-1922	Labourer	8-8-1945
E/408173	RIORDAN, William	54 Loughmore, Dungarvan, Co. Waterford.	14-4-1916	Labourer	8-8-1945
V/209104	ROACHE, Desmond	The Gardens, Athlone.	21-9-1921	Labourer	8-8-1945
V/206275	ROARTY, Edward	Falcarragh, Co. Donegal.	14-11-1909	Clerk	8-8-1945
E/423714	ROBERT, Denis	Bonehill, Ballyshannon.	5-4-1921	Farm Labourer	8-8-1945
E/403532	ROBINSON, Christopher	38 Chamber St., Dublin.	24-3-1918	Cycle Mechanic	8-8-1945
A/80118	ROBINSON, Henry	Bridge St., Downpatrick, Co. Down.	19-7-1919	Motor Driver	8-8-1945

Army No.	Name.	Last Recorded Address.	Date of Birth.	Declared Occupation prior to enlistment in Defence Forces.	Date of Dismissal from Defence Forces.
E/433495	ROBINSON, Martin	42 Glasthule Buildings, Glasthule, Dun Laoghaire.	21-3-1922	Labourer	8-8-1945
E/403033	ROBINSON, Patrick	15 Verschoyle Pce., Dublin.	3-7-1922	None	8-8-1945
79199	ROBINSON, Patrick	23 Villean Street, Belfast.	26-2-1920	Labourer	8-8-1945
E/421343	ROBINSON, William	c/o P. Hanley, Pearse St., Ballina.	1-7-1922	Draper's Assistant	8-8-1945
E/431158	ROCHE, Anthony	Newton, Enniscorthy, Co. Wexford.	12-3-1922	Labourer	8-8-1945
75804	ROCHE, Denis	41 Queen Street, Dublin.	29-5-1919	Messenger	8-8-1945
E/410917	ROCHE, James	Caherdrinna, Mitchelstown, Co. Cork.	19-4-1920	Hotel Porter	8-8-1945
E/407580	ROCHE, Michael	30 Effra Road, Rathmines Dublin.	18-8-1923	Student	8-8-1945
L/508605	ROCHE, Michael	Ahenine, Callan, Co. Kilkenny.	2-11-1924	Labourer	8-8-1945
E/431487	ROCHE, Patrick	Butlerstown, Broadway, Co. Wexford.	17-3-1919	Labourer	8-8-1945
E/435529	ROCHE, Richard	Ballinalan, Kilmacow, Co. Kilkenny.	22-12-1922	Labourer	8-8-1945
E/417368	ROCHE, Thomas	Farrahy, Broadford, Co. Limerick.	17-2-1924	Labourer	8-8-1945
V/200013	ROCHE, William	50 Shandon Street, Cork.	23-1-1920	Labourer	8-8-1945
79768	RODDEN, John	25 Friary Street, Kilkenny.	24-6-1919	Labourer	8-8-1945
E/432373	RODEN, Richard	47 Temple Bar, Dublin.	6-5-1920	Messenger	8-8-1945
E/423296	RODDY, Michael	101 Bogside, Derry.	10-4-1921	Labourer	8-8-1945
79058	RODDY, Patrick	57 Wellington St., Derry.	23-9-1915	Labourer	8-8-1945
84152	RODGER, William	St. Muir's, Fahan, Co. Donegal.	6-10-1919	Butcher's Assistant	8-8-1945
E/425258	RODGERS, James	19 Nelson Street, Derry.	29-6-1923	Labourer	8-8-1945
E/404650	RODGERS, Michael	12 Lr. Dominick Street, Dublin.	23-6-1920	None	8-8-1945
E/404083	ROE, Joseph	75 Foley Street, Dublin.	1-3-1922	Labourer	8-8-1945
V/208840	ROGERS, Bernard	10 Emmett Tce., Navan.	9-3-1921	Labourer	8-8-1945
85162	ROGERS, Charles	Ulster Bank House, Ferbane, Offaly.	18-2-1924	Student	8-8-1945
E/405071	ROGERS, Thomas G.	7 Clinches' Cottages, North Strand, Dublin.	7-7-1914	Painter	8-8-1945
85138	ROHAN, Michael	30 Iona Road, Dublin.	17-5-1925	Student	8-8-1945
82022	ROLSTON, Francis	Upper Aghada, Rostellan, Co. Cork.	14-11-1920	Lorry Driver	8-8-1945
V/205793	RONAN, Patrick	13 Brennan St., Limerick.	15-3-1922	Builder's Labourer	8-8-1945
L/508457	RONAN, William	c/o Mrs. O'Meara, Ballickboy, Ballinure, Killenaule, Co. Tipperary	1-1-1925	Farm Labourer	8-8-1945
V/203228	RONAYNE, Edmond	Ballhickey, Cahir, Co. Tipperary.	1-4-1919	Labourer	8-8-1945
E/401399	ROONEY, Daniel J.	7 Forth Road, East Wall, Dublin.	9-5-1921	Motor Driver	8-8-1945
A/78501	ROONEY, Edward	63 Bellview Buildings, Thomas Street, Dublin.	20-1-1921	Underpresser	8-8-1945
E/406251	ROONEY, Gerard	36 Boat Street, Newry.	17-2-1923	Labourer	8-8-1945
E/408357	ROONEY, Gustav	6 Artillery Street, Belfast.	13-11-1918	General Labourer	8-8-1945
204312	ROONEY, James	33 Boyne Street, Dublin.	4-5-1921	Labourer	8-8-1945
206545	ROONEY, John	9 Eccles Street, Dublin.	18-2-1918	None	8-8-1945
A/79002	ROONEY, Laurence	Nuttstown, Clonee, Co. Meath.	8-9-1920	None	8-8-1945
E/435648	ROONEY, Michael	Ryland, Clohamon, Ferns.	14-9-1923	Labourer	8-8-1945
E/422657	ROONEY, Patrick	c/o Jos. Warran, Castlehill, Carlingford, Co. Louth.	21-5-1913	Bricklayer	8-8-1945
V/207619	ROONEY, Patrick	33 Boyne Street, Dublin.	1-9-1922	Labourer	8-8-1945
E/404605	ROONEY, Thomas	104 Annamoe Drive, Cabra, Dublin.	23-10-1922	Labourer	8-8-1945
E/407122	ROONEY, William	6 Artillery Street, Belfast.	8-1-1921	Labourer	8-8-1945

Army No.	Name.	Last Recorded Address.	Date of Birth.	Declared Occupation prior to enlistment in Defence Forces.	Date of Dismissal from Defence Forces.
E/402181	ROSS, Anthony	45 Longwood Ave., Dublin.	10-6-1910	Cameraman	8-8-1945
76775	ROSSITER, James	Ballygillistown, Enniscorthy, Co. Wexford.	20-8-1919	Labourer	8-8-1945
75811	ROURKE, James	Summer Hill, Wicklow.	22-1-1919	Farm Labourer	8-8-1945
E/403055	ROURKE, John	3 Dublin Road, Roscrea, Co. Tipperary.	2-11-1921	None	8-8-1945
77753	ROUTLEDGE, Alan	11 Oxmantown Road, Dublin.	12-1-1911	Shop Assistant	8-8-1945
E/404444	ROWAN, James	Iveagh House, Bride St., Dublin.	25-10-1919	Labourer	8-8-1945
E/423694	ROWAN, Thomas	10 Robin Villas, Palmerston, Co. Dublin.	30-9-1920	Farm Labourer	8-8-1945
E/416156	ROWLEY, Christopher	Ballynockane, Ballymackey, Toomevara, Co. Tipperary.	24-12-1921	Labourer	8-8-1945
80687	ROY, David	Roundwood, Mountrath, Co. Leix.	31-3-1920	Student	8-8-1945
E/420603	RUDDY, Joseph	Glebe, Carndonagh, Co. Donegal.	28-4-1893	Labourer	8-8-1945
E/402933	RUMMEL, Henry	3 Oakfield Place, S.C.Rd., Dublin.	8-6-1922	Cabinet Maker	8-8-1945.
E/407021	RUSK, Robert	41 Upr. Sean McDermott Street, Dublin.	27-2-1913	Gardener	8-8-1945
L/506716	RUSSELL, James	44 Barrymore Ave., Cobh.	16-1-1925	Labourer	5-1-1946
76907	RUSSELL, James	Railway Road, Kilkee, Co. Clare.	4-2-1915	Labourer	8-8-1945
A/82708	RUSSELL, John	Duncummin, Emly, Co. Limerick.	20-6-1921	Labourer	8-8-1945
L/502435	RUSSELL, John	8 Usher's Island, Dublin.	22-3-1926	Messenger	8-8-1945
E/413093	RUSSELL, Patrick	Church Street, Rathkeale, Co. Limerick.	10-5-1922	Carpenter	8-8-1945
E/404642	RUSSELL, Thomas N.	21 Camac Park, Bluebell, Dublin.	25-12-1921	Machine Operator	8-8-1945
E/405050	RUSSELL, William	21 Camac Park, Bluebell, Dublin.	16-2-1921	Labourer	8-8-1945
82884	RYAN, Anthony	21 Keene Street, Killalee, Limerick.	22-1-1923	Labourer	8-8-1945
80846	RYAN, Benjamin Joseph	Accommodation Road, Carlow.	1-11-1921	Machinist	8-8-1945
77699	RYAN, Christopher	Killoo, Clarecastle, Co. Clare.	5-12-1919	Labourer	8-8-1945
E/423644	RYAN, Christopher	1 Fairhill, Galway.	4-9-1922	Student	8-8-1945
A/76695	RYAN, Daniel	c/o Mrs. Dempsey, Bank Street, Templemore.	21-3-1918	Shoemaker	8-8-1945
E/422244	RYAN, Daniel	c/o Michael McHale, Muff, Lifford.	13-12-1919	Labourer	8-8-1945
E/433088	RYAN, Daniel	Dublin Street, Monaghan.	1-12-1920	Fowl Dealer	8-8-1945
E/423977	RYAN, Denis	Garryduff, Tipperary.	5-2-1915	Foundry Worker	8-8-1945
78707	RYAN, Denis	Graiguenahoun, Spink, Abbeyleix.	14-9-1920	Farm Labourer	8-8-1945
E/432356	RYAN, Denis	581 North Circular Road, Dublin.	1-6-1921	Labourer	8-8-1945
A/77427	RYAN, Edmond	Coolnadown, Emly, Co. Tipperary.	16-6-1920	Farmer	8-8-1945
E/411469	RYAN, Edward	Boher, Caherconlish, Co. Limerick.	18-4-1921	Labourer	8-8-1945
75724	RYAN, Edward	Cannon Place, Newbridge, Co. Kildare.	18-9-1918	Cutler	8-8-1945
E/404907	RYAN, Frank J.	27 Eden Quay, Dublin.	15-4-1918	Lorry Driver	8-8-1945
202072	RYAN, Henry	The Square, Claremorris.	8-9-1910	General Labourer	8-8-1945
68275	RYAN, Hugh	35 Marymount, Ferrybank, Waterford.	8-3-1909	Labourer	8-8-1945
E/414993	RYAN, James	Ballycurrane, Thurles.	17-1-1923	Labourer	8-8-1945
74121	RYAN, James	12 Harty Place, Dublin.	25-9-1915	Tailor	8-8-1945

Army No.	Name.	Last Recorded Address.	Date of Birth.	Declared Occupation prior to enlistment in Defence Forces.	Date of Dismissal from Defence Forces.
E/413466	RYAN, James	6 Margaret's Place, Watergate, Limerick.	18-4-1922	Labourer	8-8-1945
E/435427	RYAN, James	Cooltigue, Enniscorthy, Co. Wexford.	24-5-1922	Labourer	8-8-1945
A/83692	RYAN, James	33 Botanic Ave., Dublin.	20-4-1910	Able Seaman	8-8-1945
E/405363	RYAN, James	18 Fownes Street, Dublin.	9-1-1923	Engineer Apprentice	8-8-1945
E/432976	RYAN, John	14 Tolka Park, Dublin.	19-5-1920	Labourer	8-8-1945
79905	RYAN, John	Coone, Bagenalstown, Co. Carlow.	9-9-1921	Farm Labourer	8-8-1945
E/416350	RYAN, John	Toilaclug, Cappawhite, Tipperary.	25-11-1923	Labourer	8-8-1945
76697	RYAN, John	15 Ballycurrane, Thurles.	2-12-1919	Labourer	8-8-1945
E/434325	RYAN, John	Rathfeston, Geashill, Offaly.	7-4-1916	Labourer	8-8-1945
E/432511	RYAN, John	64 Caledon Road, East Road, Dublin.	12-2-1919	Labourer	8-8-1945
E/412097	RYAN, John	County Home, Ennis.	3-5-1917	Labourer	23-11-1945
E/423867	RYAN, John	Church Street, Loughrea, Co. Galway.	17-6-1922	Garage Attendant	8-8-1945
E/405707	RYAN, John J.	131 Rathgar Road, Dublin.	1-9-1915	Clerk	8-8-1945
E/407538	RYAN, John J.	Upper Main Street, Portarlington.	30-3-1914	Clerk	8-8-1945
L/503173	RYAN, Joseph	185 Kildare Road, Crumlin, Dublin.	6-2-1927	General Labourer	4-7-1946
77938	RYAN, Joseph	Home Barracks, Ennis.	19-4-1920	Shop Porter	8-8-1945
A/72834	RYAN, Malachy	Mount Patrick Villa, Dublin Road, Limerick.	5-10-1913	Cinema Operator	8-8-1945
V/214078	RYAN, Michael	104 Carey's Rd., Limerick.	16-5-1922	Labourer	8-8-1945
V/201045	RYAN, Michael	Ballagh, Monasterevan, Co. Kildare.	1-4-1917	Labourer	8-8-1945
V/210056	RYAN, Michael	2 O'Sullivan's Place, Limerick.	28-4-1922	Labourer	8-8-1945
73393	RYAN, Myles	21 Vinegar Hill Villas, Enniscorthy.	3-7-1914	Labourer	8-8-1945
83864	RYAN, Patrick	1 Summer Place, Charles Street, Dublin.	15-8-1922	Painter's Improver	8-8-1945
V/215148	RYAN, Patrick	Cornmore, Kiltyclogher, Co. Leitrim.	17-5-1918	Farmer	8-8-1945
A/78564	RYAN, Patrick	19 Ballycurrane, Thurles.	1-1-1921	Casual Labourer	8-8-1945
V/203271	RYAN, Patrick	9 Mungret Street, Limerick.	24-4-1922	Labourer	8-8-1945
E/410808	RYAN, Patrick	65 Fair Green Cottages, Limerick.	24-10-1906	Labourer	8-8-1945
E/411853	RYAN, Patrick	Stradavoher, Thurles.	24-6-1910	Labourer	8-8-1945
204690	RYAN, Patrick	Sion, Crossabbey, Co. Wexford.	13-5-1922	Labourer	8-8-1945
E/414889	RYAN, Patrick	1 Halpin's Row, Nicholas Street, Limerick.	14-12-1922	Labourer	8-8-1945
83380	RYAN, Patrick	7 Hardwick Place, Dublin.	19-4-1922	Labourer	8-8-1945
83184	RYAN, Patrick	4 Hanover Square, Dublin.	30-1-1921	Mechanic's Assistant	8-8-1945
A/76718	RYAN, Terence	2 Back Clare St., Limerick.	16-10-1919	Labourer	8-8-1945
209325	RYAN, Thomas	Templetuohy, Templemore.	2-1-1916	Farmer	8-8-1945
E/433388	RYAN, Thomas	Iveagh House, Bride Street, Dublin.	7-4-1894	Labourer	8-8-1945
77601	RYAN, Thomas	2 Grattan St., Limerick.	9-11-1919	Labourer	8-8-1945
E/403024	RYAN, Thomas	2 Murray's Cottages, Sarsfield Road, Dublin.	13-7-1916	Motor Mechanic	8-8-1945
76954	RYAN, William	Barnett St., Bagenalstown, Co. Carlow.	17-6-1916	General Labourer	8-8-1945
L/507518	RYAN, William	19 Ballycurrane, Thurles.	16-3-1927	Labourer	8-8-1945
76200	RYAN, William	4 Fianna Road, Thurles.	25-9-1919	Carpenter	8-8-1945
E/412819	RYAN, William	31 Lower Gerald Griffin Street, Limerick.	19-6-1922	Labourer	8-8-1945

Army No.	Name.	Last Recorded Address.	Date of Birth.	Declared Occupation prior to enlistment in Defence Forces.	Date of Dismissal from Defence Forces.
L/508468	RYDER, Christopher	Newtown, Bagenalstown, Co. Carlow.	15-5-1923	Labourer	8-8-1945
L/502653	SALINGER, Martin	50 Kildare Road, Crumlin, Dublin.	15-1-1926	Turf Worker	8-8-1945
E/433175	SALMON, Thomas	1 High Street, Wexford.	11-5-1917	Blacksmith and Fitter	8-8-1945
E/403724	SAMMON, Patrick J.	Cullaville, Co. Armagh.	18-11-1900	Lorry Driver	8-8-1945
A/74786	SARSFIELD, Patrick	12 Castle Bks., Limerick.	31-10-1919	Labourer	8-8-1945
V/214031	SARSFEILD, Timothy	Cregane, Charleville.	23-4-1921	Labourer	8-8-1945
V/203291	SAVAGE, Michael J.	Gortroche, Ballyhooley, Co. Cork.	27-8-1921	Labourer	8-8-1945
E/431848	SCALLAN, James Francis	c/o Fr. McCabe, Main St., Ballyconnell, Cavan.	20-4-1915	Labourer	8-8-1945
E/423297	SCALLON, Joseph	Drumharvey, Irvinestown, Co. Fermanagh.	5-8-1914	Lorry Driver	8-8-1945
E/413941	SCANLON, Daniel	Glenmount, Ballybunion, Co. Kerry.	28-10-1920	Carpenter	8-8-1945
79611	SCANLON, John	Fermoy, Co. Cork.	17-3-1921	Labourer	8-8-1945
V/201472	SCANLON, Patrick	30 St. John's Tce., Sligo.	21-3-1920	Labourer	8-8-1945
E/434104	SCANLON, Patrick	Kilcorney, Clara, Offaly.	25-5-1915	Waiter	8-8-1945
83594	SCANTORI, John	46 Jervis Street, Dublin.	6-7-1922	Messenger	8-8-1945
A/83568	SCARFFE, William	1 James's Street, Dublin.	1-12-1919	Labourer	8-8-1945
A/72201	SCOTT, Alexander	45 Eccles Street, Dublin.	27-6-1912	Labourer	8-8-1945
E/413048	SCOTT, John	Newtown, Drangan, Co. Tipperary.	5-4-1918	Labourer	8-8-1945
83284	SCOTT, John	122 Larkhill Road, Whitehall, Dublin.	4-8-1920	Labourer	8-8-1945
80346	SCOTT, John	Coneyburrow Rd., Lifford.	3-1-1922	Motor Mechanic	8-8-1945
E/405823	SCOTT, Richard F.	18 Beechmount Crescent, Broadway, Belfast.	4-10-1921	Electrician	8-8-1945
206745	SCOTT, Richard	45 Anner Road, Inchicore, Dublin.	7-12-1921	Labourer	8-8-1945
E/405074	SCOTT, Thomas	14 Ballybough Cottages, Dublin.	22-7-1921	Motor Driver	8-8-1945
E/434706	SCOTT, Thomas	2 Wellington Square, Kilkenny.	1-10-1914	Bookmaker	8-8-1945
E/433208	SCULLY, Bernard	11 Upper Patrick Street, Kilkenny.	5-11-1913	Motor Driver	8-8-1945
82541	SCULLY, Denis	New Inn, Cahir, Co. Tipperary.	24-5-1922	Labourer	8-8-1945
A/75496	SCULLY, James	New Inn, Cahir, Co. Tipperary.	5-12-1917	Horse Trainer	8-8-1945
V/211619	SCULLY, James	17 McDowell's Avenue, McCaffrey's Estate, Mount Brown, Dublin.	1-3-1923	Messenger	8-8-1945
E/417843	SCULLY, Joseph	Deelin, Canon, Kilnaboy, Co. Clare.	29-10-1924	Labourer	8-8-1945
V/209464	SCULLY, Michael	Curtin's Lane, Hospital, Co. Limerick.	24-3-1922	Groom	8-8-1945
V/207107	SCULLY, Patrick	Knockbodly, Graiguenamanagh, Co. Kilkenny.	—-2-1922	Labourer	8-8-1945
E/405918	SCULLY, William	8 Cashel Road, Crumlin, Dublin.	15-11-1921	Labourer	8-8-1945
E/422053	SEARY, Thomas	Creeve, Walderstown, Co. Westmeath.	7-3-1916	Steel Erector	8-8-1945
E/423846	SEERY, Patrick	Porters Terrace, Arva, Co. Cavan.	4-9-1914	Mason's Labourer	8-8-1945
79719	SEMPLE, Frank	1 Upton Street, Dublin.	12-12-1919	Labourer	8-8-1945
E/433500	SEXTON, Christopher	77 Thatch Road, Drumcondra, Dublin.	25-12-1921	Motor Engineer	8-8-1945
E/411856	SEXTON, Denis	5 Castle Barracks, Limerick.	24-6-1912	Labourer	8-8-1945
V/202788	SEXTON, John	46 Mount Eden Rd., Cork.	25-4-1922	Shoemaker	8-8-1945

Army No.	Name.	Last Recorded Address.	Date of Birth.	Declared Occupation prior to enlistment in Defence Forces.	Date of Dismissal from Defence Forces.
E/432985	SHANAHAN, Francis	155 Comeragh Road, Crumlin, Dublin.	4-11-1921	Fitter	8-8-1945
E/431837	SHANAHAN, James	31 Doyle St., Waterford.	10-12-1914	None	8-8-1945
81275	SHANAHAN, Joseph	Ballinamona, Hospital, Co. Limerick.	30-8-1920	Labourer	24-9-1945
A/79126	SHANAHAN, Kevin	Main Street, Bruff, Co. Limerick.	18-11-1920	Builder	8-8-1945
80694	SHANAHAN, Kevin Jos.	4 Stradbally Road, Portlaoighise.	25-1-1921	Baker's Assistant	8-8-1945
E/415101	SHANAHAN, William	23 St. Flannan's Terrace, Ennis.	6-8-1922	Messenger Boy	8-8-1945
E/402266	SHANKS, George	14 Geraldine St., Dublin.	20-9-1920	Motor Driver	8-8-1945
E/425029	SHANLEY, John	Island, Cloghan, Offaly.	8-1-1924	Farm Labourer	8-8-1945
81935	SHANNON, James	4 O'Connell Road, Tipperary.	31-4-1924	Labourer	8-8-1945
E/405260	SHANNON, Michael	20 Chelmsford Avenue, Ranelagh, Dublin.	1-11-1918	Clerk	8-8-1945
E/404049	SHANNON, Patrick	52 Poolbeg Street, Dublin.	30-6-1919	Cook	8-8-1945
110958	SHANNON, Patrick	11 "G" Block, Married Quarters, Arbour Hill, Dublin.	28-1-1919	Labourer	9-6-1946
78630	SHARKEY, Daniel	Mullagh Road, Miltown-Malbay, Co. Clare.	22-2-1921	Hotel Attendant	8-8-1945
E/420488	SHARKEY, Edward	Gortnasade, Kincassalagh, Co. Donegal.	8-12-1904	Labourer	8-8-1945
E/400502	SHARKEY, James	2 Dungiven Road, Waterside Derry.	23-3-1914	Electrician	8-8-1945
E/421707	SHAUGHNESSY, James	Lettergonnell, Ballinalee, Co. Longford.	7-4-1922	Labourer	8-8-1945
A/77428	SHAW, James	33 Clark Avenue, Janesborough, Limerick.	12-1-1920	Labourer	8-8-1945
E/423151	SHAW, Kevin Barry	28 Annesley Ave., Dublin.	2-1-1921	None	8-8-1945
V/210057	SHAW, Patrick	33 Road B, Janesborough, Limerick.	4-10-1922	Butler	8-8-1945
76784	SHEEHAN, Denis	7 Cremin's Lane, Cork.	27-7-1919	Labourer	8-8-1945
E/414568	SHEEHAN, James J.	Oakview, Tralee.	1-3-1917	Clerk	8-8-1945
E/410919	SHEEHAN, James	23 Dominick Street, Cork.	24-5-1918	Butcher	8-8-1945
V/213116	SHEEHAN, John	34 Washbrew Lane, Cork.	10-5-1922	None	8-8-1945
E/410769	SHEEHAN, Matthew	St. Ita's Terrace, Newcastle West, Co. Limerick.	5-6-1922	Labourer	8-8-1945
E/400153	SHEEHAN, Michael	14 East James St., Dublin.	10-9-1908	Motor Driver	8-8-1945
76910	SHEEHAN, Patrick	St. Ita's Terrace, Newcastle West, Co. Limerick.	7-3-1918	Labourer	8-8-1945
112287	SHEEHAN, Patrick	Ballybricken, Kilmallock, Co. Limerick.	22-4-1916	Labourer	8-8-1945
L/507627	SHEEHAN, Thomas	16 St. Philomena's Road, Gurranebraher, Cork.	17-12-1926	Labourer	10-11-1945
81826	SHEEHAN, Timothy	Velvetstown. Buttevant, Co. Cork.	26-2-1927	House Boy	22-3-1946
E/415524	SHEEHAN, William	Tinnageragh, Watergrasshill, Co. Cork.	22-12-1922	Motor Driver and Mechanic	8-8-1945
E/404738	SHEEHY, Colm	81 Brian Road, Marino, Dublin.	25-2-1915	Bricklayer	8-8-1945
E/415067	SHEEHY, Michael	Corner House, Croom, Co. Limerick.	5-6-1918	Wireless Operator	8-8-1945
E/414879	SHEEHY, Patrick	38 Stacks Villas, Tralee.	7-6-1922	Labourer	8-8-1945
E/420725	SHEILDS, Thomas	3 Tower Terrace, Kildare.	10-11-1917	Compositor	8-8-1945
E/424286	SHEILS, Charles	Toragh Glen, Kilmacrenan, Co. Donegal.	23-1-1923	Labourer	8-8-1945
E/407332	SHERIDAN, Edward	107 St. Nicholas Avenue, Dundalk.	10-9-1921	Labourer	8-8-1945
V/204130	SHERIDAN, Felix	Lakeview House, Arva, Co. Cavan.	20-3-1918	Farm Labourer	8-8-1945
E/406863	SHERIDAN, Frederick	14 North Great Charles Street, Dublin.	18-1-1923	Labourer	16-10-1945

Army No.	Name.	Last Recorded Address.	Date of Birth.	Declared Occupation prior to enlistment in Defence Forces.	Date of Dismissal from Defence Forces.
204168	SHERIDAN, Frederick	41 Upper Rutland Street, Dublin.	2-1-1921	Messenger	8-8-1945
E/403344	SHERIDAN, James	10 O'Brien's Place, Drumcondra, Dublin.	23-3-1922	Page	8-8-1945
E/422055	SHERIDAN, John	Drung, Co. Cavan.	31-5-1922	Carpenter	8-8-1945
204028	SHERIDAN, Kevin	15 D Block, Benburb St. Buildings, Dublin.	28-11-1920	Labourer	8-8-1945
V/207087	SHERIDAN, Michael	15 D Block, Benburb St. Buildings, Dublin.	6-6-1922	Messenger Boy	8-8-1945
E/433990	SHERLOCK, John	Milestown, Dunboyne, Co. Meath.	6-2-1919	Labourer	8-8-1945
V/201495	SHERLOCK, Michael	96 Tolka Road, Dublin.	13-4-1920	Messenger	8-8-1945
E/424435	SHIELDS, Gregory	Timmock House, Bridgeland, Co. Donegal.	1-8-1922	Labourer	8-8-1945
79035	SHIELDS, James Paul	Gibbinstown, Navan.	29-6-1917	Grocery	8-8-1945
76564	SHIELDS, Joseph	Passextown, Enfield, Co. Meath.	27-4-1917	Labourer	8-8-1945
A/80328	SHIELS, James	24 Union St., Waterside, Derry.	16-1-1921	Labourer	8-8-1945
E/406016	SHIELS, Kevin	Mayne, Castlebellingham, Co. Louth.	5-4-1922	Farm Labourer	8-8-1945
E/423224	SHIELS, Michael	15 Wesley St., Rosemount, Derry.	28-9-1921	Labourer	8-8-1945
E/403808	SHIELS, Patrick	1 Herbert Cottages, Ballsbridge, Dublin.	31-3-1922	Messenger	8-8-1945
210120	SHIELS, Patrick	Coronea, Arva, Co. Cavan.	12-3-1913	Farmer	8-8-1945
E/432456	SHIELS, Philip	Mall Road, Monaghan.	28-12-1921	Motor Driver	8-8-1945
E/414381	SHINE, Michael	105 St. Michael's Road, Spangle Hill, Cork.	29-3-1922	Clerk	8-8-1945
V/206133	SHORT, James	North Street, Crossmaglen, Co. Armagh.	3-12-1910	Publican	8-8-1945
E/434858	SHORTALL, John	32 Jail Street, Kilkenny.	17-9-1922	Labourer	8-8-1945
E/404971	SHORTALL, Patrick	34 Pimlico, Dublin.	17-10-1922	Labourer	8-8-1945
78794	SHORTEN, William	8 Bankside, Milltown, Co. Dublin.	14-2-1920	Gardener	8-8-1945
77607	SHORTT, John	31 Roxtown Tce., Limerick.	1-1-1919	Farm Labourer	8-8-1945
V/217069	SHUEL, Francis	Drumsnat, Smithboro', Co. Monaghan.	24-4-1922	Farm Labourer	4-1-1946
E/421759	SIMMS, William	Doumhagord, Muff, Co. Donegal.	14-4-1922	Apprentice Iron Moulder	8-8-1945
E/400013	SIMPSON, Edward	27 Capel Street, Dublin.	29-1-1914	Butler	8-8-1945
E/431979	SIMPSON, James W.	Blandsfort, Abbeyleix.	15-6-1922	Labourer	8-8-1945
V/211302	SIMPSON, Patrick	St. Anne's, Clontarf, Dublin.	1-5-1923	Motor Mechanic	8-8-1945
202998	SINGLETON, Richard	8 White Mill Rd., Wexford.	13-12-1920	Labourer	8-8-1945
E/422247	SKEFFINGTON, Seamus	Park Street, Monaghan.	16-3-1922	Shop Assistant	8-8-1945
209165	SKEHAN, Thomas P.	Main Street, Templemore.	24-3-1918	Barber	8-8-1945
A/83827	SKELTON, John	Brackaville, Coalisland, Co. Tyrone.	4-2-1922	Labourer	8-8-1945
E/404861	SKERRET, Thomas	New Road, Ennistymon, Co. Clare.	6-1-1923	Blacksmith	8-8-1945
E/406442	SKINNER, Cameron	237 Cashel Road, Crumlin, Dublin.	4-4-1922	Boot Repairer	8-8-1945
L/507124	SLANNON, Michael	55 D Road, Killeely, Limerick.	19-5-1923	Messenger Boy	8-8-1945
E/435856	SLATTERY, Michael	21 Rathfadden Villas, Waterford.	18-1-1924	Labourer	8-8-1945
E/430031	SLATTERY, Walter	21 Rathfadden Villas, Waterford.	15-10-1921	Labourer	8-8-1945
84238	SLEVIN, John	Ballindrait, Lifford.	26-8-1921	Labourer	8-8-1945
L/503236	SLOVIA, Patrick J.	347 Clogher Road, Crumlin, Dublin.	18-4-1928	Tailor's Apprentice	1-7-1946
215240	SMID, Noel	Harrington Row, Mullingar.	25-12-1924	Labourer	8-8-1945

Army No.	Name.	Last Recorded Address.	Date of Birth.	Declared Occupation prior to enlistment in Defence Forces.	Date of Dismissal from Defence Forces.
78477	SMITH, Donald	64 Emmett Tce., Navan.	15-1-1920	Messenger	8-8-1945
E/402188	SMITH, Francis	33 Pearse Square, Dublin.	8-6-1897	Fireman	8-8-1945
E/420383	SMITH, Herbert	Blacklion, Co. Cavan.	22-9-1908	Motor Driver and Mechanic	8-8-1945
V/209327	SMITH, James	Mill St., Carrick-on-Suir.	27-12-1919	Labourer	8-8-1945
80458	SMITH, James	25 Prior's Knock, Waterford.	7-12-1920	Labourer	8-8-1945
E/405194	SMITH, Joseph	Cullies, Cavan.	31-12-1922	Labourer	8-8-1945
A/83186	SMITH, Matthew	Jobstown, Co. Dublin.	23-1-1920	Labourer	8-8-1945
E/400607	SMITH, Michael	15 Victoria Road, Clontarf, Dublin.	28-5-1895	Clerk	8-8-1945
E/405267	SMITH, Michael	131 Mourne Rd., Crumlin, Dublin.	17-7-1922	Messenger	8-8-1945
E/423108	SMITH, Michael	16 St. Michael's Road, Longford.	2-2-1920	General Labourer	11-8-1945
80315	SMITH, Michael	Clough, Gurteen, Woodlawn, Co. Galway.	28-5-1921	Labourer	8-8-1945
204430	SMITH, Owen	2 Henry Place, Dublin.	18-4-1921	Motor Driver	8-8-1945
81245	SMITH, Raymond F.	70 Lindsay Road, Dublin.	3-1-1924	Motor Driver	8-8-1945
202827	SMITH, Terence	31 Fassaugh Road, Cabra, Dublin.	22-9-1921	Central Heating Fitter	8-8-1945
E/432878	SMITH, Stephen	14 O'Sullivan's Avenue, Ballybough, Dublin.	14-10-1921	Messenger	8-8-1945
E/402977	SMITH, Thomas	70 Lindsay Road, Dublin.	20-4-1918	Radio Operator	8-8-1945
V/211219	SMITH, William	15 Leighlin Road, Kimmage, Dublin.	16-12-1919	Labourer	8-8-1945
E/424798	SMULLEN, Daniel	Aughdrumderg, Mohill, Co. Leitrim.	30-8-1923	Labourer	8-8-1945
E/420096	SMYTH, James	Mostown, Keenagh, Co. Longford.	12-2-1921	Farm Labourer	8-8-1945
204131	SMYTH, James	Glebe, Garadice P.O., Ballinamona, Co. Leitrim.	3-3-1919	Farmer	8-8-1945
E/422057	SMYTH, John	Main Street, Blacklion, Co. Cavan.	2-6-1913	Salesman	8-8-1945
83825	SMYTH, Michael	6 Parkview Street, Belfast.	10-1-1922	Labourer	8-8-1945
E/420145	SMYTH, Patrick	78 Gilmartin Road, Tuam.	9-3-1918	General Labourer	8-8-1945
E/420100	SMYTH, Patrick	Navenney St., Ballybofey, Co. Donegal.	9-7-1913	Labourer	8-8-1945
E/437829	SMYTH, Patrick	Knockbridge, Dundalk.	10-1-1916	Farm Labourer	8-8-1945
V/202312	SMYTH, Thomas	16 St. Joseph's Tce., Sligo.	16-2-1921	Labourer	8-8-1945
E/413405	SMYTH, Thomas	Scarrough House, Cahir, Co. Tipperary.	1-3-1915	Carpenter	8-8-1945
L/508312	SMYTH, Thomas	Arva, Co. Cavan.	19-12-1919	Painter	8-8-1945
E/423298	SMYTH, William	12 Donegal Street, Derry.	25-11-1920	Labourer	8-8-1945
74623	SMYTH, William	Main Street, Midleton, Co. Cork.	12-8-1918	Fisherman	29-5-1946
77872	SOMERS, Ambrose	10 Riverside Cottages, Templeogue, Dublin.	30-6-1920	Messenger Boy	8-8-1945
E/403726	SOMERS, Patrick	137 Up. Dorset St., Dublin.	6-9-1907	Labourer	8-8-1945
E/404732	SOUTHWELL, Joseph	496 North Circular Road, Dublin.	27-3-1913	Sheet Metal Worker	8-8-1945
E/412302	SPENCER, Thomas	29 Bunkershill, Roscrea.	3-8-1921	Labourer	8-8-1945
E/416898	SPILLANE, Daniel	Knocknageela, Greevnavilla, Rathmore, Co. Kerry.	17-2-1913	Labourer	8-8-1945
A/71743	SPILLANE, Joseph	6 Arthur's Quay, Limerick.	23-2-1911	Mechanic	8-8-1945
E/423290	SPRATT, Francis	Bridge Street, Irvinestown, Co. Fermanagh.	20-9-1912	Labourer	8-8-1945
E/423300	SPRATT, Thomas	Bridge Street, Irvinestown, Co. Fermanagh.	5-10-1898	Labourer	8-8-1945
E/402859	STAFFORD, James	89 Lismore Rd., Crumlin, Dublin.	1-3-1922	Cabinet Maker	8-8-1945
A/78584	STAFFORD, James	George's Street, Gorey.	14-4-1915	Farm Labourer	8-8-1945

Army No.	Name.	Last Recorded Address.	Date of Birth.	Declared Occupation prior to enlistment in Defence Forces.	Date of Dismissal from Defence Forces.
E/433241	STAFFORD, Thomas	Shelbaggan, Ramsgrange, Co. Wexford.	16-1-1919	Labourer	4-12-1945
E/404790	STANLEY, Joseph	52 Annamoe Terrace, Cabra, Dublin.	1-6-1922	None	8-8-1945
V/207496	STAPLETON, John	1 Grenville Stret, Dublin.	13-7-1921	Plasterer	8-8-1945
V/211418	STAPLETON, Patrick	1 Cloyne Road, Crumlin, Dublin.	1-5-1922	None	8-8-1945
V/200274	STARR, John	Derrygorlin, Woodford, Co. Galway.	26-2-1910	Road Labourer	8-8-1945
E/403048	STEBBINGS, John	22D St. Michan's Flats, Mary's Lane, Dublin.	26-11-1922	None	8-8-1945
E/433174	STEELE, Veirein F.	11 Abbey Street, Wexford.	1-11-1922	Fitter's Improver	8-8-1945
E/416495	STENSON, Stephen	14 Mill House, High Street, Limerick.	19-7-1923	Bricklayer	8-8-1945
E/402622	STEWART, John	139 Mount Tallant Avenue, Dublin.	29-9-1921	Motor Driver	8-8-1945
83678	STEWART, Michael	St. Bridget's Cotts., Blanchardstown, Co. Dublin.	21-2-1922	Labourer	8-8-1945
83826	STEWART, Patrick A.	46 Ardilea Street, Belfast.	24-11-1913	Railway Porter	8-8-1945
E/423301	STEWART, William	24 South End Park, Derry.	13-2-1921	Labourer	8-8-1945
E/403403	ST. JOHN, John	31 Termon Park, Boyle.	4-7-1905	Cook	8-8-1945
E/414382	STOKES, Raymond	11 Lr. Rock Street, Tralee.	31-8-1915	Commercial Traveller	8-8-1945
E/416161	STOKES, Thomas	Kilmore, Clonmel.	19-3-1920	Lorry Driver	8-8-1945
E/416065	STOUT, James	39 Spring Lane, Blackpool, Cork.	5-10-1922	Farm Labourer	8-8-1945
E/404051	STOUT, William	18 Hill Street, Dublin.	16-9-1910	Labourer	8-8-1945
E/414317	STRAND, Francis	2 Steele's Terrace, Ennis.	5-8-1921	Factory Worker	8-8-1945
78326	STRANGE, William	29 Upper Mercer's Street, Dublin.	13-1-1921	Moulder's Helper	8-8-1945
E/432075	STRINGER, Robert	Barnhill, Durrow, Co. Leix.	25-5-1915	Labourer	8-8-1945
E/412106	STUBBINS, Christopher	Road E, Prospect, Limerick.	18-9-1906	Labourer	8-8-1945
E/409241	STURDY, Michael	175 Brandon Rd., Crumlin, Dublin.	6-6-1924	Clerk	8-8-1945
E/402658	SUGARS, Thomas	18 Lavarna Rd., Terenure, Dublin.	14-12-1921	None	8-8-1945
V/209616	SULLIVAN, James	New Road, Kilcock, Co. Kildare.	1-10-1921	Labourer	8-8-1945
E/408094	SULLIVAN, John	28 St. Nicholas Avenue, Dundalk.	28-8-1924	Messenger	8-8-1945
A/82827	SULLIVAN, John	Lord's Park, Rathcabban, Co. Offaly.	21-10-1922	Farm Labourer	8-8-1945
E/412446	SULLIVAN, Patrick	Knockdure, Bonane, Kenmare, Co. Kerry.	29-6-1918	Labourer	8-8-1945
78346	SULLIVAN, Patrick	49 O'Hanlon Pk., Dundalk.	4-1-1920	Messenger	8-8-1945
77096	SULLIVAN, Thomas	10 New Buildings, Kilkenny.	10-7-1920	Farm Labourer	8-8-1945
E/414472	SULLIVAN, Thomas	Ballinard Road, Carrick-on-Suir.	21-9-1922	Labourer	8-8-1945
42789	SULLIVAN, Timothy	9 House 1 Block, M/Qrs., Collins Barracks, Cork.	21-10-1897	Fisherman	8-8-1945
E/429606	SUMMERVILLE, Martin	Kilbride, Clonbur, Co. Galway.	9-9-1921	Farm Labourer	8-8-1945
E/403810	SUPPLE, Frederick	4 Summerville Place, Rathmines, Dublin.	1-4-1918	Mechanic	8-8-1945
E/415433	SUTTON, John	Ahamilla, Clonakilty, Co. Cork.	4-2-1918	Aircraft-Part Packer	8-8-1945
L/508302	SUTTON, John	Sallins, Naas.	20-5-1923	Labourer	8-8-1945
V/204708	SUTTON, Paul	Ballinakill, Moyvalley, Co. Kildare.	14-1-1917	Labourer	8-8-1945
E/435419	SWAINE, James	Ballycarney, Co. Wexford.	2-3-1922	Labourer	25-11-1945
E/404612	SWEENEY, Charles	c/o Mrs. Reilly, Newlion, Cootehill, Co. Cavan.	24-5-1921	Motor Driver	8-8-1945

Army No.	Name.	Last Recorded Address.	Date of Birth.	Declared Occupation prior to enlistment in Defence Forces.	Date of Dismissal from Defence Forces.
A/68172	SWEENEY, Edward	Maherdrummond, Ramelton, Co. Donegal.	14-4-1908	Labourer	8-8-1945
E/420431	SWEENEY, George	Church Lane, Letterkenny.	3-6-1905	Labourer	8-8-1945
A/83196	SWEENEY, Hugh	7 "C" Block, Benburb St., Dublin.	18-12-1921	Labourer	8-8-1945
79180	SWEENEY, James	Knockeen, Pallasgreen, Co. Limerick.	28-2-1921	Labourer	8-8-1945
200820	SWEENEY, John	Main Street, Letterkenny.	18-8-1919	Labourer	8-8-1945
V/215168	SWEENEY, John	Lr. Meencornick, Crotty, Co. Donegal.	10-11-1915	Labourer	8-8-1945
E/422779	SWEENEY, John	Magherallon, Derrybeg, Co. Donegal.	4-11-1901	Seaman	8-8-1945
E/413473	SWEENEY, Joseph	23 Mountpleasant Avenue, Limerick.	5-11-1918	Labourer	8-8-1945
E/424146	SWEENEY, Louis	Drumully, Clones, Co. Monaghan.	13-6-1920	Farm Labourer	8-8-1945
E/432970	SWEENEY, Michael	18 James Road, Drumcondra, Dublin.	25-1-1922	Engineer	8-8-1945
E/421182	SWEENEY, Patrick	Newtowncunningham, Co. Donegal.	17-1-1917	Egg Tester	8-8-1945
E/423303	SWEENEY, Patrick	27 Howard Street, Derry.	17-3-1914	Labourer	8-8-1945
V/200821	SWEENEY, Patrick	Daly's Tce., Letterkenny.	9-4-1921	General Labourer	8-8-1945
E/433000	SWEETMAN, John	72 West Road, Dublin.	21-3-1916	Labourer	8-8-1945
V/211605	SWIFT, Christopher	127 Crumlin Road, Dublin.	12-2-1923	Hairdresser	8-8-1945
A/62486	SWORDS, Edward	3 Perry Square, Limerick.	11-9-1906	Messenger	8-8-1945
V/206135	SYNNOTT, Kevin	23 William St., Clonmel.	25-7-1921	Boot Repairer	8-8-1945
E/409366	SYNNOTT, William	76 Rollin's Villas, Sallynoggin, Co. Dublin.	18-4-1924	Grocer's Porter	8-8-1945
204635	TALBOT, Stephen	52 Ravensdale Road, East Wall, Dublin.	28-4-1920	Labourer	8-8-1945
V/204647	TALBOT, William	25 Gulistan Ctgs., Dublin.	25-11-1919	Slater's Apprentice	8-8-1945
A/80390	TALTY, Patrick	Killard, Doonbeg, Co. Clare.	23-1-1922	Labourer	3-1-1946
A/84237	TAULT, Laurence	47 Thornhill Road, West Croydon, England.	2-4-1917	Farm Labourer	8-8-1945
E/421998	TAYLOR, Daniel	Carrigans, Co. Donegal.	12-5-1919	Labourer	8-8-1945
A/83076	TAYLOR, John	Newtownmountkennedy, Co. Wicklow.	14-9-1921	Farm Labourer	8-8-1945
E/434072	TAYLOR, Michael	18 Gordon Place, South Richmond St., Dublin.	1-7-1913	Labourer	8-8-1945
E/409957	TAYLOR, Patrick	39 Jamaica Street, Belfast.	6-10-1924	Carter	8-8-1945
E/421536	TEDDERS, William	Shrule, Co. Galway.	19-10-1915	Post Office Asst. & Motor Driver	8-8-1945
E/408399	TEMPLE, Francis	4 Wolfe Tone Sq., Bray.	5-10-1923	Railway Porter	8-8-1945
E/409216	THACKABERY, Nathaniel	6 "D" Block, Ormond Sq., Ormond Quay, Dublin.	4-2-1917	Labourer	8-8-1945
E/403148	THOMAS, Frederick	19 Pearse Street, Dublin.	31-5-1922	Brushmaker	8-8-1945
79975	THOMAS, Terence	21 Upr. Nassau St., Derry.	1-3-1922	Bricklayer	8-8-1945
E/412825	THOMPSON, Christopher	2 Barry Lane, Boherbuoy, Limerick.	13-12-1917	Shoemaker	8-8-1945
L/502558	THOMPSON, Christopher	29 Bannow Road, West Cabra, Dublin.	29-12-1925	Labourer	8-8-1945
A/84130	THOMPSON, Henry	c/o M. Kiernan, Ballyconnell, Co. Cavan.	27-1-1921	Farm Labourer	8-8-1945
E/423466	THOMPSON, James	Fearnaught, Dromard, Co. Leitrim.	22-9-1919	Farm Labourer	8-8-1945
A/78737	THOMPSON, John	355 Galtymore Road, Crumlin, Dublin.	1-12-1921	Messenger	8-8-1945
82265	THOMPSON, Michael	Gearach, Rathcormac, Fermoy.	2-4-1913	Pipe Joiner	8-8-1945
77430	THOMPSON, Michael	Kildysart, Co. Clare.	12-8-1918	Motor Driver	8-8-1945
84914	THOMPSON, Patrick	8 Lower Wellington Street, Dublin.	11-4-1927	Messenger	16-5-1946

Army No.	Name.	Last Recorded Address.	Date of Birth.	Declared Occupation prior to enlistment in Defence Forces.	Date of Dismissal from Defence Forces.
E/423032	THORNBURY, Charles	30 Leighlin Rd., Crumlin, Dublin.	23-12-1921	Blacksmith	8-8-1945
V/208865	TIBBY, John J.	Cross, Monaghan.	27-7-1920	Labourer	8-8-1945
105807	TIERNEY, Dennis	Gortlandroe, Nenagh, Co. Tipperary.	5-8-1914	Labourer	8-8-1945
E/415621	TIERNEY, James	Main Street, Templemore, Co. Tipperary.	24-7-1910	Motor Driver	8-8-1945
E/407484	TIERNEY, John	10 Charlotte Street, Dublin.	23-12-1923	Labourer	8-8-1945
V/203625	TIERNEY, Luke	6 North Richmond Street, Dublin.	2-1-1912	Electrical Engineer	8-8-1945
A/76176	TIERNEY, Peter	64 Church Road, North Strand, Dublin.	9-6-1919	Motor Driver	8-8-1945
V/210079	TIGHE, John	Acre, Aughmore, Ballyhaunis, Co. Mayo.	13-2-1922	Labourer	8-8-1945
E/435331	TIGHE, John	233 Keogh Square, Inchicore, Dublin.	23-11-1922	Labourer	8-8-1945
E/432327	TIMMINS, George	105 Francis Street, Dublin.	7-7-1922	Labourer	8-8-1945
E/407792	TIMMONS, Patrick	283 St. Attracta Road, Cabra, Dublin.	30-4-1921	Motor Driver	8-8-1945
A/78365	TIMMONS, Patrick	29 York Street, Dublin.	31-1-1920	Labourer	8-8-1945
E/421621	TIMON, Patrick	1 Dublin Gate St., Athlone.	16-3-1919	National Health Insurance Clerk	8-8-1945
E/423314	TIMONEY, Gerard	Braeview, Pearse Road, Sligo.	16-4-1916	Telegraphist	8-8-1945
E/407154	TINNENY, James	Roslea, Co. Fermanagh.	22-5-1923	Student	18-12-1945
E/423592	TINNEY, James	Glencar, Co. Donegal.	15-7-1917	Labourer	8-8-1945
E/420220	TINNEY, John	The Bridge, Castlefin, Co. Donegal.	12-6-1907	Motor Driver	8-8-1945
E/433112	TOAL, James	North Road, Monaghan.	22-4-1921	Labourer	8-8-1945
E/404578	TOAL, Patrick J.	Grange, Carlingford, Co. Louth.	14-4-1922	Motor Driver	8-8-1945
77120	TOBIN, James	13 Upper Mountpleasant Avenue, Dublin.	15-6-1918	Farm Labourer	8-8-1945
A/77099	TOBIN, Peter	Borrismore, Urlingford, Co. Kilkenny.	10-12-1918	Farm Labourer	8-8-1945
V/203886	TOBIN, Robert	77 St. Kevin's Sq., Cork.	31-5-1917	Mechanic	8-8-1945
A/76600	TOBIN, Thomas	19 Railway Road, Temple-More, Co. Tipperary.	10-5-1919	Labourer	8-8-1945
E/405082	TOHILL, Desmond	79 Bangor Road, Crumlin, Dublin.	28-10-1918	Student	8-8-1945
E/423304	TOLAN, Owen	Tedd, Irvinestown, Co. Fermanagh.	7-10-1921	Labourer	8-8-1945
E/421538	TOLAND, Patrick	c/o M. McGranaghan, Killygordon, Co. Donegal.	23-6-1922	Labourer	8-8-1945
79729	TORMEY, James	Boher, Ballycumber, Offaly.	15-9-1921	None	8-8-1945
A/73720	TORMEY, John	Tubberhill, Westport, Co. Mayo.	11-8-1912	Bus Conductor	8-8-1945
V/204172	TORMEY, Thomas	4 Lower Fitzwilliam Street, Dublin.	4-11-1920	None	8-8-1945
E/425304	TOWNSEND, William	Bastion Street, Athlone.	3-7-1923	Motor Driver and Mechanic	8-8-1945
E/424153	TOYE, Edward	Ballindrait, Lifford.	28-9-1916	Motor Driver	8-8-1945
A/74202	TRACEY, George	Limerick Road, Naas.	16-5-1916	Messenger	8-8-1945
A/78272	TRACEY, Joseph	Drumscar, Portumna, Co. Galway.	17-3-1916	Labourer	8-8-1945
E/437670	TRACEY, Patrick	61 Milford Street, Belfast.	9-10-1925	Bricklayer's Apprentice	8-8-1945
L/507645	TRACEY, Peter	21 Parkers Range, Vizes Field, Limerick.	30-6-1926	Labourer	15-4-1946
E/422255	TRAINOR, Hugh	c/o John Barber, North Road, Monaghan.	16-4-1920	Shorthand Typist	8-8-1945
E/406477	TRAVERS, Patrick	25 Belgrave St., Glasgow.	4-4-1923	None	8-8-1945
E/434252	TRAVERS, Patrick	Ballyryan, Carlow.	20-11-1916	Labourer	8-8-1945
E/421320	TRAVERS, Peter	Rossfriar, Kinlough, Co. Leitrim.	23-6-1916	Farm Labourer	8-8-1945

Army No.	Name.	Last Recorded Address.	Date of Birth.	Declared Occupation prior to enlistment in Defence Forces.	Date of Dismissal from Defence Forces.
E/423563	TRAYNOR, Daniel	c/o Mrs. Woods, Swanlinbar, Co. Cavan.	4-4-1899	Carpenter	8-8-1945
83569	TRAYNOR, Pierce	28 Blackhall St., Dublin.	3-10-1916	Boiler Maker	8-8-1945
A/80334	TREACEY, Edward	Meenagh, Kiltyclogher, Co. Leitrim.	14-10-1918	Barman	8-8-1945
L/502961	TREACY, Brendan	178 Quarry Road, Dublin.	27-11-1927	Van Boy	8-8-1945
E/403826	TREMER, Arthur	12 Lindsay Avenue, Newry.	12-11-1921	Labourer	8-8-1945
78903	TUBBRETT, William	7 Cannon St., Waterford.	11-2-1920	Labourer	8-8-1945
E/404226	TUCK, Francis	31 Carlton Road, Marino, Dublin.	12-5-1922	Labourer	8-8-1945
V/209381	TUITE, Bernard	Oldcastle, Co. Meath.	22-12-1915	Farm Labourer	8-8-1945
E/420459	TULLY, Luke	Cloonminda, Castlerea, Co. Mayo.	28-5-1917	Farm Labourer	8-8-1945
V/206781	TUMALTY, Thomas	Cannon Street, Kells.	24-3-1920	Labourer	8-8-1945
B/3404	TUMULTY, James	98 Lr. Sean McDermott Street, Dublin.	4-3-1909	Labourer	8-8-1945
E/404995	TUOHY, Martin	Ballaghadereen, Co. Roscommon.	22-10-1907	Seaman	8-8-1945
E/410605	TUOHY, Roger	22 Lr. John Street, Cork.	4-4-1910	Auctioneer's Clerk	8-8-1945
E/407116	TURLEY, Eamon	54 Dunmore St., Belfast.	26-12-1921	Labourer	8-8-1945
84201	TURLEY, George	South Commons, Carlingford, Co. Louth.	26-3-1920	Waiter	8-8-1945
E/401735	TURLEY, Michael	6 Rampart Lane, Dundalk.	21-5-1900	Labourer	8-8-1945
E/405437	TURLEY, Robert	56 Dawson Street, Dublin.	12-9-1920	Electric Welder	8-8-1945
V/205052	TURNER, Bernard	Donardagh Lodge, Newtown Park Avenue, Blackrock, Dublin.	4-11-1920	Messenger	8-8-1945
E/401914	TURNER, James	17 Great Longford Street, Dublin.	30-3-1920	Presser	8-8-1945
E/405304	TUTTY, Peter	57 Dodsboro Cottages, Lucan, Co. Dublin.	29-6-1922	Messenger	8-8-1945
A/61093	TWOHIG, John	19 Cattle Market Avenue, Cork.	8-11-1905	Labourer	8-8-1945
E/414402	TWOMEY, Jeremiah	Pound Hill, Millstreet, Co. Cork.	5-9-1910	Labourer	8-8-1945
E/410608	TWOMEY, John	7 Vicar's Street, Cork.	16-10-1902	Labourer	8-8-1945
A/78238	TYMON, John	Termon, Boyle.	17-8-1920	Labourer	8-8-1945
E/408996	TYNAN, Patrick	Mains Court, Ballyboughal, Co. Dublin.	19-7-1924	Farm Labourer	5-12-1945
E/417506	TYNAN, Philip	Curragheeu, Horse and Jockey, Thurles.	14-11-1923	Labourer	8-8-1945
A/75518	TYNDALL, Thomas	Hartstown, Clonsilla, Co. Dublin.	2-6-1918	Schoolboy	8-8-1945
E/423305	TYRE, John	40 Nelson Street, Derry.	20-1-1922	Labourer	8-8-1945
E/408621	TYRRELL, Edward	327A Kildare Road, Crumlin, Dublin.	2-5-1924	Clerk	8-8-1945
201254	TYRRELL, Martin	55 Dooley's Terrace, Athy.	15-8-1919	Labourer	8-8-1945
E/402233	TYRRELL, Michael	94 Drumcliffe Road, Cabra, Dublin.	1-10-1921	Labourer	8-8-1945
84740	TYRRELL, William	327A Kildare Road, Crumlin, Dublin.	17-11-1923	Labourer	8-8-1945
80060	UPTON, James	1 Excise Street, Athlone.	26-2-1918	Driver's Mechanic	8-8-1945
V/211339	VARD, Harold	Whitecross, Blackrock, Dublin.	11-3-1921	Furrier	8-8-1945
E/410076	VARIAN, Henry	71 Wolfe Tone St., Cork.	14-5-1909	Shoemaker	8-8-1945
E/429544	VARLEY, Edward	Ardan, Clonbar, Co. Galway.	28-4-1919	Labourer	8-8-1945
V/203526	VENN, James	Cloncharron, Duncannon, Co. Wexford.	5-9-1915	Labourer	8-8-1945
A/83762	VICTORY, John	55 Carlton Road, Marino, Dublin.	11-9-1920	Motor Trimmer	8-8-1945

Army No.	Name.	Last Recorded Address.	Date of Birth.	Declared Occupation prior to enlistment in Defence Forces.	Date of Dismissal from Defence Forces.
E/402469	VICTORY, Thomas	18 Annadale Avenue, Fairview, Dublin.	19-10-1920	Motor Mechanic	8-8-1945
E/423306	VILLA, Laurence	9 Creggan Terrace, Derry.	22-8-1922	Butcher	8-8-1945
E/433055	WADE, Patrick	42 Tolka Rd., Ballybough, Dublin.	14-3-1922	Cinema Usher	8-8-1945
E/400612	WADE, Peter	8 Patrick Street, Dublin.	15-7-1905	Labourer	8-8-1945
A/76219	WADE, William	5 Kildare Road, Crumlin, Dublin.	10-1-1920	Messenger	8-8-1945
E/436899	WADE, William	Westown, Tramore, Co. Waterford.	26-8-1923	Farm Labourer	8-8-1945
84228	WALKER, Hugh	Castletown, Fahan, Co. Donegal.	21-12-1921	Labourer	8-8-1945
V/209382	WALL, Edmond	4 Turlough Parade, Croydon Park, Dublin.	20-10-1919	Mechanical Engineer	8-8-1945
V/209335	WALL, James	Caltra, Easky, Co. Sligo.	3-4-1921	Labourer	8-8-1945
A/82274	WALL, John	12 Staff Barracks, Tralee.	16-8-1922	Student	8-8-1945
83641	WALL, Oliver	8 Warwick Terrace, Leeson Park, Dublin.	23-7-1920	Engineer	8-8-1945
V/213219	WALLACE, James	3 Slattery's Ave., Thomas Davis Street, Cork.	17-2-1922	Labourer	8-8-1945
V/204917	WALLACE, Edmond	Killcullane, Holycross, Co. Limerick.	23-7-1920	General Labourer	8-8-1945
E/424893	WALLACE, Patrick	Derrygimla, Clifden, Co. Galway.	29-1-1918	Labourer	8-8-1945
V/208801	WALSH, Arthur	333 St. Attracta Road, Cabra, Dublin.	18-8-1921	Labourer	8-8-1945
E/434496	WALSH, Charles	41 Eccles Street, Dublin.	24-8-1919	Shop Assistant	8-8-1945
V/201171	WALSH, Christopher	6 Broad Street, Cork.	24-4-1922	Messenger Boy	8-8-1945
209633	WALSH, Christopher	Killenaule, Co. Tipperary.	20-12-1916	Labourer	8-8-1945
75455	WALSH, Daniel	627 Water Park, Kimmage, Dublin.	21-9-1918	Messenger	8-8-1945
E/400505	WALSH, Edward	16 Avondale Ave., Dublin.	6-3-1915	Mechanic	8-8-1945
E/415679	WALSH, Edward	184 Old Youghal Road, Cork.	25-7-1922	Labourer	8-8-1945
E/407885	WALSH, Frank	32 James's St., Bawnboy, Co. Cavan.	4-2-1923	Labourer	8-8-1945
A/68544	WALSH, George	99 St. Munchin's Terrace, Island Field, Limerick.	5-7-1911	Labourer	8-8-1945
E/417696	WALSH, John Redmond	Amphona, Wilton, Cork.	7-6-1925	Bank Official	8-8-1945
E/404631	WALSH, James	Fasaroe, Bray.	25-1-1907	Driver	8-8-1945
E/414024	WALSH, James	Ballalley, Carrick-on-Suir.	14-6-1920	Labourer	8-8-1945
E/417904	WALSH, James	10 St. Munchin's Terrace, Bruree, Co. Limerick.	14-4-1911	Motor Driver	8-8-1945
E/435072	WALSH, James	28 Dominick Place, Waterford.	12-11-1922	Plasterer	8-8-1945
77973	WALSH, James	Grove Street, Roscrea.	3-1-1920	Baker	8-8-1945
E/404515	WALSH, John	10 Ranelagh Road, Dublin.	25-4-1904	Bus Driver	8-8-1945
E/438357	WALSH, John	Lettermullen, Co. Galway.	30-7-1917	Farm Labourer	8-8-1945
E/401350	WALSH, John	Birney's Sq., Coalisland, Co. Tyrone.	29-3-1916	Shop Assistant	8-8-1945
E/412664	WALSH, John	Loughane, Askeaton, Co. Limerick.	6-6-1921	Draper's Assistant	8-8-1945
V/206071	WALSH, John	Craan Bree, Enniscorthy.	15-5-1910	Labourer	8-8-1945
E/431754	WALSH, Joseph	2 Dooley's Terrace, Athy.	14-7-1921	General Labourer	8-8-1945
V/215077	WALSH, Martin	Gurteenlough, Renvyle, Co. Galway.	8-11-1916	Farmer	8-8-1945
E/421067	WALSH, Martin	Upper New Street, Ballinrobe, Co. Mayo.	9-8-1921	Labourer	8-8-1945
E/404719	WALSH, Maurice	183 Pearse Street, Dublin.	29-12-1912	Clerk	8-8-1945
V/207351	WALSH, Michael	Kilmainham, Kells.	21-9-1921	Labourer	8-8-1945
74749	WALSH, Michael	Lettermullen, Co. Galway.	9-10-1915	Farm Labourer	8-8-1945
E/420959	WALSH, Michael	Knockleigh, Ballina.	11-2-1922	Printer's Mechanic	8-8-1945

Army No.	Name.	Last Recorded Address.	Date of Birth.	Declared Occupation prior to enlistment in Defence Forces.	Date of Dismissal from Defence Forces.
E/421931	WALSH, Michael	Netley Park, Crossmolina, Co. Mayo.	18-9-1898	Carpenter	8-8-1945
E/415364	WALSH, Michael	Brandon, Castlegregory, Co. Kerry.	25-5-1917	Machine Operator	8-8-1945
A/72558	WALSH, Michael	Prospect, Drangan, Co. Tipperary.	16-7-1913	Labourer	8-8-1945
A/80772	WALSH, Michael	Cooltigue, Clonroche, Wexford.	7-3-1920	Labourer	8-8-1945
201662	WALSH, Michael	4 Robinson's Lane, Waterford.	4-2-1921	Foundry Worker	8-8-1945
E/430772	WALSH, Michael	82 O'Molloy Street, Tullamore.	10-9-1918	Labourer	31-12-1945
77543	WALSH, Michael	Ahacross, Killdorrery, Co. Cork.	3-6-1919	Farm Labourer	8-8-1945
E/424271	WALSH, Michael A.	Fenagh, Foxfield P.O., Carrick-on-Shannon.	27-10-1919	Farm Labourer	8-8-1945
403273	WALSH, Patrick	67 C Block, Corporation Place, Dublin.	23-3-1922	Bootmaker	8-8-1945
A/70803	WALSH, Patrick	52 Marlboro' St., Dublin.	24-9-1910	Labourer	8-8-1945
E/423408	WALSH, Patrick	Craggagh, Balla, Co. Mayo.	11-8-1916	Labourer	8-8-1945
E/433901	WALSH, Patrick	Ballydaniel, Camolin, Wexford.	9-2-1922	Labourer	8-8-1945
E/434173	WALSH, Patrick	7 Green Street, Portlaw, Waterford.	14-3-1913	Labourer	8-8-1945
E/401915	WALSH, Peter	25A Green Street, Dublin.	14-11-1915	Labourer	8-8-1945
A/79585	WALSH, Peter	95D Corporation Bldgs., Dublin.	19-6-1921	Labourer	8-8-1945
80542	WALSH, Richard	Ballygowan, Piltown, Co. Kilkenny.	4-11-1919	Labourer	8-8-1945
A/83636	WALSH, Sean	Ballydonohue, Listowel.	16-1-1922	None	8-8-1945
L/502737	WALSH, Stephen	112 Foley Street, Dublin.	26-12-1926	Factory Hand	6-3-1946
A/77121	WALSH, Thomas	Gloughabrody, Thomastown, Co. Kilkenny.	2-2-1920	Messenger Boy	8-8-1945
V/206264	WALSH, Thomas	3 Cloumel Road, Mitchelstown, Co. Cork.	14-2-1921	None	8-8-1945
V/209635	WALSH, Thomas	Derhia, Listowel.	3-8-1920	Labourer	8-8-1945
105119	WALSH, Thomas	Ballymulrey, Ballymahon, Co. Longford.	2-2-1916	Labourer	8-8-1945
85488	WALSH, Thomas	Callafenish, Carna, Co. Galway.	24-8-1923	General Labourer	20-7-1946
79487	WALSH, William	Ballypatrick, Clonmel.	15-10-1914	Labourer	8-8-1945
V/20753	WALSH, William	Long Gardens, Killaloe, Co. Clare.	16-3-1913	Farm Labourer	8-8-1945
A/80609	WALSH, William	Ballinacourty, Ring, Dungarvan.	17-5-1919	Farm Labourer	8-8-1945
V/201224	WALSHE, Ambrose	3 Charles Street, Midleton, Co. Cork.	22-2-1916	Labourer	8-8-1945
E/422444	WARBY, Christopher	16 St. Patrick's Terrace, Athlone.	11-12-1921	Messenger Boy	8-8-1945
206292	WARD, Albert	Tullyown, St. Johnstown, Co. Donegal.	7-8-1920	Slate Splitter	8-8-1945
E/422726	WARD, Dominic	Castlehill, Carlingford, Co. Louth.	31-10-1910	Painter	8-8-1945
E/423619	WARD, Francis	The Mall, Sligo.	12-9-1916	Bar Manager	8-8-1945
E/423476	WARD, Frank	Irishtown, Athlone.	12-7-1909	General Labourer	8-8-1945
E/407101	WARD, John	James's Street, Westport.	23-7-1923	Messenger	8-8-1945
V/209735	WARD, Joseph	Curlesdaune, Ballyglass, Co. Mayo.	21-5-1921	Labourer	8-8-1945
A/83865	WARD, Oliver	Laurleen, Mornington, Drogheda.	14-9-1922	Student	8-8-1945
E/423758	WARD, Peter	Annaghmacomry, Cloono, Co. Leitrim.	29-6-1922	Labourer	8-8-1945
79532	WARD, Peter	Shark, Innisbofin P.O., Clifden, Co. Galway.	26-1-1916	Labourer	8-8-1945

Army No.	Name.	Last Recorded Address.	Date of Birth.	Declared Occupation prior to enlistment in Defence Forces.	Date of Dismissal from Defence Forces.
L/503089	WARD, Thomas	38 Jinks Avenue, Sligo.	6-7-1927	Labourer	13-2-1946
E/401010	WARDELL, James	16A Avondale House, Nth. Cumberland St., Dublin.	10-8-1921	Labourer	8-8-1945
E/420871	WARREN, George	Church St., Killeshandra, Co. Cavan.	23-6-1922	Wood Turner	8-8-1945
E/406930	WARREN, Tim	30 Carnew Street, Oxmantown Rd., Dublin.	14-4-1923	Motor Storeman	8-8-1945
E/405777	WARTEW, William	76 Slievemore Road, Crumlin, Dublin.	4-7-1915	Motor Driver	8-8-1945
83288	WATERS, Desmond	4 Hill Street, Ardglass, Co. Down.	1-4-1918	None	8-8-1945
E/410085	WATERS, Francis	2 Dean Street, Cork.	15-5-1915	Labourer	8-8-1945
V/211461	WATERS, James	Carrowcorry, Castlebar, Co. Mayo.	2-11-1919	Student	8-8-1945
E/410078	WATERS, John	56 Grattan Street, Cork.	23-3-1919	Labourer	8-8-1945
V/207040	WATERS, John	5 Bride Street, Wexford.	10-7-1922	Labourer	8-8-1945
E/437752	WATERS, Patrick	Market Street, Keady, Co. Armagh.	18-10-1925	Draper	8-8-1945
E/404973	WATSON, George	47 Rayham Ave., Upper Edmonton, London.	20-9-1922	Engineer	8-8-1945
E/407967	WATTS, James J.	170 Clonard Road, Crumlin, Dublin.	4-6-1916	Lorry Driver	8-8-1945
E/409847	WATTS, James	70 Butler Street, Belfast.	17-4-1925	Butcher's Apprentice	8-8-1945
E/423160	WEAFER, Christopher	51K Keogh Square, Dublin.	18-10-1904	Labourer	8-8-1945
110771	WEBSTER, George	Ballinacurry, Thurles.	10-4-1915	Labourer	8-8-1945
A/69708	WEIR, John	River Street, Clara, Offaly.	31-8-1909	Student	8-8-1945
A/83687	WELDON, Francis	63 Amiens Street, Dublin.	6-5-1915	Motor Driver	8-8-1945
E/401237	WELDON, James	68 Meath Street, Dublin.	10-10-1916	Motor Driver	8-8-1945
E/423162	WELDRIDGE, Patrick Joseph	4 Empress Place, Portland Road, Dublin.	7-8-1922	Labourer	8-8-1945
L/502072	WELDRIDGE, Patrick	4 Upper Buckingham, St., Dublin.	11-1-1923	Labourer	8-8-1945
A/80316	WEMYESS, Joseph	28 Crosthwaite Park, West, Dun Laoghaire.	21-8-1920	Labourer	8-8-1945
106394	WHARTON, Thomas	William St., Portlaw, Co. Waterford.	12-11-1915	Builder's Labourer	8-8-1945
E/405975	WHELAN, Christopher	11 Keogh Square, Dublin.	18-12-1922	Foundry Worker	8-8-1945
83570	WHELAN, Christopher	116 Thatch Road, Dublin.	13-1-1922	Mechanic	8-8-1945
E/402360	WHELAN, Edward	8 Hogan's Place, Dublin.	28-9-1918	Labourer	8-8-1945
E/400406	WHELAN, Francis	53 Ballsbridge, Dublin.	18-9-1921	Baker	8-8-1945
A/84272	WHELAN, George	Ardrahan, Co. Galway.	10-9-1922	Student	8-8-1945
L/508626	WHELAN, George	Mount Nugent, Oldcastle, Co. Meath.	17-5-1925	Student	8-8-1945
E/434928	WHELAN, James	Ballyhobuck, Glenmore, Co. Kilkenny.	1-1-1916	Farm Labourer	8-8-1945
V/204381	WHELAN, James	9 St. Senan's Street, Island Field, Limerick.	28-12-1916	Farm Labourer	8-8-1945
V/211422	WHELAN, John	32 Dorset Street, Dublin.	9-8-1922	Bottler	8-8-1945
E/406527	WHELAN, John	4 Spencer Terrace, Cork Street, Dublin.	18-7-1920	Labourer	8-8-1945
84534	WHELAN, John	Ballintin, Red Cross, Wicklow.	2-5-1923	Farmer	8-8-1945
76252	WHELAN, John	Woodtown, Ballycroghy, Wexford.	1-8-1917	Builder's Labourer	8-8-1945
74083	WHELAN, John	4 Cassidy's Place, James' Street, Dublin.	13-6-1913	Hairdresser and Bootmaker	8-8-1945
E/432328	WHELAN, Joseph	11B Oliver Bond House, Bridgefoot St., Dublin.	21-1-1920	None	8-8-1945
E/405122	WHELAN, Michael	6 North Richmond Street, Dublin.	18-1-1915	Labourer	8-8-1945
A/82644	WHELAN, Michael	Ballinahinch, Cashel, Co. Tipperary.	5-6-1921	Farm Labourer	8-8-1945
L/501805	WHELAN, Myles	5 Lower Jane Place, North Strand, Dublin.	30-6-1923	Labourer	8-8-1945

Army No.	Name.	Last Recorded Address.	Date of Birth.	Declared Occupation prior to enlistment in Defence Forces.	Date of Dismissal from Defence Forces.
E/407512	WHELAN, Patrick	93 Carnlough Road, Cabra, Dublin.	2-8-1923	Labourer	8-8-1945
A/83923	WHELAN, Patrick	64 Shelmalier Road, East Wall, Dublin.	8-11-1922	Plasterer	8-8-1945
L/502774	WHELAN, Richard	1A Marrowbone Lane, Dublin.	10-4-1927	Tinsmith	8-8-1945
E/405914	WHELAN, Stephen	Belleview, Finglas, Co. Dublin.	17-1-1913	Motor Driver	8-8-1945
78460	WHELAN, William	Rathkeale, Co. Limerick.	31-1-1921	Messenger	8-8-1945
E/403535	WHITBY, James	15 Bullocks Court, Lisburn.	2-6-1907	Net Weaver	8-8-1945
E/406737	WHITE, John	71 O'Connell Avenue, Listowel.	3-4-1922	Labourer	8-8-1945
E/405318	WHITE, Joseph	236 Sundrive Road, Kimmage, Dublin.	17-11-1917	Labourer	8-8-1945
V/201265	WHITE, Joseph	Rochestown, Cahir, Co. Tipperary.	19-3-1919	Plasterer	8-8-1945
79548	WHITE, Michael	8 Fairview Green, Fairview, Dublin.	14-5-1921	French Polisher	8-8-1945
A/78943	WHITE, Patrick	123 Clonliffe Ave., Dublin.	29-5-1919	Labourer	8-8-1945
E/402702	WHITE, Vincent P.	165 Mountpleasant Bldgs., Dublin.	3-7-1922	Vanman	8-8-1945
E/414256	WHITLEY, Griffith	33 Friars Road, Turner's Cross, Cork.	11-9-1921	Shoemaker	8-8-1945
E/410606	WHITLEY, John	123 Roches Bldgs., Cork.	16-10-1911	Boot Repairer	8-8-1945
V/211209	WHITLEY, Patrick	3 Monasterboice Road, Kimmage, Dublin.	29-12-1921	Messenger	8-8-1945
V/211459	WHITNEY, Frank	31 Claude Road, Dublin.	27-3-1922	Student	8-8-1945
L/508398	WHITTY, John	Heath Park, Ballinaboola, Co. Wexford.	8-6-1923	Labourer	8-8-1945
E/435070	WHITTY, William	51A Chapel Lane, Waterford.	9-12-1922	Labourer	20-8-1945
L/507911	WHYTE, John	St. Fanahan's Place, Mitchelstown, Co. Cork.	16-4-1928	Labourer	7-7-1946
E/408862	WILDING, Edward	Church Street, Cootehill, Co. Cavan.	25-3-1915	General Labourer	8-8-1945
E/410303	WILKINSON, Joseph	Boyle Street, Bandon, Co. Cork.	21-8-1918	Mechanic and Lorry Driver	8-8-1945
200902	WILLIAMS, Gerald	Brackernagh, Ballinasloe.	15-4-1921	Farm Labourer	8-8-1945
V/201522	WILLIAMS, Kevin	32 Connolly Gardens, Inchicore, Dublin.	10-11-1920	Apprentice Fitter	8-8-1945
76601	WILLIAMS, Patrick	Ballynahown, Lisdoonvarna, Co. Clare.	1-1-1920	Labourer	8-8-1945
E/407449	WILLIAMS, Thomas	10C Ross Road, Dublin.	2-12-1923	Messenger	8-8-1945
E/422666	WILLIAMS, Thomas	36 Oliver Plunkett Park, Dundalk.	15-8-1922	Messenger	8-8-1945
206779	WILLIAMS, Thomas	Castlerickard, Longwood, Co. Meath.	17-6-1916	Labourer	8-8-1945
E/434126	WILSON, Claud	New Home, Battlemount, Ballytore, Co. Kildare.	28-9-1922	Labourer	8-8-1945
V/202977	WILSON, Patrick	56 Davitt's St., Tipperary.	19-1-1921	Tailor	8-8-1945
E/403154	WILSON, Trevor	O'Leary's Cafe, Blackrock, Dublin.	24-5-1922	Bootmaker	8-8-1945
E/407251	WINTERS, John	Camlough, Newry, Co. Down.	21-4-1923	Labourer	8-8-1945
V/208299	WINTERS, Patrick	1 F Block, James' Street Flats, Dublin.	9-6-1922	Labourer	8-8-1945
E/423864	WINTERS, Patrick	c/o B. Harkin, Shanamuck, Castlefin.	15-3-1919	Labourer	8-8-1945
E/402359	WOLOHAN, William	24 Lismore Rd., Crumlin, Dublin.	8-5-1922	Messenger	8-8-1945
E/402097	WOODS, Arthur	62 Lower Dominick Street, Dublin.	20-8-1922	Labourer	8-8-1945
E/401699	WOODS, Daniel	4 Kells Road, Crumlin, Dublin.	22-2-1921	None	8-8-1945

Army No.	Name.	Last Recorded Address.	Date of Birth.	Declared Occupation prior to enlistment in Defence Forces.	Date of Dismissal from Defence Forces.
E/416213	WOODS, Michael F.	33 Connaught St., Athlone.	7-8-1921	Student	8-8-1945
E/404762	WOODS, Patrick	Kilmurray, Bray.	8-4-1920	Farm Labourer	8-8-1945
E/406392	WOODS, Thomas	Tallinavall, Ballyhanna, Co. Armagh.	2-1-1922	Farm Labourer	8-8-1945
A/83828	WOODS, Thomas	22 St. James' Gardens, Belfast.	18-11-1913	Labourer	8-8-1945
82345	WORT, Ernest	c/o Mrs. O'Connell, 13 Blackrock Road, Cork.	3-12-1914	None	8-8-1945
E/410511	WOULFE, John	15 St. Patrick's Terrace, Kilkee, Co. Clare.	16-6-1916	Blacksmith and Motor Driver	8-8-1945
E/437855	WRIGHT, Joseph	23 George's Place, Hardwicke St., Dublin.	5-1-1926	Messenger	8-8-1945
E/406023	WYKES, Peter	2 Castletown Cottages, Dundalk.	21-11-1920	Labourer	8-8-1945
E/409982	WYLIE, Cecil	Hawthorne Drive, Bangor, Co. Down.	27-12-1921	Fitter	8-8-1945
V/208429	WYMBS, Michael	Cliffoney, Co. Sligo.	12-10-1917	Labourer	8-8-1945
V/204435	WYNN, John	198 Keogh Sq., Inchicore, Dublin.	10-1-1919	Motor Driver	8-8-1945
84461	WYNNE, James	Slievenagork, Ballina.	10-7-1925	Farm Labourer	8-8-1945
E/420461	WYNNE, John	51 St. John's Tce., Sligo.	26-12-1912	Labourer	8-8-1945
84700	YORE, Richard	Charlestown, Ardee, Co. Louth.	7-10-1921	Labourer	8-8-1945
E/405774	YOUNG, Thomas	322 C Block, Marrowbone Lane, Dublin.	1-11-1921	Motor Driver	8-8-1945

Lightning Source UK Ltd.
Milton Keynes UK
UKOW020816240812

197964UK00003B/42/P